The Moral Psychology of Gratitude

Moral Psychology of the Emotions

Series Editor: Mark Alfano, Associate Professor, Department of Philosophy, Delft University of Technology

How do our emotions influence our other mental states (perceptions, beliefs, motivations, intentions) and our behavior? How are they influenced by our other mental states, our environments, and our cultures? What is the moral value of a particular emotion in a particular context? This series explores the causes, consequences, and value of the emotions from an interdisciplinary perspective. Emotions are diverse, with components at various levels (biological, neural, psychological, social), so each book in this series is devoted to a distinct emotion. This focus allows the author and reader to delve into a specific mental state, rather than trying to sum up emotions en masse. Authors approach a particular emotion from their own disciplinary angle (e.g., conceptual analysis, feminist philosophy, critical race theory, phenomenology, social psychology, personality psychology, neuroscience) while connecting with other fields. In so doing, they build a mosaic for each emotion, evaluating both its nature and its moral properties.

Other titles in this series:

The Moral Psychology of Contempt,
edited by Michelle Mason

The Moral Psychology of Compassion,
edited by Justin Caouette and Carolyn Price

The Moral Psychology of Disgust,
edited by Nina Strohminger and Victor Kumar

Forthcoming titles in the series:

The Moral Psychology of Regret,
edited by Anna Gotlib

The Moral Psychology of Admiration,
edited by Alfred Archer and André Grahle

The Moral Psychology of Guilt,
edited by Corey J. Maley and Bradford Cokelet

The Moral Psychology of Hope,
edited by Claudia Blöser and Titus Stahl

The Moral Psychology of Gratitude

Edited by Robert Roberts and Daniel Telech

ROWMAN & LITTLEFIELD
INTERNATIONAL

London • New York

Published by Rowman & Littlefield International Ltd.
6 Tinworth Street, London SE11 5AL
www.rowmaninternational.com

Rowman & Littlefield International Ltd. is an affiliate of Rowman & Littlefield
4501 Forbes Boulevard, Suite 200, Lanham, Maryland 20706, USA
With additional offices in Boulder, New York, Toronto (Canada), and Plymouth (UK)
www.rowman.com

British Library Cataloguing in Publication Data
A catalogue record for this book is available from the British Library

ISBN: HB 978-1-78660-602-0

Library of Congress Cataloging-in-Publication Data Available

ISBN: 978-1-78660-602-0 (cloth)
ISBN: 978-1-5381-5879-1 (pbk)
ISBN: 978-1-78660-603-7 (electronic)

Contents

Acknowledgments

Edited volumes, like many other projects that depend on the generosity, trust, and patience of others, are customarily preceded by words of thanks. This volume on gratitude is no exception.

We thank Mark Alfano for his attentiveness and encouragement throughout the editorial process. From suggesting possible authors to improve the breadth of the volume to ideas about acquiring funding in order to workshop the chapter drafts, Mark was generous with his advice and general support. A better series editor is difficult to imagine.

Mark suggested that we submit an application to the Templeton Foundation to fund the workshop, and their generous response enabled us to host a very fruitful meeting in the fall of 2017. They responded with an outright *gift*, obviating a detailed budget and expense reports. The Templeton Foundation's kind support enabled us to hold a three-day pre-read workshop at the University of Chicago that brought the volume contributors, as well as some local scholars, into conversation with one another while the contributors worked on their drafts.

We thank Isobel Cowper Coles and Natalie Linh Bolderston at Rowman & Littlefield International for their patient and highly professional support.

Thanks also to the participants of the gratitude workshop at the University of Chicago: Jack Bauer, Agnes Callard, David Carr, Sophie-Grace Chappell, Justin Coates, Cameron Fenton, Liz Gulliford, Bennett Helm, Christina Karns, Brian Leiter, Hichem Naar, Tony Manela, Terrance McConnell, Coleen Macnamara, Adrienne Martin, Colin Shanahan, Stephen White, Marya Schechtman, and Will Small.

Daniel would like to thank Agnes Callard, Brian Leiter, and Paul Russell for their mentorship in thinking about gratitude (and praise-manifesting attitudes generally), and Robert Roberts for showing him the ropes of volume editing and teaching him much about gratitude and philosophy in the process. Bob Roberts would like to thank Daniel Telech for doing most of the work for this volume, including securing our authors, applying for funding for the workshop, and organizing and hosting the workshop.

The Emotion-Virtue-Debt Triad of Gratitude: An Introduction to *The Moral Psychology of Gratitude*

Robert Roberts and Daniel Telech

Gratitude is a response to another's goodness. Paradigmatically, one is grateful *to* another *for* some benefit. That is, in feeling grateful, you typically construe yourself or someone you care about as a beneficiary and the other—the person to whom you are grateful—as a benefactor. But gratitude represents the benefactor as more than a supplier of benefits. It is a response not simply to beneficence but also to bene*volence*—goodwill. Natural events and malicious persons both may cause some end of mine to be fulfilled, and I may be glad *that* the beneficial state of affairs came to be, but such good fortune doesn't usually dispose me to feel grateful *to anyone*. This is plausibly because I do not take these benefits to be expressions of benevolence, or goodwill. The claim that gratitude construes another to have acted from goodwill is a mainstay in philosophical discussion of gratitude (e.g., Berger 1975: 299–300; Camenisch 1981; McConnell 1993; Roberts 2004). Gratitude is thus an interpersonal or social emotion.

We hasten to note a usage of the word "gratitude" that does not pick out an inherently interpersonal response; for example, "I am grateful *that* I got to see a shooting star." This sense of gratitude, sometimes called "propositional gratitude" (McAleer 2012), involves a relation between a person and a state of affairs, without reference to a benefactor. But little seems to be lost by redescribing instances of so-called propositional gratitude as cases of *appreciation* (cf. Carr 2013; Roberts 2015; Manela 2016). Whether or not "propositional gratitude" is gratitude only in name, this volume is about the social and agent-directed emotion that involves a triadic relation between two agents and (typically) an action, as expressed by the following kind of sentence: "Abe is grateful to Miranda for helping him move into his new apartment."

Gratitude has been studied in various aspects. It has been theorized not only as a positive emotion (alongside joy and admiration), but as both a virtue and a grounding kind of *debt* or duty. This is not an exhaustive list, but the emotion-virtue-debt triad captures a core set of questions about gratitude, so we begin here. It might not be immediately transparent how the emotion-virtue-debt triad of gratitude hangs together. For, while the idea that gratitude is an emotion fits neatly with the idea that gratitude may also be a virtue (or a trait of excellence, whereby one is stably disposed to feel the emotion in the appropriate circumstances and to the appropriate degree), the emotion-debt dyad may be less intelligible. If one's debt of gratitude is a duty to be grateful, and being grateful amounts to feeling an emotion, then, given that one cannot directly will oneself to feel an emotion, debts of gratitude will seem to violate the "ought implies can" principle. To help render the emotion-virtue-debt triad intelligible, we discuss its elements in turn. Then we briefly summarize the volume's chapters.

FEELING GRATEFUL: GRATITUDE QUA EMOTION

Gratitude is a pleasant emotion. To be grateful is to *take joy in* another's benevolently given benefit to oneself. That is, gratitude is a joyful attitude that represents another to have benefited oneself from goodwill.[1]

Morgan et al. (2014) say that some people, especially in the UK, find gratitude to be unpleasant because of the sense of indebtedness that it involves. Roberts (2016) speculates that such people may be mistaking the *situation* that calls for gratitude—a benefit has been gratuitously conferred—for gratitude itself, or supposing that any response to such a situation must be gratitude. Such people feel uncomfortable with being indebted, thus perhaps even resenting their benefactors for the benefits they have conferred. This is no doubt a common response; many people dislike feeling indebted and may not be clear about the special kind of indebtedness that goes with gratitude. Also, "benefactors" can be manipulative and domineering, and almost nobody likes being "indebted" to such people. Roberts (2016) argues that if this is what leads some to find "gratitude" unpleasant, the emotion they feel toward their benefactors is not properly called gratitude.

The exact propositional content definitive of gratitude is a matter of debate. In addition to representing another as having benefited one benevolently, it is sometimes held that gratitude represents the benefactor to have acted with the *intention* of benefiting one, and in a way that exceeds his duties toward the beneficiary (i.e., supererogatorily). Additionally, in feeling grateful, one presumably not only construes oneself as a beneficiary but also *welcomes the* benefit, and welcomes it as a benefit *from this benefactor*. What exactly it is to *be* a benefit is a large and important question in its own right (taken up in part by Macnamara, this volume), but it is worth mentioning that (1) the benefactor's benefiting the beneficiary and (2) his benevolent attitudes are not always obviously separable. This is not only because one can be grateful to another for his benevolent *omission* but also because we are sometimes grateful for benevolent *attempts*, where there is no benefit to speak of apart from the kind or generous motivating attitudes of the benefactor. Though our welfare interests might not be promoted, we sometimes recognize that, as the saying has it, it's "the thought that counts." Indeed, Seneca, being a Stoic who thinks the only real goods are attitudes, thinks *only* the thought counts:

> [a] benefit cannot be touched with one's hand; the business is carried out with one's mind. There is a big difference between the raw material of a benefit and the benefit itself. . . . Consequently, the benefit is not the gold, the silver, or any of the things which are thought to be most important; rather, the benefit is the intention of the giver. (*On Benefits*, 1.5.2)

Thus, on his view, "benevolent attitude" and "benefit" will share the same intension.[2]

As an emotion, gratitude can be considered either episodically or dispositionally. An *episode* of gratitude is the mental state experienced in joyfully thinking of oneself as benevolently benefited by another. One can count as being grateful, in the sense of having the emotion, however, even when one is not experiencing this joyful state. While being pulled over for speeding, Alex will not be joyful about much, but he can nevertheless be truly described as grateful to Ben for saving his life, assuming he is disposed to appreciate the action when reflecting on Ben's benevolent deed.

Alex's gratitude, however, will involve more than a disposition to *feel* positively about being benefited by another. To have the emotion of gratitude is also to be *motivated* to respond to one's benefactor in a way that shows him what the benefit means to one.[3] Someone who is merely happy to have been benefited by another might have no desire to reciprocate or otherwise express his joy *to* the benefactor. Such a person is easily construed as an ingrate, at least if he is aware of the benevolence from which his benefit proceeds. Alex would hardly count as grateful to Ben if, when presented with the opportunity to help Ben out of an innocent bind, Alex had no motivation to help Ben. A description of someone who is grateful must include his sense of *owing* thanks to his benefactor. A range of factors may prevent the grateful agent from *in fact* expressing thanks/reciprocating, but the person who feels grateful will at least be motivated to return the kindness previously shown him.

In many respects, gratitude is the symmetrical opposite of resentment, an angry attitude that represents another to have slighted (or harmed with ill will, or perhaps merely indifference) the resenter (see, e.g., Berger 1975; Roberts 2004). As with gratitude, one can count as resentful of (or "angry with") another for long stretches of time that include a wide range of (variously valanced) mental episodes. The contrast between gratitude and resentment is of particular importance, given that resentment is often thought to be a paradigmatic vehicle of interpersonal blame. Considered as Strawsonian "reactive attitudes," resentment and gratitude are a "usefully opposed pair" (Strawson 1962: 77) in that resentment has the affective and motivational profile we associate with second-personal blame, while gratitude has the affective and motivational profile associated with second-personal praise (or "moral credit"). That is, these attitudes are paradigmatic ways of taking others to be responsible (i.e., blameworthy or praiseworthy). But while gratitude (along with admiration and pride) are often *mentioned* as paradigmatic praise-manifesting attitudes, the nature and norms of blame have thus far received the lion's share of attention within the moral responsibility literature. Several of this volume's chapters address the status of gratitude as a reactive attitude, shedding new light on the positive aspect of our responsibility practices.

BEING A GRATEFUL PERSON: GRATITUDE QUA VIRTUE

The person who is stably disposed to develop dispositions to feel gratitude plausibly has the *trait* of gratitude. On the assumption that this trait can be, but is not necessarily, an excellence of character, the person who is stably disposed to develop dispositions to feel gratitude toward the right person, in the right circumstances, in the right way, and to the right degree plausibly possesses the *virtue* of gratitude.

Thinking of gratitude as a virtue brings into focus that gratitude involves more than experiencing an emotion. Intuitively, the grateful person not only takes joy in another's having benevolently benefited him but also—on this basis—takes the other's concerns as providing *reasons for action*. While one might count as having the emotion of gratitude even if one does not in fact *express* one's gratitude, it is often thought to be essential to gratitude that one at least be *disposed* to express one's gratitude, where this is a matter of treating the benefactor with goodwill. Sometimes we do this by saying "thank you," but we often "show our thanks" through more heartfelt and personalized actions. The expression of gratitude is often referred to under the banner of "reciprocation," though it should be distinguished from *repayment* that cancels a debt. Unlike repayment, the reciprocation involved in gratitude essentially involves sincerity. I can successfully repay a monetary debt (for example) regardless of the attitudes I have toward my creditor, but gratitude is partly constituted by the beneficiary's *wanting* to make a return of kindness (at least in part) for its own sake. This return kindness has the character of an *expression* of one's heart, and is often intended as a *communication* with the benefactor. Though sometimes benefactors don't want such communication, and so the sensitive beneficiary may refrain from it (see Dickens's characters John Jarndyce and Esther Summerson, in Roberts, this volume). Plausibly then, to be disposed to have the emotion of gratitude *in the right way* involves being disposed to reciprocate, that is, to communicate to your benefactor, *out of goodwill*, what the benefit meant to you.

We emphasize the expressive component of gratitude here for the following reason. The person who is merely joyful about having been benevolently benefited is in many cases the paradigm of *ingratitude*. It is true that we sometimes call the person who is unhappy with her lot an "ingrate," but when we say this, we are saying not only that she ought to *appreciate* what she has been given but she also has a reason to express her gratitude to her benefactor. For, suppose that the ingrate in question comes to take joy in what she has been given, yet displays indifference to her parents, teachers, and friends (perhaps out of an undue sense of self-determination). This person may very well be happy about having been benevolently benefited, but if we continue to think of her as an exemplar of ingratitude, this is because she lacks the disposition to reciprocate sincerely. The grateful person, one who has the virtue of gratitude, is not only disposed to feel the emotion at the right times, toward the right persons, and in the right circumstances, but is also disposed to feel it *in the right way*. A proper account of the virtue of gratitude will fill in what it is to have these appropriate dispositions. For now, let's say the disposition to "feel gratitude in the right way" importantly includes the motive to reciprocate or express gratitude to the benefactor. This motivational/behavioral component of the virtuous agent's grateful response is sometimes considered in isolation. As such, its fulfillment is sometimes theorized as a debt or duty of gratitude.

DEBTS OF GRATITUDE

It is widely held that being benevolently benefited can generate a debt of gratitude. How to understand "debts of gratitude," however, is a matter of much debate. These debts are often referred to as generating "obligations (or duties) of gratitude," but unlike standard obligations, those of gratitude do not seem to provide the benefactor with the *right* to demand or exact reciprocation from the beneficiary. One explanation of this is that gratitude is a response to generosity (see Chappell this volume and Roberts this volume; see also Seneca's *On Benefits*, where gratitude is tightly linked to generosity); for generosity is *free* giving, giving without requirement of return. To give generously and then turn around and demand repayment would be both inconsistent and boorish. And indeed, those who hold that "repayment of debts of gratitude is [. . .] an obligation (or moral requirement)" (McConnell

1993: Chapter 2; McConnell 2018) typically deny that the benefactor has a claim-right to the beneficiary's gratitude. What, then, does the idea "A has a duty of gratitude to B" come to? Should talk of duties/obligations/requirements here be understood in terms of *desert*, such that the beneficiary's "having a duty of gratitude" reduces to the benefactor's *deserving* the beneficiary's reciprocal return?

> These notions of deserving and owing can be connected to the idea of a right, even if not a claim right. Tony Manela (2015: especially 163–166) invokes the notion of an *imperfect right* for these cases. Although the original benefactor does not have a claim right to demand that the beneficiary reciprocate, she does have standing to remonstrate and express resentment, and this sort of standing affirms her self-respect. (McConnell, this volume, endnote 7)

But it may strike us that even to remonstrate, complain, or resent the ungrateful beneficiary is a compromise with the spirit of generosity unless the remonstrator also occupies the role of moral educator (say, that of a parent) vis-à-vis the ungrateful one. But in that case, the complaint is not justified by the benefactor-beneficiary relationship, but by the parent-child or other educator-learner relationship. We might say that the debt of gratitude is properly felt primarily or even solely by the beneficiary, and that it is felt not as needing to be paid off, but as a lasting bond of love. This would be why Seneca warns us to be careful in selecting our benefactors:

> I should be even more careful when seeking someone to be indebted to for a benefit than for money. The financial creditor only has to be paid back as much as I accepted, and once I pay him off then I am free and clear. But I have a larger payment to make to the other creditor, and even after the favor has been returned we are still linked to each other. For once I have paid him back I must start again, and a friendship persists. (*On Benefits*, 2.18.5)

On this Senecan proposal, the debt of gratitude is inextricable from the beneficiary's sense of owing reciprocation or thanks, which itself is a component of the joyful emotion of gratitude. This thought coheres with the idea that, whatever else they may be, debts of gratitude are not paradigmatically experienced by the beneficiary simply as *to-be-discharged*, but rather as opportunities to deepen the relation of interpersonal joy occasioned by the benefactor's original manifestation of goodwill.

The Chapters

The volume's first chapter challenges the idea that gratitude is inherently an affective phenomenon. Hichem Naar advances a distinction between generic and deep gratitude, where the former is a matter of merely *believing* that one has been benevolently benefited. Generic gratitude is neither affective nor does it motivate one to reciprocate. Naar's proposal is motivated in part by the peculiar features of introspecting our attitudes of gratitude. In contrast to our grasp of whom we love, our grasp of whom we are grateful to is often elusive. Naar argues that the elusiveness of self-attributions of gratitude is well explained by positing a form of ("generic") gratitude for which it is sufficient to be grateful that one have an evaluative belief with the right content, even if this belief remain largely dormant. Naar then discusses the possible grounds (or rather, the elusiveness of grounds) on which generic gratitude might appropriately become "deep gratitude," that is, gratitude that is inherently affective and motivational.

Terrance McConnell's chapter (chapter 2) focuses on a puzzle generated by cases in which an agent has sufficient reason to reciprocate gratefully ("to discharge a debt of gratitude"), but where it may nonetheless be morally desirable to act from reasons other than those of gratitude, especially those of love. When multiple values commend the same action, it is not always clear what the agent's salient motive should be, or alternatively and more specifically, whether one should benefit another qua original benefactor (i.e., from gratitude), or qua loved one. Complexity is added to the analysis by McConnell's treating love as possessed of moral content, such that the conflict between acting from love versus from gratitude is not simply a standoff between morality (understood as a burdensome source of motivation) and personal relationships.

Debts of gratitude are the focus of the next set of chapters. Adrienne Martin's chapter advances a solution to a puzzle concerning obligations of gratitude. While debts of gratitude seem to be instances of directed obligation— the beneficiary has a debt *to* the benefactor *for* being benefited—benefactors lack a claim-right to the beneficiary's gratitude. Unlike standard directed obligations, of which promissory obligations are paradigmatic, "obligations of gratitude" (if there are any) do not seem to give the benefactor the authority to *demand* the beneficiary's reciprocation. Martin proposes a novel way to anchor obligations of gratitude. On her proposal, the beneficiary has an obligation of gratitude that corresponds not to a claim-right, but to the benefactor's "personal expectation." While the agent with a claim-right (e.g., the promissee) has the standing to direct both the adoption of an end and the means to it, the benefactor has the authority to "direct the beneficiary only to adopt or maintain the broad end of being grateful." On Martin's view, the benefactor *does* have the standing to issue directives, including demands, but these are directives not to perform a particular action but a broad end, of being grateful. That is, the benefactor has the standing to direct that differs from the promisee's in *scope*. Martin contrasts her "scope strategy" with strategies that identify the difference between the promisee and the benefactor in the *force* of the kind of directive they have the standing to issue.

Agnes Callard analyzes debts of gratitude in terms of the demand to come to value something. Callard argues that such debts come in two types: debts of reciprocation, and debts of appreciation, corresponding to two forms of gratitude: assistance gratitude versus mentor gratitude. Instances of assistance gratitude are those by which the benefactor's benevolence generates an obligation that governs how the beneficiary acts, thinks, and feels *toward the benefactor*. By contrast, mentor gratitude generates an obligation that governs how one acts, thinks, and feels about *the benefit*. Callard distinguishes both assistance gratitude and mentor gratitude from a further form of gratitude that does *not* generate a debt of gratitude, namely gratitude for gifts, at least when the gift satisfies the norms of gift-giving by treading the line between the overly useful and the useless. "The perfect gift is perfect precisely in that it elicits an affective response that exhausts all the demands of gratitude. It leaves no normative remainder to stand as a 'debt of gratitude.'"

Coleen Macnamara's chapter asks whether gratitude can be owed for rights-fulfilling conduct (i.e., for benefits that the benefactor has an obligation to give). The standard, but largely unargued for, view is that gratitude is *not* owed for rights-fulfilling conduct. After considering several baselines relative to which a beneficiary may count as being benefited, Macnamara provides an argument for the view that benefits constitutive of rights-fulfilling conduct do not generate debts of gratitude. She maintains that "requiring P_1 to feel gratitude toward P_2 amounts to morally forbidding her from representing herself as possessing what morality, itself, has deemed (in a sense to be specified) normatively *hers*." Macnamara allays worries about her proposal by discussing the ways in which gratitude may be fitting and of moral significance even when it is not *owed*.

Cameron Fenton presents a view of filial gratitude that sits between the view that gratitude is owed for basic parental care and the view that it is owed for supererogatory benefits. Fenton argues that "children owe their parents gratitude only when they meet their moral parental duties and raise their children well." In reply to the objection that a gratitude-based theory of gratitude cannot specify how filial obligations are to be discharged, Fenton outlines what it may be for children to provide their parents with "commensurate benefits" that respond to their parents' genuine needs. Lastly, Fenton appeals to data measuring unpaid childcare performed by fathers and mothers to argue that filial duties of gratitude are apt to be stronger toward mothers.

Gratitude considered as a Strawsonian reactive attitude is the focus of the next set of chapters. Stephen Darwall advances an account of gratitude as a "second-personal attitude of the heart." He contrasts attitudes of the heart (which also include trust and love) with the standard "juridical" reactive attitudes (resentment, indignation, and guilt), which reflect interpersonal demands and through which we hold agents accountable for conduct. While juridical reactive attitudes are second-personal in virtue of addressing their targets with implicit demands, gratitude is a reciprocating attitude that communicates to the benefactor that the beneficiary welcomes the benefit and the benefactor's giving of it. In this way, gratitude, like other second-personal attitudes of the heart, involves "heartfelt giving and receiving."

In the next chapter, Justin Coates argues that gratitude and resentment are asymmetrical in at least three key ways: in their fittingness conditions, in the norms that govern their expression, and in their value for human relationships. First, Coates defends the view that there is an asymmetry in conditions under which agents deserve praise-manifesting and blame-manifesting attitudes, proposing that this is to be explained by a difference in the degree of moral *competence* required to deserve blame in contrast to praise. Next, Coates argues that the reasons to express blame-manifesting attitudes are more readily defeasible than the reasons to express praise-manifesting attitudes, like gratitude. Finally, he argues that there exists an asymmetry in the value of praise- and blame-manifesting attitudes, such that "a world with *n* instrumental goods and the good of being grateful to someone who genuinely deserves gratitude seems *better*—more worthy of actualization—than a world with *n* instrumental goods and the good of resenting someone who genuinely deserves resentment."

Bennett Helm's chapter focuses on gratitude's role within the broader rational network of reactive attitudes. According to Helm, this network of reactive attitudes is constitutive of a community of respect, the norms of which are sometimes made determinate through our very attitudes of gratitude and the like. He focuses on an example in which a student is grateful to her teacher for the teacher's correcting herself after first failing to use the student's preferred gender pronouns. On Helm's view, though it is not clear whether the teacher *benefits* the student, gratitude is responsive to benevolence, understood as one's being motivated by "recognition respect." On the assumption that there is indeterminacy in our gender recognition norms, the student's gratitude can be understood as further committing themselves to, and more determinately delineating, the norm, and inviting the teacher—as well as the community at large—to uphold the norm.

The next pair of chapters address the social neuroscience and social psychology of gratitude. Christina Karns provides a model for understanding how "neural systems may work together to support an experience of gratitude and how the plastic and changeable nature of the brain might be used to promote gratitude." She begins by offering a conceptual analysis of gratitude similar to what a philosopher might provide, but she uses it to generate hypotheses about the neural processes that underlie the experience of this socially complex and morally implicated emotion. Her assumption is that in such conditions as that the grateful person feels joyful rather than guilty about receiving the benefit from the benefactor and that she feels begraced by, rather than entitled to, the benefit correspond to distinguishable neural and biological processes that can be empirically identified. And she suggests that an understanding of these physiological processes might be useful for helping people to grow in gratitude.

Jack Bauer and Colin Shanahan offer a developmental account of gratitude rooted in a narratival understanding of self identity. According to their account, the traits of existential authenticity and gratitude interact reciprocally over the decades of the lifespan in such a way that individuals become increasingly appreciative of the depth of their interdependency with others. Furthermore, their sense of what it means to "be oneself" evolves from merely not putting on a false façade socially to an incorporation of ethical values that determine the core of being human as their moral tradition construes them. Young people can be grateful, but their gratitude is largely behavioral, consisting in the disposition to "recognize" others' contributions by *expressing* gratitude. But as their narrative self-awareness extends and complexifies and ethically deepens over time, they come both to feel and to understand how interlaced their lives and their identities are with those of others, thus rendering their gratitude deeper and more genuine.

The final set of chapters addresses a range of questions concerning gratitude as a virtue and the various ways of manifesting the vice of ingratitude. Sophie Grace Chappell proposes that virtues be divided into those primarily oriented toward good/right action, and those oriented toward good/right feeling. She argues that gratitude should be understood as belonging to the latter class. After providing a self-standing analysis of gratitude, on which gratitude is understood as responsive to *generosity*, Chappell challenges the standard view that gratitude is not among the Aristotelian virtues. She argues that Aristotle's treatment of gratitude must be understood against the background of Athenian client-patron relations, and that a more positive Aristotelian stance on gratitude, between equals, can be extracted from Aristotle's discussion of friendship in the *Nicomachean Ethics*, read alongside his discussion of gratitude between unequals in the *Rhetoric*. Chappell concludes by making a case for the appropriateness that we, like St. Paul, "give thanks in every circumstance," and so makes a case for "cosmic gratitude," or at least the intelligibility of a mind-set of cosmic gratitude.

Drawing on an example from Graham Greene's novel *Brighton Rock*, David Carr addresses the question whether gratitude is a virtuous response to "benefits" that turn on some kind of deceit. The well-meaning person who lies to her friend for the latter's benefit may strike us as both belittlingly dishonest or as compassionate. To help with the analysis of gratitude for "benefits" based on lies, Carr proposes that we distinguish talk of virtue from talk of morality. On this basis, he argues that we can understand the deceitful friend as a proper object of gratitude (though perhaps not unambivalent gratitude) insofar as she has the other's interests in mind, even if these are not *moral* interests.

Liz Gulliford provides conceptual grounds and evidence for thinking that gratitude belongs to a mutually reinforcing set of benevolent virtues, that is, an "allocentric quintet" comprised of generosity, gratitude, forgiveness, compassion, and humility (Gulliford and Roberts 2018). Focusing in particular on the exercises making up Twelve Step programs and the practice of *lojong* (from the Tibetan Buddhist tradition), Gulliford's chapter outlines how spiritual and self-examination practices promote cross-pollination from one allocentric virtue to another within a person's character. Gulliford concludes with "some suggestions as to how psychological interventions to promote strengths of character might be enriched by fostering mutually reinforcing strengths, rather than targeting virtues individually."

Tony Manela's chapter focuses on the various ways in which one can fall short (or long) of the virtue of gratitude. After providing an account of the virtue of gratitude as a "meta-disposition" or the "disposition to perceive benevolence and to form the proper grateful beliefs and affective and behavioral dispositions vis-à-vis the source of that benevolence," Manela provides a taxonomy of the ways one can fail to be a grateful agent. According to Manela, there are three ways an agent can fail to be properly grateful: he can fail to be properly sensitive to evidence of benevolence (failures of attunement); he can fail to establish the proper beliefs and dispositions when gratitude is called for (failures of establishment); and he can fail to preserve those beliefs and dispositions for a proper or reasonable amount of time (failures of duration).

In the volume's final chapter, Robert Roberts explores the emotional depth of Charles Dickens's *Bleak House* to illustrate how gratitude must be understood in its connection with other virtues, especially generosity, but also humility, justice (injustice), friendship, and practical wisdom. By attending to the characters of John Jarndyce, Esther Summerson, and Harold Skimpole, Roberts maintains that it is only in combination with the concept of justice that the notions of generosity (in contrast to liberality, which construes gratitude as servile) and gratitude are intelligible. The generosity-gratitude dynamic is especially central to Roberts's contribution as he, following Dickens, identifies these as complementary virtues: gratitude is a proper or canonical response to genuine acts and attitudes of generosity and such generosity is satisfied and completed, so to speak, by expressions of gratitude. Roberts proposes that we call this pair the *virtues of grace*, since both are about gifts—giving and gracious receiving.

NOTES

1 Although, to say that "gratitude an essentially pleasant emotion . . . is fully compatible with someone's finding the *idea* of gratitude unpleasant" (Roberts 2015: 888).

2 At least where the benevolent attitudes are weighty enough to motivate action, as benevolent intentions are, though benevolent but idle or fleeting desires, say, are not. That is, even if it's the "thought that counts," it is not clear that we ought to be grateful to the person who merely *desires* (even for our own sake) that another would help us, when the desirer is in a position to help us himself with little effort.

3 For simplicity's sake, we do not distinguish here between (1) seeing (being disposed to see) the benefactor's interests and circumstances as providing reasons for (beneficent) action and (2) being motivated to act beneficently, toward one's benefactor.

REFERENCES

Berger, Fred (1975). "Gratitude." *Ethics* 85: 298–309.

Camenisch, Paul (1981). "Gift and Gratitude in Ethics." *The Journal of Religious Ethics* 9: 1–34.

Carr, David (2013). "Varieties of Gratitude." *Journal of Value Inquiry* 46: 17–28.

Gulliford, Liz and Robert C. Roberts (2018). "Exploring the 'Unity' of the Virtues: The Case of an Allocentric Quintet." *Theory and Psychology* 28: 208–226.

Manela, Tony (2015). "Obligations of Gratitude and Correlative Rights." *Oxford Studies in Normative Ethics* 5: 151–170.

Manela, Tony (2016). "Gratitude and Appreciation." *American Philosophical Quarterly* 53(3): 281–294.

McAleer, Sean (2012). "Propositional Gratitude." *American Philosophical Quarterly* 49(1): 55–66.

McConnell, Terrance (1993). *Gratitude*. Philadelphia, PA: Temple University Press.

McConnell, Terrance (2018). *Gratitude's Moral Status*. Unpublished manuscript.

Morgan, B., L. Gulliford, and K. Kristjánsson (2014). "Gratitude in the UK: A New Prototype Analysis and a Cross-Cultural Comparison." *The Journal of Positive Psychology* 9: 281–294.

Roberts, Robert C. (2004). "The Blessings of Gratitude: A Conceptual Analysis." In *The Psychology of Gratitude*, eds. R. A. Emmons and M. E. McCullough, pp. 58–78. New York: Oxford University Press.

Roberts, Robert C. (2015) "The Normative and Empirical in the Study of Gratitude." *Res Philosophica* 92(4): 883–914.

Roberts, Robert C. (2016). "Gratitude and Humility." In *Perspectives on Gratitude: An Interdisciplinary Approach*, ed. David Carr, pp. 57–69. New York: Routledge.

Seneca (2011). *On Benefits*. Trans. M. Griffin and B. Inwood. Chicago: University of Chicago Press.

Strawson, Peter (1962/1974). "Freedom and Resentment." In *Freedom and Resentment and Other Essays*, pp. 1–25. London: Methuen & Co Ltd.

Part I

REASONS AND ACTION

Chapter 1

Gratitude: Generic versus Deep

Hichem Naar

THE ELUSIVENESS OF GRATITUDE

In this chapter, I argue that gratitude is not necessarily affective or motivating. Against a common trend in recent philosophical treatments of the notion, indeed, I argue for the introduction of an important but neglected kind of gratitude that is simply a matter of believing that one has been benefited by a benevolent benefactor. I will call this non-affective, non-motivating kind of gratitude "generic," and the kind—taking center stage in the literature—that is affective and motivating, "deep." After defending the distinction, I explore the connection between these kinds of gratitude.

Suppose I asked you to recall as many people as you can to whom you are grateful. How many would you be able to bring to mind? And how long would it take you? How difficult is the task? Is it easier than bringing to mind people you love, or harder? My experience is that it is much harder to bring to mind people I am grateful to. Besides a couple of obvious answers—which may not have been obvious to me until I actually tried—I find it a daunting task to come up with names of people to whom I am grateful. For one thing, *many* people have benefited me in the past; for another, rarely anything as deep as a state of love was formed as a result of having been benefited from them. Nonetheless, there may appear to be a fact of the matter as to whether, for any given person X, I am grateful to X for having done something for me. The problem is that it often takes some effort to come up with a satisfactory answer to the question "Whom are you grateful to, and why?", giving the impression that, as one is thinking deeply about one's past, one is not really grateful to the people one will ultimately cite. When you are pondering over whom you are grateful to, are you engaged in a bit of introspection, or are you, quite literally, *making up your mind* as to whether you are, or should be, grateful to this or that person? The fact that it takes so much effort—and what looks like genuine deliberation—to come up with names may suggest that, prior to being asked the question, you were not really grateful to the people you were hard put even to remember.

Things may look a bit less alarming when you don't have the initial task of remembering a specific person. Suppose I ask you, for any given person X, whether there is anything for which you are grateful to X. You would probably come up with a definite answer much more easily. Since you now remember X, it is much easier for you to think of the various ways X may have contributed to your life. Perhaps X has helped you carry your furniture when you moved into your new apartment. Or perhaps X has often been there when you needed advice on relationships. Or perhaps X bought you a nice meal last weekend. In any case, provided the relevant person has already been brought to your attention, it is rather easy to remember what he may have done for you which appears to render gratitude appropriate. In such cases, one can then declare "I am grateful to X for A." Although it might have been easier to come up with an answer to the question "Are you grateful to X?" than it is to answer the question "Whom are you grateful to?", there remains the suspicion that one's answer is not really revelatory of a prior state of gratitude. Indeed, if no one had asked you this question, you probably would never have given much thought to the fact that the person has benefited you. Perhaps, then, gratitude is such as to be held on the basis of effortful conscious deliberation. If true, this would imply a fairly robust form of skepticism about gratitude formed spontaneously and effortlessly, of the sort we take to be paradigmatic, the sort of gratitude we take to be revealed rather than created when reflecting on the impact other people have had on one's life, and therefore the sort of gratitude the knowledge of which can be a matter of genuine discovery.

Perhaps, however, this sort of skepticism should not be accepted just yet. Suppose I asked you, not whether you are grateful to X for having done something or other (that you would then need to think about), but whether you are grateful to X for having done A in particular—thereby sparing you the trouble to search for ways you may have benefited from X in the past. It appears that the answer will be extremely easy to come by. Suppose you believe you were benefited by X's action, and also believe that X's motives were good. I can easily imagine you reply: "Sure, I'm grateful." And this could be repeated for any agent-action pair I give you. For any such pair, it seems you will immediately know what answer to give. If you don't believe you were benefited by a person, for instance, then you are highly likely to answer the question "Are you grateful to X for A?" with a firm "No." By contrast, if you believe you were benefited by X, that X did something good for you, then arguably you are just as likely to give the positive answer. It appears, then, that there is a fact of the matter whether you are antecedently grateful to a person for something they have done, a fact that you are able to access if prompted in the right sort of way. Maybe you were not aware that you were grateful before being prompted, but the immediacy with which you are able to answer the question suggests that your gratitude was there all along, waiting to manifest itself.[1]

But what exactly was "there all along" that would require you to get all the relevant information in full view in order for the gratitude to be triggered? I don't need to give you the name of someone in particular in order for you to tell me whom you love spontaneously and effortlessly. So why do I need to do this to have a spontaneous and effortless answer to a query about whom I am grateful to? I think this has to do, not with the fact that I may have failed to be grateful prior to being asked the question, but rather with the fact that gratitude is, in many cases, rather *cheap*, requiring something much less sophisticated than contemporary accounts of gratitude claim it requires. As I argue in the section "Being a Grateful Person: Gratitude Qua Virtue," although there is a fact of the matter whether you are grateful at a particular time to a person for having benefited you, this fact is often hard to pin down precisely because it is *trivial*—in particular, it is a trivial consequence of having further, temporally persisting, and often dormant, mental states. Calling these mental states to mind, however, can have psychological *consequences* that are *not* trivial, which is why it may be important to attend to the various ways other people have benefited us. In particular, doing so might lead to a *deeper* form of gratitude of a sort associated with the affective and the motivational. In section "Deep Gratitude," I discuss this sort of gratitude, which I call *deep gratitude*, to be contrasted with the *generic gratitude* of the sort discussed in the previous section. I argue that, in addition to the mental states involved in generic gratitude, deep gratitude involves an essentially affective-cum-motivational element, and I tackle the question of what turns a merely generically grateful person into a deeply grateful one. In the section "When Is Deep Gratitude Appropriate?" finally, I ask what might make deep gratitude appropriate over and above generic gratitude. As we will see, it is difficult to draw a principled distinction between appropriate and inappropriate instances of deep gratitude, and skepticism about conditions of appropriateness for deep gratitude is difficult to avoid.

GENERIC GRATITUDE

In presenting a previous version of this chapter to various audiences, I have had many comments, some very helpful, others a bit less so. In any case, I take myself to have benefited from the people who reacted to the chapter. Also, I'm assuming that many of these people really wanted to help me improve the paper, and that they didn't do it for any self-interested ulterior motives, or at least not just for these reasons (McConnell, 1993). For simplicity, I'll call the attitudes in a benefactor that appear to be presupposed by the grateful beneficiary "benevolent attitudes," leaving it open what exactly these are.[2]

But am I grateful to them, now, several weeks or months after receiving the comments, comments my benefactors may not even remember? At first sight, it may appear that I am not genuinely grateful to them. For one thing, nothing in my behavior appears to suggest that I am grateful to them. To be sure, I may actually *use* some of the comments I received to improve the chapter. Although this might make my commentators happy, should they come to realize the impact they had on the chapter, I may do so in a way that disregards completely the origin of these comments. At least while I am writing the paper, what matters is that I improve it, and if the comments I received may help me do that, then I will use them. Otherwise, I won't. If I don't, however, this doesn't mean that I am not really grateful to my commentators.

Perhaps, however, we should look at what I am disposed to feel and do with respect to my commentators. But then again, I don't find myself experiencing anything in particular when I think about the moment I received the comments, or my commentators themselves. I might find the comments useful in and of themselves, but I might not feel anything toward the commentators who gave them. Neither am I particularly disposed to help them should they need some comments. The next time I see any of them talk, I do not think I will be particularly inclined to give a comment over and above my prior inclination to give comments whenever I find it relevant to do so. I am not, in other words, disposed to return the benefit.

To be sure, I might happen to feel differently about the various people who reacted to my chapter. I might like, or take pleasure in the company of, some more than others. I might want to keep in touch with some but not others. I might even appreciate the feedback given by some people more than I appreciate the feedback of others. And there might be commentators I actually feel, for various reasons, negatively about. And some reasons might have to do with the comments I received. Perhaps someone expressed a forceful objection to my argument, which, not knowing how to answer it, led me to form an irrational dislike of that person.

But what I happen to feel about my commentators need not be indicative of an underlying state of gratitude that I formed in response to the comments I received. I think that I am genuinely grateful to the people who reacted to my chapter, a fact whose only external sign will probably be an acknowledgment in a footnote, and that I am grateful to all these people *equally*. In expressing my thanks in a footnote, I take myself to be expressing the *same* kind of attitude to both those people I generally feel positively about and those people I generally feel negatively about. And, assuming talk of "strength" is appropriate here, such attitude may have the same strength in both cases, regardless of what I happen to independently feel. In addition, the attitude expressed need not lead me to be motivated one way or another to benefit my commentators.[3]

At this stage, one might object that I am not *really* grateful to my commentators if I am not disposed to benefit them in return if the occasion presents itself or do not feel a certain way with respect to them (e.g., McConnell, 1993). If this is right, then my acknowledgment would not be an expression of gratitude. At best, the objection goes, this would simply be compliance with a norm of etiquette.[4] Just as saying "Thanks" when someone is holding the door for us does not imply that I am grateful to that person for doing so, acknowledging the help of someone in a footnote need not indicate any attitude of gratitude toward her. In doing so, I may just be doing what's conventionally expected of me, and nothing more than that, especially if I am not disposed to return a benefit or to feel in a certain way in response to having been benefited.

Suppose it is true that my "thanks" in response to someone holding the door is not a genuine expression of gratitude, but rather mere compliance with a norm of etiquette. Does my thanking my commentators have the same structure such that it is plausible that I am not expressing any sort of gratitude in this case either? I think that there are at least two differences between the two cases that would explain why I should be grateful to my commentators but not grateful to the person who holds the door for me. First, there appears to be a social norm such that, if you are entering a building and someone is not too far behind you, then you should hold the door for them. It is therefore expected that we hold doors for others when this condition obtains. In fact, it is often *because* of our perception of this expectation that we hold doors, and not because we want to benefit the person behind us. By contrast, giving a comment at a conference is not expected in this way. There is no social norm enjoining us to give a comment when attending a talk, especially when the number of people is large enough so that not everyone is going to have a chance to give a comment anyway. In giving a comment at a conference, to a certain extent one thereby goes *out of one's way* in a way that someone holding a door for us doesn't.[5] There are, therefore, differences in what motivates the two actions that would explain why I should be grateful for only one of them, differences that would be reflected in my attitudes toward the relevant agents.[6] Second, it is not quite clear that having the door held for one is significant enough to be called a "benefit" at all. It would clearly count as a benefit if it were somewhat burdensome to open the door ourselves. Since for most of us it is not, calling it a benefit is a bit of a stretch. At any rate, since I don't believe that the door's being held for me is a benefit, it is pretty clear that I am not grateful to the agent.

I have pointed to two differences between holding the door for someone and giving a comment at a conference that appear to indicate that I should be grateful only to my commentators. The two situations are therefore normatively different. One might insist, however, that the sort of gratitude called for in the conference case should involve certain dispositions—affective and motivational—that I don't have, implying that I am not genuinely grateful. Perhaps, indeed, I should be disposed to give a comment in return, or to feel a certain way about my commentators. If I am not so disposed, the thought goes, I am not really grateful to them.

I have two responses to this argument to the effect that, given my dispositions, I am not genuinely grateful to my commentators even if I sincerely judge that I am. First, we should distinguish between the grateful response that one *should* form in a given context and the grateful response that one *actually* forms. Perhaps I should have the relevant sort of dispositions to be appropriately grateful to my commentators. This, however, does not entail that I am not grateful if I lack any of these dispositions. To appreciate this point, consider a situation in which a person merits the deepest gratitude there could ever be for an extraordinary benefit conferred on one (the person saved one's life, say). It seems that one should be extremely grateful to that person, and thereby should be disposed to do much more than say "thanks." Suppose, however, that one is in fact disposed to do a bit less than what the benefit calls for. Is one ungrateful? In a sense, yes. But it may still be true that one is grateful, albeit not as grateful as one should be. Perhaps, then, I am genuinely grateful to my commentators, albeit not as grateful as I should be.[7] If this much is accepted, however, then gratitude of the sort I take myself to have toward my commentators really exists, implying that gratitude does not necessarily involve the rather complex and deep dispositions— involving both motivational and affective aspects—posited in the contemporary literature (Berger, 1975; McConnell, 1993). Second, it is not even clear that I should be disposed to act and feel in certain ways to be appropriately grateful to my commentators. To be sure, I may have a sense of indebtedness, or may feel positively about my commentators, but this does not seem to be something the situation calls for. I would not be open to criticism if I failed in these respects. Nor would I be open to criticism if I did not give a comment while attending a talk delivered by any of my commentators. All the situation appears to call for, when it comes to my behavior, is a public acknowledgment of the help they have provided.

But in order for this acknowledgment to be a genuine expression of gratitude, rather than (say) compliance with a norm of etiquette, there still must be in my psychology something that makes it true of me that I *am* grateful, and that I have been grateful *all along*. Intuitively, I have been grateful ever since I have benefited from them and the acknowledgment was simply the occasion to express that gratitude. In addition, it seems that the acknowledgment does not mark the end of my gratitude, as if my gratitude was something, like thirst, to be quenched. But, as pointed out earlier, it shouldn't be always easy for me to bring the relevant people to mind.

To get to my account of the nature of gratitude of this minimal, generic sort—which I call *generic gratitude*—I'd like to make explicit what I take to be an attractive general conception of gratitude. I think that gratitude is a particular mode of *recognition* of the impact other people have on one's life and of the quality of their character.[8] In being grateful, I recognize that certain people have a certain *concern* for me—or at any rate, that they had such concern at some point in the past—and that it is such concern that motivated them to benefit me. I recognize the good things they do for me out of a concern of this sort. If one recognizes such things, then one can be truly said to be grateful. There are, however, different ways to recognize the good others bring to our lives in a way expressive of benevolent attitudes such as a concern. A particularly extreme way to do this is to commit oneself to do everything one can to improve their lives. In response to a (perhaps extraordinary) benefit I receive, I may form the disposition to be on the constant lookout to help my benefactor. Another form of recognition may involve only having a certain concern for the well-being of one's benefactors, although not one that will lead us to constantly try to benefit them. Still another form of recognition may involve being disposed to return a benefit.

Now, I think that there is a clear sense in which I recognize the good that my commentators brought to my life, a recognition I express by thanking or acknowledging them in my chapter.[9] This recognition, I have suggested, does not necessarily involve any particular sort of motivational or affective disposition. What must be true of me, then, for me to recognize the value of what my benefactors have done for me if not being disposed in these ways? All that seems needed, I contend, is that I hold certain *beliefs* about the benefactor and the benefit I received. In particular, I should believe that the thing my benefactor has done was a benefit and that it was motivated by benevolent attitudes.[10] Having a belief of this sort, by itself, is a way of recognizing that you have done something good for me out of attitudes that indicate that you have a benevolent concern for me. My sincere "thanks" or acknowledgment is a way of showing you that part of my conception of you—the part that I get from the fact that you benefited me (from the relevant benevolent motives).[11] Although more details about the cognitive states involved here should be ultimately given, I think that, if gratitude is a recognition of some sort, and if recognition of this sort can be realized by cognitive states of the sort just alluded to, then there is a kind of gratitude—generic gratitude—which someone has in virtue of holding certain beliefs, and that is appropriate only if such beliefs are in fact true.[12] It is important to notice that, on this account, generic gratitude is not something over and above the relevant beliefs. Rather, it is a logical consequence of holding these beliefs. If one holds the relevant beliefs, one is *thereby* grateful in the generic sense.

This account of generic gratitude seems to explain why I can be grateful to my commentators for a long time, including long after I have publicly acknowledged their help. So long as I hold the relevant beliefs, then it is true of me that I am grateful to my commentators. The account also explains why complete failure to remember being benefited by a certain person will imply a failure to be grateful to them, as presumably such a failure would imply the absence of some of the relevant beliefs. How about a temporary failure to remember? Since such a failure is compatible with the presence of the relevant beliefs, and it often takes a little bit of reflection to bring to mind the content of our beliefs, the account implies that we can be grateful, at a given time, to certain people even if we would not remember them if prompted at that time. The account, therefore, allows cases in which reflection is needed to know whom we are grateful to, thereby avoiding skepticism about the sort of gratitude we spontaneously and effortlessly form (which will often be unconscious, if the relevant beliefs are unconscious) as a result of benefiting from others.

I have argued that gratitude comes in both generic and non-generic forms in virtue of the fact that gratitude is a mode of recognition of other people, their character, and the things they do for us. Given that a belief of a certain sort is sufficient to constitute this recognition, such belief is sufficient to count as gratitude (or, rather, to make it true that one is grateful). I have not given reasons to believe this inclusive conception of gratitude as recognition, however. Neither have I given any argument to the effect that, if the account of gratitude as recognition is wrong, an inclusive account is preferable to a non-inclusive one. Instead of giving an argument for the account of gratitude as recognition in particular, though, I will point to three reasons for preferring an inclusive conception of gratitude—one that allows the holding of merely cognitive states to count as sufficient for gratitude. First, I think that an inclusive account better accommodates our ordinary self-attributions of gratitude. It takes at face value my sincere judgment that I am grateful to my commentators. It also takes at face value the judgment of those who take themselves to be grateful to others for extremely minor benefits. I may be grateful to my friend for buying me breakfast last weekend. It seems, indeed, that if you believe someone else has benefited you—even in a minor way— out of benevolent attitudes, you will thereby be disposed to sincerely assent to a proposition of the form *I am grateful to X for A*, regardless of any other attitude you might have toward your benefactor. Second, and relatedly, an inclusive account of gratitude gives a proper account of those cases of minor benefit such that it is clear that the beneficiary has pretty much nothing to do. Most advocates of non-inclusive accounts of gratitude would presumably agree that being benefited out of benevolent attitudes is sufficient for gratitude to be called for, and this regardless of how much one was benefited. It turns out that most of the ways other people benefit us do not appear to call for any deep change in motivational or affective profile, much less to generate a "debt of gratitude." The advocate of the non-inclusive account would therefore be forced either to deny that it is being benefited *simpliciter* that matters or deny that the relevant "benefits" are genuine benefits. Neither option, however, is particularly promising. Third, the inclusive account emphasizes that the evaluative beliefs other people have about us and about what we do already *matter*, and that they need not feel anything toward us to properly acknowledge us. If my feelings about you are significant in a way that does not derive from their disposing me to do certain things, I don't see why my beliefs about you cannot be significant in a similar way. We certainly care about what others think of us, we care about their conception of us, and we seem to care about it for its own sake. This suggests that we attach some significance to evaluative thought over and above feeling and action. Although I do not have an account of the normative significance of thought, I find it hard to deny.

To conclude this section, gratitude is often elusive because our evaluative beliefs about others are elusive. In many cases, it takes some effort and reflection to come to know what we think of other people and their actions. The fact that beliefs do not seem to be as phenomenologically salient (if they are so at all) as emotions and motivations may explain why philosophers tend to construe gratitude nongenerically, that is, as necessarily involving precisely those dispositions (motivational and affective) whose manifestation is very difficult to ignore. If the argument in this section is on the right track, this tendency should be avoided if we want to do justice to the full spectrum of ways we can properly recognize the impact other people have on us.

DEEP GRATITUDE

At first sight, it might be thought that gratitude is the response one forms *after* one has formed certain beliefs about the world—in particular, after having formed the belief that one has been benefited and that the benefit was given out of benevolent attitudes (or some such). If my argument in the previous section is on the right track, it is a mistake to think that one is not yet grateful when one has formed the relevant beliefs. As I have argued, gratitude is *already* present when one has those beliefs. In other words, holding the relevant beliefs is sufficient for gratitude.

This claim has an important implication, namely that affect and motivation are not necessary for gratitude. It is not true that gratitude implies a certain kind of goodwill toward one's benefactor (*contra* Herman, 2012; Walker, 1980–1981), or any sort of affective disposition (*contra* Berger, 1975; Camenish, 19801; McConnell, 1993; Roberts, 2004). One can be grateful without having these dispositions, or at any rate without having dispositions that one didn't already have before being benefited. Neither must one be inclined to benefit one's benefactor to be grateful. Gratitude, therefore, does not entail reciprocity (*contra* Manela, 2015, Section 3.4.1). Such descriptive claims have normative counterparts. It is not the case that to be appropriately grateful, one should have rather deep affective and motivational dispositions. If gratitude was indeed called for in response to receiving comments at a conference—which I think it was—what would be called for would be no more than the holding of certain beliefs and, if the occasion arises, a public acknowledgment of the benefit one received.

Now, not all cases of gratitude will be "generic." In fact, the clearest cases of gratitude are those that will also involve the sort of affective or motivational disposition often taken by philosophers to be essential to gratitude. The paradigmatic case of gratitude, one might argue, is not generic but *deep*. It is deep in the sense that it plays a rather pervasive role in one's psychology. A deeply grateful person would not only hold certain beliefs about her benefactor but would also be disposed to feel and be motivated in ways characteristic of gratitude. Such a person would also be disposed to emphatically express one's gratitude with claims such as that she is *deeply* grateful to X, or that she will *always* be grateful to X, for something X has done—something the generically grateful person would not typically say.[13]

I think deep gratitude—by contrast with generic gratitude—is essentially *affective*.[14] What this means is that it has a strong connection to the emotions. At first blush, we might take deep gratitude to *be* an emotion. This claim, although plausible, should be taken with a certain degree of care. For it is quite common in the literature on emotions—both in philosophy and the sciences—to take emotions to be *episodic* mental states, that is, mental events of some sort that are typically experienced for a relatively short period of time. On this understanding of the notion of emotion, the idea of gratitude as an emotion would be understood as about something we experience over a short period of time. Although there might exist a distinctive *feeling* of gratitude (a claim that itself may be doubted), gratitude as an *attitude* appears to be something that endures in a way that a mere emotional episode does not. As noted previously, one may *be* grateful for a really long time, even a lifetime. Deep gratitude, therefore, should be understood as an emotion in a rather different sense, that of an *affective attitude* or *sentiment* (Naar, 2018).[15] Just as one can love someone for a lifetime—even if it is not the case that one will constantly feel a particular way about the individual over a lifetime—one may be deeply grateful to someone for a lifetime.[16] Why should a sentiment be conceived as affective? Presumably, this is because it is connected to affective *episodes* in some way. Elsewhere, I argue that the nature of this connection is dispositional (Naar, 2018, see also Helm, 2001). Love, for instance, is (inter alia) a disposition to experience a certain range of emotions in various situations (Naar, 2013). Similarly, if deep gratitude is a sentiment, it will involve a disposition to experience various emotions in relevant situations.[17]

Several questions could be asked about the proposal just outlined. One might ask how we should understand the notion of disposition at play here. For instance, should it be understood in realist or antirealist terms? Although I have a view on this (Naar, 2013, 2018), I think that it is not crucial for my purposes, which is to propose a plausible distinction between two ways one can be grateful and an account of how these two sorts of gratitude are related. One might also ask how gratitude differs from other sentiments such as love. In particular, one might wonder how deep gratitude and love differ in their manifestations. Admittedly, I do not have an answer to this question.[18] In fact, I suspect that a fully satisfactory account is difficult to come by. The reason is that both deep gratitude and love appear to be species of *caring*. Both attitudes, indeed, appear to dispose their bearer to feel positively when things go well for the target and negatively when things go badly, and both attitudes appear to involve an inclination to advance the interests of the target. This set of dispositions, it seems, is sufficient for the subject to be properly said to care about the target, at least in some minimal way.

If true, the claim that deep gratitude is a species of caring raises important descriptive and normative questions. On the one hand, we might ask what explains that a subject could come to care about a benefactor, as opposed to merely holding the beliefs constitutive of generic gratitude as a result of having been benefited. On the other hand, we might ask what could make deep gratitude appropriate over and above generic gratitude. Why should one come to care about a benefactor in some cases and not others? Why, in other words, should being deeply grateful to someone be an appropriate way of recognizing the impact they have had on our lives? In the rest of this section, I will briefly spell out what I take to be the basic structure of deep gratitude, thereby going some way toward answering the descriptive question. In the next section, I will tackle the question of what might make deep gratitude an appropriate response to a benefactor.

The question of what explains the formation of deep gratitude is an instance of the question of what explains the formation of a special concern for someone. Why does one come to care about a person as opposed to many others one doesn't particularly care about? It appears that having certain beliefs about them may not be sufficient. I am fully aware that there are really wonderful people out there. I might even believe—perhaps on the basis of testimony—that that person over there is wonderful. Yet, believing this won't motivate me to care about them in the way I care about my friends. What would be needed, then, for me to be so motivated? Presumably, I would need to interact with them over a certain period of time. This would allow me to learn more about the particular way the person is wonderful. But even then, I might not be motivated to come to care about them the way I care about a friend. I think that what I learn about the person needs to *resonate* with me in some way. To come to care about them, indeed, what happens between us should bear on my own likes and dislikes, my desires, my personality, and my cares, namely traits I have had before meeting the person. The nature of this "bearing" relation is difficult to specify, but it is clear that without the addition of such factors, we won't be able to fully explain why I come to care about some people rather than others.[19]

The structure of deep gratitude that appears to emerge involves two main elements. First, one must form an adequate conception of the benefactor, the considerations that motivated her, and the benefit, something I've suggested should count as gratitude of a certain—generic—sort. When receiving comments at a conference, I formed certain beliefs about my commentators, their motivations, and the benefit I received. But I am not disposed to feel and act in ways characteristic of deep gratitude with respect to most people who gave me comments. Suppose, however, that one of the comments somehow bears on my cares. Perhaps one innocuous comment led me to the discovery of an important insight, the sort of thing I value greatly. In such a case, the fact that the comment has bearing on what I care about will make it much more likely for me to be deeply grateful to the person who gave it. Deep gratitude, therefore, is likely to occur when (1) one has the beliefs constitutive of generic gratitude and (2) some aspect of the benefit one has received—as represented by the beliefs mentioned in (1)—bears on one's cares, desires, likes, and so on.

Before moving on, three remarks are in order. First, the account of deep gratitude just sketched allows certain kinds of explanation that we would ordinarily give for our cares. Suppose you have come to care about someone in particular as a result of having benefited from her in the past. To my question "Why do you care about her?" you might at first point to features of the person that make your care for her appropriate or fitting. But suppose what I'm asking is that you give me a *psychological* explanation of your care, that is, what it is about your mental life that would have made your caring about her particularly likely to happen. It might then make sense to simply say, "Because I am grateful to her for what she has done for me." If deep gratitude is a species of caring, in saying this, you might be doing one of two things. On the one hand, you might be *specifying* the sort of care you have toward the person—it is an instance of gratitude rather than love (say). On the other hand, you might be pointing to the fact that you are *generically* grateful to the person and that this explains, at least in part, why you care about her, that is, why you are deeply grateful to her. In a way, indeed, it is *because* you are grateful that you care about the person, and the account I sketched allows us to say precisely this. Second, and relatedly, the account gives a straightforward story as to how deep gratitude is a distinctive kind of care. What motivates deep gratitude is indeed different from what motivates love. It is because I believe the things I believe about some of my friends that I am deeply grateful to them rather than in love with them. More generally, the fact that generic gratitude is a basic element of deep gratitude allows us to draw a principled distinction between those mental states that stem from gratitude and those that do not. Although it is quite easy to list things that appear to be "involved" in gratitude, it is relatively difficult to distinguish those that are really constitutive of it from those that are not. On my account, the difference has to do with the source of the relevant mental states. If I come to care about a given person (a care which will dispose me to feel and act in various ways) as a result of holding the beliefs constitutive of generic gratitude (together with deeper motivational features), then my caring for her will count as gratitude. Third, I think that the account of the structure of gratitude I sketched out gives a plausible story of the role of *reflection* in the generation of deep gratitude. In particular, it explains why reflecting on facts about the world—as represented by our beliefs—might motivate us to care about other people. Consider the practice of keeping a gratitude journal. To be sure, the value of doing so has in part to do with the fact that realizing or remembering that other people really care about us has a clear impact on our well-being; upon remembering what someone has done for me today, I might feel good in some way. As a result, there are clear reasons of self-interest to keep a gratitude journal. These are not the only reasons, however. In trying to remember what other people have done for us, and what motivated their action, we are putting ourselves in a position in which we might end up positively caring about them.[20] For, what they have done may in fact bear on what we care about in some significant way, in which case having the facts in plain view—absent some countervailing conditions (such as fatigue)—makes it likely that one will come to care about them.[21]

WHEN IS DEEP GRATITUDE APPROPRIATE?

At this stage, one might worry that, given that most of the benefits we receive will bear on deeper motivational features in one way or another, we should care about just about anyone who benefits us, however, minor the benefit may initially appear to be. This, it seems, would be an undesirable consequence of my account. The account, however, does not have this consequence. Recall that what I have done in the previous section is sketch out a *descriptive* account of deep gratitude, that is, an account of what deep gratitude is and how it might arise. The account didn't claim that, whenever deep gratitude is present, it is appropriate. On that issue, the account is silent. In fact, it might be the case that while deep gratitude depends on the presence of certain deeper traits, its appropriateness is a completely objective—attitude- or trait-independent—matter. Perhaps, indeed, one should be deeply grateful even when there is no trait that could lead one to be in that state (perhaps, then, one should have cared about different things).

Ignoring completely the relevant traits in an account of the appropriateness of deep gratitude may be a mistake, however. For one thing, what counts as a *benefit* generally depends on the presence of such traits. Whether a meal containing meat counts as a benefit for one will vary from one case to the next—whether or not, for instance, the recipient is a meat-eater or a vegetarian, and if she is a meat-eater, whether or not one in fact likes the relevant kind of meat. If the recipient is a vegetarian, presumably she would have absolutely no reason to be grateful,[22] let alone deeply grateful. For receiving the dish would not even count as a benefit in the first place. Furthermore, if what one receives indeed counts as a benefit, it may have a different impact on different people. In fact, the magnitude of a benefit (minor vs. major) appears to depend on what people happen to like, dislike, care about, and so on. If I like chocolate a little, but you are extremely fond of chocolate, being given the best Belgian chocolate will count as a significant benefit for you but not for me.

Now, the problem is that most benefits will be major—and thereby making deep gratitude appropriate—under *some* description or other. I may only like chocolate a little, but I deeply care about staying alive—and chocolate might contribute to that. So, chocolate counts as a major benefit if seen in light of its nutritional value but not if seen in light of its gustatory value. Furthermore, the practice of keeping a gratitude journal may in fact promote searching for a description under which the benefits we receive are major and thereby make deep gratitude appropriate. If I reflect on the comments I received at the conference, it appears that there is a description under which they are all very significant. For instance, the comments I received all constitute an occasion for me to sharpen up my intellectual and critical skills—something I deeply care about. Should I therefore be deeply grateful to each of my commentators? If being appropriately grateful is a matter of responding to the actual significance of a benefit, and if the actual significance of a benefit depends on some trait or other of the beneficiary, then it seems that I should be deeply grateful not only to my commentators but also to anyone who benefits me in a way that taps into some or other of my deeper cares.

The apparent conclusion, then, is that deep gratitude is almost always appropriate, so long as the benefit one receives is significant under some description.[23] Although some might not find this conclusion too implausible, many would probably want to avoid it. For accepting it would force us to accept that deep gratitude is almost never *in*appropriate. Clearly, though, forming the deep dispositions characteristic of caring as a result of being bought a meal looks like a disproportionate response to the benefit one receives. Being appropriately grateful, quite generally, does not seem to lie in the eye of the beholder in this way. At the same time, there appear to be cases in which the personal significance of a benefit should be taken into account in our assessment of the appropriateness of an instance of deep gratitude. Consider a piece of advice you have received a few years ago. As you see it, it radically changed the course of your life. You would not be the person you are today if you hadn't received it, and you deeply care about the sort of person you have become. It seems that being deeply grateful to the relevant person would be completely appropriate. The problem is that, under some description, most benefits can come to be seen a similar way as having great personal significance. Even being bought a meal may—by way of a rather complex story—be seen as contributing to the sort of person one is. If this is right, then we should conclude that, provided one has gone through a process whereby one finds some special significance in a benefit, deep gratitude is almost always appropriate, a conclusion many would find quite disturbing.

There are at least three possible responses to this problem, none of which is fully satisfactory. First, one might simply decide to bite the bullet and claim that deep gratitude is appropriate just in case it is supported by a story we tell ourselves, and perhaps this story is true (i.e., it is indeed true that the benefit is personally significant under the relevant description). Second, one might try to argue that, among all the descriptions under which a given benefit falls, there is a *right* (or relevant) one, and it is that description that determines whether deep gratitude is appropriate. The problem, however, is that it is really difficult, if not impossible, to find a principled way to distinguish between relevant and irrelevant descriptions. Should relevant descriptions be a matter of what we—observers—consider most salient, as opposed to what the beneficiary herself may see as salient as a result of a process of reflection? One possibility is that the relevant description is partly fixed by the *intention* of the benefactor, thereby introducing an external condition on relevant descriptions. For instance, if the benefactor didn't intend the meal she bought me to contribute to my flourishing in some important way, then perhaps the benefit itself should not be seen in this light—even if, in fact, it has had such an impact. But making the appropriateness of a benefit dependent in this way on the intention of a benefactor would rule out cases of seemingly appropriate gratitude in response to clearly extraordinary benefits the benefactor didn't intend.[24] If something someone told you a while ago quite literally saved your life, I don't see why you should not be deeply grateful to her. A third response would be to go back to the objectivist account of the appropriateness of deep gratitude introduced but discarded earlier in this section. On that account, one should be deeply grateful when certain attitude-independent conditions obtain. Perhaps, for instance, what counts as a benefit is determined by factors independent of one's attitudes. On this view, whether a sandwich counts as a benefit for one won't depend on how much significance one assigns to it, or indeed on whether or not one sees it as a benefit in the first place. This account would thereby imply that sometimes one should be grateful even if one doesn't see any value in the thing one has received. Although it might deal with cases where it is possible for us to reason our way to recognition of a benefit, this account comes with the risk of having to admit that we should sometimes be deeply grateful even if it is virtually psychologically impossible to form that attitude (because we have no cares on which the benefit bears in any way), in turn divorcing the normative profile of deep gratitude from its attitude-dependent nature.

All in all, we seem to be caught in a certain dilemma: either the appropriateness of deep gratitude is determined by what one happens to think—in which case one could bootstrap oneself into a situation in which deep gratitude is appropriate (or into one in which it is inappropriate, if one decides to take as relevant a description on which a benefit ends up being minor rather than major)—or else deep gratitude is determined, at least in part, by factors (e.g., the actual intention of the benefactor or other objective conditions) that might be in some way alienating to the beneficiary (either enjoining her to be deeply grateful when nothing in her cares could motivate her to form the attitude, or enjoining her to stop being grateful even if she assigns great personal value to the benefit). This leaves us with a challenge: that of showing that deep gratitude indeed has conditions of appropriateness. For as the discussion suggests, it might just be true that benefits by themselves never give us reasons to be deeply grateful—as opposed to generically grateful—to others for what they have done for us. Perhaps, then, deep gratitude—as a mode of recognition—is outside the domain of things we should do or should not do. Like a gift, it might simply be completely free.[25]

NOTES

1 Of course, you might realize that you have been benefited much later after the fact, perhaps as a result of reflecting about the impact a given person has had on your life. In cases like this, it is certainly not the case that you have been grateful all along. The question in the text will be what must be true of you for it to be the case that you have been grateful prior to the relevant acknowledgment. Thanks to Robert Roberts for the discussion.

2 Here I follow Manela (2016).

3 Of course, I may be motivated to benefit them for reasons that do not have anything to do with my gratitude to them.

4 Alternatively, it might be an acknowledgment of a positive causal contribution, as when one is grateful *that* it is sunny. If what I call "generic gratitude" does not exist, then perhaps what is going on in the conference case is that I am grateful *that* I received the comments, rather than being grateful—in the generic sense—to my commentators for the comments I received. I don't think we should resort to this move, however, unless a positive argument is given to the effect that the broadly intuitive considerations given in the text can be explained away. Thanks to Daniel Telech for discussion.

5 To be sure, at a conference, there might be a norm that *somebody* gives a comment when nobody in the audience says anything. Assuming you are not the only person in the audience, giving a comment would be going out of your way, for some other person in the room could have done it instead of you. Generic gratitude may thereby be called for in such a case. Thanks to Robert Roberts for the discussion.

6 As Daniel Telech pointed out, it is unclear that people give comments at conferences out of concern for the speaker rather than from interest in the philosophical question at issue. I do not wish to deny that this might be what's going on in many cases. When this happens, on my view, saying "thanks" would be a matter of compliance to etiquette. I do believe, however, that at least some of the people who comment on my papers do so out of a concern for me. If the readers find the conference paper case misleading, they are free to switch to the case of an internal seminar designed to improve a colleague's paper, a context where arguably a desire for the success of the speaker is more likely to be in place.

7 See Manela (this volume) for a discussion of the range of such possible kinds of failures of gratitude.

8 For an account of gratitude as recognition, see Berger (1975). It should be noted that Berger's notion of recognition is richer than the minimal one I endorse in the text. As a result, Berger may disagree with my claim that there is the sort of gratitude I call "generic."

9 For a view along these lines, see Macnamara (2013).

10 As pointed out by Daniel Telech, a further condition on generic gratitude might be that the benefit be "welcome," where this implies not only that I believe that my benefactor benefited me benevolently but also that I desire that the benefactor so benefits me. In response, I do not wish to deny that certain desires must be present in order for generic gratitude to form. For one thing, it is plausible that, in order for something to count as a benefit at all, it must relate to my desires in a certain way (see next section). Similarly, for a benefit to be welcome, it may need to relate to my desires in some way. It is important to note, however, that the relevant desires are plausibly independent of the generic gratitude I form in response to a benefit, for they seem to belong to the conditions that must be satisfied for it to form in the first place. Just as I need to be alive to be grateful, I need to have certain background desires. I take it that accepting this much is compatible with holding a purely cognitive account of generic gratitude. At any rate, I don't mind adding a further claim to the

account to the effect that the benefit must be welcome in the relevant sense. So long as this does not entail any of the desires authors typically associate with gratitude, the core thesis of this section is preserved.

11 Perhaps holding this conception of you would itself count as a benefit for you; I'm not sure.

12 A further condition might be that the belief should be justified. I would like to remain silent on the question whether the belief must also constitute knowledge.

13 Notice as well that it will be much easier for us to call to mind someone we are deeply grateful to.

14 It might also be essentially motivational if affective states are essentially motivational. At any rate, since affective and motivational states often come together, the present account could be adequately cast as an "affective-cum-motivational" account.

15 For the claim that the term "emotion" is ambiguous between two senses, see Goldie (2000).

16 Of course, the explanation of why *generic* gratitude persists a similar way will have to do with the fact that the relevant beliefs persist in that way.

17 If there is such a thing, a way deep gratitude might manifest itself is in an episodic *feeling* of gratitude. It might also issue in episodic consternation if one becomes aware of some behavior of one's benefactor that is inconsistent with one's gratitude to her. It should also be noted that the sort of disposition involved in deep gratitude is different from the sort of disposition involved in gratitude the *trait*, which is not directed at anybody in particular. Thanks for Robert Roberts for a discussion on this issue.

18 My own suspicion is that the primary difference between deep gratitude and love lies in part in the considerations that make them appropriate. Whereas love is made appropriate by facts about the beloved, gratitude is made appropriate in part by facts about oneself—such as the fact that one has benefited. For an account of reasons for love as completely disinterested, see Naar (2017).

19 This is in fact an instance of a more general point about the formation of various affective states. As Deonna and Teroni (2012) point out, emotions do not just have a "cognitive base"—namely the set of representational states that give us the information necessary for an emotion to be triggered (i.e., the belief that there is a wild animal nearby). Emotions also have a "motivational base"—namely the set of motivational states, which explain why the thing represented by the relevant cognitive states should be something we are likely to be afraid of, sad about, and so on. For instance, after having formed the belief that there is a wild animal nearby, and that he could hurt me, I won't be afraid unless I care for my life.

20 As pointed out to me by Robert Roberts, in remembering what other people have done for me, and caring as a result, I may also be doing them "justice," or giving them their "due." If, as I suggested in the previous section, gratitude is a mode of recognition, this is unsurprising.

21 If one does not care yet, one may instead form the commitment to care about them at some point in the future. In this case, enthusiastically thanking someone or claiming publicly that one is deeply grateful may work as a commissive speech act rather than as an expressive one (Camenish, 1981).

22 Unless an expression of goodwill or benevolence can itself constitute a benefit. In the case at issue, however, any benefit one might get from such an expression would arguably be outweighed by the negative aspect of being given meat. Thanks to Daniel Telech for pointing out this possibility.

23 And perhaps so long as that description is present to the beneficiary's mind.

24 It should be pointed out that this is compatible with claiming that the benefactor must have at least intended to benefit me in some way. Recall that, on my view, a necessary condition on gratitude is that one believes that the benefactor has acted out of concern for one. This, however, is not the same as saying that the benefactor must be believed to have intended to benefit one in the way she did. Thanks to Daniel Telech for discussion.

25 I am—generically but potentially deeply—grateful to Bob Roberts, Daniel Telech, Michele Palmira, and two audiences at the University of Chicago and the University of Montreal, for reactions and comments on previous versions of this chapter, in particular: Jack Bauer, Paul Boswell, Etienne Brown, Agnes Callard, David Carr, Sophie Grace Chappell, Justin Coates, Willem van der Deijl, Cameron Fenton, Martin Gibert, Valéry Giroux, Liz Gulliford, Richard Healey, Bennett Helm, Christina Karns, Tony Manela, Angie Pepper, Marya Schechtman, Will Small, Christine Tappolet, and Stephen White.

REFERENCES

Berger, F. (1975). "Gratitude," *Ethics*, 85, 4, 298–309.

Camenish, P.F. (1981). "Gift and Gratitude in Ethics," *Journal of Religious Ethics*, 9, 1, 1–34.

Deonna, J.A. & Teroni, F. (2012). *The Emotions: A Philosophical Introduction*. New York: Routledge.

Goldie, P. (2000). *The Emotions: A Philosophical Exploration*. Oxford: Oxford University Press.

Helm, B. (2001). *Emotional Reason: Deliberation, Motivation, and the Nature of Value*. Cambridge: Cambridge University Press.

Herman, B. (2012). "Being Helped and Being Grateful: Imperfect Duties, the Ethics of Possession, and the Unity of Morality," *Journal of Philosophy*, 109, 5/6, 391–411.

Macnamara, C. (2013). " 'Screw you!' & 'Thank you,' " *Philosophical Studies*, 165, 893–914.

Manela, T. (2015). "Gratitude," *Stanford Encyclopedia of Philosophy*, https://plato.stanford.edu/entries/gratitude/.

Manela, T. (2016). "Gratitude and Appreciation," *American Philosophical Quarterly*, 53, 3, 281–294.

Manela, T. (this volume).

McConnell, T. (1993). *Gratitude*. Philadelphia, PA: Temple University Press.

Naar, H. (2013). "A Dispositional Theory of Love," *Pacific Philosophical Quarterly*, 94, 3, 342–357.

Naar, H. (2017). "Subject-Relative Reasons for Love," *Ratio*, 30, 2, 197–214.

Naar, H. (2018). "Sentiments," in Naar, H. & Teroni, F. (eds.), *The Ontology of Emotions*. Cambridge: Cambridge University Press, pp. 149–168.

Roberts, R.C. (2004). "The Blessings of Gratitude: A Conceptual Analysis," in Emmons, R.A. & McCullough, M.E. (eds.), *The Psychology of Gratitude*. Oxford: Oxford University Press, pp. 58–78.

Walker, A.D.M. (1980–1981). "Gratefulness and Gratitude," *Proceedings of the Aristotelian Society*, 81, 39–55.

Chapter 2

Acting from Gratitude

Terrance McConnell

INTRODUCTION

My focus in this chapter is on some cases where it is not clear that an agent's acting from gratitude is morally admirable. Before getting to these cases, let me set the scene.

I start from the premise that repayment of debts of gratitude is both an obligation (or moral requirement)[1] and a virtue (McConnell 1993: Chapter 2; McConnell 2018b). I also assume that being morally motivated is primarily acting from virtue (Audi 1995: 462–463, 467, 469; Hursthouse 1999: 123–126; Tiberius 2015: 108) and that virtuous agents choose virtuous acts for their own sake. Since Aristotle, this is the canonical position (Aristotle 1985: 1105a 28–35 [39–40] and 1144a 15–20 [168–169]). Aristotle frequently asserts that virtuous agents perform the right acts, with the right feelings, at the right times, toward the right people (Aristotle 1985: 1106b 20–25 [44]; 1120b 1–5 [88]; and 1125b 30–35 [105]). According to this approach, "Gratitude would only count as appropriate when felt 'at right times, about right things, towards the right people, for the right end and in the right way'" (Morgan et al. 2015: 101). This requires saying when gratitude is owed and why.

Gratitude is the response of a beneficiary to his benefactor.[2] But gratitude is not due for the mere receipt of a benefit. If my walking by frightens a would-be mugger and thereby saves you from an assault, you owe me no gratitude (Simmons 1979: 170–171). And if I realized that my walking by would frighten the assailant but I did not care whether that fortuitous result happened, again my act lacks moral quality (Berger 1975: 299). In neither case did I intend to provide you with the benefit. Furthermore, if I benefit you only so that I can hurt some third party, or if I benefit you only for the purpose of putting you in my debt, no gratitude is due (McConnell 1993: 22–23). Gratitude is not a response merely to the provision of a benefit; it is a response to benevolence, and that requires that the act be done intentionally and for the right reasons (Berger 1975: 299–300). Adam Smith's account of gratitude in *The Theory of Moral Sentiments* (1982/1790: Part II, 67–108) recognizes all of these elements. Smith argues that gratitude is a response to moral merit; the benefactor's actions deserve recognition and reward (69). The benefactor's motives and reasons for action must be admirable; trivial motives lack moral merit (72–75). The beneficiary must acknowledge and appreciate the benefactor's act and be willing to compensate her in suitable circumstances (68, 75). The point of gratitude is "to make him [the benefactor] conscious that he meets with this reward on account of his past conduct, to make him pleased with that conduct" (95). Smith's position—one with which I concur (McConnell 1993: Chapter 1)—holds that the gratitude of a beneficiary is *conceptually connected* with her moral evaluation of the benefactor's act.[3] Viewed this way, gratitude is in part a form of respect. Kant says explicitly, "Gratitude consists in honoring a person because of kindness he has done us. The feeling connected with this recognition is respect for the benefactor (who puts one under obligation)" (Kant 1964/1797: Ak 453 [123]). Anthropologist Margaret Visser puts it this way: "Gratitude, like giving, is about regard and respect" (Visser 2009: 316; see also, 53, 63, 218, 227, 355). This is an instance of what Stephen Darwall calls "appraisal respect" (Darwall 2006: 122–123).[4] So gratitude involves not only an emotion on the part of the beneficiary but also a belief (that he has been benefited intentionally) and an evaluation (that the benefactor's act is morally admirable).

ACTING FROM GRATITUDE: COMPLICATIONS

In what I will take to be the prototypical case of acting from gratitude, the (virtuous) beneficiary will acknowledge and appreciate the benefactor's act and in some way express this to her; a sincere "thank you" is one way to do this. He will also be prepared to reciprocate if appropriate circumstances obtain; the concept of *gratitude to* another entails a willingness to make a return (Manela 2016a: 283, 290). He is acting from gratitude if he acts for the sake of the relevant value. When acting from virtue (in general), the agent need not have the occurrent thought that virtue V is relevant to her circumstances; rather, her reasons must reflect appreciation of the relevant underlying value (Hursthouse 1999: 127–128 and 233; MacIntyre 1999: 159; and Russell 2009: 84–85). Robert Audi articulates this idea by suggesting that each virtue has characteristic "targets" it aims at, "such as the well-being of others in the case of beneficence." So an agent might be thinking of her action as "relieving suffering" rather than specifically in terms of beneficence. Thus, "One can act *from* a virtue by acting from its grounds without having that very virtue in mind" (Audi 1995: 458, 461). This can be true when the beneficiary acts from gratitude. He may be thinking generally about the benefactor's goodwill toward him, and in particular about the provision of a benefit to him by way of a morally admirable act. Though some have held that the benefactor's act must be supererogatory before gratitude is due, I deny this. Whether the provision of a benefit is morally admirable in a suitable way is context-dependent. In some cases, gratitude is due even if the benefactor had a duty to provide the benefit, and in some cases, gratitude is due even when the beneficiary had a right to the benefit (McConnell 2017). (For an opposing view on this last point, see the chapter by Coleen Macnamara in this volume.)

There can be cases where a beneficiary does what a grateful person would do but does not act *from* gratitude. If the beneficiary (or the original benefactor) has ulterior motives, such as the desire to impress others, that is not acting from virtue in general, or gratitude in particular (Hursthouse 1999: 125; Visser 2009: 338). If the beneficiary (or the benefactor) acts from whim or for frivolous reasons, that is not moral motivation (Hursthouse 1999: 124; Smith 1982/1790: 72). If the beneficiary acts for the purpose of angering or harming some third person, that too is not acting from gratitude.

Moreover, not all cases where someone might describe himself (or others might describe him) as acting from gratitude are cases that reflect the appropriate values. Cases of misplaced gratitude fit here. One example is the so-called Stockholm syndrome, situations in which victims come to sympathize with their captors and sometimes experience gratitude for small benefits (e.g., food) or even for those times when they are not being assaulted or victimized. The subjective feeling may be akin to gratitude, but the relevant beliefs and evaluations are either not present or are badly mistaken. Some will say that what the victim is experiencing in this case is not gratitude proper because all three elements are not properly aligned; others will say, based on the feeling alone, that it *is* gratitude but it is *not warranted*. While I favor the former view, I don't think that anything I say here hinges on how this is resolved.

Consider a second case where someone's apparently acting from gratitude is not morally admirable. Suppose the benefit provided is morally tainted, what we might call an ill-gotten gain (Carr 2015: 1481). Robert Roberts (2013: 124) provides a provocative case. The physician of a man who is badly in need of a kidney transplant is willing to falsify documents so that her patient will be given priority over other patients who have been waiting longer and whose medical conditions are more desperate. The man feels grateful to the physician both because of the magnitude of the benefit and that she was willing to engage in risky conduct to help him. According to Roberts, though the man's gratitude may show some good things about him, it is nevertheless in this case "intrinsically bad" (125). This is correct if the man recognizes the wrongness of the physician's conduct; and even if he does not recognize this, gratitude is unwarranted because the physician's actions were not morally admirable.

What is common to these two cases is that gratitude is *not due*; there are no doubt other such examples. There can also be cases where gratitude is due but where acting from gratitude may not be admirable. This can occur when gratitude conflicts with some other principle, and in the particular case, the other principle takes priority. This is what Rosalind Hursthouse calls "resolvable dilemmas" (Hursthouse 1999: Chapter 2); the requirements of two different virtues are in *conflict*. Imagine a situation in which an agent can assist either P_1 or P_2 but not both. P_1 is due gratitude from the agent, but P_2 is in grave danger and P_1 will suffer only minor inconvenience if the agent does not assist her. In this case, beneficence takes priority over gratitude, and if the agent were to help P_1 and to do so from gratitude, it would be morally problematic.

For the remainder of this chapter, however, I will focus on cases where an agent has an all-things-considered reason to discharge a debt of gratitude, but where the agent's acting from gratitude may nevertheless not be morally desirable. The situation I am envisioning is where two (or more) principles support doing the same act and it seems that we have moral reasons to hope that the agent will act for the sake of one of the principles (or the values underlying the principle) rather than the other. The principles are not in conflict because they prescribe the same act. We might say that they are *competing for salience*. Suppose that a judge is prepared to rule in a case. She believes that justice (understood here as following the law) supports decision D_1, but she also notices that decision D_1 will be good for the defendant, supported by beneficence. Acting from justice, we think, is what is called for here. Suppose that an instructor is calculating final grades for his class. Based on all of the work submitted, he believes that student S_1 has earned an A. He believes, correctly, that fairness requires assigning S_1 an A, but he also believes that this will promote her interests and help her achieve her career goals. Fairness should be the salient motive in this case. And suppose that a physician must convey a dire diagnosis and prognosis to her patient. Even if she believes that the patient's long-term interests are best advanced by telling him the truth about his condition, honesty, not beneficence, should be her salient motive. These examples demonstrate the broader point that an agent's salient motives reveal what her values and commitments are and why these are morally important (Badhwar 2014: 175; Frankfurt 2004: 43). If the agent acts *only* or *primarily* from beneficence in these cases, it is problematic.

Agents can, of course, have multiple reasons for performing actions and have cooperating multiple motives. But even when these reasons and motives are cooperative—that is, direct us to perform the same action—we can sensibly ask whether for the virtuous person one of these motives will be salient; for while it is possible that each of the motives is equally efficacious, that is unlikely (Ross 1930: 168–173). Consequentialists may hold that it does not matter which if either of these motives is salient; what is important is that the right action is performed. For some deontologists and for virtue ethicists, however, it does seem important which motive is salient. This is the issue underlying the two main cases that I shall discuss here.

BENEFICENCE OR GRATITUDE?

Let us consider the person whom Kant calls a "friend of mankind." As Kant depicts this person, he is simple-minded and instinctively kind. Perhaps he possesses what Aristotle calls a natural virtue (Aristotle 1985: 1144b 5–15 [170]). Here is part of Kant's description.

> To be beneficent where one can is a duty; and besides this, there are many persons who are so sympathetically constituted that, without any further motive of vanity or self-interest, they find an inner pleasure in spreading joy around them and can rejoice in the satisfaction of others as their own work. But I maintain that in such a case an action of this kind, however dutiful and amiable it may be, has nevertheless no true moral worth. (Kant 1983/1785: Ak 398 [11])

Kant continues this thought experiment by imagining that "all sympathy with the lot of others is extinguished" in this person due to ill fortune; nevertheless he performs some acts of beneficence "from duty." Kant infamously says that "then for the first time his action has genuine moral worth" (Kant 1983/1785: Ak 398 [11]). I am not advocating this position, but I do want to consider a modified version of the case.

Let us say that our "friend of mankind" routinely performs acts of beneficence. She is motivated by some of the usual "targets" of beneficence, such as the desire to promote another's well-being or to relieve suffering. She possesses either the natural virtue or the moral virtue of beneficence; it may be difficult for casual observers to determine which (Frankfurt 2004: 72). Gratitude, however, is not one of her prominent moral traits. Either she has not cultivated the moral virtue of gratitude or its strength is minimal. But she is a paragon of beneficence.[5] Now let us imagine that this kind person, P_1, owes gratitude to a second individual, P_2. P_1 is now in a position to provide P_2 with a benefit, and she does so. Her motivation is beneficence; the opportunity to help another person is what prompts her conduct. She gives no thought to the fact that P_2 had previously helped her. In this case, not only is beneficence the salient motive, it is the only motive. What difference does it make, one might ask? The right person, P_2, received help and P_1 did the right act, in some sense of "right."

Let's approach this issue in a slightly circuitous way. Let's ask a different question. If an agent has adopted the principle of beneficence and has culti-vated this virtue "to the full extent" (Aristotle 1985: 1140b 14 [170]), does that render gratitude superfluous? Two simple cases show that the answer to this question is negative. First, suppose that our beneficent agent encounters a situation in which two people need help, she can help either but not both and one of the two is a prior benefactor,[6] but helping the other person would produce slightly more good. Beneficence dictates helping the stranger, but if gratitude has any moral force the prior benefactor should be favored. This is a case of *conflicting* motivations (rather than competing) because the two principles pull the agent in different directions. So it is not the test case we need, but it does show that beneficence does not make gratitude superfluous. Second, suppose that our agent encounters a situation in which several people need help, she can help any but only one of them, and one of those in need of help is a prior benefactor. Suppose further that the amount of good that will be produced is the same, no matter which person she chooses to help. Gratitude requires the agent to help her prior benefactor, while beneficence presumably requires her to help one, but any one, of those in need. In one sense, this is not a conflict; but beneficence merely permits what gratitude requires. This is still not the test case, but it is closer.

The test case is when the two principles direct the agent to help the same person. This case will obtain if there is only one person in need of help and he is a prior benefactor, or if there are multiple people in need of help but assist-ing the prior benefactor will produce the most good. This is where the "What difference does it make?" response may seem to have some punch. But it does make a difference. The grateful person acknowledges that she benefited from the morally meritorious conduct of the benefactor. The prior benefactor *deserves* her help and the moral motivation of the virtuous agent will reflect this. I should clarify what I mean by "deserves" here. It is commonplace in the literature about gratitude to say that the benefactor does not have a claim right against the beneficiary. I agree with this; that is one of several things that distinguish contractual relationships from those of gratitude. But in some contexts, we can correctly say that P_1 *owes* P_2 something, or that P_2 *deserves* to be treated in a certain way without thereby implying that P_2 possesses a claim right against P_1. "Owing" sometimes denotes that an attitude or conduct is morally fitting, appropriate, or deserved, even if there is no correlative right (Card 1988: 121). We owe compassion to the suffering even if they have no claim right to that (MacIntyre 1999: 116); so too an organ recipient owes gratitude to the donor's family even though the family has no right to demand this.[7]

Two qualifications are in order. First, I am not claiming that gratitude always takes priority over beneficence in situations where those norms *conflict*. A variety of cases can occur here, and which of the conflicting norms prevails will vary with the circumstances. Second, other cases of (what I am calling) *competition* can be imagined, and I am not claiming that in all such instances, the motive of gratitude, rather than a competitor, should be salient. It depends on the values in question. Suppose that my supervisor owes me gratitude for some past favor or benefit. Suppose too that she has determined that this year my job performance has been especially good and that I deserve a generous raise. In such a case, the motive for giving me a raise should be fairness; gratitude should play no role.

LOVE OR GRATITUDE?

If someone acts from duty in general, or from gratitude in particular, the person toward whom the action is directed may feel undervalued, or believe that the relationship is being diminished. This sense of disconcertion is most likely to be experienced in the relationship between loved ones. Here by "loved ones" I mean spouses, other life-partners, close adult friends, adult siblings, and parents and adult children (Velleman 1999: 351).[8] I assume here that in most cases, the conditions necessary for creating an obligation of gratitude are satisfied in the relationship between loved ones (or have been on various past occasions). Or, more modestly, I am concerned only with those cases where the conditions are satisfied. Anecdotally when I have asked people about gratitude in their own lives, they most often mention family, parents, spouse, and friends (McConnell 2018a: 51).[9] In these relationships, when one party acts from duty, or from gratitude, it may seem that something has gone wrong. Michael Stocker articulates this point clearly.

> Duty seems relevant in our relations with our loved ones and friends, only when our love, friendship, and affection lapse. If a family is "going well," its members "naturally" help each other; that is, their love, affection, and deep friendship are sufficient for them to care for and help one another (to put it a bit coolly). Such "feelings" are at times worn thin. At these times duty may have to be looked to or called upon (by the agent or by others) to get done at least a modicum of those things which love would normally provide. (Stocker 1976: 465, note 8)

This suggests that when the motive of duty must be called upon in loving relationships, something has gone wrong. That would also seem to apply if one of the parties in the relationship acted from gratitude, acted because she believed that reciprocation was morally owed to the other.

Another reason for feeling discomfort in appealing to duty in loving relationships is spelled out by Rosalind Hursthouse. She asks us to consider a person who visits a friend, or a mother who jumps into the river to save her child. If we asked this person why she performed the action in question, and she said, "This would be the right thing to do" or "This is my duty," her answer would be "repellently self-righteous." "The right reason is, say, 'She's lonely', 'She's my child' . . . that should be sufficient to prompt the action in the circumstances" (Hursthouse 1999: 132). Indeed, if a third party were to "credit" the friend or the mother for acting from duty, that friend or mother would likely take offense. The same would seem to be the case if the motive of gratitude were attributed to a party in a comparable relationship.

The relationship between parents and their adult children provides another instance of the awkwardness of duty-talk in loving relationships. There is a robust debate about whether adult children owe their parents gratitude (McConnell 1993, Chapter VII; McConnell 2018a; and the references therein; Fenton, this volume). One aspect of this debate concerns what parents want from their adult children. Visser observes, "Research has confirmed that elderly parents rarely think of their children as 'owing' them anything. . . . They want not a 'return' for what they did for their children, but relationship in love" (Visser 2009: 198). Norvin Richards also notes that "gratitude is not ordinarily what parents want from their grown children" (Richards 2010: 229). He later returns to this topic and writes:

> But what is it that parents want from their children beyond gratitude for what they once did and how deeply they cared for them? I would say it includes a further place of their own in the affections of their grown sons and daughters. I will argue that this is what grown children *owe* their parents if certain further conditions are met. (Richards 2010: 233)

If Visser and Richards are correct, parents may be disappointed or offended if their adult children provide them with help from a sense of gratitude (understood as a moral requirement). These attitudes are likely to be present in other loving relationships. Let us call this "the complaint." But why do people have this attitude? I suspect that the underlying belief here is that people who act from duty somehow have to be prompted; the action is in some way burdensome, one they would rather not do. By contrast, when someone acts from love, that person does so joyously; it is no burden at all.[10]

There is another reason that parents may be offended if their adult children feel, express, and act from gratitude toward them. They may retort, "I didn't expect a return" or "I was only doing my duty." Claudia Card explores this idea as it applies to those who rescued persons who were fleeing from the Nazis during World War II. She calls such an individual "the decent rescuer." She quotes from Holocaust rescuer Ari Van Mansum, who says, "There was nothing special about what I did. I did what everyone should have done" (Card 2016: 101). We might note here that we are viewing this from the perspective of the original benefactor. She is saying, "I only did my duty; therefore, no gratitude is due." The same idea can come from the perspective of the beneficiary. Visser sums it up succinctly.

> Gratitude *might* be fitting where a parent has been outstandingly gifted at child rearing, or has made exceptional sacrifices on behalf of her young. But gratitude, strictly speaking, is not owing for what is done for us out of duty. . . . Parents are obviously obliged to take care of their children; but if they do only what parents are supposed to do, and are not perceived by their offspring as having shown excellence, then gratitude is not required. (Visser 2009: 192)

What is common to each perspective is the belief that duty-fulfilling conduct cannot generate a debt of gratitude.[11] There is something a bit odd here. It is likely that the parents themselves acted often from love, but sometimes from duty, in raising their children. Yet, if Visser and Richards are correct, they prefer that their adult children act from love rather than from duty (gratitude). The idea seems to be, per Stocker, that the relationship is on firmer grounds when the motive of love is sufficient.

There is a tension here. It would be bizarre to hold that the agent who acted from love rather than gratitude in a loving relationship was thereby morally lacking. On the other hand, it seems clear that gratitude can be due in such relationships. A proper understanding of this kind of case requires showing that love can be the agent's salient motive without thereby shortchanging other morally applicable norms, such as gratitude.

One answer to this challenge is provided by Thomas Hill Jr. Writing in the context of trying to show that the gap between Kantian ethics and virtue ethics is not as great as many believe, he addresses the objection that Kant had an implausible account of moral motivation because he held that only acts done from duty have moral worth. He thinks instead that Kant can allow that acting from some motives other than duty can be both appropriate and commendable. "A virtuous person, for example, may be commendable for caring for her children out of love, rather than duty, assuming that duty would move her if love should fade" (Hill 2012: 157; see also, Velleman 1999: 341). Hill here proposes a *counterfactual test*. If P_1 is morally required to treat P_2 in a certain way, and does indeed do so from love, P_1's act exhibits proper moral motivation provided she would have acted in the same way even if love were not present. If the counterfactual is true, it suggests that P_1 has adopted appropriate principles and cultivated relevant moral virtues.

A second answer to the challenge (compatible with the first) suggests that love encompasses various other moral norms. When friends interact with each other, it would be odd if they did not exhibit the virtues of kindness, generosity, compassion, honesty, and fidelity. This is, in part, what friendship is. I allude here to what Neera Badhwar has called the "limited unity of the virtues," the claim that the existence of a virtue in one domain of a person's life does not imply its existence in some other domain, but that every virtue does require the others in the same domain (Badhwar 1996: 308; 2014: 172–173).[12] Whether love itself is a moral emotion is a contested question; but it is clear that various norms have a special application in loving relationships (Badhwar 1996: 320–321; 2014: 189–195). As noted earlier, while there are differences among romantic love, filial love, and the kind of love that friends have for each other, nevertheless we expect that our treatment of someone in any one of these relationships will be virtuous in all (or most) respects: that we will exhibit to the beloved kindness, generosity, compassion, honesty, *and* gratitude.

One aspect that these two answers to the challenge have in common is a picture of how agents in loving relationships are morally prepared. Decisions are made constantly in these relationships, and often there is little time to contemplate or reason. Henry Sidgwick makes this point, though in a broader context.

> [I]n order to fulfil our duties thoroughly, we are obliged to act during part of our lives suddenly and without deliberation: on such occasions there is no room for moral reasoning, and sometimes not even explicit moral judgment; so that in order to act virtuously, we require such particular habits and dispositions as are denoted by the names of the special virtues: and it is a duty to foster and develop these in whatever way experience shows this to be possible. (Sidgwick 1981/1907: 227)

Daniel Russell makes a similar point.

> When someone helps a parent with a pram out of kindness, he makes a decision and acts, and the decision has a deliberative structure. . . . But that is not to say that he had to stop and search over that specification; he did not have to, since certain patterns of end-specification have already become habitual. Simply put, deliberation takes time, *until* a deliberative pattern becomes habitual. (Russell 2009: 13; see also, 82)

Along these same lines, writing about generosity, Alasdair MacIntyre says, "But insofar as I have in fact acquired that virtue—it, like other virtues, can be acquired in varying degrees—I will have learned to act without thought of any justification beyond the need of those given into my care" (MacIntyre 1999: 159). Not surprisingly, Aristotle has expressed this same idea. "If an action is foreseen, we might decide to do it [not only because of our state of character, but] also by reason and rational calculation; but when we have no warning, [our decision to act] expresses our state of character" (Aristotle 1985: 1117a 21–23 [78]). Such a trait is a moral virtue, rather than a natural one, because of the manner in which it was acquired (Aristotle 1985: 1144b 5–16 [170]). So combining this point about moral preparedness with the idea of the limited unity of the virtues, we might reasonably expect that a person will more or less automatically treat someone she loves with kindness, generosity, honesty, and the like; and we might reasonably expect gratefulness to the beloved for his beneficent acts would be a part of this package.[13]

But this reveals another tension. There is some indication that gratitude is often not expressed between loved ones who live together or associate frequently (Watkins 2014: 43–44 and 111). A possible explanation of this phenomenon appeals to one way of understanding an aspect of human psychology. When we regularly receive benefits from another, we tend not to recognize them for what they are. What has been called *the emotional law of habituation* (Frijda 1988: 353–354) suggests that most human emotions are responses to change. Receiving a benefit that was not expected may trigger an emotion akin to gratitude; but if a person receives benefits regularly from the same source, such emotions are less likely to be experienced. So it may be all too easy for persons in loving relationships to fail to notice or to appreciate some of the benefits that the other person provides, or the effort she exerts in doing so. It may appear, then, that such a person is lacking in gratitude.[14]

On the other hand, in loving relationships, it seems inappropriate "to keep score" of who has done what.[15] This is conveyed strongly in an amusing though bizarre anecdote relayed by Frans de Waal.

> When, at a conference on reciprocity, a senior scientist revealed that he kept track on a computer spreadsheet of what he had done for his wife and what she had done for him, we were dumbfounded. This couldn't be right. The fact that this was his third wife, and that he is now married to his fifth, suggests that keeping careful score is perhaps not for close relationships. (de Waal 2009: 174)

Taking for granted benefits provided by a loved one seems to reveal a lack of gratitude, but keeping score seems very bad for such relationships. Where does that leave us?

Perhaps we should not be too hard on those who do not always express gratitude to a beloved. If each party in a loving relationship treats the other with kindness, generosity, compassion, honesty, and the like, no particular benefit stands out. It is not just the law of habituation that is at work here. In some sense, an underlying norm in loving relationships is to each according to his needs (Bloomfield 2014: 221). De Waal observed this phenomenon occurring among chimps.

> Chimps seem to recall previous favors, such as grooming. . . . During the mornings before every feeding session, we had recorded spontaneous grooming. We then compared the flow of both "currencies": food and grooming. If the top male, Socko, had groomed May, for example, his chances of getting a few branches from her in the afternoon were greatly improved. We found this effect all over the colony: Apparently, one good turn deserves another. This kind of exchange must rest on memory of previous events combined with a psychological mechanism we call "gratitude," that is, warm feelings toward someone whose act of kindness we recall. (de Waal 2009: 173–174)

Socko and May were not close within the colony, and so this interaction tracks an ordinary case of gratitude. But this kind of relationship did not hold across the board among chimps.

> Interestingly, the tendency to return favors was not equal for all relationships. Between good friends, who spend a lot of time together, a single grooming session carried little weight. They both groom and share a lot, probably without keeping careful track. Only in the more distant relationships did small favors stand out and were specifically rewarded. (de Waal 2009: 174)

This is an "is" that does not prove any "oughts", but it may suggest that these different behaviors in different relationships are rooted in evolutionary moral psychology. So if the law of habituation is credible and if relationships among loved ones typically involve acts of kindness, generosity, and the like, then it may not be surprising that gratitude is not expressed all of the times that it is called for in these relationships. We are not forced to conclude, however, that the parties in these relationships lack the virtue of gratitude. Hill's counterfactual test can be applied here. If gratitude would move the agent to reciprocate if love were to fade, we still have proper moral motivation.

ASSESSING THE COMPLAINT

We saw in the section "Beneficence or Gratitude?" that beneficence, even perfect beneficence, does not render gratitude superfluous. This is not only because beneficence and gratitude do not always direct the agent to perform the same action but also because even when they counsel the same act, gratitude should (at least sometimes) be the salient motive. One way of understanding love is that it is an emotion that is morally encompassing, one that embraces all (or most) moral norms (Badhwar 2014: 195 and 215). So does love render gratitude superfluous? Is the relationship among de Waal's chimps what we should expect among humans?

Following Smith and Kant, I have maintained that gratitude is a crediting norm that includes a certain kind of (appraisal) respect reserved for prior benefactors. Love too involves selection and valuing. But, as David Velleman puts it, "Loving some but not others entails valuing them differently but not attributing different values to them" (Velleman 1999: 372; see also Frankfurt 2004: 38–39). Since love does not seem to be a crediting norm or emotion, we might reasonably think that love does not render gratitude superfluous.

It may be helpful to reflect on how some close relationships develop. Psychologists tell us that gratitude both promotes and sustains close human relationships (Algoe et al. 2008; Emmons 2007: 10–11, 44–45, 49–50; Watkins 2014: 142–149).[16] We might reasonably expect, then, that gratitude expressed between intimates would positively contribute to their relationship. And indeed there is empirical evidence to support this idea. One study purports to show that gratitude in romantic relationships increases relationship connection and satisfaction (Algoe et al. 2010). Another study concludes that expressed gratitude contributes to the successful maintenance of intimate bonds (Gordon et al. 2012). Other researchers have shown that expressing gratitude to an intimate enhances each partner's perception of the relationship's strength (Lambert et al. 2010) and makes each partner more comfortable in expressing relationship concerns (Lambert and Fincham 2011). Since all of this comports with common sense, it seems reasonable to concede that expressing gratitude in loving relationships enhances those relationships in various ways. But bearing in mind the law of habituation, we might suspect that people who live together and relate daily will sometimes take each other for granted. The antidote for this may be a commitment to some of the so-called gratitude exercises, such as count your blessings (Watkins 2014: 44), focused specifically on the conduct of the beloved. If the psychologists are right, this should result in better relationships.

What the psychologists tell us highlights the *instrumental* value in expressing gratitude. But is this called for ethically? The answer seems to be yes because gratitude expresses warranted appraisal respect; its value is not merely instrumental. But if this is correct, why might a loved one be bothered by the fact that the other acted from gratitude rather than from love? In short, what is the basis of the complaint? My guess is that the complaint is based on a contested conception of moral motivation. Recall Kant's discussion of the friend of mankind. When he was acting from what Kant called "inclination," when he helped others simply because he enjoyed doing so, his actions were said to be in accord with duty but not done from duty. According to Kant, proper moral motivation is acting from duty. Kant opens himself to parody when he goes on to say that if this friend of mankind is overcome by sorrow and his sympathy for others is extinguished, but he nevertheless tears himself from this insensibility and helps another *because* duty requires it, "then for the first time his action has genuine moral worth" (Kant 1983/1785: Ak 398 [11]). Such an account pictures moral motivation as burdensome. (It was to this account of moral motivation attributed to Kant that Hill was responding in the discussion in section "Love or Gratitude.") There is a similar (though less extreme) view of obligation and moral motivation in some of the psychological literature. Philip Watkins, for example, distinguishes sharply between gratitude and indebtedness, in part because he sees gratitude as a positive emotion.

> After receiving a benefit, if one feels an "obligation to repay," and feels discomfort until they are able to do so, it seems reasonable to suppose that the individual will have difficulty enjoying the gift, and thus will have difficulty recognizing the goodness of the gift, which consequently should result in less gratitude. (Watkins 2014: 215)

Yet Watkins's own research shows that when people feel grateful, they feel somewhat indebted. He resolves this tension by arguing, "I submit that in gratitude the 'debt' is incurred, not by the giver, but by the receiver. . . . [O]ne does not feel obliged to return the favor, rather one is intrinsically motivated to benefit their benefactor" (Watkins 2014: 216). So, according to this picture, feelings of obligation are burdensome because they are externally imposed, whereas the grateful person is "intrinsically motivated" to reciprocate. This presents us with a false dichotomy.

Aristotle's account of moral motivation avoids this dichotomy. A virtuous person aims at what is fine, does what is fine, and does so with pleasure, whether this involves temperance (1104b 4–6 [37]), generosity (1120a 27–28 [87]), justice (1173b 30–32 [272]), or any virtue (1157b 25–36 [217]). This does not mean that it is always easy to perform a virtuous action, but it does mean that the virtuous agent characteristically enjoys doing so. Watkins' own research suggests that "thought/action tendencies" associated with gratitude (as determined in vignette studies) include adoring, approaching, praising, and desiring to help (Watkins 2014: 150). Moreover, Watkins says, "I submit that the cognitions that typically produce genuine grateful emotion are fairly quick, fluent, and effortless appraisals" (Watkins 2014: 43).[17] This fits with the picture of moral preparedness described earlier in the quotes from Sidgwick, Russell, and MacIntyre. The morally prepared agent need not regard required actions as burdensome; they may characteristically be pleasant.[18]

Where does this leave "the complaint"? If I do something nice for a loved one and I do so from gratitude, why might she be disappointed or offended?

There are, I think, two points at the heart of the complaint. First, if I acted from gratitude and I understand gratitude to be a moral requirement, then I must have found the act burdensome to perform, and it should not be (characteristically) burdensome to do nice things for a loved one. Second, if I really love her, love should be enough; I should not need whatever motivation accompanies moral norms to be moved to act. If I need additional motivation, it seems that my love is wanting. The thought seems to be that affection alone should be sufficient. One is reminded of Bernard Williams's point that sometimes reasoning morally involves "one thought too many" (Williams 1981: 18); this is also the suggestion in the quote from Michael Stocker cited earlier. The first point rests on an understanding of moral motivation that I have rejected. Doing one's duty because it is one's duty—or, putting it in a less Kantian way, acting for the sake of the underlying value—need not be burdensome; and for the virtuous agent it is typically not burdensome. The second point requires more extensive discussion.

When the complainant says that love should be enough, the implication is that there is a sharp distinction between moral motivation and acting from love. But I have suggested (citing Badhwar earlier) that persons in loving relationships are committed to a constellation of moral norms vis-à-vis each other. Love without kindness, generosity, honesty, and gratitude is hard to comprehend. Moreover, it is in these relationships that such norms are likely to be well cultivated. Acts of kindness and generosity will often be performed without giving the matter a second thought. When we interact with others regularly, sometimes "there is no room for moral reasoning, and sometimes not even explicit moral judgment" (Sidgwick 1981/1907: 227); we are kind without deliberating because "a deliberative pattern becomes habitual" (Russell 2009: 13); and we are generous to loved ones "without thought of any justification beyond the need of those" whom we love (MacIntyre 1999: 159). Affection is present too, but it is intermingled with norms in a way that makes separating them artificial. Love includes affection, but moral norms too. The complaint is based on a false dichotomy.

There is another aspect to the "love should be enough" objection. When it comes to helping behavior—providing assistance, visiting, extricating the loved one from a difficult situation, and the like—*love is enough*. As just noted, people in such relationships typically perform helpful acts without much thought, and so observers cannot tell what motivates the act. Whatever it is, the loved one gets help. If providing help were the whole of gratitude, it would not matter what motivated the agent. But reciprocation is not the whole of gratitude; as a crediting norm, it also includes *acknowledgment* and *appreciation* of the other's morally meritorious acts. Perhaps often in loving relationships these things can go unstated; the appreciation is felt and each party knows that. But circumstances can change in ways that may make overt expressions important. This is most significant, I think, in relationships that have significant periods of time when the exchange of benefits is asymmetrical. The most obvious case is the relationship between parents and children. When children are young, parents are the benefactors and children are the beneficiaries. When children are young adults, the relationship may be more equal. In some cases, as the parents age, they become disabled and dependent on others; in a subset of these cases, adult children provide significant assistance for their parents. This can take a toll on both parties, but let's think of the perspective of the parent. As the situation goes on, the parent may feel guilt and believe that he is a burden to his children, in spite of their claims to the contrary. Reminding the parent that the situation was once reversed and that gratitude is part of love can be appropriate; and if conveyed properly, it need not leave the parent with the impression that conduct motivated in part by gratitude is thereby burdensome for the children.

But in interactions with loved ones, must agents *always* act from gratitude when it is applicable? The question contains a problematic presupposition, namely, that in these cases, we always know whether it is gratitude or beneficence that is the applicable norm. Typically, multiple norms are simultaneously applicable. In any given case between loved ones, it does not matter whether the agent regards the provision of a benefit as reciprocation or just beneficence. But, as just noted, reciprocation is only one aspect of gratitude. Acknowledging and appreciating the benefactor's meritorious acts are also core elements; the simple act of saying "thank you" expresses these elements. So in relationships with loved ones, it seems reasonable to hold that we help them when they need help (and we are in a position to help). It does not matter whether this is beneficence or reciprocation. But if one of our loved ones has benefited us in an especially meritorious way, expressed gratitude in the form of acknowledgment and appreciation is in order; and, as the previously cited psychological literature demonstrates, this also enhances relationships.

CONCLUSION

In Chapter VII of *The Right and the Good*, W. D. Ross writes, "Suppose, now, that love and sense of duty incline us to the *same* act. Will our action be morally better if we act from the first motive or from the second? It seems clear that since the sense of duty is recognized as the better motive when the two are in conflict, it is still the better when they are in agreement" (Ross 1930: 164). In this passage, Ross presents the choice as an "either-or," and says that acting from a sense of duty is morally better than acting from love. He gives two reasons to support this claim. One reason is that "instinctive affection is a more wayward, capricious motive than sense of duty." The other reason is more important, however: "the sense of duty is different in kind from, and superior in kind to, any other motive" (Ross 1930: 164). Ross moves beyond the "either-or" choice, however, and considers cases that he calls "the co-operation of motives." He says that some of these cooperating motives are morally indifferent and some are positively good (though not as good as the motive of duty). An example of the former is "desire of an innocent sensuous pleasure"; an example of the latter is love (Ross 1930: 171). Ross assigns positive value to the motive of love but not to the desire for one's own pleasure, but does not explain why. He holds that some acts involving "the co-operation of motives" may be overdetermined; that is, "there may be some [motivation] to spare" (Ross 1930: 172). When the cooperating motive is morally indifferent, the act is "as good as if it had been done from sense of duty alone," as long as sense of duty itself is sufficient to produce the act. When the cooperating motive is "an inferior good motive," the value of the action is *greater* than if it had been done from duty alone, "as long as the sense of duty is strong enough to have secured by itself the doing of the act" (Ross 1930: 172). The former claim is the counterfactual test; the latter claim is the counterfactual test plus the idea that additional value accrues when the act is overdetermined and the extra motive is good.

My position differs from Ross's in that I regard the motive of love as one imbued with moral content; it is not merely affection. It involves a commitment to kindness, generosity, compassion, and the like. It also involves a commitment to gratitude. Gratitude, like kindness and generosity, has the well-being of the beloved as its target. But gratitude, unlike kindness and generosity, is due because of the benefactor's prior morally meritorious acts. This results in a tension. We associate regularly with many of our loved ones. If gratitude in these relationships were never expressed, proper appraisal respect would be missing. But if gratitude were expressed on every occasion when warranted, it could become robotic and lose its meaning. There is a fine line to be walked here.

It should be clear that the "beneficence or gratitude" case arises in a relationship between the agent and a stranger or casual acquaintance. Acting from gratitude in that case is important because in some sense, the benefit is owed to the would-be beneficiary. The "love or gratitude" case is far more complicated.[19]

NOTES

1 In this chapter, I use the expressions "obligation of gratitude," "duty of gratitude," and "the moral requirement of gratitude" interchangeably.

2 This paragraph is based on McConnell (2018b, Section 5).

3 For someone who strongly *denies* the connection between gratitude and the goodwill of the benefactor, see Fitzgerald (1998).

4 Gratitude is the appraisal respect that the beneficiary has for the benefactor. Third parties might also have appraisal respect for the benefactor, but it is something like honor or praise rather than gratitude. See Card (2016: 99). For the view that gratitude is tied to what Darwall calls "recognition respect"—rather than appraisal respect—see Helm (this volume).

5 This is a caricature, as is Kant's "friend of mankind." This is permissible in thought experiments, I assume, in order to flush out various concepts.

6 Throughout the remainder of this chapter, when I write "prior benefactor," I am assuming that whatever conditions are necessary for generating a debt of gratitude have been satisfied.

7 These notions of deserving and owing can be connected to the idea of a right, even if not a claim right. Tony Manela (2015: especially 163–166) invokes the notion of an *imperfect right* for these cases. Although the original benefactor does not have a claim right to demand that the beneficiary reciprocate, she does have standing to remonstrate and express resentment, and this sort of standing affirms her self-respect.

8 I am aware that in each of these cases, the relationship is not always one of love. I also understand that there are different senses of love involved here.

9 Here we need to distinguish between "grateful to" and "grateful for" (McAleer 2012), where only the former involves an obligation to reciprocate if a suitable opportunity arises. Parents may be grateful for the fact that they have a young child without (yet) being grateful to that child.

10 I have argued elsewhere that this conception of duty (obligation) as burdensome is present in some of the positive psychology literature and is based on too narrow of an understanding of acting from duty. See McConnell (2018b, Section 4).

11 I have argued against this claim. See McConnell (1993, chapter I) and McConnell (2017).

12 For some explanation of the notion of a domain, see Badhwar (1996: 316–317).

13 I am not assuming here that possession of the virtues requires perfection. But someone who possesses virtue V will *characteristically* act in accord with that virtue.

14 One might think that if the benefactor acted from love, then no gratitude is due because the benefactor has not acted for morally admirable reasons. But as I argue, love is not mere affection but also encompasses moral norms.

15 Even between strangers, we do not *keep* score if the original benefit was provided freely. But that does not mean that the original benefactor cannot later *determine* the score. See McConnell (1993: 24–25).

16 In terms of affection and intimacy, clearly relationships are on a continuum. The term "friend" seems loose enough to cover a broad array of relationships. I do not assume that all cases of friendship involve love.

17 Watkins delineates four "cognitive conditions of gratitude." They are recognizing the gift, recognizing the goodness of the gift, recognizing the goodness of the giver, and recognizing the gratuitousness of the gift (2014: 42–49).

18   Some may think that if the beneficiary experiences the debt as burdensome, his gratitude is mitigated or entirely missing. But I think that is mistaken. Acknowledging and appreciating the benefactor's act should not be burdensome for a grateful beneficiary. But it is a contingent matter when an apt occasion for reciprocating arises, and it is possible that in some circumstances, reciprocation is difficult or burdensome for the beneficiary. There are other ways in which negative feelings may be associated with gratitude. Gratitude may also be burdensome if the beneficiary does not want a further relationship with the benefactor (Card 1988: 124–125), and the beneficiary is apt to feel grief if the benefactor experienced significant harm in providing the benefits (Manela 2016b).

19   **Acknowledgments:** I thank Robert Roberts, Daniel Telech, and participants in the Moral Psychology of Gratitude Workshop (September 8–10, 2017) for comments and suggestions on earlier versions of this chapter.

REFERENCES

Algoe, Sara, Haidt, Jonathan, and Gable, Shelly. (2008). Beyond Reciprocity: Gratitude and Relationships in Everyday Life. *Emotion* 8, pp. 425–429.

Algoe, Sara, Gable, Shelly, and Maisel, Natalya. (2010). It's the Little Things: Everyday Gratitude as a Booster Shot for Romantic Relationships. *Personal Relationships* 17, pp. 217–233.

Aristotle. (1985/4th century BC). *Nicomachean Ethics* (T. Irwin, trans.). Indianapolis: Hackett Publishing.

Audi, Robert. (1995). Acting from Virtue. *Mind* 104, pp. 449–471.

Badhwar, Neera. (1996). The Limited Unity of Virtue. *Nous* 30, pp. 306–329.

Badhwar, Neera. (2014). *Well-Being: Happiness in a Worthwhile Life*. New York: Oxford University Press.

Berger, Fred. (1975). Gratitude. *Ethics* 85, pp. 298–309.

Bloomfield, Paul. (2014). *The Virtues of Happiness*. New York: Oxford University Press.

Card, Claudia. (1988). Gratitude and Obligation. *American Philosophical Quarterly* 25, pp. 115–127.

Card, Claudia. (2016). Gratitude to the Decent Rescuer. In D. Carr (ed.). *Perspectives on Gratitude: An Interdisciplinary Approach* (pp. 99–111). New York.

Carr, David. (2015). Is Gratitude a Moral Virtue? *Philosophical Studies* 172, pp. 1475–1484.

Darwall, Stephen. (2006). *The Second-Person Standpoint*. Cambridge, MA: Harvard University Press.

De Waal, Frans. (2009). *The Age of Empathy*. New York: Three Rivers Press.

Emmons, Robert. (2007). *Thanks: How the New Science of Gratitude Can Make You Happier*. Boston: Houghton Mifflin Co.

Fitzgerald, Patrick. (1998). Gratitude and Justice. *Ethics* 109, pp. 119–143.

Frankfurt, Harry. (2004). *The Reasons of Love*. Princeton: Princeton University Press.

Frijda, Nico. (1988). The Laws of Emotion. *American Psychologist* 43, pp. 349–358.

Gordon, Amie, Oveis, Christopher, Impett, Emily, Kogan, Aleksandr, and Keltner, Dacher. (2012). To Have and to Hold: Gratitude Promotes Relationship Maintenance in Intimate Bonds. *Journal of Personality and Social Psychology* 103, pp. 257–274.

Hill, Thomas Jr. (2012). *Virtue, Rules, and Justice: Kantian Aspirations*. New York: Oxford University Press.

Hursthouse, Rosalind. (1999). *On Virtue Ethics*. New York: Oxford University Press.

Kant, Immanuel. (1964/1797). *The Doctrine of Virtue*, Part 2 of *The Metaphysic of Morals* Mary Gregor, trans.). Philadelphia: University of Pennsylvania Press.

Kant, Immanuel. (1983/1785). *Grounding for the Metaphysics of Morals* (James Ellington, trans.). Indianapolis: Hackett Publishing.

Lambert, Nathaniel, Clark, Margaret, Durtschi, Jared, Fincham, Frank, and Graham, Steven. (2010). Benefits of Expressing Gratitude: Expressing Gratitude to a Partner Changes One's View of the Relationship. *Psychological Science* 21, pp. 574–580.

Lambert, Nathaniel, and Fincham, Frank. (2011). Expressing Gratitude to a Partner Leads to More Relationship Maintenance Behavior. *Emotion* 11, pp. 52–60.

MacIntyre, Alasdair. (1999). *Dependent Rational Animals*. Chicago: Open Court.

Manela, Tony. (2015). Obligations of Gratitude and Correlative Rights. *Oxford Studies in Normative Ethics* 5, pp. 151–170.

Manela, Tony. (2016a). Gratitude and Appreciation. *American Philosophical Quarterly* 53, pp. 281–294.

Manela, Tony. (2016b). Negative Feelings of Gratitude. *Journal of Value Inquiry* 50, pp. 129–140.

McAleer, Sean. (2012). Propositional Gratitude. *American Philosophical Quarterly* 49, pp. 55–66.

McConnell, Terrance. (1993). *Gratitude*. Philadelphia: Temple University Press.

McConnell, Terrance. (2017). Gratitude, Rights, and Moral Standouts. *Ethical Theory and Moral Practice* 20, pp. 279–293.

McConnell, Terrance. (2018a). Gratitude in Special Relationships. In J. Tudge and L. Freitas (eds.). *Developing Gratitude in Children and Adolescents*. Cambridge: Cambridge University Press (pp. 42–62).

McConnell, Terrance. (2018b). Gratitude's Moral Status. Unpublished manuscript.

Morgan, Blaire, Gulliford, Liz, and Carr, David. (2015). Educating Gratitude: Some Conceptual and Moral Misgivings. *Journal of Moral Education* 44, pp. 97–111.

Richards, Norvin. (2010). *The Ethics of Parenthood*. New York: Oxford University Press.

Roberts, Robert. (2013). *Emotions in the Moral Life*. New York: Cambridge University Press.

Ross, W.D. (1930). *The Right and the Good*. Oxford: Oxford University Press.

Russell, Daniel. (2009). *Practical Intelligence and the Virtues*. New York: Oxford University Press.

Sidgwick, Henry. (1981/1907). *The Methods of Ethics*. 7th edition. Indianapolis: Hackett Publishing.

Simmons, John. (1979). *Moral Principles and Political Obligations*. Princeton: Princeton University Press.

Smith, Adam. (1982/1790). *The Theory of Moral Sentiments*. Indianapolis: Liberty Classics.

Stocker, Michael. (1976). The Schizophrenia of Modern Ethical Theory. *The Journal of Philosophy* 73, pp. 453–466.

Tiberius, Valerie. (2015). *Moral Psychology: A Contemporary Introduction*. New York: Routledge.

Velleman, J. David. (1999). Love as a Moral Emotion. *Ethics* 109, pp. 338–374.

Visser, Margaret. (2009). *The Gift of Thanks: The Roots and Rituals of Gratitude*. Boston: Houghton Mifflin Harcourt.

Watkins, Philip. (2014). *Gratitude and the Good Life*. Dordrecht: Springer.

Williams, Bernard. (1981). *Moral Luck*. New York: Cambridge University Press.

Part II

GRATITUDE, RIGHTS, AND DUTIES

Chapter 3

Obligations of Gratitude: Directedness without Rights

Adrienne M. Martin

THE QUESTION

A person who feels an obligation of gratitude toward her benefactor typically feels obliged *to* her benefactor. That is, their obligation feels *directed* toward the particular person who generously helped them.[1] Jay Wallace describes this directedness as a "relational" structure[2]: with such an obligation, "The very things that give us reasons to do (say) *X* also give another party a claim against us that we should do *X*, and a privileged basis for objecting if we should fail so to act" (2012, 194). Even if the beneficiary finds that the best way to express their gratitude is to "pay it forward," by doing something *for a third party*, they do so in order to fulfill an obligation *to the original benefactor*.[3] For a contrast, consider the possibility that the original benefaction was a response to a felt general obligation to help others. The recipient of the beneficence happens to present an opportunity to fulfill this general obligation but, if the potential benefactor were to choose a different opportunity, they would do equally well, as far as the obligation is concerned. Not so, for the beneficiary's obligation of gratitude, which ties the beneficiary to their benefactor and no one else.

One familiar kind of directed obligation is a *debt*, such as the obligation *to the lender* to repay a loan. Another is a directed *duty*, such as the duty *to the promisee* to keep a promise. For all that we talk about "feeling indebted to" or "owing" gratitude to our benefactors, however, the notion that obligations of gratitude could be debts or duties has been met with skepticism by many philosophers. This is in part because it is standard to think that *rights* are the correlates of debts and directed duties, and there is a strong intuitive resistance to the possibility that benefactors might have a right to gratitude. Here is a small sample from the recent literature, on this point:

- Herman: "Curious debts [debts of gratitude] are, since they are owed to the benefactors but cannot be claimed or waived by them" (394).
- Berger: "While we have no hesitation in saying there is an obligation to show gratitude . . . we do not feel at ease in saying it is something owed to the grantor in the sense that he has a right to demand it" (300).
- Card: "The benefactor does not have a *right* to one's acting in accord with [responsibilities of gratitude] but only deserves it (or doesn't)" (120).
- Wellman: "Since gratitude does not offer the beneficiary the discretion typically associated with freestanding duties, then, it seems that if gratitude generated duties, it would also create corresponding rights. As a result, our recognition that there are no rights to gratitude signals that there can be no duties of this type either" (289).

A lender has a *right* to repayment according to the terms of the loan; a promisee has a *right* to the promiser's fidelity to their promise. These rights are the poles centered in the people to whom the obligations are owed, the correlates of the debts and duties centered in the obliged parties. Such rights have certain standard features: in the case of debts, they are both waivable and transferrable by the rights-bearer. But an obligation of gratitude does not seem to be waivable or transferrable by the benefactor. More broadly, it is at least not often in the spirit of the kind of generosity that produces an obligation of gratitude, for the benefactor to insist on a *right to*, or a *claim on*, the beneficiary's gratitude.

Now, as Claudia Card points out, debts—and duties, insofar as they are assimilated to or modeled on debts (more on this, later)—are not the only kind of obligation.[4] Trustees have obligations in virtue of being entrusted, and Card argues that obligations of gratitude are more readily modeled on trustee obligations than on debtor obligations. Trustee obligations are frequently not transferrable or waivable; and depending on what has been entrusted, they might not be dischargeable, either, which is another feature of obligations of gratitude that many have found striking: the fact that we often feel obliged *forever*.[5] Card also emphasizes that the "responsibilities of trusteeship and guardianship are not closely correlated with others' rights" (121), if rights are understood in Hart's sense of justifications for interfering with the freedom of others.

Although Card does not emphasize it, trustee obligations are also directed, or relational. If you entrust me with the care of something that matters to you, I am obligated *to you* to provide that care. What Card does not provide, however, is an account of that directedness—within this model, debtor and promissory obligations correlate to *rights*; to what do trustee obligations correlate? Her conception of obligations of gratitude is, as far as directedness is concerned, purely negative: the obligations do not correlate to rights. Without a positive account of directedness, though, the conception of gratitude is importantly incomplete, and it is not possible to adequately compare the debtor/duty and trustee models as frameworks for obligations of gratitude.

Having an obligation to another person is being in a relationship with them—a normative relationship that contours how you should see that person and how you should treat them, and what they may legitimately hope for, ask for, expect from, even extract from you. Understanding directed obligation, then, means understanding it from both sides of the relationship. That is what I aim to do, in this chapter: provide a positive characterization of the directedness of obligations of gratitude in terms of the benefactor claim—a claim that is not a right—to gratitude. I will call this non-right claim the "anchor" of the obligation. Thus, my central question is: *What is the benefactor anchor in directed obligations of gratitude?*

In the section "Imperfect Duties," I consider some of the reasons for and against categorizing obligations of gratitude as imperfect duties, and what it would take to make an imperfect duty directed. This leads to the Natural Law concept of an imperfect right, which I present in the section "Imperfect Rights" as generally associated with *nonenforceability*. In the section "Enforcement and Sanction," however, I argue that sorting rights into enforceable and nonenforceable claims does not produce a taxonomy with a clear place for obligations of gratitude. I thus leave behind the vocabulary of perfect and imperfect duties and rights for purposes of the rest this chapter, and proceed with less historically burdened terms, where the benefactor anchor is a *non-rights-based personal expectation* or, more simply, *personal expectation*.

In the sections "Demand and Speech Acts" and "Directing versus Blaming," I consider and reject proposals to draw the distinction between rights and personal expectations by appeal to the legitimacy or illegitimacy of performing directive speech acts. In the section "Directives of Different Forces," I examine in detail a proposal to associate rights with the standing or permission to *demand* compliance, and personal expectations with the standing or permission to direct or encourage compliance through less forceful speech acts. I conclude that this proposal, though it has promise, faces some significant obstacles. In the section "Directing means versus Directing ends," I propose that, instead of a force-based distinction, we need a scope-based distinction. According to the scope-based distinction, a person who has a personal expectation has the standing or permission to direct the obligated person to adopt or maintain a broad *end*, while a person who has a right also has the standing or permission to direct the obligated person to take a particular *means* to the obligatory end. In the concluding section, I sketch a couple of the interesting implications of this proposal for the conceptual relationship between rights and personal expectations, and for thinking about interpersonal obligations on a more general level.

IMPERFECT DUTIES

When Card critiques the debtor model of obligation, she presents it as a simultaneous critique of the possibility that obligations of gratitude could be *duties*. Deontic or duty-centered moral philosophy is, she asserts, obsessed with the idea that moral obligations are debts or debt-like. This move is, however, too quick, for at least two reasons. First, there are right-duty pairs perfectly at home within standard deontic frameworks that do not resemble debts. For example, inalienable rights are non-transferrable and non-waivable and imply reciprocal, non-dischargeable duties. Second, and more important for our purposes here, *imperfect duties* are standard elements of deontic moral philosophy, and do not resemble debts. Card even acknowledges that trustee obligations share some central features with imperfect duties: both "tend to be abstractly defined, allow room for latitude, and call upon discretion and judgment to a greater extent than what Kant called 'perfect duties'" (121). Nevertheless, she resists the idea that obligations of gratitude might *be* imperfect duties, because she thinks the concept of a duty is thoroughly infected with the sensibility of debts, at least as a matter of contingent fact about the history of deontic moral philosophy.[6]

Others are more sanguine about the possibility that obligations of gratitude might be imperfect duties. In arguing that there are at least some "defeasible and contextually dependent" duties of gratitude, Samuel Bruton highlights the fact that John Stuart Mill's definition of duty includes the conceptual space for duties that do not correlate with rights (13). Terrance McConnell argues directly that the requirement of gratitude is a "narrow imperfect duty": a duty to adopt the principle of helping prior benefactors when the opportunity presents itself [imperfect] that does not permit the duty-bound person to skip out on such an opportunity on the grounds that they have helped or will help other benefactors [narrow] (68). And Barbara Herman locates obligations of gratitude at the level of imperfect duties within a "lattice" of duties streaming down from "innate right," the marker of the core human values of self-governance and equal moral status (406).

However, none of these advocates of imperfect duties of gratitude provide any clear resources for answering the question of this chapter. They turn to the idea of an imperfect duty in part to account for the *negative* point on which all agree that benefactors have no *right* to gratitude. But this provides no insight into how an imperfect duty of gratitude could be *directed*, or what that directedness could consist in.[7] Indeed, the most prevalent way of characterizing imperfect duties excludes the possibility of their being directed or owed to anyone in particular. Mill describes them this way: "[Imperfect duties are] those . . . which . . . we are indeed bound to practice but *not toward any definite person*, nor at any prescribed time" (49, my emphasis). He then equates being obligated but not "toward any definite person" with "moral obligations which do not give birth to any right." According to this way of understanding the distinction between perfect and imperfect duties, imperfect duties are *never* directed and, indeed, the only way a duty *could* be directed toward a definite person is if that person has a correlative right. This conception is also commonly attributed to Kant, who said that imperfect duties are duties to adopt maxims, rather than to perform specific actions.[8] The assumption informing this attribution is that the "latitude" of adopting a maxim must include not only how, when, and where to pursue the end, but also with regard to whom. Not coincidentally, this is how Card, in her argument that obligations of gratitude challenge the entire traditional deontic conception of moral obligation, understands imperfect duties, as well. She writes, "Kant treated moral obligation as a supreme indebtedness, an owing of duties to someone or other, if only to ourselves. When we cannot specify what must be done to carry out the duty or the party to whom the duty is owed (as in the 'duty of benevolence'), we have an 'imperfect duty,' an imperfect debt" (115).

Notice, however, that there's not actually anything conceptually problematic about having a duty to adopt a maxim—one that is broad or vague enough not to dictate many of the terms of its achievement—relative to a given individual. There's nothing puzzling, for example, about the idea that I have a duty to my partner to adopt the end of committing some time to "us," which leaves latitude for choice about which concerts we will attend together, or whether we will go to concerts or go hiking or watch TV. Conceivably, then, an imperfect duty of gratitude would be consistent with the beneficiary having a directed duty to the benefactor—there is no necessary tension between having a duty to a particular person and having some choice about how to fulfill it. In short, a person could have a claim on you to do something, without having a claim on *how you do it*. Thus, there is a conceptual space, perhaps somewhat neglected, where imperfect duties might provide a comfortable home for debts of gratitude that are owed to particular individuals but not claimable by those individuals as rights.

Some of "the philosophic jurists" developed a similar conceptual space. In Grotius, we find the distinction between perfect and imperfect *rights*, which Pufendorf then develops into a distinction in duties.[9] Tony Manela retrieves this concept of an imperfect right and proposes that it is the key to understanding the directedness of obligations of gratitude, so I will turn to his proposal next.

IMPERFECT RIGHTS

Manela proposes that the beneficiary's obligation of gratitude corresponds to "*some* kind of standing for [the] benefactor—not license to demand or enforce, but license to resent and remonstrate in the face of non-compliance. Reviving a term from the natural lawyers, I propose to call such standing an *imperfect* right" (2016, 16).

Manela argues that the possessor of a perfect right is someone who is licensed to force the duty-bound person to do their duty, and punish them if they don't. These are things it is *not* legitimate for the benefactor to do to encourage gratitude from their beneficiary, so the benefactor does not have a perfect right to gratitude. It is, however, legitimate for the benefactor to do other things—Manela proposes "resent[ment] and remonstrat[ion] in the face of [ingratitude]." And this is what the imperfect right constitutes: the legitimacy or permissibility of resentment and remonstration.

In associating perfect rights with enforcement and sanction, Manela stays true to the natural law tradition. Grotius, Pufendorf, and many philosophers in the Modern period who followed them connect perfect rights and duties with the legitimate use of force. As Schroeder writes, in this tradition, "[A] perfect right includes the authorization to use force and coercion to ensure it is respected. To have an imperfect right, on the other hand, is to be genuinely owed something, but not to have license to use force to get it" (6). Furthermore, although the concept of an imperfect right has mostly dropped out of usage in moral philosophy, the notion that rights are enforceable and their violations sanctionable, in some way that other kinds of moral claims are not, plays a fairly major role in many philosophers' skepticism about rights to gratitude. For example:

- Manela: "When a beneficiary . . . fails to return a benefit, or do a much-needed favor for a benefactor when begged, we do indeed condemn him; but we do not call such a beneficiary *unjust* because of this failure. Nor do we think he should be liable to punishment, as those who perpetrate injustice typically are" (2016, 283).
- Berger: "[W]e do not, generally, *punish* people for failing to show gratitude" (306).
- Fitzgerald: "It is never possible to exact gratitude. We can never force someone to be grateful" (138).
- Bruton insists that gratitude cannot, in Mill's term, be "exacted," and that ingratitude is not "the proper object of punishment" (13).

Despite this estimable backstory, I will argue that appeals to the legitimacy of enforcement and sanction cannot help answer the question of this chapter. Perfect duties and obligations of gratitude do not sort neatly into categories of enforceable and non-enforceable obligations. At the end of the next section, I thus conclude that imperfect rights, despite their initial appeal, do not readily provide an account of the benefactor anchor of directed obligations of gratitude.

ENFORCEMENT AND SANCTION

My argument takes the form of a dilemma. The first horn grows out of the proposition that the relevant forms of enforcement and sanction are *legal* in nature. The possibility of *the state* enforcing gratitude and punishing ingratitude through the force of law does indeed seem beyond the pale. This does not, however, drive the wedge between perfect and imperfect rights in a helpful way, insofar as our aim is to understand the obligations of gratitude as directed imperfect duties. What we need is a conception of perfect versus imperfect rights that distinguishes the benefactor anchor from other *moral rights*, which may or may not be enforceable by law—rights that Mill famously described: "When we call anything a person's right, we mean that he has a valid claim on society to protect him in the possession of it, either by the force of law *or by that of education and opinion*" (66, my emphasis). For example, it is generally believed, and I will stipulate here, that a non-contractual promise gives the promisee a moral right to the promiser's fidelity. Such a right is not legally enforceable or sanctionable, but that doesn't stop us from marking it out through social means. But the right of a promisee is exactly the kind of right that skeptics about benefactor rights to gratitude have in mind. In other words, appealing to legal enforcement and sanction leaves paradigmatic examples of rights meant to be withheld from benefactors on the wrong side of the perfect-imperfect divide.

The alternative, and second horn of the dilemma, is that we define perfect rights as those that are enforceable and sanctionable in the full breadth Mill describes, including non-state-backed punishment such as the punishment a parent might impose on his child, personal and social sanctions like expressions of blame, and as Mill says "by education and opinion." But then gratitude appears to be as enforceable as is fidelity to a promise. We educate our children in gratitude, at home and at school (including public school, so that the state turns out to have a role here, too, though not through lawgiving and enforcement). As to "opinion" and blame, the unappreciated benefactor often gets to express hurt and angry feelings. Third parties, too, are often in a position to aptly criticize ingratitude. As Mill says, and Bruton emphasizes, the "opinion of one's fellow creatures," and "the reproaches of one's conscience" are forms of punishment. So now it appears benefactors *do* have a perfect right to gratitude.

Either way we understand enforcement and sanction, we fail to distinguish the benefactor anchor in obligations of gratitude from the kind of moral right it is assumed benefactors lack.[10] Thus, insofar as the distinction between perfect and imperfect rights is a matter of enforceability and its absence, the concept of an imperfect right does not help answer my question about the benefactor anchor. It's certainly conceivable that other ways of drawing this distinction might be more serviceable, but for purposes of this chapter, I want to proceed without terms that have such complex historical associations. For the rest of the chapter, therefore, I will use the following vocabulary:

A directed obligation: An obligation owed to a particular person, who thereby has some sort of special standing relative to the obliged party—as Wallace says "a privileged basis for objecting" if the obligated party fails to act in accordance with the obligation.

A right-based obligation: A directed obligation that is owed as a matter of right—someone has a claim right against the obliged party. For example, a promissory obligation.

A non-right-based obligation: A directed obligation that is not owed as a matter of right. The assumption of this chapter is that rights are not the only form of special standing, since obligations of gratitude are directed but do not correlate to rights.

A right: In this chapter, I use this term interchangeably with "claim right" and "claim of right," meaning not to import any particular theory of claim rights but rather to intuitively invoke the sort of claim associated with being the recipient of a promise or the party to a contract. A person with a right has special standing relative to a person with a directed obligation.

A non-right-based personal normative expectation or, more simply, *personal expectation*: The reciprocal of a directed obligation, like the obligation of gratitude, that is not owed as a matter of right. I take the term "normative expectation" from Jay Wallace (1998), who says that to have a "normative expectation" of a person is to hold them responsible—as in "I expect you will keep your promise," said to direct rather than predict. Importantly for current purposes, some normative expectations are *impersonal*: when I blame a person in a faraway land or time for some bad deed, I am holding them to a normative expectation, but not pressing any sort of *special* standing relative to them, such that they could be said to have failed in an obligation *to me*.[11] So the normative expectations that are the subject of this paper are *personal*, involving this special standing or privileged basis for objection. The anchor of a directed obligation of gratitude is a non-right-based personal normative expectation. Technically speaking, a (claim) right is another kind of personal normative expectation, but for the sake of brevity, I reserve the term "personal expectation" to refer to *non-right-based* expectations.

DEMAND AND SPEECH ACTS

Let's briefly revisit Manela's proposal: "gratitude provid[es] *some* kind of standing for a benefactor—not license to demand or enforce, but license to resent and remonstrate in the face of non-compliance" (2015, 164). Manela explicitly associates the legitimacy of forcing someone to do something, and of punishing them for failing to do it, with the legitimacy of *demanding* that they do it. Hence, he also argues that the possessor of a (perfect) right is someone who is licensed to *demand* that the duty-bound person do their duty. The benefactor, he argues, is not licensed to demand gratitude from their beneficiary. Remonstration and resentment are the alternatives. This suggests that even if appealing to the legitimacy or illegitimacy of enforcement and punishment does not help us characterize the benefactor pole of an obligation of gratitude—what I am now calling a non-right-based personal normative expectation—appealing to the legitimacy or illegitimacy of *speech acts* might.

The notion that it is not legitimate for a benefactor to demand gratitude is also a prominent motif in recent work on gratitude:

- Manela: "Intuitively it seems that acts of gratitude, despite how beneficiaries should deliberate about them, may never be *demanded*" (2015, 161).
- Berger: "There are no acts which the benevolent person may *demand* as a grateful return for his largess" (306).
- Bruton: "It seems that gratitude cannot be *demanded* by the one to who[m] it is owed" (14).
- Camenisch: "Certainly the good giver will not *demand* any . . . return and indeed cannot do so without radically changing the gift relation into something else" (29).
- Walker: "Though we speak of obligations of gratitude we feel that their fulfillment cannot be *demanded*" (52).

It's interesting, this focus on *demand*. It is certainly true that, in many circumstances, a benefactor who demands gratitude strikes us not a very *good* benefactor. But the suggestion in the aforementioned references is not just a claim about how to be an excellent benefactor, but a conceptual claim that the benefactor anchor of an obligation of gratitude precludes the legitimacy of demanding gratitude—that is, if a benefactor demands gratitude, they are thereby not owed gratitude. There are two versions of this claim. The first builds the illegitimacy of demanding gratitude into the definition of demand, itself. On this version, demand, as a speech act, has among its felicity conditions a certain authority or standing,[12] so that a person who lacks this standing cannot successfully make a demand. That is to say, if a person without the necessary standing attempts to perform this speech act, it will "misfire." So the claim amounts to saying that the holder of a right has the standing to demand compliance from the duty-bound party, while benefactors lack the standing to demand gratitude from their beneficiaries. Alternatively, the illegitimacy of demanding gratitude may be a matter of the *permissibility* of issuing a demand. On this view, anyone may successfully make a demand—demand's felicity conditions do not include any particular standing or authority—but only some may permissibly do so. A pirate can successfully but not permissibly demand a ransom payment, for example.[13] So now the claim is that the holder of a right may permissibly demand whatever it is they have a right to, while benefactors may not permissibly demand gratitude from their beneficiaries. Either way, the view under consideration is that a benefactor who demands (or purports to demand) gratitude, by contrast with a person who demands compliance with their rights, thereby oversteps the bounds—of either their legitimate authority or what they may permissibly do.

Now, demands are *directive* speech acts; they are in the same family of speech acts as commands and requests—acts that try to influence their addressees' actions. So perhaps the key to the distinction between rights and personal expectations is the legitimacy and illegitimacy of *directives*. Perhaps the holder of a right gets to direct the duty-bound person, while the holder of a personal expectation gets to do something short of direction.

DIRECTING VERSUS BLAMING

There is broad agreement among the opponents of demanding gratitude that other negative reactions to an ungrateful beneficiary may be entirely appropriate for the benefactor: Many commentators allow that benefactors get to be *offended by* or *complain of* ingratitude; they get to feel *insulted* or *mistreated* or *undervalued*; they get to chastise or, in Manela's term, "remonstrate" with the ungrateful beneficiary.[14]

These legitimate responses are bound up with blame—blaming attitudes and blaming actions. So we might consider the possibility that a benefactor who has a non-right-based personal expectation of gratitude, while lacking the authority or permission to *direct* the beneficiary to show gratitude, nevertheless has the standing or permission to *personally blame* an ungrateful beneficiary.

Now, as we saw in the earlier discussion of normative expectations, there are forms of legitimate blame that do not presuppose any particular or personal standing other than, say, that of fellow member of humanity. Anyone (or at least anyone who is not a hypocrite) may legitimately blame, in one sense, a murderous dictator for their crimes, no matter how geographically or temporally removed. Certain forms of blame, by contrast, seem to presuppose the sort of standing or privileged basis I have been associating with both rights and personal expectations. These are the forms of blame that are bound up, for example, with feelings of resentment.[15] *Not* just anyone gets to resent the dictator—that response is reserved for his victims, those who loved them, and perhaps their descendants. Hence, in considering the possibility that the difference between a holder of a right and a holder of personal expectation is a difference in standing to direct versus to blame, we need to specify that it is this second kind of blame—call it "personal" blame—that is at issue.

Even with this specification, however, I think we will not get far with this possibility. First, non-demanding kinds of directives *do* seem legitimate in anticipation of or in response to ingratitude. Benefactors may legitimately, for example, *entreat* or *urge* the recalcitrant and inconsiderate beneficiary to show gratitude: "Are you really going to treat me like this? After all I've done for you?" Let me say a bit more about this.

A rough-and-ready indicator that one person has the standing or permission to *direct* another through the performance of directive speech acts is what I like to call the "Who are *you* to?!" test. In general, the incredulous exclamation, "Who are *you* to . . .?!" challenges the presumption of a relationship. If your nosy neighbor pries into your personal business, and you think to yourself "Yeesh, who the hell does he think he is?" that marks your feeling that he has overstepped his bounds, and presumed a degree of intimacy that is, at least as far as you are concerned, not a part of your relationship. Having the standing to direct a person is a kind of normative relationship, and "Who are *you* to!?" marks the would-be directee's feeling that that the agent attempting to direct them is acting presumptuously. You can see this in many American children, who are raised to believe only their parents have the standing to issue commands or even requests of them: Try asking a stranger's child to pick up the candy wrapper they have just dropped on the ground—you may very well get a "Who are *you* to?!" eyebrow raise.

Now imagine the beneficiary of a great act of kindness, poised to act in a way most would think ungrateful—perhaps some petty backstabbing of their benefactor. A disinterested onlooker lacks the standing or permission to *direct* the beneficiary away from ingratitude; if they were to say, for example, "C'mon, don't let me down; I know you're better than this!" the beneficiary could reasonably enough respond, "Who are *you* to talk to me that way?" The onlooker would be overstepping their bounds, presuming a normative relationship they do not have with the beneficiary.

It is true that the bystander may, at least in some circumstances, appropriately *point out the reasons* for the beneficiary to refrain from the backstabbing: "This does seem an ungrateful way to act. You realize you're hurting the person who helped you?" But the bystander is still not the person who has some kind of claim to the beneficiary's gratitude.

By contrast, the benefactor has the standing or permission to direct. If the benefactor were to say, "I'll really be disappointed in you if you join in with those gossipy backstabbers at the next party," it would be strange for the beneficiary to respond, "Who are *you* to say that?" (assuming that the benefactor is not displaying an insulting level of distrust by issuing this warning). There is a normative relationship there, one that gives the benefactor the standing or permission to direct the beneficiary, lacked by other parties. Thus, if what the benefactor has is a *non-right-based* personal expectation of gratitude, it will not do to exclude standing or permission to perform all directive speech acts from such expectations.[16]

A second point against the possibility that personal expectations imply the standing to blame but not direct, which is essentially a generalization on the first point, is that directing and blaming cannot be so readily separated. If anyone has the standing to resent a rights-violation, and to blame the violator by expressing that resentment, it is the person with the claim of right that has been violated. Thus, it also seems likely that a person with a personal expectation thereby has the standing to personally blame the person who flouts that expectation. Personal blame in the form of reactive attitudes like resentment and feeling let down, and the expression of these attitudes, plausibly bears a conceptual link to directive speech acts.[17]

I conclude that the essential difference between claims of right and non-right-based personal expectations is not the difference between having the standing or permission to perform directive speech acts and having only the standing or permission to personally blame. Thus, if the idea that demands are beyond the benefactor's standing or permission is the key to distinguishing rights and personal expectations, the distinction will have to trace a difference *within* the category of directive speech acts, most likely between directives of different *forces*.

DIRECTIVES OF DIFFERENT FORCES

Within the family of directive speech acts, there are many different kinds of acts, with differing registers or forces. Making a demand of someone has a different force from issuing a request, and again from offering, entreating, encouraging, or urging the importance of something. So perhaps having a right means having the authority or permission to perform directive speech acts with the force of demands, while having a personal expectation means having standing or permission to perform directive speech acts with a different force (e.g., the force of urging).[18] This seems a promising way of capturing the intuitions at the start of section "Demand and Speech Acts," whereby, on the one hand, benefactors overstep their bounds if they demand gratitude from their beneficiaries but, on the other hand, benefactors nevertheless have some sort of special standing relative to their beneficiaries, a privileged basis for complaining about, or feeling let down or hurt by, ingratitude.

The concerns I am going to raise about this view are not dispositive, I think. Indeed, I consider this idea an interesting proposal, worth further development and exploration.[19] However, I do want to indicate one hazard of articulating a distinction among kinds of directed obligations—such as the distinction between rights and personal expectations—in terms of distinctions among speech acts. That hazard is the risk of circularity, for a likely way of distinguishing among the relevant forms of speech acts relies on distinctions among obligations.

To see this risk, consider Manela's argument that demanding gratitude undermines any beneficiary obligations of gratitude:

> A benefactor's belief that she could (permissibly) demand a return in the future . . . undermine[s] her standing to demand an act of *gratitude*. . . . When a benefactor demands fulfillment of an obligation of gratitude . . . what is problematic is . . . that it presupposes and entails . . . a belief on the part of the benefactor that in conferring her original benefit, she became *entitled* to demand a return. This presupposition undermines her desert of gratitude, renders gratitude no longer owed. (2015, 162–63, my emphases)

This argument is different from Berger's related argument that an act performed out of an expectation of return cannot generate an obligation of gratitude. Demanding gratitude, on Berger's account, indicates that the benefactor's original helping act was not motivated in the right way—not in the right way to merit gratitude (300). Manela's argument, by contrast, does not depend on how the benefactor saw their helping act at the time of performance, or what motivated them.

The first step in Manela's argument is the claim that a person who issues a demand implies they are *entitled* to whatever it is they demand. I'm not convinced this is true. If, for example, pirate demands are genuine (though impermissible) demands—and not misfires—then this claim says pirates are implicitly committed to believing they are *entitled* to ransom payments. And if pirate demands are not genuine demands, and some kind of authority is among the felicity conditions of demands, then we need to wonder whether this standing is the same as entitlement. Could a person nevertheless be placed to legitimately demand, say, recognition for an accomplishment, even if she is not *entitled* to that recognition?

Suppose, however, that we set aside these objections, and grant that demands imply the belief that one is entitled to whatever one demands. The next step in the argument is the claim that a person who believes—or is implicitly committed to the belief—that she is *entitled* to gratitude cannot deserve, or be owed, gratitude. I take it the idea is that, if a person interprets an act of beneficence as generating an entitlement to certain treatment, she thereby interprets the act as the first step in something like a *transaction*—as Manela says, such an interpretation turns the act into "an odd sort of lending" (162). So, the benefactors who see themselves as entitled to certain treatment in virtue of their beneficence thereby become strange lenders or perhaps traders—trading the benefit for the treatment to which they are now entitled. In turn, this self-conception is supposed to undermine the legitimacy of seeing themselves as deserving or meriting gratitude. Why? It certainly seems I can be grateful to someone for lending me money in a time of need, even while knowing she thinks of the loan as pure transaction and expects me to return the money (perhaps with interest). Perhaps, however, the *repayment of my debt* cannot itself be an expression of that gratitude; it can be only the repayment of a debt. If that's right, then the benefactor who sees themselves as entitled to certain treatment specifically undermines the legitimacy of seeing *that treatment* as an obligation of gratitude—they cannot both say "I am entitled to better treatment" and "It is ungrateful—that is, a failure to live up to your obligation of gratitude—to treat me this way."

Again, though, we might wonder about a gap between concepts. Seeing myself as entitled to certain treatment precludes gratitude for that treatment only if entitlement entails the kind of claim produced by a trading transaction—that is to say, a claim of right. So this inference precludes the coherence of proclaiming that one is entitled to, say, the things one deserves or merits, where that is not a claim of the sort generated by trading transactions. It may sound arrogant to proclaim that one is entitled to admiration for an impressive accomplishment (but maybe not, if one has regularly been denied such acknowledgment), but it is not obvious that it is *incoherent*.

Most importantly for the current discussion, if we do *not* think there are conceptual gaps between demands and entitlements or between entitlements and transactional claims (claim rights), then we cannot use the picture Manela sketches in this argument for purposes of distinguishing rights and personal expectations. If we did, the result would be circular: having a right means having the standing or permission to direct through demand, which means being entitled, which means having the kind of claim produced by a trading transaction, which means having a right. To be clear, Manela does not forward this argument in the context of distinguishing rights and personal expectations (or, more on point for his purposes, imperfect rights)—his account of this distinction is not circular (his account is the sanction account I argued against in section "Enforcement and Sanction"). My point is that one tempting way to characterize the force of a demand—through connection with concepts like entitlement—risks relying on the concept of a right.

Compare, for example, Paul Portner's pragmatic approach to distinguishing varieties of directives: directive speech acts contribute to the common ground by updating the addressee's "To Do List," and different kinds of directives update different sublists (2007, 2012). As Harris, Fogal, and Moss describe the view: "a command proposes an update to the part of the To-Do List that corresponds to the addressee's duties, [while] a request proposes an update to the part of the To-Do List that corresponds to the speaker's desires" (21). In keeping with this approach, if we wanted to distinguish commands and demands, we might consider that both propose updates to the part of the To Do List that corresponds to the addressee's duties, but commands more specifically to the duties resulting from the speaker's exercise of a normative power and demands to the duties correlating to the speaker's rights. But now the circularity arises again.

I believe this is one of the most important challenges to the kind of approach I've been considering in this section. If we aim to distinguish among different kinds of directed obligation by appealing to different forces of directive speech act, we have to be able to distinguish between speech acts without relying on different kinds of obligations, or on concepts tightly linked to those obligations.

Add to the risk of circularity an intuition that cuts against the intuition that demanding gratitude is out of bounds: Benefactors do *sometimes* get to demand gratitude, don't they? They get to demand it in a general way of truly crummy beneficiaries: "You need to straighten up and show some gratitude! You simply cannot go on treating me this way!" And, in certain cases, they get to demand specific actions or omissions. Manela's own example of a strict duty of gratitude strikes me as such a case. He argues that beneficiaries have strict duties of non-maleficence to their beneficiaries. For example, it may be a case of impermissible ingratitude for a beneficiary to enter into a fair business competition that aims to put their benefactor out of business. Although Manela says the benefactor in this case still does not get to *demand* that the beneficiary refrain from this competition, it's difficult to see why not: "Don't you dare!" they could legitimately say. Threatening severe sanctions seems appropriate, too: "If you do this, I will make sure everyone knows what an ungrateful scumbag you are."[20]

It is true that many of the cases where demand seems legitimate are actually cases of demanding that the beneficiary not act in an *un*grateful way: in the case I take from Manela, the demand is that the beneficiary refrain from actively seeking to damage the benefactor's interests. Another case that seems plausible to me is where the beneficiary is simply oblivious, and does nothing either intentionally or unintentionally to damage the benefactor's interests, but also does nothing, ever, to acknowledge the benefactor's generosity. I suppose it could be argued that the benefactor has an interest in being acknowledged or in appreciation, and the oblivious beneficiary's ongoing silence harms that interest—so that any demand the benefactor might legitimately make is still a demand for refraining from ingratitude. At this point, though, the line between refraining from ingratitude and expressing gratitude becomes pretty fine. Perhaps, however, there is a basis here for maintaining that it is never legitimate for a benefactor to demand gratitude from their beneficiary. I'll say a bit more about this in the section "Directing Means versus Directing Ends."

As noted earlier, it seems to me that despite the worries I have raised here, the project of distinguishing rights and non-right-based personal expectations by appeal to different forces of directive speech act is still a live one. However, these worries should encourage us to explore alternative approaches, which is what I want to do in the next section. In particular, I will propose that the distinction we want might be better grounded in the *scope* of directive standing or permission, rather than force.

DIRECTING MEANS VERSUS DIRECTING ENDS

The proposal I want to put forward is that rights entail the standing or permission to direct specific actions, or means to ends; while personal expectations entail only the standing or permission to direct the adoption of broad ends, leaving latitude regarding the means to be taken.

I think we already have in hand the right account of *directedness*: a directed obligation is one where someone else has the standing or permission to perform directive speech acts regarding the performance of the obligation. A promissory obligation and an obligation of gratitude share this aspect: The person who is obliged to keep a promise is obliged to the person to whom they made the promise, which is to say that the promisee may legitimately direct the promiser to do as they promised. The beneficiary who is obliged to be grateful to their generous benefactor is obliged to the benefactor, which is to say the benefactor may legitimately direct the benefactor to be grateful.

What we still require is the wedge between rights and personal expectations. I want to propose that the distinction is between having two forms of standing relative to a person. The first form of standing entails the legitimacy of directing *both* the adoption of an end *and* the means taken to that end, and the second form entails the legitimacy of directing only the adoption of an end. That is, the difference between rights and personal expectations is a matter of *scope*: the rights-holder gets to direct quite narrow choices on the part of the obliged party, while the person who holds a personal expectation gets to direct only relatively broad choices or commitments.[21] Hence, the key difference we have been trying to mark throughout this chapter, between the promissee's position and the benefactor's, is that the promissee can legitimately direct the promiser to *do as they promised*[22]—that is, to fulfill the end of fidelity through specific performance—while the benefactor can legitimately direct the beneficiary only to adopt or maintain the broad end of being grateful.[23]

What does it mean to be able to direct only the adoption or maintenance of a broad end? It means that the means the beneficiary takes to being grateful are to be specified not by the benefactor, but by circumstances, opportunities, and the beneficiary's choice. This, then, is the answer to the question with which we began: *The benefactor anchor in directed obligations of gratitude is the benefactor's standing or permission to direct, through the use of directive speech acts, the beneficiary to adopt the end of being grateful.*

I now want to perform an initial test of this answer, by considering whether it *explicates*—that is, not only fits with, but provides a deeper understanding of—one of the central intuitions found in the gratitude literature: namely, the conviction that it is generally inappropriate for a benefactor to demand gratitude from the beneficiary. I think that it does.

First, the benefactor generally *does not* get to direct the means the beneficiary takes to being grateful. They do not have standing or permission to direct *in any way*—by demanding or entreating or urging or nudging or encouraging or whatever—the beneficiary's particular grateful actions. And this seems right: it would be as inappropriate to *urge* the beneficiary "Really, you should say 'thank you' to me"; or *cheer*, "C'mon, you can do it! Get me a gift! G-I-F-T!" as it would be to demand any such thing.

Second, the benefactor *does* get to direct the beneficiary to adopt the end of gratitude. All else being equal, that means the benefactor gets to issue demands as well as "gentler" or more positive directive speech acts. However, as Card points out, "It is not all right to prod people to fulfill their obligations when they have not had a chance to do so on their own initiative" (1988, 121). It is inappropriate to demand either the performance of a particular action or the adoption of an end, when one does not have adequate reason to doubt that the target is going to comply. It is also inappropriate to urge, nudge, or cheer for it. Given that it can be much more difficult to discern whether a person has adopted a broad end than whether they are considering shirking a specific means to an obligatory end, it is unsurprising that demand is more frequently associated with rights than personal expectations. There are simply more occasions where Card's point does not apply, in the case of rights and their correlative obligations. If you promise to return my book to me tomorrow no later than noon and then turn to the person next to me and commit to lending it him when you are done with it, I know you are not planning to follow through on your promise: "What the—?! What are you doing? You promised to return it tomorrow!"

Compare the beneficiary who fails to offer a simple "thank you" to a benefactor who has, out of care and with no concern for reciprocation, generously helped them. Absent excusing or mitigating circumstances, existing social conventions entail that such a beneficiary has failed to be grateful. What are the available legitimate responses from the benefactor? First, there may very well be excusing or mitigating circumstances. If the beneficiary needed help, they may be distracted or distraught or otherwise reasonably have their attention elsewhere. This is why a benefactor who is truly tuned into and motivated by their beneficiary's need is unlikely to quickly prompt, "You're *welcome?*" The benefactor simply will not perceive the failure to say "thank you" as evidence of a lack of gratitude.

But suppose time passes: the beneficiary has recovered from their misfortune, and multiple apt moments for a simple "thank you" have passed unmentioned. Nor has the beneficiary expressed gratitude or appreciation in any other way. It would surely be legitimate for the benefactor, at this point, to begin to feel hurt. Then, one day, the beneficiary begins to regale the benefactor with a self-congratulatory narrative about their recovery from that original misfortune, giving no credit to the benefactor. At this point, the hurt feelings bloom into resentment, and a little direction would not be amiss: "You know, you've never even said 'thank you' for the help I gave you then?" This direction is legitimate not because the beneficiary suddenly has a claim on a performance of this particular social convention, but because enough evidence has accumulated that the beneficiary has no notion that they ought to be grateful.

Similarly, there are circumstances where the opportunity to take certain *necessary* means arises, such that, if the beneficiary fails to take them, they thereby demonstrate that they have not adopted the end of being grateful. Manela's examples of non-maleficence are cases-in-point. On this account, the benefactor *does* get to demand that the beneficiary refrain from seeking to put them out of business—such restraint is a necessary part of having the end of gratitude at all. There are also means that are not necessary but are *excellent opportunities*, and the beneficiary who fails to take such means thereby provides defeasible evidence that they do not have an adequate commitment to the obligatory end of gratitude. For example, if the opportunity to easily assist the benefactor presents itself, a person with a genuine commitment to the end of gratitude will take this opportunity; if they do not, they call into question their understanding of their obligation to the benefactor, and it may be legitimate for the benefactor to make a demand: "Show some appreciation for what I did for you!"

I conclude that the proposal to characterize the benefactor anchor, the personal expectation, as the standing or permission to direct broad ends or commitments and not narrow means does well, at least by this initial test.

CONCLUSION

By way of conclusion, I want to note two interesting implications of my proposal. First, it is intuitive to think of rights and personal expectations as distinct *kinds* of claim; or, to think of promissory obligations and obligations of gratitude as distinct kinds of obligation. The proposal I have put forward implies that they rather occur on a spectrum, stretching from directed obligations correlative to the standing or permission to direct precise means to an end, to those correlative to the standing or permission to direct a broad and general end, leaving latitude for the obliged party to choose from a wide variety of means. Consider, for example, what I have been taking as a clear example of a right-based obligation, throughout: the obligation of fidelity to a promise. Many instances of this obligation fall on the right-based end of the spectrum, because people often promise to perform fairly specific actions. However, there are other instances that fall closer to the non-right-based end. If I promise a friend to lead an authentic life, for example, the result is that they have standing or permission to direct me to adopt or maintain quite a broad end. Their position therefore resembles the benefactor's: They rarely have standing or permission to direct me to take particular means to leading an authentic life—there may be many paths, values, and commitments that will contribute to this end. They *do* have standing or permission to direct me to adopt and stay committed to this end, but it will often not be easy to discern whether I am slipping. When my choices *do* provide good evidence that my commitment is slipping—say I am on the verge of "selling out" by my own lights—my friend has, in virtue of my promise, standing to demand or otherwise direct me not to do so. So here we have a case of a promissory obligation that resembles obligations of gratitude much more than transactional obligations.

The second implication is a general recommendation for philosophical accounts of obligation, which I'll come at by way of a potential objection to my proposal: For some, the idea of an *end of being grateful* might not seem a good fit with what benefactors typically want from their beneficiaries. The benefactor who feels slighted and unappreciated usually feels that the ungrateful beneficiary has *treated* the benefactor in a way that neglects the value of the assistance provided—and perhaps more importantly, neglects the value of the care and concern that the benefactor demonstrated in providing that assistance. Moreover, the feeling of having been slighted often includes a sense that the beneficiary does not *perceive* the benefactor in an appropriate way; the benefactor's assistance, care, and concern—indeed, the benefactor themselves—are inadequately salient to the beneficiary (perhaps the beneficiary is too wrapped up in themselves, or has a misplaced sense of entitlement). In short, what we often want, when we help or support others, is *to be appreciated*—that is, to be perceived in a certain way, and to be treated in a way that reflects that perception. *Adopting an end*, goes the objection, is really about *having a project*, or goal-to-be-realized. It may often, as a contingent matter, involve seeing people and things in particular ways, but what we need to fully capture the nature of obligations of gratitude is an immediate obligation of perception and motivation shaped by that perception.

For those who think gratitude is more about vision than agency, I want to suggest that there is a general lesson of this chapter that extrapolates to different frameworks. The lesson is that, whatever moral or ethical framework we adopt, it should contain the conceptual space for articulating different ways in which people may be bound to each other through directed obligations and some of these ways of being bound together differ in terms of *scope*. Some relationships contain quite strict and narrow parameters of obligation, while others are significantly more open-ended. The latter, of course, tend to be the more "personal" relationships. This is not just because personal relationships work better with this kind of open-endedness but also because this open-endedness provides the opportunity for creativity and particularity. It allows an obliged person to develop his own beautiful ways of instantiating his understanding and appreciation of his obligation and the person to whom he is obliged. It also leaves open the opportunity for the person to whom he is obliged to be pleasantly surprised by the care and creativity taken in response to the obligation. Such obligations thereby provide the opportunity for the relationships they shape to become deeper and more distinctively meaningful.[24]

NOTES

1 In this chapter, I focus on gratitude to benefactors—though I do not assume that there are not other forms of gratitude—and I assume that obligations of gratitude arise as a result of something like *generous* benefaction (e.g., see Chappell in this volume). I assume nothing further about either the acts that generate obligations of gratitude or what adequate gratitude involves. The account I develop of directedness should travel across different conceptions of gratitude and different views about whether obligations of gratitude are primarily obligations to *be* grateful, obligations to *feel* grateful, obligations to *show gratitude*, obligations to act as a grateful person would act, and so on.

2 Another prevalent term that picks out this structure is "bipolar": the obligation has one "pole" centered in the beneficiary, linked to the other pole, centered in the benefactor. See Stephen Darwall, "Bipolar Obligation."

In "Duties of Love," Wallace actually puts forward the view that *all* obligations are relational, but I do not assume this view is either true or false in this chapter. Perhaps some obligations are general and undirected.

3 For one way of understanding the connection between obligations of gratitude and "paying it forward," see the section "Gratitude and Obligation" of Helm (this volume).

4 Card, "Gratitude and Obligation."

5 See Kate Moran, "Much Obliged."

6 Kant's and Hobbes's own ways of talking about "sacred" and "eternal debts" certainly lend some credence to Card's view. On the other hand, they are also at some pains to specify the ways in which "debts" of gratitude are unlike more familiar, transaction-based debts. See Moran, "Much Obliged." In her 2016 essay, "Gratitude to the Decent Rescuer," Card seems more open to the possibility that obligations of gratitude are imperfect duties.

7 Perhaps Barbara Herman's account, in "Being Helped and Being Grateful," provides some resources. Her view is that beneficence creates an imbalance in independent agency, and beneficiaries create or adopt the duty of gratitude toward their benefactors in order to compensate for this imbalance. What's missing from this account is that gratitude is largely about *appreciating* the benefactor or the care they demonstrate. Herman's account also seems to require, implausibly, that appropriate expressions of gratitude are limited to actions that amount to helping the benefactor—thereby restoring the balance of independent agency. See Moran, "Much Obliged," for an argument that, for Kant, gratitude is a dutiful acknowledgment of human—and thus the beneficiary's own—neediness and insufficiency.

8 See Hill.

9 For Grotius, see especially §§II.I.i–vii, II.XI.iii–iv, II.XXII.xvi. For Pufendorf, §§I.i.19–20, I.vii.x-11, III. iv.5–7.

10 Something like this dilemma makes sense of why Kant ultimately conceives of all ethical duties as imperfect, and reserves perfect duties—understood as externally enforceable duties of action—for the juridical realm.

11 There are, of course, plenty who would say that all obligations are directed to a moral community that encompasses all of humanity, so that the faraway wrongdoer did in some sense violate an obligation to me. Even if such a view is correct, it remains true that there are obligations directed not (only) to all members of the moral community but (also) to some specific person or persons who are positioned to assert a distinctive kind of standing relative to the obligated party.

12 Specifically, possessing this standing would be among what Searle and Vanderveken call the "preparatory conditions" for a felicitous demand. See Searle and Vanderveken (1985).

13 On pirate demands, see Manela (2015), 161.

14 For example, see Berger 306, Herman 393–394, Wellman 290.

15 The distinction between impersonal and personal blame parallels the distinction between impersonal and personal normative expectations, discussed in the section "Enforcement and Sanction."

16 What about those in close relationships with the beneficiary who are *not* the benefactor? Couldn't the beneficiary's romantic partner reasonably "urge" them to treat the benefactor better? I think so, but that this does not show that directives like urging do not presuppose the standing or "normative relationship" I have been

talking about. I see two possibilities. The first is that the partner's "urging" is in fact a different, non-directive kind of speech act, such as *advising*. Alternatively, perhaps the partner does have the standing to direct the beneficiary in this context. If so, however, the partner must have some kind of personal stake in the beneficiary's gratitude, or perhaps in their character more broadly, so that what is being urged is responsiveness to an obligation to the partner (a tacit commitment to be a better person, say) *by way of* responsiveness to the obligation of gratitude to the benefactor. Such a stake explains why, for example, parents often have the standing to urge their children to do better in their relationships with others: the parents are invested in the children's character in such a way that the children's treatment of others reflects on their relationship with their parents. So if a teenager does something terrible to a teacher who has always been a supportive and caring mentor, the teenager thereby does wrong by both the teacher and the parent. Thanks to Daniel Telech for pushing me on this point.

17 My view is that directive and personally blaming speech acts have different felicity conditions: a personally blaming speech act has a personal reactive attitude (or at least the belief that a personal reactive attitude would be appropriate) among its *sincerity* conditions, while a directive speech act does not—for example, even a person who would not resent or believe it appropriate to resent a broken promise may be positioned to felicitously demand fidelity. Personally blaming and directing are nevertheless conceptually linked, I believe, because the person who has the standing to aptly feel a personally blaming reactive attitude thus has the standing to direct the target of that attitude, and vice versa. But my point in the main text does not rely on this particular view of the conceptual relations among attitudes and speech acts; it relies only on the more general proposition that personal blame and directive speech acts bear some kind of conceptual link.

18 At first consideration, it seems natural to mark the differences in the forces of these various directives in terms of *strength*, and thus think that a person who has standing to demand must also have standing to, say, urge or request. I'm not certain, however, that the *degree of strength* fully accounts for differences in force. For example, it can sometimes seem quite presumptuous for a person with a claim right to *urge* the duty-bound person to comply with the right: "Don't let me down" is reserved for people with some kind of personal investment in the urged action.

19 In *How We Hope: A Moral Psychology*, I propose that investing hope in a person—what I call "normative hope"—should be understood as "aspiring on their behalf" rather than "making a demand" of them, and argue that such investment grounds an interpersonal standing or authority distinct from the authority manifested in demands. The standing of normative hope, I propose, is the standing to *urge aspiration*, rather than *demand compliance*, and it is associated with being *disappointed in* a person, by contrast with *resenting* noncompliance. My aim in the present chapter is to take seriously the shortcomings of such a view, and consider an alternative.

20 Indeed, Manela's own articulation of "remonstration" in this case sounds a lot like demand, to me: "She seems to have special standing to *remonstrate* with [the ungrateful beneficiary]. 'How could you do this to me?' she might ask. 'Have you forgotten that I saved your life? How dare you drive me out of business just so you

can have a new Maserati! All I ask is that you have the decency to leave my client base alone—and I will not forgive you if you don't' " (2015, 163). In conversation and in forthcoming work, Manela proposes that demands are "proto-threats"—speech acts where the next move is to threaten coercive sanctions. For reasons I articulated in the section "Enforcement and Sanction," I am not optimistic about relying on concepts like enforcement, coercion, or sanction to distinguish perfect and imperfect rights.

21 Schroeder argues that maxim-based accounts of imperfect duties are unable to give an adequate account of the *specificity* of these duties—they are unable to say, that is, what exactly the duty-bound person must do, or why they must do it. See especially pages 564–565. My broad-scope conception of non-right-based personal expectations may face a similar challenge, but I make an effort to suggest how such a challenge may be surmounted.

22 Barring an overriding excuse on the part of the promise-maker, of course.

23 The inspiration here is, obviously, Kant, who says a perfect duty is a duty to perform an "action," while an imperfect duty is a duty to adopt a "maxim." As I've said, I want to lay aside the historical burdens of the concepts of perfect and imperfect duty, for purposes of this chapter.

24 I presented previous versions of this chapter and benefited from audience comments at: the 2016 Philosophy Colloquium Series at St. Mary's University, the 2017 Philosophy Colloquium Series at UC San Diego, the 2017 Rocky Mountain Ethics Congress, and the 2017 Moral Psychology of Gratitude Workshop at the University of Chicago. I am also grateful to Daniel Telech and Robert Roberts for both their comments on a draft of this paper and their careful work shepherding this volume.

WORKS CITED

Fred R. Berger, "Gratitude," *Ethics* 85, no. 4 (July, 1975): 298–309.

Samuel V. Bruton, "Duties of Gratitude," *Philosophy in the Contemporary World* 10, no. 1 (2003): 11–15.

Paul Camenisch, "Gift and Gratitude in Ethics," *Journal of Religious Ethics* 9, no. 1 (Spring, 1981): 1–34.

Claudia Card, "Gratitude and Obligation," *American Philosophical Quarterly* 25, no. 2 (1988): 115–127.

———, "Gratitude to the Decent Rescuer," in *Perspectives on Gratitude: An Interdisciplinary Approach*, ed. David Carr (New York, NY: Routledge, 2016): 99–111.

Stephen Darwall, "Bipolar Obligation," in *Morality, Authority, and Law* (New York, NY: Oxford University Press, 2013): 20–29.

Patrick Fitzgerald, "Gratitude and Justice," *Ethics* 109 (October 1998): 119–153.

Hugo Grotius, *On the Law of War and Peace* (1625).

Daniel W. Harris, Daniel Fogal, and Matt Moss, "Speech Acts: the Contemporary Theoretical Landscape," in *New Work on Speech Acts*, edited by Harris, Fogal, and Moss (forthcoming from Oxford University Press). Accessed at http://www.danielwharris.com/papers/HarrisFogalMoss-SpeechActsTheContemporaryTheoreticalLandscape.pdf on May 23, 2018.

Barbara Herman, "Being Helped and Being Grateful: Imperfect Duties, the Ethics of Possession, and the Unity of Morality," *The Journal of Philosophy* CIX, no. 5/6 (2012): 391–411.

Thomas E. Hill, Jr., "Kant on Imperfect Duty and Supererogation," *Kant Studien*, 62 (1971): 55–76. Reprinted in his 1992 *Dignity and Practical Reason in Kant's Moral Theory*, Ithaca: Cornell University Press, 147–175.

Tony Manela, "Obligations of Gratitude and Correlative Rights," *Oxford Studies in Normative Ethics* 5 (2015): 151–170.

———, "Gratitude and Appreciation," *American Philosophical Quarterly* 53, no. 3 (July 2016): 281–294.

Adrienne M. Martin, *How We Hope: A Moral Psychology* (Princeton, NJ: Princeton University Press, 2013).

Terrance McConnell, *Gratitude* (Philadelphia, PA: Temple University Press, 1993).

John Stuart Mill, *Utilitarianism*, Second Edition, ed. George Sher. (Indianapolis, IN: Hackett 2001).

Kate Moran, "Much Obliged: Kantian Gratitude Reconsidered," *Archiv für Geschichte der Philosophie* 98, no. 3 (2016/9/27): 330–363.

Paul Portner, "Imperatives and modals," *Natural Language Semantics* 15 (2007): 351–83.

———, "Permission and choice," In Grewendorf, G. and Zimmermann, T., editors, *Discourse and Grammar: From Sentence Types to Lexical Categories*. (Mouton de Gruyter, 2012); 43–68.

Samuel Pufendorf, *On the Law of Nature and of Nations* (1672).

S. Andrew Schroeder, "Imperfect Duties, Group Obligations, and Beneficence," *Journal of Moral Philosophy* 11 (2014): 557–584.

John Searle and D. Vanderveken, *Foundations of Illocutionary Logic* (Cambridge: Cambridge University Press, 1985).

A. D. M. Walker, "Gratefulness and Gratitude," Proceedings of the Aristotelian Society, New Series, 81 (1980–1981): pp. 39–55.

R. Jay Wallace, *Responsibility and the Moral Sentiments*. (Cambridge, MA: Harvard University Press, 1998).

———, "Duties of Love," Proceedings of the Aristotelian Society, Supplementary Volume, 86 (2012), pp. 175–198.

Christopher Heath Wellman, "Gratitude as a Virtue," *Pacific Philosophical Quarterly* 80, no. 3 (1999): 284–300.

Chapter 4

Debts of Gratitude[1]

Agnes Callard

Gratitude is a positive emotion, typically classified with joy, pride, and admiration. But unlike those emotions, gratitude often comes with uncomfortable strings attached—the so-called debt of gratitude. Imagine you were on dialysis, and your eager young coworker, having learned that she is a match, offered to donate a kidney. I stipulate that you suspect no ulterior motive, nor do you think she feels pressured into offering; you are satisfied that she has thought through the implications. Nonetheless, you might be so pained by the prospect of what gratitude calls for in response to such a massive act of beneficence that you have difficulty bringing yourself to accept. And if you do accept, your gratitude to her will be tinged with a feeling of indebtedness. In such a case, that feeling of being burdened by how much you owe her is part and parcel of gratitude.

The debt of gratitude points to the existence of norms governing the reception of benefits. But we can make a corresponding point about the other positive emotions: it is possible to respond inadequately or excessively in respect of joy, pride, or admiration. And yet we don't speak of a "debt of joy" or a "debt of pride." What is special about the norms that govern being benefited, such that they generate an uncomfortable feeling of indebtedness?

In some cases, they don't. Suppose my best friend gets me, for my birthday, the quirky dress only she could have known I'd love. I am delighted; I feel grateful; I thank her—or perhaps the look on my face is thanks enough. I do not feel myself to be under any sort of standing normative burden. The demands of gratitude are exhausted by what I feel and express in reaction to the dress. She'll be happy that I'm happy, and that will be all. In this case, there is no debt of gratitude, no discomfort. My gratitude is a purely positive emotion, akin to joy, admiration, and pride.

In this chapter, I explain what a debt of gratitude is, and why there is no debt of gratitude in the birthday dress case. I also argue that when there *is* a debt of gratitude, it needn't take the form of the kidney-donation case. Debts of gratitude come in two variants, corresponding to the two "objects" that the feeling of gratitude takes. In the kidney-donation case, beneficence generates an obligation that regulates how one acts toward, thinks of, and feels about *the person* who gave you something. I will call this a "debt of reciprocation." In another kind of case, the obligation in question governs one's feelings, thoughts, and behavior in relation to *the thing* given by someone. I will call this a "debt of appreciation." Let me begin by describing in detail a debt of this second kind.

MY TEACHER

I have been taught by many good teachers, and one great teacher. Her name was Amy Kass, and her classes—more specifically, her questions—were the centerpiece of my college education. Her special talent was to treat a work of literature as a jumping-off point for exploring issues in ethics, metaphysics, and areas of human life and thought that are impossible to classify. She once asked me why I wouldn't want to be Helios, the sun god. Another time, she asked whether the lyrics of the Simon and Garfunkel song "Blessed" are true to the message of their biblical source: "Did they understand what Jesus was trying to say?" She had a lot of questions about eating: does it matter what we eat? Who we eat it with? How we eat it? And *why* do these things matter? She wondered whether I'd be satisfied with having an immortal soul that was not personalized to me: "Do you think your immortal soul has to have your name written in the corner?" She wanted to know whether Socrates was guilty as charged, whether Ahab's quest to kill the whale was noble or foolish, and what I thought about Cordelia's refusal of Lear's demand for a profession of love—was she principled or cold-hearted?

She would ask a question, and then she would give you *this look*. I have spoken to many of her students about this moment, so I know that my reaction was not idiosyncratic. When her eyes fall on you, and you are poised to answer, something about her face conveys the following thought: she has been waiting her whole life for this moment, to encounter *you*, the one person who knows the answer to this deeply important question. As absurd as that sounds, she sold it. Hers is the countenance, the demeanor, the mood that I project onto Socrates, when I imagine him asking his interlocutors: "What is X?" I model my Socrates on her because when it came to eliciting answers people never dreamed were in them, I have never met anyone more earnest or more ruthless.

This questioning helped me see the meaning in everyday human practices, in philosophy, in literature, in community, in teaching and being taught. The list could go on and on. Her classes exposed the connection between thinking and living: that thinking about something could make doing it more meaningful, and that much of what was worth thinking about could be thought about only by drawing on one's lived experience in the relevant domain.

She once told me that someone once told her that whenever you teach a class, you should imagine that someone much smarter than you is in the classroom. After I left college for graduate studies in Classics, I often found myself imagining her. Having been assigned a massive amount of Greek reading, I'd be tempted to peek at the translation to speed myself up; sitting in a seminar on material I didn't really understand, I'd wonder whether I should raise my hand. I knew what she would tell me to do, and when I didn't take her "advice," I felt guilty. Teaching my first class—Intro Greek—I often felt her presence, advising me to be patient, to admit ignorance, to make sure that I conveyed something of the beauty of the language and not only the grammar.

I felt I owed it to her to do all these things—that any less would constitute ingratitude. And this feeling was uncomfortable, in that it blocked the easy way forward. I subjected myself to criticism; I monitored for self-indulgence; I never felt that I had done enough. To give just one example: in view of what I perceived to be the deficiencies in the textbook assigned for the class, I felt obliged to write my own Greek textbook for my students.

My life both during and after college was suffused with a feeling of indebtedness, but little of this debt took the form of a desire to reciprocate, benefit, or even come into contact with my college teacher. What I felt obligated to do—what I felt I owed her, in view of her beneficence to me—was the completion of the project we began together.

Gratitude has two targets—we are grateful *to* someone—our benefactor— *for* something—the benefit. Gratitude is a response to benefit, not per se, but more specifically to the fact that some benefit is received *from another* as opposed to self-generated or the product of chance. Gratitude is a response to another's goodwill toward us, not per se, but as manifested *in some action* they take for the sake of our good.[2] Gratitude expresses the second-personal thought: "it means something to me that you did this." We are touched by the fact that the well-being that we are experiencing was the intentional object of another person's agency. My claim in this chapter is that the debt of gratitude I feel toward my teacher is a matter of being called upon to appreciate *what* she gave me—the benefit—whereas in the kidney donation case described earlier, the debt is primarily a matter of appreciating (the goodwill of) the benefactor. Before I describe the difference between these cases, however, it will be useful to differentiate both of them from a case of gratitude in which there is no debt at all, such as the birthday dress example sketched earlier. For this reason, I turn now to a discussion of the gratitude we feel for gifts.

GIFT-GRATITUDE

It is hard to give a good gift, because the gift-giver must navigate two pitfalls of gift-giving—the overly useful gift and the useless gift. The reason why these are bad gifts is that in either case, one generates a debt of gratitude. The art of gift-giving calls for one to be beneficent without generating a debt of gratitude.

Overly useful gifts fail to allow the gift-giver to shine. When I was 12, my prize possession was a Polaroid camera. I told my mother all I wanted for my birthday—from her, from relatives, from family friends—was film for the camera. My mother had to explain to me that people don't want to give me packages and packages of film. Such a request did too much to instrumental-ize the gift-giver into subservience to my ends. The purely instrumental gift makes it hard to appreciate the gift-giver. The pleasure one takes is too much a pleasure simply in the object, rather than in the fact that one received it *from so and so*.[3] Unlike the case of the birthday dress described earlier, one's reaction to the instrumental gift does not already contain an appreciation of the giver. One is, therefore, liable to feel that one still "owes" the giver some kind of debt in this regard. A gift that leaves the recipient feeling indebted is, under most circumstances, defective *qua* gift.

At the other extreme is the useless gift, such as a kitchen implement given to someone who doesn't cook. If you give me such a failed gift, my "thank you" will be a bit strained. When I say "it's the thought that counts," I'm appreciating the fact that you had goodwill toward me, rather than the benefit in which that goodwill materialized. Here the outstanding "debt of gratitude" will be in relation to the object—I may feel obligated to *try* to like it, and feel somewhat bad for not doing so. I may think I *ought* to display it (or at least to do so when you visit . . .). This outstanding debt, once again, indicates a defect in the gift.[4]

Gifts can be useless even when they are not tools. It is risky to give some-one, for example, an objet d'art, because the recipient may not have the same tastes as the giver. Such a gift is "useless" in the broader sense: it cannot be enjoyed. The educational gift is an especially interesting species of useless gift. If you are not interested in poetry or painting, it will usually be a mis-take for me to gift you, for example, a book collecting my favorite poems or paintings. It may be true that your life would be vastly improved if you took to poetry or painting, but it is (usually) inappropriate for me to try to effect the change via a gift. In this case, there is too much, as opposed to too little, of the giver in the gift; and this is likely to be felt by you as an imposition. A good gift, such as the birthday dress, allows the recipient's gratitude to take the form of an immediate pleasure or happiness in response to what she has been presented with. That means it must speak to her current ends, rather than those ends one would desire her to be educated into.

The perfect gift strikes a kind of mean between drawing our attention toward the benefit given and toward the person giving it, and it does so by being neither too useful nor utterly useless. A holy grail of gift-giving is to discover something the recipient never knew existed, but which ideally serves one of their idiosyncratic standing ends. The gift-giver makes her mark on the gift by presenting the recipient with something that reflects the giver's efforts, tastes, and ingenuity, but the receiver can immediately appreciate the gift as directed to them in particular, by way of being subordinated to some peculiar concern of theirs. In this sort of case, a heartfelt "this is just what I've always wanted!" can obviate even the need to add, "thank you." The perfect gift is perfect precisely in that it elicits an affective response[5] that exhausts all the demands of gratitude. It leaves no normative remainder to stand as a "debt of gratitude."

The intentional avoidance of a "debt of gratitude" stems from the fact that gifts are, ideally, *expressions* of gratitude, appreciation, or love. We give gifts to those people whose presence in our lives we want to mark in some positive way. The disposition to give to those people is part and parcel of the fact that (1) we are affectively vulnerable to both how they treat us and what happens to them; (2) we believe that it is good to have our lives implicated with theirs; (3) we are motivationally disposed to act in ways that protect and benefit both the people themselves and our connection to them; and (4) we reflectively endorse the above set of attitudes[6]. In short, we *value* our relationship with them and the gifts we give them are one way of marking this fact.[7] (Given that forms of the word "value" are often ambiguous as to whether they pick out a feature of the object valued or the subject doing the valuing, I will often use the word "valuation" or "valuational" to mark the condition of the subject specifically.)

Gift-giving is a recognition of the existence of such a shared valuational structure binding two people together. The excellent gift marks and celebrates ties that are already present; this project cuts against that of generating new ones. This is why educational gifts, or "motivational" gifts prompting the recipient to take up, for example, cooking or exercise, are problematic. To give such gifts is to suggest that one is not happy with the way things are, but it is precisely such happiness that gift-giving ought to express. The normative remainder prohibition does not apply to the two other forms of beneficence I would like to discuss, and this is because they represent the opening rather than the closing act of a valuational story. Gift-gratitude comes *from* valuing; the debt of gratitude, by contrast, is felt when gratitude moves one *toward* valuing.

ASSISTANCE GRATITUDE

If the aforementioned description of gift-giving is persuasive, it will be acceptable to restrict the word "gift" to mark an act of beneficence that is subject to the demand that the recipient's affective response exhaust all demands of gratitude. Not all that is given is, in my sense, a gift. The account of gift-gratitude given earlier is not a complete account of gratitude. Sometimes it is no defect in the act of benefaction that it provides something purely instrumental:[8] when we save the life of a drowning stranger, or bring food to our recently bereaved colleague, we provide them with help that is not inflected by the demand that the giver's idiosyncrasies be recognized. Call the gratitude one experiences in response to such benefaction "assistance-gratitude."

Assistance gratitude is typically not exhausted by a person's emotional reaction to having received assistance. Even after the beneficiary has made full use of the benefactor's gift by, for example, spending the money in a way that was profitable to herself—she feels she still owes the benefactor some kind of debt. Her enjoyment of the benefit he provided her does not contain within itself an acknowledgment of the fact that this enjoyment was secured by way of another's concern for her. In addition to enjoying the benefit, she feels she owes it to him to (become disposed to) make corresponding sacrifices on his behalf. I will call this a "debt of reciprocation."

Consider the following example from my own life. An editor of a journal went out of his way to expedite the refereeing process for a paper I submitted shortly before my tenure file was due. Two years later, I still never turn down his referee requests, no matter how inconvenient; I owe him. The debt of gratitude in such a case constitutes a normative remainder from the action that was done, such that her benefactor's ends, needs, and interests become, in some way or other, a source of normative demands for the beneficiary.

Whether benefaction generates a debt of gratitude is not simply a matter of the benefactor's choice—I may feel indebted to your assistance even if you wish that I didn't. There are, however, means benefactors can take to mitigate the beneficiary's feeling of indebtedness. Some charitable donors choose to remain anonymous, so that there is no target to whom the beneficiary might take herself to be indebted. Other benefactors might cast certain forms of assistance as a loan, in order to establish specific terms, the satisfaction of which would constitute repayment and cancellation of any debt. Here the normative debt of gratitude is transmuted into a financial debt—and, under some circumstances, this might make it more feasible for the beneficiary to accept the assistance. Another strategy is for the benefactor to minimize the cost of the benefit to himself, downplaying his own role in such a way as to try to get the beneficiary to see her situation as close to that of a person who has received a chance windfall.

Notice that in a case of gift-gratitude, the benefactor would have no inclination to subtract herself from the equation in any of these ways: I would not want to give a birthday present anonymously, or to treat it as a loan, or to downplay my role in getting it. Gift-gratitude is not beset by the problem these mechanisms are designed to address. Gift-gratitude doesn't put someone under a standing normative burden; it doesn't leave a remainder.

We can explain the source of the difference in terms of the relation to the practices of shared valuation described earlier: in the gift case, the benefaction comes from a place of already secured shared valuation, whereas in the assistance case, it moves one toward that place. When someone assists a stranger, this expresses a care or concern that the beneficiary who feels the debt of gratitude experiences herself as obligated to return. Likewise in the case where someone assists a friend or colleague in a way that goes beyond the already established terms of that relationship. The feeling of gratitude is the feeling that the benefactor has initiated the proceedings of a new form of valuation in which it behooves one to participate. When the benefactor tries to subtract herself from the equation in the ways described earlier, her aim is to benefit without thereby eliciting such a feeling in the beneficiary.

RECIPROCATION IS NOT PAYBACK

Gratitude is structured in such a way as to have a dual target: we are grateful to someone for something. Well-chosen gifts elicit an emotional response of gratitude that exhausts any normative demands toward either target; this is possible because both giving and receiving are governed by a pre-existing valuational state, namely mutual valuation of the interpersonal relationship in question. By contrast, in the case of assistance (and, as we will see later, mentorship), the grateful person experiences beneficence as an invitation to enter (more deeply) into valuation: her gratitude calls not for the expression, but rather for *the acquisition* of a practical disposition.

In the case of assistance-gratitude, the disposition to be acquired is one of valuing her relationship with her beneficiary. If she had such a disposition, she would be inclined to make (certain kinds of) sacrifices for her beneficiary and to act for the sake of (some of) her beneficiary's interests. Which kinds of sacrifice and which kinds of interests? The answers to these questions will depend on the kind of relationship they have, and on this point the beneficiary takes her cue from the benefactor's act of beneficence. The result is that gratitude often calls for a person to become disposed to do the kind of deed that was done for her; hence, I will call this kind of debt, a "debt of reciprocation."

But it is important to see that gratitude does not point toward paying someone back for what she did. Usually, our attitude toward debts is to discharge them, with a view to returning to our earlier, unindebted condition. The "debt of gratitude" is one that draws us up into normative demands rather than promising any kind of release from them. I do not deny that sometimes the beneficiary's goal is to do just *enough* to "balance out" what her benefactor did for her, with a view to thereafter being freed from any connection to him. In this sort of case, the beneficiary wishes to convert the debt of gratitude into one more closely resembling a financial debt. But such a motivational makeup can be the grounds for an accusation of ingratitude.

Reciprocation is not payback; hence the debt of reciprocation doesn't necessarily involve doing the sort of thing that was done for one. If a teenager's wealthy neighbor pays for him to take an expensive summer photography course, he might write her weekly letters detailing what he learns there. This is an appropriate expression of his valuation of the distinctive kind of tie that binds them, which is some species of what the Romans called a "patron-client relationship." It would make no sense for him to aim to pay for *her* education. He is not trying to undo the favor she did him; he is trying to play his part in the new relationship to which he reads her beneficence as an invitation. In the next section, I will discuss a debt of gratitude in which one's benefactor invites one to "step up" into valuing something other than a relationship with him- or her-self.

MENTOR-GRATITUDE

Assistance leaves a normative residue of gratitude to be directed toward the giver. If someone expresses a valuation of your welfare that goes beyond your current relationship to them, your gratitude is the feeling of being pulled into (a deeper) community with that person. You feel that you ought to value your relationship with them in a way that corresponds to the way in which their act of beneficence demonstrates that they do. I have used the phrase "debt of reciprocation," to describe the object of this feeling.

Mentorship generates a different sort of normative demand. The mentee's debt of gratitude points toward deepening her relationship with the gift rather than the giver. The job of a mentor is to help us acquire new ends by sharing their own; what their benefaction leaves behind is a *debt of appreciation* for what they have shared with us.

When reviewing the case of gift-gratitude, we noted that it is problematic when people give you gifts designed to educate you into their interests. It doesn't follow that it is inappropriate to try to educate someone—merely that it is, at least typically, inappropriate to do so on an occasion of gift-giving. Gifts express appreciation for what is already there; and this sentiment is incompatible with the desire to see someone change.

How, then, does one come to "give" someone a new end, desire, project, or passion? We don't usually educate people by handing them things—not even when the things are tickets or course-registrations. One helps another come to value something by sharing one's own passion for it in such a way as to guide the other's efforts to come to acquire it. Usually, this kind of support is received not from peers but from elders: the parents, teachers, coaches, and religious counselors who are further along than we are with respect to the relevant end. Let me use the word "mentor" to cover all of these various categories. I propose that what makes someone an excellent mentor with respect to some domain of human value is the fact that, for that person, sharing the value with others is a, perhaps even the best, way of realizing or fulfilling that value on a personal level. My teacher was someone who valued Homer *by* teaching others to value him.

Could someone be good at causing others to care about, for example, music without finding that educative activity to be musically fulfilling, or even without caring at all about music? Perhaps. But if such a person agreed (perhaps reluctantly) to do what it took to induct you into the world of music, and if she succeeded, you would not feel that you owed it to her to become musically excellent. At most you owe her assistance-gratitude for having been willing to do you the favor of making you musical. In this case, the person was making a sacrifice to educate you; my teacher made no such sacrifice.

My claim is that we feel a special kind of gratitude to those whose valuational projects are pursued by helping us acquire those values. Mentoring is not a zero-sum game: one doesn't lose anything by giving another person an end.[9] The help our mentors gave us did not alienate them from their own interests and so we don't, as in the cases of assistance-gratitude, feel obliged to develop a corresponding concern for those interests. I didn't owe my teacher personal favors. Her ministrations were an initiation into value—not that of our relationship, but of Homer and Plato, of literature and human reason and culture. My feeling of gratitude to her for those overtures is the feeling that I ought to become a full-fledged valuer of those things.

Just as it is not all the same whether I found the money as opposed to receiving it from a kind benefactor—in the second case, I have a debt of gratitude—it is likewise not all the same whether I discovered Homer and Plato on my own or whether I had them entrusted to me by someone to whom I likewise owe a debt of gratitude. I have a debt of appreciation when, as a result of what someone has done for me, I ought to (more fully) acquire some value.

CONCLUSION: WHY DO DEBTS OF GRATITUDE EXIST?

The beneficiary of assistance feels that she ought to acquire a disposition that would move her to benefit her benefactor in ways that correspond to the benefits she has received from him. I have called this kind of debt of gratitude, a "debt of reciprocation"; it is directed at the giver as opposed to the gift. In the case of mentor-gratitude, the disposition in question is one that would move her to properly value whatever value the mentor was helping her acquire. I have called this kind of debt, the "debt of appreciation"; it is directed at the gift as opposed to the giver.[10]

Why don't gifts and assistance give rise to debts of appreciation? There is, to be sure, a norm of appreciation that applies here: those who receive assistance or gifts ought to appreciate what they have been given. So, for instance, if someone gives me money because I need it for an operation, I ought to use the money for the operation. If, instead, I gamble it away, I'm failing to appreciate what they have given me. But it is also true that I will tend to use the money for the operation—and not because I appreciate the gift, but because I need the money. Likewise, if you give me a book for my birthday, I ought to read it; whereas if I had simply found the same book lying on the sidewalk, I would have no obligation to read it. But if you chose well, I will not experience the obligation to read the book as demanding, since I will *want* to start reading. I will already have the values that (are partly constituted by the dispositions that) motivate me to read it. I do not need to become a new or different person—to change in value—in order to appreciate what I should appreciate; for these reasons, I refrain from describing the fact that I ought to appreciate gifts and assistance as a "debt of appreciation."

Parallel claims apply with respect to reciprocation. We owe it to the gift-giver to *express* our delight, to make them see that we see the care and love with which the gift was chosen. Once again, in the case of a good gift and a good relationship, the recipient already has the disposition from which such a reaction will spring. Likewise, if we have been touched by the care and attentions of our mentors over the course of their mentorship, we will have developed the valuational disposition that inclines us to communicate how much they have meant to us. What we may not yet be fully inclined to do is to love Homer and Plato; this may still strike us as onerous and guilt inducing, insofar as it is a form of valuation we have not fully internalized, but feel that we ought.

A debt of gratitude is generated when beneficence gives rise to a duty to come to care about someone or something. Valuing, as described earlier, is a complex disposition: it contains cognitive, motivational, affective, and self-reflective attitudes.[11] To value is not merely to believe that something is valuable and it is not merely to act as though something were valuable. To value is to feel, believe, and be motivated in a new way. When our values change, we become, to just that extent, different people.

How could it be that a simple act of beneficence—either one of mentorship or assistance—generates a duty to become a different person? I have not tried to answer this question, and I admit I view it as one of the great mysteries of life that human beings feel moved to rise to the occasion in this particular way. Let me indulge in a conjectural answer to this question. Perhaps the reason we read the actions of others as beckoning us to enter a new normative space is that we are all, in one way or another, antecedently looking for opportunities to grow in respect of value.

Unless we had feelers out, how could we increase our stock of values in anything but an accidental way? It is not irrational[12] to entrench oneself in what one currently cares about; to focus one's attentions on one's present concerns; to close oneself off from coming to care about anything that would detract from a full pursuit of what one has already committed oneself to. Indeed, sometimes rationality dictates this move—when, for instance, we find ourselves stressed out, overcommitted, and close to the breaking point. But even when rationality doesn't dictate it, it is always open to us to close the circle of caring and say "this is what I care about, and I'm satisfied with that." And the rational availability of this move doesn't depend on the size of the circle. What, then, prevents human beings from shutting themselves tight into hermit-like balls of self-concern? Even if rational egoism is false, and there exists an argument for caring about more than the pursuit of self-preservation and (narrowly conceived) pleasures, it usually isn't *argument* that breaks through that wall. It's emotion.

My claim throughout this chapter has been that the debt of gratitude is a call for the opening out of the self; my concluding conjecture is that we hear this call because we are listening for it. We are striving to strive. The existence of this standing disposition to become more than we are makes it possible for others to treat us, proleptically, as though we already were the people we might become. They assist us in ways that would be appropriate if we already were in a certain kind of community with them, and we correspondingly experience this treatment as beckoning us into that community. If we posit a standing disposition to become valuers of other people, we can explain the debt of gratitude as a case where that disposition is activated by the beneficence of another.

When I showed up in my teacher's classroom, I was an awkward, insecure teenager who knew nothing of great books or big ideas. But I wanted to be more—I strove to strive. My teacher saw that, and it led her to treat me not as the person I was, but as the person I could become. If she could envision me as a lover of Plato, then I could become one. And if I could, I should: when you're itching to move, the fact that someone is making a destination available to you is enough to give you reason to get going.

NOTES

1 I would like to thank the participants of the September 2017 Moral Psychology of Gratitude workshop for their questions on an earlier draft of this chapter. I am also grateful to Daniel Telech and Robert Roberts, whose insightful queries and objections are responsible for a number of important points of revision and clarification in the final version.

2 Should we feel grateful to those who *intended* to benefit us, but are prevented from doing so by forces outside their control? I leave the question for the reader.

3 The exception might be the *secretly useful* gift—where the knowledge that this gift was useful betrays an intimate connection. The secretly useful gift allows the beneficiary to appreciate the benefactor in the gift in spite of its usefulness.

4 There are also cases in which the feeling of indebtedness is traceable to faults in the recipient's oversensitivity to issues of debt rather than to any fault in the gift.

5 Note that I include expression of the emotion as part of the affective response.

6 For an account of valuing as having these four components, see Scheffler (2010) and Callard (2018, pp. 117–123).

7 The phrase "value our relationship" can be understood in two ways. The first is to see the relationship as a historical or biological connection that exists independently of the attitude of valuation directed at it. The second is to see the relationship as identical to the evaluative connection between its participants. On this second view, relationships are constituted by an activity of shared valuation. "I value my relationship with her" becomes another way of saying, "I have a relationship with her" and "I engage in valuing with her." For the first view, see Kolodny (2003). For the second view, see Callard (2017, pp. 130–132).

8 I am setting aside cases of minor assistance—holding the door open for the person behind you, picking up something that someone on line in front of you has dropped. It is also worth noting that the "size" of one's assistance depends on the relationship in question—in the context of a close personal relationship, someone's giving you money or cooking you dinner or driving you to the airport might be something small. Cases of minor assistance do not call for much in the way of gratitude, a fact that is interesting in its own right but which I do not seek to explain here.

9 Though one might well, by taking on a mentee, make oneself vulnerable to new forms of loss, e.g., disappointment if one's mentee fails to make the most of her talents, or sadness if her development is cut short by factors outside her control.

10 All debts are owed to people and not things; what I'm marking with the phrase "directed at the giver/gift" is the difference between owing someone a favor and owing it to someone to apply myself in some domain; in the first case what I owe are debts of reciprocation and in the second, debts of appreciation.

11 See note 2 and corresponding text.

12 Here I use the word "rational/irrational" as a gloss for "what I have (no) internal reason to pursue," rather than in the broader way I argue for in Callard (2016). There, I try to show that reasons-internalism is false because we have (what I call) "proleptic reasons" to come to acquire new values. In Callard (2016), I argue that we sometimes have reason to pursue something precisely to the extent that it doesn't (yet) serve any of our standing desires, interests, or values; for the purposes of the present paper, I have relinquished the terminology of "rationality."

REFERENCES

Callard, A. 2016. "Proleptic Reasons," *Oxford Studies in Meta-Ethics* vol. 11, pp. 129–154. New York: Oxford University Press.

———. 2017. "The Reason to Be Angry Forever," in *The Moral Psychology of Anger*, Myisha Cherry and Owen Flanagan, eds. Lanham, MD: Rowman & Littlefield, pp. 123–137.

———. 2018. *Aspiration*. New York: Oxford University Press.

Kolodny, N. 2003. "Love as Valuing a Relationship," *Philosophical Review* vol. 112, pp. 135–189.

Scheffler, S. 2010. "Valuing," In *Equality and Tradition*. Oxford: Oxford University Press, pp. 15–40.

Chapter 5

Gratitude, Rights, and Benefit[1]

Coleen Macnamara

INTRODUCTION

Imagine that Meghan has a right to Luke giving her the bread and Luke acts accordingly. Does Meghan owe Luke gratitude for providing the bread? On the received view, she does not. It is widely agreed that when P_1 has a right to P_2 φ-ing, P_1 does not owe P_2 gratitude for φ-ing. Paul Camenisch—both paraphrasing and endorsing Daniel Lyons's (1969) view—writes, "[W]e do not owe gratitude to others for respecting our rights" (1981: 13). Or again, Roslyn Weiss claims that a necessary condition "for an obligation of gratitude toward A on the part of B" is that "B has no right to, or claim to x" (1985: 493). Similarly, Joel Feinberg, in a piece worth quoting at length, imparts the following:

> There are in general two distinct kinds of moral transaction. On the one hand there are gifts and services and favors motivated by love or pity or mercy and for which gratitude is the sole fitting response. On the other hand there are dutiful actions and omissions called for by the rights of other people. These can be demanded, claimed and insisted upon without embarrassment or shame. When not forthcoming, the appropriate reaction is indignation; when duly done there is no place for gratitude, an expression of which would suggest that it is not simply one's own or one's due that one was given. (1970: 143–44)[2]

But while most theorists seem to agree that when P_1 has a right to P_2 φ-ing, P_1 does not owe P_2 gratitude for φ-ing, the conversation about the normative status of gratitude for rights-fulfilling conduct is still very much in its infancy. Few take the topic of gratitude and rights head on; claims are instead made in the context of broader discussion about gratitude. Consequently, key terms are rarely specified, and theorists tend merely to assert, rather than defend the claim that gratitude is not owed for rights-fulfilling conduct. Indeed, to my knowledge, this claim has not yet been defended. Most theorists simply list P_1 not having a right to P_2 φ-ing as a condition of owed gratitude. We thus come away from the literature wondering why it is that when P_1 has a right to P_2 φ-ing she does not owe gratitude to P_2 for φ-ing. What, precisely, about the nature of gratitude on the one hand and the nature of rights on the other explains this?

In this chapter, I take the question of the normative status of gratitude for rights-fulfilling conduct head on. I provide a defense of the claim that if P_1 has a right to P_2 φ-ing, P_1 does not owe P_2 gratitude for φ-ing. Call this the *Rights Exemption Claim*, or REC for short.[3]

My argument unfolds as follows. In the section "Gratitude and Rights," I clarify the key terms in REC: gratitude and rights. In the section "Benefit and Baselines," I turn to the notion of *benefit*, a concept at the heart of gratitude. In brief, I show that all benefit is relative to a baseline and that when P_1 has a right to P_2 φ-ing, P_2 does not benefit P_1 from the perspective of a rights-based baseline. In the section "The Rights Exemption Claim," I present my argument for REC. I argue that requiring P_1 to feel gratitude toward P_2 amounts to morally forbidding her from representing herself as possessing what morality, itself, has deemed (in a sense to be specified) normatively *hers*. Since this would be a highly implausible result, we have good reason to accept REC. I conclude by considering two potential counterexamples to REC put forth by Terrance McConnell in his recent work on gratitude. I not only argue that my defense of REC withstands these cases, but I show how the framework that I offer here can accommodate and explain (some of) the driving intuitions behind them.

GRATITUDE AND RIGHTS

My defense of REC relies on widely held but nonetheless particular understandings of our two key concepts: gratitude and rights. To start, gratitude comes in both propositional and interpersonal varieties. It is one thing to be grateful *that* a state of affairs obtains—for example, grateful that the weather was stunning on my wedding day. And it is another to be grateful *to* an agent for performing some action—for example, grateful to a friend for volunteering to proof my manuscript. Propositional gratitude has a dyadic structure: it is a two-place relation between some person and a state of affairs. In contrast, interpersonal gratitude has a triadic structure: it is a three-place relation between two people and an action: P_1 is grateful to P_2 for φ-ing (Manela 2015). For the purposes of this chapter, REC refers exclusively to interpersonal gratitude.[4]

Sometimes, when theorists state that P_1 owes interpersonal gratitude to P_2, they mean that P_1 owes P_2 some kind of *material* acknowledgment of the benefit bestowed. P_1 may discharge this duty by saying "Thank you," or an act of returned beneficence may be required. Owing gratitude is not, though, in the first instance about material acknowledgment. Rather, it is about emotion— that is, the feeling of gratitude that is supposed to be expressed in one's thank you or returned kindness. Principle REC, then, centrally concerns gratitude qua emotion. To say that P_1 owes P_2 gratitude for φ-ing is to say that P_1 owes it to P_2 to respond to her φ-ing with the feeling of gratitude.

Gratitude, like all emotions, is a way of recognizing or apprehending a feature of the world under an evaluative guise (de Sousa 1987, 2004; Helm 1994; Nussbaum 2001; Roberts 1988; Sherman 1997; Solomon 1973; Stocker 1996). When Amanda is grieving over the death of her mother, or again, John is afraid of the patch of ice that he is approaching, Amanda and John are each apprehending a feature of the world in evaluative terms. Amanda is recognizing her mother's death as a terrible loss, and John the ice as dangerous.[5] So, too, with gratitude. To feel gratitude is—whatever else it is may be—to recognize or apprehend a feature of the world under an evaluative guise: it involves evaluating, or appraising, the feature of the world that it is about. Where the evaluative term defining of fear is danger, and of grief, loss, the evaluative terms defining of gratitude are benefit and benevolent motive. For P_1 to feel gratitude toward P_2 for φ-ing is for P_1 to construe P_2 via φ-ing (feature of the world) as benefiting her from a benevolent motive (evaluative guise) (Roberts 2015; Berger 1975).[6]

Finally, let's turn to rights. While the function of rights (i.e., what rights do for those who have them) is hotly contested, theorists tend to agree on the *structure* of rights (Wenar 2015). Most accept Wesley Newcomb Hohfeld's (1913) seminal analysis of rights in terms of four incidents: powers, claims, privileges, and immunities. For the present discussion, we need only focus on powers and claims.[7]

Power-rights can take many forms, but the power-right relevant for us is the power of P_1 to change P_2's normative situation by making it the case that P_2 ought to φ.[8] Imagine, for example, a sergeant and his soldiers. If the sergeant orders his soldiers to drop and give him fifty pushups, he changes their normative situation. The sergeant via his demand makes it the case that the soldiers now face a requirement to drop and give him fifty pushups. The sergeant's demand has this normative upshot because he has the *normative power* to impose this duty on his soldiers. This point is thrown into stark relief when we contrast the sergeant's demand with the demand from my toddler that I buy him a toy. My toddler's demand does not succeed in imposing a requirement on me because he, unlike the sergeant, lacks the normative power needed to render his demand normatively potent.

Thus, one thing that we may mean when we say that P_1 has a right to P_2 φ-ing is that P_1 has a power-right: the power, via her speech act, to make it the case that P_2 ought to φ. A second thing that we may mean is that P_1 has a *claim-right* to P_2 φ-ing. To say that P_1 has a claim-right that P_2 φ is to say that P_2 has a duty *to* P_1 to φ. In other words, a claim-right against an agent logically entails that agent's duty to perform the relevant action. As Feinberg puts the point, "The creditor's right against his debtor, for example, and the debtor's duty to his creditor, are precisely the same relation seen from two different vantage points, as inextricably linked as two sides of the same coin" (1970: 249–50). But this does not give us a full picture of the relation between claim-rights and their corresponding duties. Again, in Feinberg's words, "[The above] fails to do justice to the way claim-rights are somehow prior to, or more basic than, the duties with which they are necessarily correlated. If Nip has a claim-right against Tuck, it is because of this fact that Tuck has a duty to Nip. It is only because something is *due* Nip (directional element) that there is something Tuck *must* do (modal element)" (1970: 250). What Feinberg is emphasizing is that P_2's duty is *sourced* in P_1 and her claim-right.

Thus, both power-rights and claim-rights mark out the rights-bearer as the *source* of another's duty to perform some action. In the case of a power-right, when P_1 issues the relevant speech act, she—in virtue of her normative power—generates P_2's duty to φ. When P_1 has a claim-right to P φ-ing, she need not utter a word, as the mere existence of the claim-right suffices to generate P_2's duty.

BENEFIT AND BASELINES

As we saw earlier, to feel gratitude toward an agent for some action is, inter alia, to construe that agent as having *benefited* oneself via her action (Berger 1975; Roberts 2015). Determining benefit, though, is far more complicated than it might appear. This is because benefit, like harm, is a comparative notion. To say that P_2 benefits P_1 by φ-ing is to say that P_2, in virtue of φ-ing, makes P_1 *better off*. But this raises a crucial question: "better off than what?" In Wertheimer's words, "Without some benchmark, there would be better and worse alternatives, but no better and worse off" (1988: 204–5). The core idea here is that to determine whether P_2 by φ-ing benefits P_1, we need a starting level of well-being from which to determine whether P_2 by φ-ing has brought about an *improvement* in P_1's well-being. This starting point is typically referred to as the baseline level of well-being (Feinberg 1984; Hanser 2008; Nozick 1969; Wertheimer 1988; Wilkinson 2003).

Though we find discussion of myriad varieties of baselines in the literature, they are often helpfully sorted into two categories: non-moral and moral baselines. Included in the former are the pre-interaction and statistical base-lines. And the types of moral baselines include both oughts-based and rights-based baselines (Feinberg 1984; Hanser 2008; Nozick 1969; Wertheimer 1988; Wilkinson 2003).[9]

Let's start with the pre-interaction baseline. Imagine that after two years of working for company X, your boss gives you a 4% raise. If you construe mat-ters from a pre-interaction baseline, you will take as your baseline the level of well-being you possess prior to your boss giving you the raise. Assuming that having more money satisfies some of your interests, your boss, by giving you the raise, will have benefited you. She will have benefited you because your level of well-being after she gives you the raise is greater than your baseline level of well-being—that is, your level of well-being before the raise.

Imagine instead that you work for company X and that in the past, your boss has reliably given you a 6% raise every two years. You have just com-pleted your tenth year at the company, and naturally, you are expecting your bi-annual raise. In this case, you might use what is often called the "statistical baseline" in order to determine benefit. To do this, you would take as your baseline the level of interest satisfaction that you predict you will have when you receive your biannual raise. Imagine, though, that this year, your boss gives you only a 4% pay increase. If you construe matters from a statistical baseline, your boss will not have benefited you. Your baseline well-being—the level you predict you will have when you receive your biannual 6% raise—is in fact higher than the level of well-being you have after a 4% raise. From the perspective of the statistical baseline, then, not only has your boss failed to benefit you, but also she has actually harmed you. Relative to a 6% raise, a 4% raise leaves you worse off.

Turn now to our moral baselines, starting with the oughts-based baseline. Imagine that you are an overworked and underpaid employee of company X. Let's assume that your boss morally *ought* to give you a 4% raise. Assume further that she does as she ought and increases your pay by 4%. If you con-strue matters from an oughts-based baseline, you will take as your baseline the amount of interest satisfaction you would have if your boss does as she ought—that is, gives you a 4% raise. From this baseline, you will not construe your boss as having benefited you. After all, even after taking into account your boss's provision of a 4% raise, your level of well-being is merely identi-cal to, as opposed to greater than, your baseline level of well-being. There is no improvement and thus no benefit.

Finally, imagine that you have been working for company X for two years and that your contract stipulates that you will receive a 4% raise after two years. In this case, it is not just that you *ought* to get a 4% raise; rather it is that, in virtue of your contract, you have a *claim-right* to said raise. If you construe matters from a rights-based baseline, you will take as your baseline the amount of well-being you would have when your boss gives you that to which you have a right, namely a 4% raise. From this baseline, your boss will not benefit you by giving you a 4% raise. If you compare the level of interest satisfaction you would have when she honors your right to the level of interest satisfaction you have when she honors your right, there is obviously no change in your well-being. Once again, your level of well-being upon receiving the raise equals, but does not surpass, the level of well-being represented by your baseline.

Let's sum up. If P_1 uses a *pre-interaction* baseline to determine whether P_2 benefits her by φ-ing, she takes as her baseline the level of well-being that she possesses prior to P_2 φ-ing. If P_1 uses a *statistical* baseline, she takes as her baseline the level of well-being that she predictively expects to possess in the relevant context. If P_1 uses an *oughts-based* baseline, she uses as her baseline the level of well-being that she ought to possess: that is, the level of well-being she would have when P_2 does as she ought. Finally, if P_1 uses a *rights-based* baseline, she uses as her baseline the level of well-being that she would have when P_2 honors her right.

As these cases illustrate, benefit is a perspectival notion. Whether or not P_1 benefits P_2 depends on the baseline that one uses. Sometimes, different baselines will deliver the same verdict. For example, in contexts in which people can be predicted to do as they ought, both the statistical and oughts-based baselines will yield the same answer. Other times different baselines will yield different answers. For example, in cases where P_1 has a right to P_2 giving her a good, P_1 will have benefited from the perspective of the pre-interaction baseline, but not from the perspective of the rights-based baseline.

Finally, and importantly for us moving forward, if P_1 has a right to P_2 φ-ing and P_1 uses a rights-based baseline to determine benefit, the answer will always be the same: P_2 will *not* have benefited P_1 via φ-ing. To see this, we need only recognize that whenever P_1 compares her (rights-based) baseline level of interest satisfaction to the amount of interest satisfaction that she has when P_2 honors her right, she will invariably conclude that there has been no improvement in her well-being and in fact, no change at all. Thus, when viewed through the lens of a rights-based baseline, P_2 cannot, via honoring P_1's right, benefit her.

THE RIGHTS EXEMPTION CLAIM

The aforementioned has familiarized us with the nature of gratitude, rights, and the perspectival character of benefit. With these preliminaries in hand, we are now in a position to defend the rights exemption claim: when P_1 has a right to P_2 φ-ing, P_1 does not *owe* P_2 gratitude for φ-ing.

To start, note that the work done earlier suggests that if P_1 has a right to P_2 φ-ing, and P_1 owes P_2 gratitude for φ-ing, then P_1 is morally forbidden from using a rights-based baseline to determine benefit. The reasoning is as follows. First, to say that P_1 *owes* P_2 gratitude, is to say that P_1 has a directed duty to P_2 to feel gratitude.[10] It is to say, in other words, that P_1 is morally required to feel gratitude toward P_2 and wrongs her if she fails to do so. Second, recall that to feel gratitude, is whatever else it may be, to construe another as having benefited oneself from a benevolent motive (Berger 1975; Roberts 2015). Thus, if P_1 is morally required to feel gratitude in response to P_2's φ-ing, she is morally required to construe P_2 as having benefited her by φ-ing. Finally, as we saw earlier, if P_2's φ-ing is an instance of honoring P_1's right and P_1 employs a rights-based baseline to determine benefit, P_1 will not construe P_2 as having benefited her. Taken together, these points imply that if P_1 has a right to P_2 φ-ing and P_1 is morally required to construe P_2 as having benefited her by φ-ing, then P_1 is morally forbidden from using a rights-based baseline.

In what follows, I argue that it is doubtful that morality would forbid P_1 from using a rights-based baseline to determine whether P_2 has benefited her. This is because, as I will show, to use a rights-based baseline is to represent oneself as (in a sense) possessing a level of well-being of which morality itself has assigned one possession. There is, doubtless, an ineluctable tension in the idea that the norms of morality would instruct against construing oneself as possessing what morality itself has already deemed one's own.

To see, first recall that theorists often sort baselines into two categories: non-moral and moral baselines. In doing so, they highlight the similarity between the pre-interaction and statistical baselines on the one hand, and the oughts-based and rights-based baselines on the other. The latter, but not the former, are concerned exclusively with *moral* norms.

We can, though, categorize baselines along a different dimension. When an agent adopts a baseline, she is *representing herself as possessing* a particular amount of well-being. Sometimes, when an agent adopts a baseline, she is representing herself as possessing a level of well-being that she does (or did) in fact possess. Other times, she is representing herself as possessing a level of well-being that she does not (and never did) in fact possess, but rather one that she *would have* under different circumstances corresponding to some statistical or moral norm.

Both statistical and oughts-based baselines are examples of the latter sort of baseline. If P_1 uses a *statistical* baseline, she takes as her baseline the level of well-being she predictively expects to possess in the relevant context. If P_1 uses an *oughts-based* baseline, she uses as her baseline the level of interest satisfaction she ought to possess: that is, the level of interest satisfaction she would have if P_2 does as she ought to. While these representations are counterfactual, they are nonetheless reasonable. The representation of the statistical baseline is, as Wertheimer puts it, "based on a reasonably rich and complex account of the future" (1988: 210). The representation of the oughts-based baseline is based on an account of what morality prescribes. But as reasonable as these representations are, the crucial point for us here is that to so represent oneself is to represent oneself as possessing a level of well-being one does not in fact possess.

Matters are obviously different when one adopts the pre-interaction baseline. When one adopts a pre-interaction baseline, one represents oneself as possessing the amount of well-being that one in fact possesses prior to the interaction. What is not so obvious is that when one adopts a rights-based baseline, one is—as when she adopts a pre-interaction baseline—representing oneself as possessing a level of well-being that one does in fact possess.

To see that she is so representing herself, we need to remind ourselves that material possession is not the only kind of possession. If my wallet falls from my pocket as I am walking down the street, I no longer have material possession of it. But this of course does not mean that the wallet is no longer mine. It is still my wallet even though it is not in my physical possession. If you happen to find my wallet and return it to me, you have not made it the case that something that was not mine now is, even though you put something back in my physical possession.

Or again, I may have a book in my physical possession that is not mine. Perhaps you kindly lent me the book. When I go to return it to you, you say, "Oh keep it, it is now yours." In this case, I did not gain material possession of the book; it was already in my possession. However, my normative position did change. The book is now mine; I now normatively possess it, whereas I did not before.[11]

Material possession is then one thing and normative possession another. On a common understanding, material possession of concrete objects amounts to having a kind of physical control over the object, relative to the kind of physical manipulation of which the object admits (think here of having material possession of one's wallet versus one's house). On my view, one can also materially possess non-concrete objects—including attributes, conditions, or properties—in virtue of "having" or "enjoying" them. For example, we might say that an intelligent person possesses intelligence, or again, that a healthy person has or possesses health. It is in the first sense that I materially possess my wallet; it is in the second sense that I materially possess a level of well-being.

Turn now to the concept of normative possession or ownership. At the core of the concept of normative possession is *the right to materially possess*. If I normatively possess or own X, I have a right to materially possess X (Honore 1961: 371). Thus, my normatively possessing my wallet, whatever else it amounts to, amounts to my right to materially possess my wallet, that is, to have physical control over it.

What's more, the owner's right to materially possess some object amounts to the owner having a bundle of Hohfeldian incidents (claim-rights, immunities, powers, and privileges) that facilitate her gaining or retaining material possession of the object. For example, I have a claim-right against others that they not interfere with my physical control of my wallet. Or again, if you have physical possession of my wallet, I have the normative power to demand that you put me in physical possession of it.

What I want to suggest is that when P_1 has a right to P_2 φ-ing, it makes sense to say that P_1 normatively possesses the piece of interest satisfaction that results from P_2's φ-ing. It makes sense to say this because insofar as P_1 has a right to P_2 φ-ing, she has a Hohfeldian incident that facilitates her material possession of said piece of interest satisfaction.

Recall that for our purposes, to have a right to P_2 φ-ing is to have either the normative power to make it the case that P_2 is morally required to φ, or a claim-right that P_2 φ. Both of these Hohfeldian incidents give P_1 normative control over P_2's φ-ing. Since P_2's φ-ing will result in P_1's material possession of said piece of interest satisfaction, both of these Hohfeldian incidences facilitate P_1 gaining material possession of said piece of interest satisfaction.

So return to the scenario in which you have a contract to receive a 4% raise after two years on the job. In this case, after two years of work, you have a claim-right to a 4% increase in pay. What I am urging is that after two years on the job, you normatively possess the piece of interest satisfaction that the 4% raise will bring. You normatively possess this piece of interest satisfaction because to possess something normatively is to have a Hohfeldian incident that facilitates your material possession of that thing. Your claim-right to the raise precisely is a Hohfeldian incident that facilitates your material possession of the piece of interest satisfaction that a 4% raise will bring.

If I am right about this, then a rights-based baseline is, in a core respect, similar to a pre-interaction baseline. When one uses a pre-interaction baseline, she represents herself as possessing the amount of well-being that she materially possesses. When an agent uses a rights-based baseline, she represents herself as possessing the amount of well-being that she normatively possesses. In both cases, she is representing herself as possessing a level of well-being that she does in fact possess.

We are now in a position to see why it is so difficult to swallow the claim that morality requires P_1 to feel gratitude toward P_2 for merely doing what she has a right to P_2 doing. For morality to require gratitude in this case would be for morality to forbid P_1 from using a right-based baseline. But given the above work, we now see that for morality to forbid P_1 from using a rights-based baseline is for morality to forbid P_1 from representing herself as possessing the interest satisfaction of which morality itself assigns her possession. This would be odd indeed. One would think that by assigning her possession of a particular amount of interest satisfaction, morality would be endorsing rather than forbidding her from representing herself as possessing said piece of interest satisfaction.[12]

GRATITUDE AND MORAL STANDOUTS

With my defense of REC in hand, I turn now to Terrance McConnell's work in "Gratitude, Rights, and Moral Standouts." In this piece, McConnell describes two cases that seem to challenge REC: the honest shopkeeper and Hirose.[13]

Let's start with the former. McConnell points out that practitioners in some occupations easily and often cheat their customers by overcharging or providing unneeded services (2017: 284). The rare shopkeepers that deal honestly with their customers are what McConnell calls moral standouts. McConnell suggests that customers of these honest shopkeepers owe them gratitude for the honest service that they receive. Gratitude is owed, he urges, because the honest service is morally significant. The practitioner is a moral standout, and the honest service provided is likely the result of the shopkeeper not experiencing the temptation to cheat or successfully resisting said temptation (2017: 287).

Turn now to the Hirose case. McConnell draws our attention to prison camps in Japan during World War II. While the prisoners in the camps were routinely tortured, in some cases, they were shown mercy. The following is an excerpt from Laura Hillenbrand's *Unbroken.*

> Though under great pressure to conform to a culture of brutality, a few guards refused to participate in the violence. In one incident, a captive was clubbed so savagely that he was certain he was going to be killed. In the middle of the assault, the attacking guard was called away, and a guard known as Hirose was ordered to finish the beating. Out of sight of other guards, Hirose told the captive to cry out as if he were being struck, then pounded his club harmlessly against the floor. The two acted their parts until it seemed enough "beating" had been done. The captive believed that Hirose might have saved his life. (Hillenbrand 2010: 196)

According to McConnell, the captive may owe Hirose gratitude.[14] If he does, it is because his conduct—like the honest shopkeeper's—is morally significant. Hirose, too, is a moral standout. He respects the captive's rights when most in the context flagrantly violate them. Hirose also helps the prisoner at great risk to himself. When guards showed kindness to prisoners, they were often beaten themselves (2017: 285).

One might wonder how my defense of REC fares with regard to these interesting cases. To start, as one might expect, I disagree with McConnell that gratitude is owed in these cases. Assuming that the shopkeeper's customers and the unjustly imprisoned captive retain their rights not to be cheated and beaten, respectively, then they do not owe their would-be wrongdoers gratitude for not wronging them. To see this more clearly, consider that to say that gratitude is owed in these cases is to say that the shopkeeper and prisoner go *wrong* in not feeling gratitude and thus, that they are *morally criticizable* for their respective failures.[15] This seems an especially dubious suggestion with respect to the customer who fails to feel gratitude toward the shopkeeper who simply resists the temptation to cheat her. Many of us are often well-positioned to abuse another's trust toward our own advantage at little risk or cost to ourselves, but we are not entitled to demand gratitude from our would-be victims for overcoming the temptation not to so use them. If, for example, upon learning that, in order to save time and energy, most of my colleagues frequently just input "best guess" grades in lieu of taking the time to read student essays, I should not expect gratitude from my own students for merely resisting the temptation to follow suit. Consider the absurdity of addressing my ungrateful students with the complaint, "Hey, I actually *read* your papers, when I could have just quickly manufactured your grades and lounged on the couch watching my favorite *Netflix* series. How about a little gratitude here!"

Similarly, it seems more than a little wrongheaded to deem the severely beaten prisoner morally criticizable for failing to feel gratitude toward Hirose for refraining from participating in his torture. If, for example, the prisoner—in an effort to maintain his self-respect in the context of constant degradation—insists on seeing matters from the perspective of his rights, then it certainly seems like he is doing nothing morally wrong. This point is thrown into stark relief once we imagine the similar plight of a woman held captive and repeatedly raped by gang members who insist that all members of the gang take part. Most would not, I think, deem the woman criticizable for failing to feel gratitude toward the single gang member who refrains from raping her but only pretends to do to so to appease the others.[16]

That said, I am sympathetic to some of the intuitions that, at first glance, might seem to support McConnell's claim that the customer and prisoner owe gratitude. In specific, I agree that gratitude in these cases is in some sense(s) appropriate, and again, that the moral significance of the shopkeeper and Hirose's actions affect the normative status of gratitude. In what follows, I show how the framework that I offer earlier can accommodate and explain these intuitions. First, I show that REC is compatible with both the fittingness (i.e., rational endorsement) and praiseworthiness (i.e., moral endorsement) of gratitude in these cases. I show further how the morally significant features mentioned by McConnell—moral standout status, preventing or resisting temptation, and potential costs—may play a crucial role in explaining why gratitude might be rationally and/or morally endorsed in these cases.

Let's start with the notion of an emotion's fittingness. As we saw in the section "Gratitude and Rights," emotions are ways of recognizing or apprehending a feature of the world under an evaluative guise. When Amanda is grieving over the death of her mother or Charlie is feeling gratitude toward Chris for helping her out of a jam, Amanda and Charlie are each apprehending a feature of the world in evaluative terms. Amanda is recognizing her mother's death as a terrible loss, and Charlie is recognizing Chris as having benefited her from a benevolent motive.

Emotions, then, are in one important way like beliefs. Like beliefs, emotions are ways of giving uptake to the way that the world is, and thus both have mind-to-world direction of fit. As such, emotions, like belief, are subject to norms of rationality. Just as a belief is *true* if its conceptual content is veridical, so too an emotion is *fitting* just in case its conceptual content is veridical. Justin D'Arms and Daniel Jacobson make precisely this point when they write

> Emotions present things to us as having certain evaluative features. When we ask whether an emotion is fitting . . . we are asking about the correctness of these presentations. The relevant considerations, then, are just those that count as evidence for the evaluations an emotion presents to us. In this respect, the fittingness of an emotion is like the truth of a belief. (2000: 72)

Thus, Amanda's grief is fitting just in case her mother's death is in fact a loss, and Charlie's gratitude is fitting just in case Chris benefited her from a benevolent motive.

Of course, the question of precisely when gratitude is fitting is complicated by the perspectival nature of gratitude. Whether or not it is true that the shopkeeper or Hirose benefit the customer or prisoner respectively will depend upon which baseline is used. Consider first the pre-interaction baseline. The customer's and prisoner's pre-interaction baselines are the levels of well-being that they possess prior to being cheated by the shopkeeper and beaten by Hirose, respectively. If we compare these levels of well-being to the levels of well-being that the customer and prisoner possess after the interaction—after not being cheated or beaten—there will be no benefit. The levels of well-being that they possess before the relevant interaction are merely identical to, rather than greater than, the levels that they possess after the interaction.

Both the oughts-based and rights-based baselines also yield the verdict of no benefit. The shopkeeper and Hirose *ought* not cheat and beat the customer and prisoner, respectively. More than that, the customer and prisoner have a *right* not to be cheated and beaten by the shopkeeper and Hirose, respectively. Thus, the customer's and prisoner's oughts-based and rights-based baselines are the levels of well-being that they would have when they are not cheated or beaten. Here, again, even after taking into account the fact that the shopkeeper and prisoner did not cheat or beat them, their levels of well-being after their respective interactions with the shopkeeper and Hirose are merely identical to, as opposed to greater than, their baseline levels of well-being.

Interestingly, a statistical baseline yields a different answer. The shopkeeper and Hirose are, as McConnell emphasizes, moral standouts: most shopkeepers and guards cheat and brutalize, respectively. What this means is that the customer and the prisoner can predictively expect to be cheated or beaten. The customer's and prisoner's statistical baselines are, then, the levels of well-being that they would have if they were cheated or beaten, respectively. Thus, from the statistical baseline, both the customer and the prisoner are benefited. Relative to being cheated or beaten, not being cheated or beaten is a better state.[17]

There is, then, at least one reasonable baseline from which the customer and prisoner are benefited. I now want to urge that this fact—assuming that the shopkeeper and Hirose act from a benevolent motive—makes gratitude fitting in these cases. As we saw earlier, an emotion is fitting just in case its conceptual content is veridical. Given that the answer to whether P_2 has benefited P_1 is always relative to a baseline, it seems natural to say that the conceptual content of P_1's gratitude is veridical just in case P_2 has acted from a benevolent motive and there is at least one reasonable baseline from which she benefits P_1. On this proposal, it is accurate to construe another as benefiting oneself whenever there is at least one reasonable baseline from which said benefit occurs.

Notice, moreover, the critical role that the shopkeeper's and Hirose's moral standout status plays in establishing the fittingness of gratitude in these cases. Of the reasonable baselines we discussed, *only* the statistical baseline yields an affirmative determination of benefit. What's more, the statistical baseline yields this result precisely because the shopkeeper and Hirose are moral standouts. It is only because most others are cheating and beating that on a statistical baseline the customer and prisoner possess the levels of well-being that they would have if they were cheated or beaten. In a world where most were doing as they ought, the customer's and prisoner's statistical baselines would be the levels of well-being they would have when they are *not* cheated or beaten. As we saw earlier, when the customer's or prisoner's baseline is the level of well-being that he does or would have when not cheated or beaten, then not cheating or beating him confers no benefit.[18]

Notice, then, that I agree with McConnell's claim that moral standout status can impact the normative assessment of gratitude. We part ways, though, on the issue of the precise kind of impact said status has. On McConnell's view, the shopkeeper and Hirose are *owed* gratitude (in part) because they are moral standouts in their respective situations. In contrast, my account suggests that their status as moral standouts explains (in part) why gratitude in these cases is *fitting*.

Importantly, nothing I have said about the fittingness of the customer's and prisoner's gratitude entails that REC is false: gratitude's fittingness does not entail a rational or moral requirement to feel gratitude. Start with the notion of a rational requirement to feel a certain emotion. To say that an emotion is fitting is to say that it is "rationally eligible," or again, "consistent with rationality." It is to say, in other words, that it is *rationally permissible*. But rational permissibility is one status, and rational requirement quite another. The former implies that it is not irrational to experience the emotion, while the latter implies that it is irrational not to feel it. Thus, in urging that the customer's or prisoner's gratitude is fitting, I am not implying that an absence of gratitude in these cases is rationally suspect (Allais 2008: 59–61). For example, the fact that my husband is lovable makes loving him consistent with but not required by rationality. And so too (assuming she acts from a benevolent motive) the fact that P_2 has, from the perspective of at least one reasonable baseline, benefited P_1 makes gratitude directed at P_2 consistent with but not required by rationality.

Turn now to the notion of a morally required emotion. First, as a conceptual matter, an emotion can be fitting without being morally required. This is because the considerations sufficient to render the emotion fitting are not sufficient to generate a moral requirement to feel the emotion. The fact that one is the victim of another's wrongdoing is sufficient to render one's resentment fitting. Said fact is not, though, sufficient to make it the case that one is morally required to feel resentment. One would face this moral requirement, only if, in addition to one being the victim of another's wrongdoing, moral norms mandated emotional uptake of said fact.

Not only is it conceptually possible for an emotion to be fitting without being required, it is often in fact the case that an emotion is fitting without being required. Again, consider resentment. Though resentment is fitting whenever one is the victim of another's wrongdoing, resentment is not similarly required whenever one is the victim of another's wrongdoing. This is because there is no general moral norm requiring emotional uptake of one's having been wronged. Morality often not only permits but encourages mercy.[19]

Of course, things may be different with gratitude: one might think that moral norms mandate gratitude whenever it is fitting. After all, the positive sentiments and pro-social dispositions internal to gratitude would seem to make it just the sort of emotion that morality might aim to promote whenever rationally appropriate. While this is possible, the above defense of REC suggests that this is not the case. Recall, I have urged that it is fitting for P_1

to feel gratitude toward P_2 whenever P_2 has acted from a benevolent motive and there is least one reasonable baseline from which P_2 has benefited P_1. If this is right, then fitting gratitude and required gratitude will have the same extension only if there is a general moral norm stating that whenever it is the case that P_2 has acted from a benevolent motive and there is a reasonable baseline along which P_2 has benefited P_1, P_1 is required to feel gratitude. Call this moral norm RG for short.

My defense of REC entails that RG is not a valid norm. Let me explain. Recall that to feel gratitude is, inter alia, to *construe* another as having benefited oneself. P_1 will construe P_2 as having benefited her only if she construes matters from a baseline along which she is benefited. Thus, RG amounts to a moral norm stating that whenever it is the case that P_2 has acted from a benevolent motive and there is a reasonable baseline along which P_2 has benefited P_1, P_1 is morally required to construe matters from one of the reasonable baselines along which she benefits. Importantly, though, to require P_1 to construe matters from one of the reasonable baselines along which she benefits is to forbid her from using a baseline along which she does not benefit. I defended REC by showing that it is highly implausible that morality would forbid P_1 from using a rights-based baseline to determine whether P_2 has benefited her. If this is right, then in cases where P_1 has a right to P_2 acting as she has, it may be true both (1) that P_2 has acted from a benevolent motive and there is a reasonable baseline along which P_2 has benefited P_1 and (2) that P_1 is *not* required to construe matters from one of the reasonable baselines along which she has been benefited. In other words, if my defense of REC succeeds, then RG is not a valid norm.

Thus far, I have focused on how my account can accommodate and explain the *rational* endorsement (i.e., fittingness) of gratitude in McConnell's cases. I now want to briefly turn to the fact that my account can also accommodate the *moral* endorsement (i.e., praiseworthiness) of gratitude in these cases. When describing the shopkeeper and Hirose cases, McConnell emphasizes not only that the shopkeeper and Hirose are moral standouts but also that the former resists temptation and that the latter puts himself at risk. He urges, further, that these features of the shopkeeper's and Hirose's respective acts are *morally significant*. On McConnell's view, the upshot of this moral significance is that gratitude is owed. While I disagree with McConnell's conclusion, I do not want to deny—nor does REC require me to deny—that the features that McConnell highlights are morally significant and might affect the moral status of gratitude.

To say that gratitude is not owed is merely to say that it is morally permissible *not* to feel gratitude in these cases. This leaves open not only the possibility that feeling gratitude is morally permissible, but also the possibility that feeling gratitude in these cases is morally admirable or praiseworthy. For all that I have said so far, the shopkeeper's resistance to temptation, or again, Hirose's willingness to endanger himself, might have a kind of moral significance that renders gratitude an ideal moral response. Importantly, though (and thankfully, for most of us), we are not always required to do what is morally ideal or morally best.[20]

The chief aim of this section was to show that one can accept that gratitude is not owed in the shopkeeper and Hirose cases, without denying either that gratitude in these cases is appropriate or that the moral significance of the shopkeeper and Hirose's actions affect the normative status of gratitude. One can at once accept that gratitude is not owed and hold that the morally significant features of the shopkeeper's and Hirose's respective actions in part explain why gratitude is fitting and morally praiseworthy. I think that once we fully acknowledge this, the idea that gratitude is *owed* in these cases loses much of its appeal.

In conclusion, I want to make a final point about the Hirose case in particular. At this point, one might be willing to accept my analysis of the shopkeeper case and yet still have lingering reservations about the Hirose case. After all, the Hirose case is fundamentally different in that Hirose puts himself at risk. Some might hold that the prisoner owes Hirose gratitude because Hirose risked his own safety for him.

In what follows, I explain how one can hold this and still accept my defense of REC. This, though, requires denying that the prisoner has a right that Hirose not beat him. While this is not the interpretation that I endorse, it nonetheless has a basis in the literature. Hirose and the prisoner find themselves in exceptional circumstances and on one widely held view of rights; exceptional circumstances can preclude it from being the case that a right obtains.

To see, consider a famous vignette from Feinberg.

> Suppose that you are on a back-packing trip in the high mountain country when an unanticipated blizzard strikes the area with such ferocity that your life is imperiled. Fortunately, you stumble onto an unoccupied cabin, locked and boarded up for the winter, clearly somebody else's private property.
>
> You smash in a window, enter, and huddle in a corner for three days until the storm abates. During this period you help yourself to your unknown benefactor's food supply and burn his wooden furniture in the fireplace to keep warm. (1978: 102)

While we colloquially speak of an owner's claim-right against others that they do not use his property, many hold that this right, on closer examination, is far more complex: it has a number of exception clauses built into it (e.g., see Shafer-Landau [1995] and Wellman [1995]). What the owner has is a claim-right that others not use his property *unless* doing so is necessary to save their lives, or again necessary to prevent mass destruction, and so forth. On this view, the owner does not have a right against you not to use his property because one of the exception clauses obtains.[21] Just as the owner does not have a right against you not to use his property, so, too, one might think that the prisoner lacks a right against Hirose not to harm him. Perhaps, the (would be) right not to be physically harmed does not obtain because the circumstances are exceptional. If, for example, the right not to be physically harmed is more precisely a right not to be physically harmed *unless* the potential harmer will suffer terrible consequences as a result of not harming, then it very well might be that the prisoner does not have the relevant right in this context. As we said, guards who showed sympathy to the prisoners were subject to harsh treatment.

My own view is that the prisoner does have a right and that gratitude is not owed. The aforementioned section, though, illustrates another way in which my view can handle cases in which there appears to be a right and there is the intuition that gratitude is owed. If these cases are such that the burdens of fulfilling another's (would-be) right are exceptionally high, then it very well might be that the right does not obtain.[22]

NOTES

1   Thanks to Michael Nelson, Joshua Hollowell, and Maggie Little for helpful discussions on the issues discussed in this chapter. Thanks also to Daniel Telech, Roberts C. Roberts, and the other participants at the 2017 Moral Psychology of Gratitude Workshop for helpful comments. I owe a special debt of gratitude to Monique Wonderly for countless conversations about the material in this chapter and for reading and commenting on numerous drafts.

2   See also McAleer (2010).

3   The claim here is that P_1 does not owe gratitude to P_2 simply in virtue of the fact that P_2 has φ-ed. I leave it open that there may be considerations external to the action itself that make it the case that P_1 is required to feel gratitude in the relevant cases. Also, in what follows when I speak of "rights-fulfilling conduct," I am specifically referring to cases of conduct that amount to one person fulfilling a right another person has *against her*. It is possible to understand rights-fulfilling conduct more broadly. Imagine that P_1 has a right against P_3 that she φ. If P_2 φ-s, it may be correct to describe P_2's φ-ing as rights-fulfilling conduct. In this chapter, I do not use rights-fulfilling conduct in this broader way.

4   Henceforth, the term "gratitude" refers to interpersonal gratitude.

5   The fear of ice example is from Stocker (1983 and 1987).

6   Some hold that feeling gratitude may alternatively involve construing another as having *attempted to* benefit oneself from a benevolent motive. I am inclined to

think that this is correct. In what follows, I speak only of benefit and not also of "attempted benefit" for simplicity's sake. The forthcoming arguments are not affected by this omission.

7 Since our aim here is to explicate what it means to say that "P_1 has a right to P_2 φ-ing," privileges and immunities are not relevant. Privileges and immunities are rights that entitle P_1 "(not) to perform certain actions, or (not) to be in certain states" (Wenar 2015).

8 Whenever I use the term "power-right," I am referring to this particular power-right.

9 Theorists often fail to distinguish rights-based baselines from oughts-based baselines. This distinction will be important for us here.

10 To say that P_1's duty is a directed duty is to say that it is a duty "directed at" P_2. One core upshot of the directedness of P_1's duty is that if she fails to feel gratitude in response to P_2 φ-ing, she not only does wrong, but *wrongs* P_2. The claim that one has a directed duty to feel gratitude raises a number of puzzles. See, for example, Manela (2015). The more minimal claim that one is *required* to feel gratitude is also controversial. Many hold that deontological concepts such as duty or requirement do not apply to emotions because we lack the requisite voluntary control over our emotions. My own view is that deontological concepts can apply to emotions. For theorists who argue that control is not needed for deontological concepts to apply, see, for example, Hieronymi (2006, 2008), McHugh (2012), and Basu (manuscript).

11 Thank you to Josh Hollowell for suggesting these examples.

12 This argument does not imply the moral permissibility of using an oughts-based baseline. Forbidding the use of an oughts-based baseline does not amount to forbidding P_1 from representing herself as possessing what morality itself assigns her possession of. When one adopts an oughts-based baseline, one is representing oneself as possessing the amount of well-being one ought to possess. One is, in other words, representing oneself as possessing a level of interest satisfaction that one does not in fact possess. It is one thing for morality to say that a piece of interest satisfaction *ought* to be yours and quite another for morality to say that it *is* yours. The argument presented here does not, then, defend the supererogatory condition on owed gratitude.

13 McConnell presents a number of other cases. Two of McConnell's cases—the DNA case (2017, 283–284) and the Northup/Bass case (2017, 285)—do not challenge my view because though P_1 has a right that P_2 honors, the right is not a right *against* P_2. McConnell's Northup/Master Ford and Northup/McCoy cases are not relevant because, as McConnell himself admits, they arguably better fit a dyadic model of gratitude (2017, 285–286). I provide a detailed discussion of McConnell's Levi/Lorenzo case (2017, 286–287) in endnote 22.

14 McConnell acknowledges that in the Hirose case, propositional gratitude may be all that is called for (2017: 287).

15 Thanks to Monique Wonderly for helping me see the force of this point.

16 Thank you to Monique Wonderly for helping me develop these examples.

17 There is reason to believe that both Feinberg (1966) and McAleer (2012) hold that when P_1 feels gratitude toward P_2 for her rights-fulfilling conduct, P_1's gratitude

is not fitting. I have offered reasons to think that gratitude in these cases can be fitting. A full defense of the fittingness claim, though, will have to wait for another day.

18   This discussion may help us better understand the normative status of P_1's gratitude in cases where P_2 is aptly described as merely refraining from harming P_1. See Smilansky (1997).

19   For an excellent and in-depth discussion of the difference between fittingness claims and moral claims, see D'Arms and Jacobson (2000).

20   The moral significance of the shopkeeper's ability to resist temptation and Hirose's self-risk might also affect how we morally assess *their actions*. We might want to say that resisting temptation to do the right thing, or again subjecting oneself to potential harm in doing the right thing renders one's action morally admirable and thus praiseworthy. Thus, there are many ways to acknowledge the moral significance of the shopkeeper's and Hirose's actions while still denying that gratitude is owed.

21   This view of rights is often called the specificationist view. Some reject this view holding instead what might be called the *pro tanto* view of rights (e.g., see Feinberg [1980] and Thomson [1990]). On this view, your action in the cabin case is permissible not because the owner lacks a right against you, but rather because the ought correlated with his right is outweighed in this context. Thus, while his right very much exists and makes it *pro tanto* wrong for you to make use of his cabin, it does not, in these circumstances, render your action all things considered impermissible.

For the sake of simplicity, this chapter assumes the specificationist view of rights. If the *pro tanto* view of rights is correct, then REC needs modification. What I defend here is the claim that when P_1 has a *conclusive* right to P_2 φ-ing, P_1 does not owe P_2 gratitude for φ-ing. A conclusive power or claim-right is one that generates a duty that is, in the relevant context, not overridden by countervailing considerations. Conclusive power or claim-rights, in other words, are rights correlated with duties that are in the relevant context all things considered impermissible not to fulfill. The original wording of REC spoke of rights and not conclusive rights because on the specificationist view, all rights are conclusive in this sense. For discussions of these two different views of rights, see Wenar (2015) and Frederick (2014).

22   McConnell also presents the Levi/Lorenzo case. In *Survival in Auschwitz*, Primo Levi describes his interaction with Nazi guards and civilian workers in the concentration camp (McConnell 2017, 286). While most did not treat the prisoners with the dignity they deserved, one man stood out: Lorenzo. In Levi's words, Lorenzo "brought me a piece of bread and the remainder of his ration every day for six months; he gave me a vest of his, full of patches; he wrote a postcard on my behalf to Italy and brought me the reply" (1958: 119). Levi credits Lorenzo with helping him survive the camp. Levi writes,

"However little sense there may be in trying to specify why I, rather than thousands of others, managed to survive the test, I believe that it was really due to Lorenzo that I am alive today; and not so much for his material aid, as for his having constantly reminded me by his presence, by his natural and plain manner of being good, that there still existed a just world outside our own, something and someone still pure and whole, not corrupt, not savage, extraneous to hatred and terror; something difficult to define, a remote possibility of good, but for which it was worth surviving" (1958: 121).

McConnell argues that Levi owes Lorenzo gratitude even if much of Lorenzo's conduct was merely rights-fulfilling. Gratitude is owed, McConnell urges, because Lorenzo's actions were of deep moral significance. Lorenzo's conduct is morally significant because (1) his conduct displays a kind of moral insight that in those circumstances it may have been difficult to obtain, (2) he may have feared being punished for his kindness, and thus helping required that he "overcome stressful circumstance" (2017: 289), and (3) "kindness in a sea of cruelty is clearly morally significant" (2017: 289). In other words, Lorenzo was a moral standout.

This case is tricky because it is hard to identify precisely what right is implicated. Levi explains that Lorenzo brought him food, a vest, and facilitated Levi's contact with his family via postcard. It is hard to see how Levi had a right to Lorenzo giving him the vest or facilitating contact with his family. Lorenzo very well might have had a right to minimal sustenance, but this right is likely *in rem* and not a right *in persona*—or more specifically—not a right *against* Lorenzo in particular. *In rem* rights are rights, as it were, against the world. *In persona*, rights are rights against a specific person. I am inclined to think that Levi, like all people, has a right *in rem* to minimal sustenance. But it is not clear to me that Levi has a right *against* Lorenzo for minimal sustenance. REC is about *in persona* rights. Thus, it is not clear that Lorenzo fulfilled any rights that Levi had against him. If he did not, then it is perfectly compatible with my view that Levi owed Lorenzo gratitude.

We might, though, construe matters differently. The quote from Levi suggests that what was most significant about Lorenzo's conduct was that Lorenzo treated him with dignity and respect. Levi certainly had a right to Lorenzo treating him with dignity. If this is the relevant right, I would deal with this case in the same way I dealt with the shopkeeper and Hirose cases. Levi did not owe Lorenzo gratitude for treating him with dignity. Nonetheless, gratitude may have been fitting and morally praiseworthy. Note further that if we understand the Lorenzo case as a case of honoring another's right to respect, it shares core similarities with McConnell's Lincoln case (2017: 292). McConnell urges that gratitude is not owed in the Lincoln case.

REFERENCES

Allais, Lucy. "Wiping the Slate Clean: The Heart of Forgiveness." *Philosophy and Public Affairs* 36 (2008): 33–68.

Basu, Rima. *Beliefs that Wrong*. PhD Thesis, University of Southern California, 2018.

Berger, Fred. "Gratitude." *Ethics* 85 (1975): 298–309.

Camenisch, Paul. "Gift and Gratitude in Ethics." *The Journal of Religious Ethics* 9 (1981): 1–34.

D'Arms, Justin and Jacobson, Daniel. "The Moralistic Fallacy: On the 'Appropriateness' of Emotions." *Philosophy and Phenomenological Research* 61 (2000): 65–90.

de Sousa, Ronald. "Emotions: What I Know, What I'd Like to Think I Know, and What I'd like to Think." In *Thinking about Feeling: Contemporary Philosophers on Emotions*, edited by Robert C. Solomon, 61–75. Oxford: Oxford University Press, 2004.

———. *The Rationality of Emotion*. Cambridge, MA: MIT Press, 1987.

Feinberg, Joel. "Duties, Rights, and Claims." *American Philosophical Quarterly* 3 (1966): 137–144.

———. "The Nature and Value of Rights." *Journal of Value Inquiry* 4 (1970): 245–257.

———. *Rights, Justice, and the Bounds of Liberty*. Princeton: Princeton University Press, 1980.

———. *Harm to Others: The Moral Limits of the Criminal Law*. Oxford: Oxford University Press, 1984.

———. "Voluntary Euthanasia and the Inalienable Right to Life." *Philosophy & Public Affairs* 7 (1978): 93–123.

Frederick, Danny. "Pro-Tanto versus Absolute Rights." *Philosophical Forum* 45 (2014): 275–94.

Hanser, Matthew. "The Metaphysics of Harm." *Philosophy and Phenomenological Research* 77 (2008): 421–450.

Helm, Bennett. "The Significance of Emotions." *American Philosophical Quarterly* 31 (1994): 319–331.

Hieronymi, Pamela. "Controlling Attitudes." *Pacific Philosophical Quarterly* 87 (2006): 45–74.

———. "Responsibility for Believing." *Synthese* 161 (2008): 357–373.

Hillenbrand, Laura. *Unbroken*. New York: Random House, 2010.

Hohfeld, Wesley. *Fundamental Legal Conceptions*. Edited by W. Cook. New Haven, CT: Yale University Press, 1919.

Honore, A. M. "Ownership." In *Oxford Essays in Jurisprudence*, edited by A. G. Guest, 370–375. Oxford: Oxford University Press, 1961.

Levi, Primo. *Survival in Auschwitz*. New York: Simon & Schuster, 1958.

Lyons, Daniel. "The Odd Debt of Gratitude." *Analysis* 29 (1969): 92–97.

Manela, Tony, "Gratitude." In *The Stanford Encyclopedia of Philosophy*, edited by Edward N. Zalta, (Spring 2015 Edition). https://plato.stanford.edu/archives/spr2015/entries/gratitude/.

———. "Obligations of Gratitude and Correlative Rights." In *Oxford Studies in Normative Ethics Volume 5,* edited by M. Timmons, 151–170. Oxford: Oxford University Press, 2015.

McAleer, Sean. "Propositional Gratitude." *American Philosophical Quarterly* 49 (2012): 55–66.

McConnell, Terrance. "Gratitude, Rights, and Moral Standouts." *Ethical Theory and Moral Practice* 20 (2017): 279–293.

McHugh, Conor. "Epistemic Deontology and Voluntariness." *Erkenntnis* 77 (2012):65–94.

Nozick, Robert. "Coercion." In *Philosophy, Science and Method: Essays in Honor of Ernest Nagel*, edited by S. Morgenbesser, P. Suppes, and M. White, 440–472. New York: St Martin's Press, 1969.

Nussbaum, Martha. *Upheavals of Thought*. Cambridge: Cambridge University Press, 2001.

Roberts, Robert C. "What an Emotion Is: A Sketch." *The Philosophical Review* 47 (1988): 183–209.

———. "The Normative and Empirical Study of Gratitude." *Res Philosophica* 92 (2015): 883–914.

Shafer-Landau, Russ. "Specifying Absolute Rights." *Arizona Law Review* 37 (1995): 209–224.

Sherman, Nancy. *Making a Necessity of Virtue*. Cambridge: Cambridge University Press, 1997.

Smilansky, Saul. "Should I Be Grateful to You for Not Harming Me?" *Philosophy and Phenomenological Research* 57 (1997): 585–597.

Solomon, Robert. "Emotions and Choice." *Review of Metaphysics* 27 (1973): 20–41.

Stocker, Michael. "Emotional Thoughts." *American Philosophical Quarterly* 24 (1987): 59–69.

———. "Psychic Feelings: Their Importance and Irreducibility." *Australasian Journal of Philosophy* 61 (1983): 5–26.

Stocker, Michael and Elizabeth Hegeman. *Valuing Emotions*. Cambridge: Cambridge University Press, 1996.

Thomson, Judith. *The Realm of Rights*. Cambridge, MA: Harvard University Press, 1990.

Walker, A. D. M. "Gratefulness and Gratitude." *Proceedings of the Aristotelian Society* 81 (1980): 39–55.

Weiss, Roslyn. "The Moral and Social Dimensions of Gratitude." *The Journal of Southern Philosophy* 23 (1985): 491–501.

Wellman, Carl. "On Conflicts between Rights." *Law and Philosophy* 14 (1995): 271–295.

Wenar, Leif, "Rights." In *The Stanford Encyclopedia of Philosophy*, edited by Edward N. Zalta (Fall 2015 Edition). https://plato.stanford.edu/archives/fall2015/entries/rights/.

Wertheimer, Alan. *Coercion*. Princeton, NJ: Princeton University Press, 1988.

Wilkinson, Stephen. *Bodies for Sale: Ethics and Exploitation in the Human Body Trade*. London: Routledge, 2003.

Chapter 6

Do Children Owe Their Parents Gratitude?

Cameron Fenton

INTRODUCTION

The following are three important questions about filial gratitude. First, do children owe their parents gratitude? Second, if so, for what benefits do children have duties of gratitude to their parents? Third, what do duties of gratitude require children to do for their parents? I argue that many children have duties of gratitude to their parents based on the benefits their parents have provided while raising them well. I then argue that, while it's difficult to be specific, duties of gratitude require children to acknowledge and appreciate the benefits their parents have provided for them and to be willing to benefit their parents if they are in need.

I begin by introducing Terrance McConnell's (1993) four conditions that anyone must meet to be owed gratitude. I then use these conditions to evaluate three versions of the gratitude theory of filial obligations: (1) gratitude for birth, (2) gratitude for basic care, and (3) gratitude for supererogatory benefits. The gratitude theory of filial obligations tells us that children owe their parents gratitude. Alternative theories of what children owe their parents are the friendship theory, which claims that children owe their parents what they would owe a good friend (English 1999), and the special goods theory, which claims that children owe their parents goods that can only be acquired in a parent-child relationship (Keller 2006).

I argue that children owe their parents gratitude only when they meet their moral parental duties and raise their children well. This means that children do not have duties of gratitude merely for being born or for being raised poorly. My view falls somewhere between gratitude for basic care and gratitude for supererogatory benefits. Parents have extensive duties to their children just in virtue of being parents and they must discharge these duties to be owed gratitude by their children.

I then respond to an objection to the gratitude theory of filial obligations posed by Brynn Welch (2012). Welch argues that the gratitude theory of filial obligations isn't a good theory because it cannot specify what children ought to do for their parents. Duties of gratitude are not specific, so the gratitude theory cannot provide us with guidance about what we must do for our parents. In response, I argue that McConnell's conditions for discharging a duty of gratitude can provide us with much of the guidance Welch is looking for.

In the final section, I argue that the gendered division of parenting also has implications for the gratitude theory of filial obligations. We live in a society in which mothers do more care work than do fathers. This means that mothers are more likely than fathers to provide benefits for their children, so children tend to have stronger obligations to their mothers than they do to their fathers.

GRATITUDE

Before discussing whether children owe their parents gratitude, it is important to say a few things about gratitude. As the nature of gratitude is not my focus in this chapter, I only have a few clarificatory points to make.

First, because I am interested in gratitude between parents and children, I am interested in prepositional gratitude. Prepositional gratitude takes the form C is grateful to E for X-ing. Or, less abstractly, a beneficiary is grateful to a benefactor for some benefits or beneficence. Prepositional gratitude occurs between two or more people. For example, Catori is grateful to Ellie for fixing her leaky roof. I am not interested in propositional gratitude, where C is grateful that X. Or, less abstractly, a beneficiary is grateful that some beneficial state of affairs has occurred. For example, Catori is grateful that she is healthy. Tony Manela suggests that propositional gratitude is more like appreciation than it is like genuine gratitude (Manela 2015).

Second, I am assuming that gratitude is an emotion, though also that it is not only a brute feeling. Genuine gratitude requires certain beliefs, feelings, expressions, and behaviors. Beneficiaries must believe that they have received a benefit and that someone is the source of that benefit. They must have positive feelings for the benefactor and an absence of contempt. Finally, they must do something that demonstrates their gratitude to the benefactor or, at least, be willing to do something if the appropriate circumstances arise (Manela 2015).

CONDITIONS FOR A DUTY OF GRATITUDE

If we want to know why children might owe their parents gratitude, we need to know how obligations of gratitude are formed. In this section, I will explain Terrance McConnell's theory of gratitude (McConnell 1993).[1]

McConnell argues that there are four necessary conditions that must be met for an obligation of gratitude to be formed. He notes that though these conditions are necessary to form an obligation of gratitude, they are not always jointly sufficient. I will briefly explain and evaluate these conditions in this section before applying them to filial obligations in the next section.

McConnell's first condition requires that someone is benefited (a) voluntarily, (b) intentionally, (c) freely, and (d) not for disqualifying reasons. This condition is quite complex, so it's worth examining each of the subconditions individually.

Subcondition (a) states that a benefit must be given voluntarily. Benefits must be given voluntarily because it's difficult to see why anyone should be grateful to you if you are forced to help them. For example, if you help Tim only because John is threatening to punch you in the nose if you do not, then Tim doesn't owe you gratitude for your help because you are acting to avoid a punch in the nose rather than to benefit Tim.

Subcondition (b) states that a benefit must be given intentionally. This subcondition ensures that accidental benefits do not create obligations of gratitude. McConnell gives an example where a passerby on the street scares off a mugger (McConnell 1993, 26). If Jim happens to be walking by while Johan is being mugged and Jim's presence scares off the mugger, then Johan doesn't owe Jim gratitude because Jim didn't do anything to benefit Johan intentionally. Jim's walking past happened to benefit Johan, and Johan might be very glad to receive the benefit, but since Jim did not intend to benefit Johan, Johan doesn't have an obligation of gratitude.

McConnell notes that actions must only be weakly intentional to qualify the benefactor for gratitude. A beneficent act is weakly intentional so long as the act itself is performed by the benefactor intentionally and to benefit someone. A beneficent act is strongly intentional when the act is performed by the benefactor both intentionally and specifically for my benefit. If Jones saves Mel from drowning without recognizing her, then his act is weakly intentional. Jones's action was meant to confer a benefit upon someone, but it was not meant to benefit Mel specifically. Jones couldn't have meant to benefit Mel specifically because he didn't know the identity of the person he was saving. Even if Jones would have let Mel drown if he had recognized her, his act is still weakly intentional. That is, Jones intended to rescue someone. His action being weakly intentional means that Mel has an obligation of gratitude to Jones for the benefit he provided her. If, in the same situation, Mel's coworker Robert recognizes her and acts with the intention to benefit her specifically, then Robert's act is strongly intentional. In this case, part of Robert's motivation comes from knowing Mel. While Mel might feel better being saved by Robert than by Jones, she would have an obligation of gratitude to either of them if they saved her.

Subcondition (c) states that the benefit must be given freely.[2] This subcondition ensures that someone cannot manipulate others into having obligations of gratitude. Freely, in this case, does not mean that the benefactor is acting in the absence of external pressures, but rather that the benefit is given without the expectation of a return. For example, if Aida helps Dietrich only so she can later call on him to help her, then the benefit she provided was not given freely. She is extending credit to Dietrich that he will later have to repay rather than providing him with a benefit for his own sake. If the benefit Dietrich receives from Aida is provided only under terms, then he owes Aida repayment, not gratitude.

Subcondition (d) requires that benefits are not provided from disqualifying motives. McConnell says that maliciously motivated benefits would fall under this subcondition. Suppose Hans gives all of his money to Jasmine when he learns he has a terminal illness. Hans dislikes his son's choice of career and doesn't want him to get any money when he dies. Hans thinks that if he gives Jasmine the money, then his son will have no claim to it. Hans tells Jasmine that he is giving her the money only so that his son does not receive anything when he dies. While Jasmine will receive a great deal of money from Hans, and this is a benefit to her, Hans isn't trying to benefit Jasmine; rather he is trying to hurt his son. Because Hans is motivated to benefit Jasmine by his malice for his son, Jasmine does not have a duty of gratitude regardless of how much she benefits.

McConnell's second condition states that benefits must not be forced on the beneficiary against his will. For example, if Nilay's grandfather insists on giving him an old hunting rifle even though Nilay has told him several times that he has no interest in hunting or guns, then Nilay doesn't owe his grandfather gratitude for his gift. While Nilay's grandfather might think he is providing Nilay with some benefit, Nilay has expressed his desire not to have the gun and doesn't receive anything he considers beneficial. If his grandfather is seeking to give Nilay something to remember him by, then his grandfather should select something more appropriate. Another example is that of parents who force their child to go to piano lessons even though the child hates the lessons. The child makes it clear that he does not value the lessons and would rather do other things with the time, but the parents force the child to go to the piano lessons. While the parents may genuinely believe they are benefiting the child, the child does not want this benefit and so does not owe the parents gratitude. If, later in life, the child comes to value piano lessons, then the situation may change, but if the child continues to hate the piano lessons, then he has no duty of gratitude. This condition prevents others from forcing duties of gratitude on us that we would rather not have.

McConnell's third condition states that the beneficiary either must accept the benefit or would accept the benefit if certain impairing conditions were corrected. Drunkenness or ignorance of important facts are two of McConnell's examples of impairing conditions (McConnell 1993, 38). McConnell makes a distinction between accepting a benefit and wanting a benefit. He argues that we can accept a benefit without wanting it. For example, suppose that Novak's parents would like him to attend university, but they are unable to pay for him to attend. Novak has no interest in attending university, so he is unwilling to pay for it himself, but he does want to please his parents and so would attend if his parents could afford to pay. If a wealthy family friend offers to pay for Novak's education, then he will be in a situation where he will accept a benefit without wanting it. Novak would prefer that the family friend had never offered the money since he could then avoid both attending university and disappointing his parents. However, once the family friend offers the money, Novak will accept it because he values pleasing his parents more than he disvalues attending university. Even though he would prefer that the family friend never offered the money, he will nonetheless accept it (McConnell 1993, 34–35). According to McConnell's theory, accepting the benefit is enough to create an obligation of gratitude to the family friend, given the satisfaction of the other conditions.

McConnell's fourth condition states that the person to whom gratitude is owed must have provided a benefit or made a great effort or sacrifice in an attempt to provide a benefit. The first part of this condition simply requires that a benefit must be provided to form a duty of gratitude. We don't owe anyone gratitude unless she provides us with a benefit. The second part of this condition adds an exception to this rule. If someone makes a great effort or sacrifice in an attempt to provide us with a benefit, then we may still owe them gratitude even if they fail to benefit us. For example, suppose that while Asher is swimming with his friends Josh and Emil, he gets caught by a rip-tide and drawn far from the shore. Asher is a competent swimmer, but while caught in the rip-tide, he hits his head on a submerged rock and loses consciousness. Josh sees what happened to Asher before Emil and begins to swim out to help him. Josh is not a strong swimmer and cannot get to Asher despite his best effort. Fortunately, Emil is an excellent swimmer and is able to reach Asher and bring him safely back to shore. Asher certainly owes Emil gratitude since Emil provided him with a great benefit when he saved his life. However, it seems that Asher owes Josh at least some gratitude as well. Though Josh did not manage to save Asher, he made a great effort to save him and risked his own life in the process.

DO CHILDREN OWE THEIR PARENTS GRATITUDE?

In this section, I will examine three versions of the gratitude theory of filial obligations.

The gratitude theory of filial obligations is based on the claim that children owe gratitude to their parents for past benefits. Parents usually provide their children with many benefits, especially when their children are young and dependent. The gratitude theory claims that these benefits create obligations of gratitude for children. Further, parents often continue to provide benefits for their children even after the children become independent, and these continuing benefits provide even more reason to think that children owe their parents gratitude.

The gratitude theory of filial obligations is the most popular in the existing literature, and, as a result, there are several variations of the theory. The most important difference between the variations of the gratitude theory concerns which parental actions create obligations of gratitude. I will evaluate three versions of the gratitude theory. The first claims that children owe their parents gratitude for being born. The second claims that children owe their parents gratitude for discharging their duties of parenthood and providing care. The third claims that children owe their parents gratitude only for super-erogatory benefits. I argue that the second version is the minimum required for gratitude. However, the more parents do for their children, the stronger the children's obligations of gratitude will be.

Gratitude for Birth

The most demanding variation of the gratitude theory claims that children owe their parents gratitude simply for being born. This variation has its roots in Aristotle and Aquinas (Aquinas, 1975) who claim that being born is such a great benefit that children owe their parents unending gratitude (Hoff Sommers 1986).

The problem with this variation of the gratitude theory is that it only accounts for weak duties of gratitude in very specific circumstances because the intentionality condition makes it difficult for birth to warrant significant gratitude. As Nancy Jecker argues, many parents do not have children with the primary intention to benefit the future child (Jecker 1989, 74). There are many reasons parents might decide to have a child, including for their own benefit, but only those parents who are primarily motivated by a desire to benefit their future child deserve gratitude. Parents who have children for other reasons may benefit them by doing so, but their benefit is not intentional.

Having a child with the primary intention to benefit the future child is not strongly intentional, as it is impossible to intend to benefit specifically someone who doesn't exist yet. While McConnell's first condition only requires a benefit to be weakly intentional, presumably weakly intentional benefits create weaker duties of gratitude than do strongly intentional benefits, other things being equal. Knowing that a benefactor acted to benefit me specifically adds to the gratitude I feel. It suggests there is something about me that is worthy of receiving a benefit. Knowing that a benefactor acted to benefit someone who happened to be me doesn't suggest anything about my worth to the benefactor.

These considerations suggest that a duty of gratitude for birth will be weak, even in rare cases where parents have a child with the sole intention to provide benefits for the future child. Far more common will be cases of mixed motivations where parents have children both to benefit the future children and to benefit themselves. In these cases, any duty of gratitude will be weaker still.

Gratitude for Care

The gratitude for care variation of the gratitude theory claims that children owe their parents gratitude for discharging their duties of parenthood and providing care.[3] By duties of parenthood, I mean things that any parent must do to be a successful parent. Minimally, this includes providing food, shelter, and basic care to one's children and taking some interest in facilitating their development. Beyond that, parents ought to provide their children with a nurturing environment.

If a parent consistently fails to provide any of the benefits required by the minimal duties of parenthood, then he is neglectful, abusive, or otherwise unfit.[4] It seems clear to me that children do not owe gratitude to parents who fail to discharge the minimal duties of parenthood. Even if these parents do some beneficial things for their children, but fail to provide basic necessities, it is impossible that they have done enough to be worthy of gratitude.

Parents who discharge only the minimal duties of parenthood might do enough to fulfill McConnell's conditions. Providing basic care to a child is certainly a benefit, so if the parents provide basic care voluntarily, intentionally, freely, and not for disqualifying reasons, then the child plausibly owes his parents gratitude. However, as I'll discuss in a later section, the strength of the duty of gratitude, that is, how much the duty requires the child to do for his parents, is quite weak in cases like this.

Moving beyond minimal duties of parenthood further increases the demandingness of being a parent. For example, creating a safe and nurturing environment for a child requires a lot of time, energy, and, in many cases, money. Parents must read with their children and take them to have potentially enriching experiences at museums and parks. Parents must also be patient with their children while they learn new things and discipline them properly when they do bad things. In many cases, these are enjoyable activities for parents, but that doesn't mean they aren't also demanding.

Parents who discharge these more demanding duties of parenthood are better candidates for duties of gratitude. They do more to benefit their children and they fulfill McConnell's four conditions. However, we might worry here that the gratitude for care variation of the gratitude theory is too quick to assign obligations. For example, we might think that very young children don't accept benefits from their parents in the way required by McConnell's theory of gratitude.[5] Very young children don't have much choice about which benefits they receive from their parents and lack the capacity to accept the benefits in the relevant way. If this is true, then children don't owe their parents gratitude for these benefits because they didn't accept them.

While this is a concern, the gratitude for care variation of the gratitude theory can deal with this challenge. We can accept that benefits provided to very young children don't lead to obligations of gratitude while still accepting that discharging parental duties and providing care can lead to obligations of gratitude. We might have to discard all the benefits parents provide before their children can accept them, but parents continue to provide many benefits while discharging their parental duties long after children begin to be able to accept them. The gratitude for care variation of the gratitude theory can claim that obligations of gratitude are based on the benefits provided after children gain the capacity to accept benefits.

Gratitude for Supererogatory Benefits

Before discussing the supererogatory version of the gratitude theory of filial obligations, it is important to be clear what I mean by supererogatory benefits. I mean morally supererogatory benefits. In the previous section, I argued that parents have extensive duties to their children. Parents have both legal and moral obligations to care for their children. For example, parents have legal obligations to feed their children and provide them with a safe living space.[6] Parents have moral obligations to feed their children nutritious food, to provide a nurturing environment, and to help them develop into healthy adults. Moral obligations usually hold parents to a higher standard than do legal obligations.

Nancy Jecker provides a good account of the supererogatory version of the gratitude theory. She argues that supererogatory parental actions typically fall into two categories. Parents may either perform beneficial actions that they are not obligated to perform, or they may discharge their existing parental duties in a way that greatly exceeds the minimum standards of those duties (Jecker 1989, 75).[7] An example of a parental action that is beneficial but not obligatory is paying for a child's university education. While parents are expected to support their children until they complete high school, parents have no obligation to pay for their children's postsecondary education. If parents choose to provide such a large benefit to their children, then they have provided a benefit that they were not obligated to provide.

Jecker has an excellent example of a parent discharging his duty in a way that greatly exceeds expectations. A father takes the day off of work to care for his daughter when she is sick. He makes his daughter her favorite snack, tells her favorite jokes, and watches her favorite movies with her (Jecker 1989, 75). Though we might expect a father to take care of his child when she is sick, this father goes well beyond what is minimally required. Rather than just making sure she is properly taken care of, he goes out of his way to cheer her up and make her ordeal as tolerable as possible. Of course, a one-off case is not enough to influence significantly what the daughter owes her father. For the daughter to have any significant duties of gratitude for this kind of supererogatory benefit, her father would have to benefit her like this frequently.[8]

Parents who provide their children with supererogatory benefits are almost certainly owed gratitude. Not only do they fulfill McConnell's conditions, but they do more than is required of them to benefit their children. In the next section, I'll discuss what duties of gratitude require children to do for their parents, but it's worth noting here that supererogatory benefits increase the benefits children ought to provide to their parents.

It's important to point out that even supererogatory actions will not create duties of gratitude for children if parents fail to uphold the minimal duties of parenthood. For example, abusive parents are not owed gratitude even if they choose to pay for their children's university tuition. Any value the supererogatory benefit provides will be outweighed by the harm caused by failing to fulfill their duties. Abusive parents have fundamentally failed at their parental duties, and it's difficult to see how any act could make up for this failing. The children of abusive parents may decide to forgive them, but they do not owe them anything.

Parents have extensive duties to provide their children with a good life, which limit opportunities for supererogation. Some children will owe their parents gratitude for one large benefit, such as paying for their university education. However, many parents are unable or unwilling to pay for their children's university education, or provide an equivalently significant benefit. Most children will owe their parents gratitude for many small supererogatory benefits provided over many years. For example, parents might help their adult children take care of their young children. As grandparents, they aren't obligated to care for their grandchildren, at least not in the same way parents are, and doing so consistently can be a great benefit for their children.

What Does a Duty of Gratitude Require of Children?

It is difficult to be specific about what duties of gratitude require children to do. Much will depend on the properties of the particular parent-child relationship in question. Children who have received many benefits from their parents will, other things being equal, owe their parents more than children who received only a few benefits. However, it is clear that a duty of gratitude will almost never require an equal return. Requiring an equal return would make a duty of gratitude too much like a debt that requires repayment (McConnell 1993, 50–51). This is problematic because it would collapse a duty of gratitude into a simple debt.

Further, in filial relationships, an equal return would often be inappropriate. If the daughter from Jecker's earlier example of supererogatory parental actions attempted to show her gratitude to her elderly father by taking the day off of work, making his favorite snacks, telling his favorite jokes, and watching his favorite movies with him, we would very likely think her actions were inappropriate. While her father might have the same illness she did as a child, her father is an adult and does not need the same kind of care that he provided for her when she was a child. He is likely to see an attempt to provide the same kind of care as demeaning and condescending. The daughter should spend time with her father, but she should not treat him exactly as he treated her when she was a child.

Brynn Welch's Objection

Brynn Welch argues that a duty of gratitude can tell us that we should do something for our parents, but not that we must do anything in particular. She suggests that, at best, the gratitude theory of filial obligations can guide us away from extremes (Welch 2012, 723). For example, suppose we accept that Niles has a duty of gratitude to his parents. It would not be appropriate for Niles to say to his parents, "Thank you for your care and support while I was growing up" and think he had discharged his duty of gratitude to them. If he has a duty of gratitude in the first place, he seems to be obligated to do more than express his thanks only once. The gratitude theory can tell us that such a minimal expression of gratitude is insufficient. It guides us away from duties of gratitude requiring too little of children.

The gratitude theory of filial obligations can also tell us that some expressions of gratitude are inappropriately extravagant because they demonstrate a lack of self-respect. If Niles devotes his whole life to satisfying even the most outlandish requests of his parents, then it's difficult to believe he values himself as an end independent of his parents. Fred Berger calls this pathological gratitude and suggests that expectations of such behavior can be oppressive (Berger 1975, 304–305). In this case, the gratitude theory can tell us that Niles shouldn't be doing as much as he is doing, or at least that he doesn't have a duty to do as much as he does. The gratitude theory guides us away from duties of gratitude requiring too much of children.

What the gratitude theory can't do, according to Welch, is provide us with specific actions to perform to discharge duties of gratitude. You might think this standard is too high. Perhaps we shouldn't expect obligations of gratitude to be this specific. However, Welch argues that the gratitude theory can't even provide us with a range of actions that would discharge duties of gratitude because the gratitude theory cannot explain the type of action required to discharge a duty of gratitude (Welch, 723). Welch claims that even if we accept that a child owes his parents gratitude, it's not clear what the child must do for them. There are three possibilities in Niles's case: he is obligated to (1) express genuine gratitude, (2) behave as though he were experiencing gratitude even if he is not, or (3) feel gratitude.

Expressing genuine gratitude would involve Niles performing some action to demonstrate the gratitude he feels for his parents. In this case, we're supposing that Niles feels gratitude to his parents and that his feeling of gratitude motivates him to do something to benefit them. This is perhaps the most intuitive way to think about what a duty of gratitude requires, though again Welch argues that gratitude theory can do no more than guide us away from extremes when determining what actions Niles must perform to demonstrate his gratitude.

The other two possibilities occur when Niles doesn't feel gratitude to his parents, even though the gratitude theory says he has duties of gratitude to them. In this case, the gratitude theory might either require Niles to pretend he genuinely feels gratitude, or it might require him to feel gratitude. If the gratitude theory of filial obligations can't tell us what actions a person with a duty of gratitude should perform, it also cannot tell us what it would be like for Niles to behave as though he were experiencing gratitude.

Finally, it seems strange to require Niles to feel gratitude. If Niles genuinely does not feel gratitude to his parents, it's not clear how he could develop the feeling. Perhaps he could make an effort to develop his character in such a way that he does feel gratitude toward his parents, but the gratitude theory gives us no guidance on how he might do so.

If, as Welch argues, the gratitude theory of filial obligations cannot identify what duties of gratitude require children to do for their parents, then it fails to provide a satisfactory answer to one of the most important questions a theory of filial obligations should answer. In addition to telling us why children have obligations to their parents, a good theory of filial obligations should also tell us what these obligations are.

Responding to Welch

The gratitude theory of filial obligations can give a better account of what children must do for their parents than Welch suggests. Again, I turn to

McConnell's theory of gratitude. According to McConnell, a beneficiary must do three things to discharge a duty of gratitude. First, the beneficiary must acknowledge and appreciate the benefit provided by the benefactor. Second, the beneficiary must be willing to provide a commensurate benefit to the benefactor, should the opportunity arise. Third, the benefit provided by the beneficiary must respond to a genuine need of the benefactor (McConnell 1993, 56).[9]

If McConnell is correct, duties of gratitude require both an action and a proper attitude. The act is being prepared to provide one's benefactor with a commensurate benefit if an opportunity presents itself. For an opportunity to present itself, my benefactor must have a genuine need for something I can provide. This means that if my benefactor is fortunate enough never to find herself in need of a benefit I can provide, then I haven't failed to fulfill my duty of gratitude (McConnell 1993, 63–64).[10] As long as I'm willing to provide the benefit were the opportunity to arise, I have done what gratitude requires.

The other aspect of discharging a duty of gratitude is having the right attitude about providing a benefit for my benefactor. I must acknowledge and appreciate what my benefactor has done for me. This means that I can't properly discharge a duty of gratitude by simply providing a commensurate benefit. If I fail to acknowledge and appreciate what my benefactor has done for me, then I've failed to discharge my duty of gratitude. McConnell's example involves him throwing a party for his friend who has recently achieved something important. He says, "It is a very fine party, and you are overcome with a sense of gratitude to me. As you are leaving, you say, 'Please, let me show my gratitude,' and you slip me fifty dollars" (McConnell 1993, 51). In this case, McConnell argues that the friend's action isn't a proper way to express gratitude. The friend seems to miss something important about the benefit the host provided for him. He fails to appreciate the benefit provided, so he has failed to discharge his duty of gratitude.

McConnell argues that duties of gratitude are narrow imperfect duties. Narrow imperfect duties require one to adopt a maxim and do not allow one to "refrain from acting on that maxim simply because he has recently done so or will do so on some other occasion" (McConnell 1993, 68–69). This explains why, when an opportunity to benefit our benefactor arises, we must benefit our benefactor, so long as doing so does not violate any perfect duties.[11]

McConnell's theory provides an answer to Welch's concern about the gratitude theory of filial obligations. According to McConnell, a beneficiary must express genuine gratitude to discharge a duty of gratitude. Being willing to provide a commensurate benefit is not enough to discharge a duty of gratitude. Similarly, merely feeling gratitude is not enough to discharge a duty of gratitude. It is only a combination of attitude and action in response to the genuine need of one's benefactor (should that arise) that can discharge a duty of gratitude. This means that McConnell's theory can tell us what Niles is required to do. In Welch's terms, he must express genuine gratitude to his parents for the benefits they have provided to him.

Commensurate Benefits

McConnell's theory can also explain how the gratitude theory can do more than guide us away from extremes. It may still be unable to provide specific actions, but, again, that's asking a lot of a moral theory. McConnell's second and third conditions help determine how demanding duties of gratitude will be for children. Children must provide a commensurate benefit or, more likely, a series of commensurate benefits to their parents in response to a genuine need.

What constitutes a commensurate benefit will depend on the history of the parent-child relationship. As I suggested earlier, parents who provide their children with supererogatory benefits as well as the benefits required to discharge their parental duties will be owed the most. Individual supererogatory benefits tend to be more beneficial than individual regular benefits, so a commensurate return for a supererogatory benefit will require more of children than a commensurate return for a regular benefit.[12] Further, since parents must fulfill their duties of parenthood to be owed gratitude at all, duties of gratitude for supererogatory benefits can only add to the duties of gratitude owed for basic care benefits.

Parents who provide only the benefits required to discharge their parental duties may still be owed quite a lot. As I mentioned earlier, duties of parenthood are extensive and demanding. Discharging them leads to a lot of benefits for children. There are obvious benefits, like being provided the necessities of life, but parents who do a good job facilitating their children's development into adulthood provide less obvious benefits as well. For example, parents help their children develop social skills, learn to read and write, and understand how to cope with failure. These benefits all contribute to a good adult life. This suggests that providing commensurate benefits for being raised well could still require a lot of children.

However, it's important to keep in mind that children are required only to provide benefits in response to a genuine need of their parents. This helps to alleviate worries about filial obligations being too demanding. Without a limiting condition like this, we might worry that children of exceptional parents could have almost unlimited obligations of gratitude. If children need only respond to the genuine needs of their parents, then children aren't obligated to provide benefits to their parents that they can obtain themselves. For example, children don't have to do a lot to meet their obligations of gratitude if their parents are healthy and financially secure. In cases like this, children might do enough to meet their obligations by keeping in touch with their parents and remaining willing to help should their parents need something.

But what does the gratitude theory say about exceptional parents who are ill and in need of care? For example, suppose Niko's parents provided him with extensive benefits when he was growing up and continue to do so. Now, Niko's father has passed away and his mother has developed severe dementia. She is no longer able to take care of herself. Providing the care she needs is time consuming, often frustrating, and expensive. However, given that Niko's mother was an exceptional parent, the gratitude theory of filial obligations suggests he must do whatever he can to care for her. He received extensive benefits from her, and she is now in need of commensurate benefits. Exactly what he can provide will depend on his circumstances—"ought" implies "can," after all—but the gratitude theory suggests he should do all he can.

Summary

In this section, I have argued that parents must discharge their moral duties of parenthood to be owed gratitude from their children. I then argued that the more benefits parents provide for their children, the stronger the duties of gratitude they are owed will be. Next, I defended the gratitude theory from Brynn Welch's objection that it cannot tell us what children ought to do for their parents. I argued that McConnell's conditions for discharging a duty of gratitude can tell us that children must provide a commensurate benefit in response to a genuine need of their parents. Finally, I discussed what providing a commensurate benefit might require children to do for their parents.

GENDERED GRATITUDE

As a result of the gendered division of household and childcare labor in most Canadian and American families, children are both more likely to have obligations of gratitude to their mothers, and more likely to have stronger obligations of gratitude to their mothers than they do to their fathers.

The Statistics

In Canada, in 2010, women spent an average of 50.1 hours per week on unpaid childcare (Statistics Canada 2015). Men spent an average of only 24.4 hours per week. Thus, women spend, on average, more than double the time men do on childcare.[13] Similarly, women in Canada in 2010 spent an average of 13.8 hours per week on unpaid household labor while men spent an average of only 8.3 hours per week (Statistics Canada 2015). Together, these statistics suggest that mothers in Canada are doing far more care work than fathers.

The situation is similar in the United States, though the data available measure time spent "caring for and helping household children as their main activity," rather than unpaid work (United States Department of Labor 2016). In 2016, mothers with children under age six spent an average of 17.92 hours per week caring for and helping household children as their main activity. For mothers with children under age eighteen, this number drops to 12.32. Fathers with children under age six spend an average of 10.29 hours per week caring for and helping household children as their main activity (United States Department of Labor 2016).[14] For fathers with children under age eighteen, this number drops to 6.86 hours per week. Women also spent an average of 15.68 hours per week on household labor compared to an average of 9.66 per week for men (United States Department of Labor 2016). In all cases, mothers do significantly more work than fathers.

Why Most People Owe Their Mothers More

As I argued in an earlier section, most children owe their parents gratitude for the benefits they receive while growing up. The strength of obligations of gratitude depends on the benefits provided to the beneficiary. The more valuable the benefit a beneficiary receives, the more a commensurate benefit will be, which leads to stronger obligations of gratitude. Parents who spend more time with their children are more likely to provide them with benefits. That is, parents who spend more time with their children tend to provide them with more benefits than parents who spend less time with their children. So, parents who spend more time with their children are more likely to be owed gratitude because they provide more benefits. In Canada and the United States, this means children typically have stronger obligations of gratitude to their mothers than to their fathers.

Neither Statistics Canada nor the United States Department of Labor asks questions directly about benefits. However, it is reasonable to think that there is a strong correlation between time spent caring for a child and benefits provided to a child. A parent who does most of the cooking, cleaning, playing, reading, and other child care activities with their children provides them with more benefits than the parent who spends less time on these activities.

Parents who spend more time caring for their children are also more likely to have a close relationship with them. A close relationship is more likely to create strong duties of gratitude for two reasons. First, parents who have close relationships with their children are more likely to desire to benefit their children. A strong desire to benefit one's children will make one more likely to provide them with the kind of benefits that lead to strong duties of gratitude. For example, parents might volunteer to help their children move to a new city for university or to look after their children regularly. Without a close relationship, it's less likely the parents would be motivated to provide these benefits. Second, parents who have a closer relationship with their children will be in a better position to benefit their children. For example, if a parent has a close relationship with his or her children, the children will be more likely to turn to their parent for help when they are in need. Without a close relationship, the parent likely won't have an opportunity to benefit his or her children because they will seek help elsewhere.

Mothers spend more time than fathers caring for their children, so mothers are more likely to have a close relationship with their children. Close relationships facilitate benefits, which lead to duties of gratitude. This means that mothers are more likely than fathers to provide benefits to their children and therefore their children are more likely to have strong duties of gratitude to their mothers.

CONCLUSION

In the introduction, I posed three questions about filial gratitude. First, do children owe their parents gratitude? I argued that most children do. Second, if so, on what parental actions are duties of gratitude based? I argued that children owe their parents gratitude for the benefits they have been provided. I suggested that parents must, at minimum, discharge their duties of parenthood to be owed gratitude from their children. Parents who do more than is required of them are owed more gratitude than parents who do only what is required. Third, what do duties of gratitude require children to do for their parents? I argued that children must provide their parents with commensurate benefits in response to genuine needs.

In the final section, I argued that most Canadian and American children owe their mothers more gratitude than they owe their fathers. Mothers do the majority of care and household labor, which leads to them providing more benefits to their children.

NOTES

1 McConnell's theory of when gratitude is owed is based on John Simmons's work (Simmons 1979).

2 McConnell makes a distinction between acting voluntarily and acting freely. Acting voluntarily involves providing a benefit without any external threats, while acting freely involves providing a benefit without the expectation of a return.

3 I'm not aware of anyone who explicitly defends this variation of the gratitude theory, but it serves as a plausible middle ground between the gratitude for birth version and the gratitude for supererogatory benefits version.

4 I add the consistently qualifier to account for normal human error. Parents might occasionally forget to pack their child's lunch, and while this is in some sense failing at their parental duty, it's not abusive or neglectful in the sense I'm worried about.

5 McConnell suggests that childhood may be an impairing condition. He says, "Many of the benefits that we have received from our parents and former teachers are ones that at the time we neither wanted nor accepted but only later came to appreciate. And while gratitude may not be due for all of these benefits, it certainly seems that it is due for some of them. In cases of this sort it is plausible to say that gratitude was owed all along, but the agent did not realize this until later" (McConnell 1993, 38). If he's right, then children can retroactively accept benefits once their impairment has been resolved. I think this is a very strange way to talk about childhood. Childhood is a time of development, not an impairment that ought to be resolved. Further, this seems like a stretch of what it means to accept something. It seems clear from his example that the children don't accept the benefit when it was provided to them. They may later come to realize that they should have, or that with their current knowledge they would have, but it's not clear that such a realization means they accepted the benefit.

6 Legal obligations can vary significantly between countries and even within countries. However, at least in North America, parents are expected to do at least this much.

7 Assuming parents aren't morally required to have children, it is plausible that being born is a supererogatory benefit. However, this benefit will only lead to a weak duty of gratitude, as explained in the section "Gratitude for Birth."

8 Each small supererogatory benefit grounds a weak duty of gratitude. The strength of these duties is additive so the more parents provide supererogatory benefits to their children, the stronger the duty of gratitude will become.

9 Presumably, the benefit could respond to a genuine want of the benefactor, not only a genuine need. McConnell's intention here seems to be to require the benefit to respond to the particular circumstances of the benefactor.

10 One of McConnell's examples is a very rich benefactor saving the life of a very poor beneficiary. It's unlikely the very poor beneficiary will ever be able to provide a commensurate benefit to his beneficiary. However, he can be prepared to provide commensurate benefit, if the opportunity presents itself. McConnell says that in this case, the beneficiary has "done all that gratitude demands at that point" (McConnell 1993, 62–63).

11 McConnell's example of violating a perfect duty in an attempt to discharge a duty of gratitude is killing my benefactor's bitter enemy (McConnell 1993, 68). We have a perfect duty not to kill, which overrides our imperfect duty of gratitude.

12 In aggregate, regular benefits, like those provided while discharging minimal duties of parenthood, can be more valuable than supererogatory benefits.

13 This ratio remains consistent across almost all working arrangements. The only exception is "dual earner couples; respondent working part-time" in which women do an average of 59.4 hour per week and men do an average of 40.5 hours per week.

14 I suspect the difference in reported total hours spent on childcare in the Canada and the United States is a result of the questions asked, rather than much

actual difference. The American survey only accounts for time when childcare is the primary task, while the Canadian survey accounts for any childcare. I don't think this difference is problematic for my purposes. I'm not trying to compare inequality between Canada and the United States, rather I'm trying to show that both have an unequal distribution of childcare and household labor.

WORKS CITED

Aquinas, Thomas. 1975. *Summa Theologiae*. Translated by J. Batten. Vol. 34. New York: Blackfriars.

Berger, Fred. 1975. "Gratitude." *Ethics* 85 (4): 298–309.

Brake, Elizabeth. 2010. "Willing Parents: A Voluntarist Account of Parental Role Obligations." In *Procreation and Parenthood: The Ethics of Bearing and Rearing Children*, by David Archard and David Benatar, 151–177. Oxford: Oxford University Press.

English, Jane. 1999. "What Do Grown Children Owe Their Parents?" In *Morals, Marriage, and Parenthood: an Introduction to Family Ethics*, by Laurence D. Houlgate, 267–271. Belmont, CA: Wadsworth.

Hoff Sommers, Christina. 1986. "Filial Morality." *The Journal of Philosophy* 83 (8): 439–456.

Jecker, Nancy S. 1989. "Are Filial Duties Unfounded?" *American Philosophical Quarterly* 26 (1): 73–80.

Keller, Simon. 2006. "Four Theories of Filial Duty." *Philosophical Quarterly* 56 (223): 254–274.

Manela, Tony. 2015. "Gratitude." *Stanford Encyclopedia of Philosophy*. March 21. https://plato.stanford.edu/archives/spr2015/entries/gratitude.

McConnell, Terrance C. 1993. *Gratitude*. Philadelphia, PA: Temple University Press.

Simmons, A. John. 1979. *Moral Principles and Political Obligations*. Princeton, NJ: Princeton University Press.

Statistics Canada. 2015a. "Time Spent on Household Domestic Work, by Working Arrangement, Canada, 2010." *Statistics Canada*. 11 30. http://www.statcan.gc.ca/pub/89-503-x/2010001/article/11546/tbl/tbl007-eng.htm.

———. 2015b. "Time Spent on Unpaid Care of a Child in the Household, by Working Arrangement and Age of Youngest Child, Canada, 2010." *Statistics Canada*. 11 30. http://www.statcan.gc.ca/pub/89-503-x/2010001/article/11546/tbl/tbl006-eng.htm.

United States Department of Labor. 2016a. "Average Hours Per Day Parents Spent Caring for and Helping Household Children as Their Main Activity." *American Time Use Survey*. https://www.bls.gov/charts/american-time-use/activity-by-parent.htm.

———. 2016b. "Average Hours Per Day Spent in Selected Household Activities." *American Time Use Survey*. https://www.bls.gov/charts/american-time-use/activity-by-hldh.htm.

Welch, Brynn F. 2012. "A Theory of Filial Obligations." *Social Theory and Practice* 38 (4): 717–737.

Part III

GRATITUDE AS A REACTIVE ATTITUDE

Chapter 7

Gratitude as a Second-Personal Attitude (of the Heart)

Stephen Darwall

1. "Gratitude" can mean several different things. In so-called gift economies, where gifts put recipients under obligation to make a return of equal or greater value, it can refer to the obligatory return. Along not entirely dissimilar lines, many philosophers, including Aquinas, Pufendorf, Kant, Sidgwick, and Ross, have argued for a moral duty of gratitude. Here again, "gratitude" refers to beneficial activity that responds appropriately to an initial gift. My concern in what follows, however, will not be with gratitude conceived of as anything that might discharge such a social or moral duty. Neither will I be concerned with gratitude as a virtue or with what constitutes a grateful person. My focus will be entirely on the emotion or attitude of gratitude, that is, the attitude that grateful actions are normally taken to express.[1]

P. F. Strawson famously included gratitude as a "reactive attitude" (Strawson 1968: 75, 76). Reactive attitudes all involve a distinctive standpoint from which they are had or felt, what Strawson called the "participant" perspective of "participation in a human relationship," by contrast with an observer's "objective" point of view (Strawson 1968: 79). Strawson also called this an "interpersonal" perspective, though I prefer "second-personal" to keep track of the fact that the attitude is had not just from *within* some relationship, but also implicitly relates *to* its object (and so implies the second-person pronoun [Darwall 2006, 2013a, 2013b]). Strawson's point was that in taking these attitudes toward someone from a second-person perspective, we are committed to certain presuppositions about their capacities of will.

The most often discussed examples of Strawsonian reactive attitudes are *juridical* attitudes like resentment, indignation (or moral blame), and guilt. These are attitudes through which we hold others or ourselves accountable for their conduct; the attitudes reflect expectations and demands to which we take ourselves to be in a position to hold people. Indeed, they partly constitute our so holding them (Strawson 1968: 92–93). Accountability is, I argue, always implicitly reciprocal or mutual (Darwall 2006, 2013a, 2013b). In holding someone accountable through blame, for example, we must see them as capable of holding themselves accountable, as we implicitly demand they do. The juridical reactive attitudes invariably come with an implicit RSVP. They call on their object to acknowledge a blameworthy wrong and to hold themselves accountable for it.

I argue that juridical reactive attitudes are conceptually linked to the juridical moral concepts of right, wrong, duty, rights, and the like, and vice versa. It is a conceptual truth that if an action is morally wrong, the violation of a moral obligation, then it is an action of a kind that it would be *blameworthy* to do without adequate excuse (Darwall 2006, 2016b). Similarly, if an action violates an obligation owed *to* someone (a "directional" or "bipolar" obligation), or a right held by them against someone else, then it is something that that person would fittingly resent (Darwall 2012). And both conceptual truths hold in the reverse direction also.

Gratitude is clearly not a juridical reactive attitude. Even if there are debts or duties of gratitude, gratitude is not itself an attitude through which we hold people accountable for their conduct.[2] So if gratitude is a reactive attitude, it cannot be because the essential feature of reactive attitudes is that they implicitly address claims and demands and hold their objects accountable. If gratitude is a reactive attitude, not all do.

Reactive attitudes, for Strawson, are second-personal responses to "the qualities of [someone's] will" (Strawson 1968: 84).[3] Juridical reactive attitudes respond to what is taken to be their object's "ill will or indifference" toward someone, as, for example, when they violate that person's legitimate demands and thereby fail to respect, and so injure, the person. Strawson calls an "other-reactive" juridical attitude *personal* when the object of indifference or ill will is oneself. The distinctive personal other-reactive attitude is resentment. Blame, by contrast, is an "impersonal" rather than a personal reactive attitude.[4] It is felt, not as if from the perspective of a wronged victim, but from a putatively impartial position that, in principle, anyone can share. Guilt is a personal reactive attitude because it is "self-reactive" (Strawson 1968: 86). It shares, however, the distinctive feature of impersonal juridical attitudes that the perspective one takes on one's own conduct is one that one shares with any member of the moral community. Guilt is self-blame.

Whereas juridical reactive attitudes respond to conduct that manifests ill will or unjustifiable "indifference" to legitimate demands on someone's conduct, Strawson clearly thinks of gratitude as a personal second-personal response to goodwill's having been intentionally shown to one. If someone intended, he writes, "to benefit me because of his general goodwill toward me, I shall reasonably feel a gratitude which I should not feel at all if the benefit was an incidental consequence" (Strawson 1968: 75–76).

Strawson does not, however, tell us what he thinks makes gratitude a "participant" attitude in the sense that it is *itself* second personal. Even if we agree that intentional benefits involve a way of relating to the beneficiary, what makes a positive *response* to that benefit second personal itself? Resentment and blame are second-personal attitudes because they implicitly *address* demands to their objects; they come with an RSVP (Strawson 1968: 92–93, Darwall 2006). In what, however, does the second-personal character of gratitude consist?

My aim in what follows is to address this question. I shall be arguing that gratitude is, like the juridical attitudes, but also like other "positive" reactive attitudes such as love and trust, a *reciprocating* attitude (Darwall 2016a, 2017, 2018a). Reciprocating attitudes mediate forms of reciprocal relationship; they implicitly call for or invite reciprocation or reciprocate such a call within an implied relationship (even if only aspirationally). Whereas, however, the form of reciprocation that juridical attitudes like blame and guilt mediate is one of mutual accountability and respect, I shall argue that gratitude mediates more heartfelt and personal forms of relationship. As I have argued elsewhere is true of love and trust, I shall argue here that gratitude is a second-personal attitude "of the heart" (Darwall 2016a, 2017). Through such second-personal attitudes, a person makes themselves vulnerable to another in heartfelt ways, either in response or with an invitation to the other to be similarly open to them.

2. To see better what I mean by a *reciprocating attitude*, consider first the more widespread category of *reciprocal attitudes*. Reciprocal attitudes are attitudes that share the same evaluative content but are felt from different perspectives, one attitude being felt from the perspective of the person who is the object of the other. With reciprocal attitudes, the object person's attitude reflects back the same evaluative content as the attitude of which they are the object.

For example, suppose someone esteems you for your trombone playing. What Roberts calls the evaluative "construal" of this esteem is that you are estimable on account of your trombone playing (Roberts 1988). The reciprocal attitude to this esteem might be pride, the feeling that *one* is estimable. Pride would be the reciprocal of esteem in the sense that pride shares the same evaluative content as the esteem but is felt from the perspective of the person who is (appropriately) an object of the esteem.

Similarly, contempt or disdain and shame are reciprocal attitudes. They share the same evaluative content: that someone is contemptible. But shame is felt as if from the perspective of someone who feels as if they are the objects of justified contempt. To someone who views another with contempt, the other's shame reflects back to the contemptuous person the other's contemptible character (Darwall 2018b).

Finally, blame and guilt are reciprocal attitudes also. To feel guilt is to feel that one is to blame for some wrong, that something one has done is culpable. This is the shared evaluative content of both attitudes. As pride does to esteem, and shame to contempt, so also does guilt reflect back a shared evaluative content to the person who views the guilt-feeling person with blame.

However, whereas blame and guilt are reciprocals, like esteem and pride and contempt and shame, they are also *reciprocating* attitudes in ways that the other pairs are not (Darwall 2018a). This is a consequence of the fact that blame and guilt are second-personal attitudes that implicitly *address* their objects with an implied RSVP. Blame calls on its object to hold themselves accountable for culpable wrongdoing, for example, through feeling guilt. So guilt *reciprocates* blame, since it not only reflects back the same evaluative content but also partly constitutes the blamed person's holding themselves accountable as blame *calls* on them to do. Blame and guilt have a "call and response" structure, with blame providing the "call" and guilt the "response."[5]

Esteem, by contrast, is a third-personal attitude. It is felt as if from the perspective of an observer. Consequently, when its object feels the same evaluative content as pride, they internalize a third-personal view. And similarly for contempt and shame. Contempt does not normally implicitly address its object; to the contrary, it often excludes its object from address. So it has no implicit RSVP. And although second-personal attitudes like blame and guilt presuppose the capacities of will that were Strawson's hallmarks of reactive attitudes, nothing like that need be true of contempt and shame. It is impossible coherently to blame someone for something when (one thinks) they lack the capacities to understand the wrongness of what they have done or hold themselves accountable for it. Nothing like this is required for contempt. To the contrary, not being able to grasp one's contemptibility may seem to make one even more contemptible and shameful (Darwall 2018b).

The "call" of a juridical attitude like resentment or blame presents itself as mandatory. Blame does not invite a reciprocating response so much as demand it. The call and response character of reciprocating attitudes of the heart, by contrast, is invitational rather than mandatory. Trust invites its acceptance, and trust in return, if only trust in the initial trust (Darwall 2017). Love invites its acceptance and reciprocal love in response; otherwise it is unrequited (Darwall 2016a). Gratitude, I shall argue, is the invited reciprocal response to an initial benefiting act conceived not simply as an improvement in the beneficiary's situation, but as a heartfelt expression to the beneficiary, as an opening of the benefactor's heart with the beneficiary's gratitude being a reciprocal opening in return.

3. Before, however, attempting further to articulate and develop this idea, it will be useful for comparative purposes to consider other discussions of gratitude that also seem to treat it as a reactive, second-personal attitude. One that interestingly anticipates Strawson's treatment is Adam Smith's discussion of gratitude and resentment as structurally analogous responses to intentionally benefiting and harming conduct, similarly to Strawson's good and ill will. Smith's discussion of gratitude and resentment comes in Part II of *The Theory of Moral Sentiments* in which he discusses "Merit or Demerit; of the Objects of Reward and Punishment," more specifically, in section I concerning the "Sense of Merit and Demerit" (Smith 1982: 67–78).

Smith's anticipation of Strawson throughout section I is uncanny. Elsewhere I have discussed the second-personal aspects of Smith's account of resentment and its conceptual connection to injustice (Darwall 2004, 2006). Injustice, for Smith, is conduct that is a fitting (Smith's term is "proper") object of resentment, where resentment is (as with Strawson) an attitude ("sentiment") through which the unjust act is challenged and its agent held accountable (Darwall 2006: 178–179). "A moral being," Smith writes, "is an accountable being," one who "must necessarily conceive himself accountable to his fellow creatures" (Smith 1982: 111).

As I have argued elsewhere is also true of Strawson, accountability for Smith is fundamentally a relation of mutual respect (Darwall 2006: 61). When we resent others for wronging us, what "chiefly enrages" us is their disrespect: "the little account which he seems to make of us, the unreasonable preference he gives to himself above us" (Smith 1982: 96). But though Smith does tie resentment to punishment, he is nonetheless clear that its aim is not retaliation, but, as Kant would put it, to "exact respect" (Kant 1996: 6: 434). What resentment "is chiefly intent upon," Smith writes, "is not so much to make our enemy feel pain in his turn, but to make him . . . sensible that the person whom he injured did not deserve to be treated in that manner" (Smith 1982: 95–96).[6]

The implied framework of juridical reactive attitudes like resentment for Smith and Strawson is one of mutual accountability and respect. But what does Smith think is the implied relational background for gratitude? Gratitude and resentment, for Smith, are what give us the "sense of merit and demerit," respectively: "The sentiment which most immediately and directly prompts us to reward, is gratitude; that which most immediately and directly prompts us to punish, is resentment" (Smith 1982: 68). Not everything that actually causes gratitude or resentment has merit or demerit, respectively. Smith is clear that merit and demerit are tied only to *proper* or fitting gratitude and resentment. Merit is what justifies or merits gratitude and demerit is that to which resentment is the proper response.

Also like Strawson, Smith holds that gratitude and resentment presuppose specific agential capacities:

> Before anything, therefore, can be the complete and proper object of either gratitude or resentment, it must possess three different qualifications. First, it must be the cause of pleasure in the one case, and of pain in the other. Secondly, it must be capable of feeling those sensations. And thirdly, it must not only have produced those sensations, but it must have produced them from design, and from a design that is approved in the one case, and disapproved in the other. (Smith 1982: 96)

This goes neither as far as Strawson, nor, I think, as far as it should. Indeed, it does not go as far as Smith's remark about the object of resentment being to make its object "sensible" of his disrespect would require. An agent might intentionally injure and be able to feel, even empathically, the pain they create without having the capacity for either guilt or self-blame that would be requisite for them to feel "the person whom he injured did not deserve to be treated in that manner." In other words, they might lack a conscience.

Taken only this far, reward and punishment become but benefits and costs that agents can expect *epistemically* when they intentionally aid or harm.[7] In order to be able to be held accountable for their harm, it is necessary that agents have the capacity to hold themselves accountable. They must have the capacity to take up an impartial second-person perspective (conscience) on and blame themselves. They must be able to *empathically internalize* and so receive and acknowledge their victim's resentment as justified or *proper*, to see it as expectable, not just epistemically, but morally.

But what agential capacities are necessary to be an appropriate object of gratitude? Smith writes that "though animals are not only the causes of pleasure and pain, but are also capable of feeling those sensations, they are still far from being complete objects, either of gratitude or resentment" (Smith 1982: 95). Smith does not explicitly say why (other) animals are not apt or "complete objects" of gratitude. However, he goes on to make a point analogous to his claim that resentment is "chiefly intent" on making a wrongdoer feel, not just resentment's sting but also its communicative (so, second-personal) content, namely, that the victim had a justified claim not to be so treated.

> What gratitude chiefly desires, is not only to make the benefactor feel pleasure in his turn, but to make him conscious that he meets with this reward on account of his past conduct, to make him pleased with that conduct, and to satisfy him

that the person upon whom he bestowed his good offices was not unworthy of them. (Smith 1982: 95)

Like resentment, therefore, gratitude has a (second-personal) communicative function. For Smith, gratitude "prompts reward" not just in the sense of involving a (third-personal) desire that a benefactor be benefited. It also implicitly seeks to communicate that the benefit is bestowed as a justified response to an estimable bestowal of a benefit on a worthy recipient. The response is thus a *reward* that recognizes the benefaction's *merit* and that seeks to communicate the worth of each, as benefactor and beneficiary, respectively.

This makes gratitude, like resentment, a second-personal attitude; both presuppose a relationship within which they respectively function. Resentment presupposes a relationship of mutual accountability and respect and demands treatment as an equal within that relationship. Gratitude, by contrast, presupposes a relationship of benefactor and beneficiary within which both seek a merit or worth that is different than the equal dignity presupposed by resentment, namely, as benefactor and worthy beneficiary, respectively. The beneficiary's rewarding response simultaneously recognizes the benefactor's worth and aspires to make the benefactor feel the beneficiary's worth as well. So conceived, initial benefaction and grateful response are both *bestowals* that are "in the gift" of benefactor and beneficiary, respectively. Both are thus outside the sphere of the juridical, of what can be legitimately claimed or demanded.

In this way, Smith's account differs fundamentally from Kant's, which squarely places gratitude within the juridical domain. For Kant, gratitude is a duty owed to the benefactor whose benefaction obligates the beneficiary.

> *Gratitude* consists in *honoring* a person because of a benefit he has rendered us. The feeling connected with this judgment is respect for the benefactor (who puts one under obligation), whereas the benefactor is viewed only in a relation of love toward the recipient. (Kant 1996: 6: 454–55)

Not only is gratitude a duty, but also it is, Kant says, a "sacred duty," since its violation "(as a scandalous example) can destroy the moral incentive to beneficence in its very principle" (Kant 1996: 6: 455). Although the benefactor's love is decidedly outside of the realm of the juridical, gratitude is not; it is an obligatory response.

Kant is clear that gratitude involves not love but respect (Kant 1996: 6: 458). Although Kant does not make these distinctions, he evidently takes gratitude to include a combination of both recognition and appraisal respect (or moral esteem) (Darwall 1977). Gratitude simultaneously *recognizes* the obligation to the benefactor that the benefaction imposes *and* honors and esteems them for their benevolent act. Indeed, Kant says, it honors a *greater* relative merit in the benefactor that the beneficiary can never attain, "since the recipient can never win away from the benefactor his priority of merit, namely having been the first in benevolence" (Kant 1996: 6: 455).

For Smith, resentment and gratitude both aim at mutuality or reciprocity. Resentment calls for mutual respect as equal, mutually accountable persons, whereas gratitude insinuates mutual esteem for benefactor and beneficiary as worthy occupants of their respective relational roles. Although Kant's account of gratitude agrees with Smith (and Strawson) that gratitude has a communicative function, what gratitude expresses, for Kant, is nothing mutual. Rather, it is that the beneficiary is obligated to the benefactor in a way that the benefactor is not to the beneficiary *and* that the benefactor thereby gains or manifests a merit that the beneficiary cannot have.

4. Both Kant and Smith agree, however, with Strawson's claim that gratitude is a reactive attitude with a second-personal communicative function. More recently, Coleen Macnamara has offered an account of gratitude as a reactive attitude that seems close to Smith's (Macnamara 2013). Macnamara emphasizes the "call-and-response" character of reactive attitudes in general and stresses that Strawson's category extends beyond the more usually discussed juridical examples. She holds that it is, as I would myself now put it, the recognizing and "reciprocating" character of reactive attitudes that is their most general defining feature. Reactive attitudes either make a call to which they expect or invite a response, or respond to such a call—they either reciprocate a call or call for reciprocation.

For gratitude to be a reactive attitude, it must fit this reciprocating, call-and-response structure. We should agree with Macnamara that *recognition* is fundamental to any call-and-response. Something cannot count as a "response" in the relevant second-personal sense unless it is to something the person having it *recognizes* (indeed, *acknowledges* to the other) as a call. All reactive attitudes, according to Macnamara, are "modes of recognition" that seek (reciprocal) recognition by their targets of having been thus "appropriately recognized" (Macnamara 2013: 893).

Macnamara distinguishes between attitudinal or emotional forms of "receptive recognition," and communicative (second-personal) expressions of these in speech through what she calls, following Kukla and Lance, "recognitives" (Kukla and Lance 2009). Recognizing someone "in a particular guise" (as Charlie, or as blameworthy) is a distinctive kind of speech act that is taken to express the receptively recognizing attitude.

"Negative" attitudes like blame receptively recognize their objects as blameworthy, and are publicly expressed with recognitive speech acts, like blaming. Recognition, pure and simple, might not call for a reciprocally recognizing response. But reactive attitudes do, and Macnamara holds that negative ones like blame call for their objects to respond with attitudes like guilt or remorse that implicitly recognize that blame is warranted and thereby reciprocate them.

Gratitude, for Macnamara, is a "positive" reactive attitude that receptively recognizes a benefactor as having benefited the grateful beneficiary. It can be expressed in speech with the recognitive "thank you," which publicly "discursively recognizes" the benefactor as having done one "a good turn" (Macamara 2013: 908). Like blame and resentment, gratitude calls for its own reciprocating response. According to Macnamara, the attitude that responds appropriately to gratitude is the benefactor's feeling "self-approbation" (Macnamara 2013: 909). Gratitude calls on its object (the benefactor) to have this response. And a public expression of gratitude, for example, with "thank you," calls, Macnamara says, for the benefactor's "discursively registering her self-approbation" by saying "you're welcome" (Macnamara 2013: 909).

There are recognizably Smithian elements in Macnamara's account. For both Smith and Macnamara, gratitude recognizes the merit in a benefaction and aims, in Smith's words, to make the benefactor "pleased with [their] conduct." This seems right, as far as it goes. But although saying something like "that was nice of you" can be a way of thanking someone, and although, we can agree, gratitude recognizes the goodness or merit of the benefactor's benevolent act, it seems doubtful that this can be all there is to gratitude, or even indeed, what gratitude is primarily about.

Notice first that an observer can also say "that was nice of you" with the aim of making a benefactor feel self-approbation without that being an expression of gratitude. Only a beneficiary, or someone with the requisite personal (perhaps caring) relation to them, has requisite standing to thank or have the feeling of gratitude that thanks are normally taken to express. Moreover, notice how odd "you're welcome" seems as a way of "discursively registering . . . self-approbation." "You're right; that was good of me" might more accurately register that, however inappropriate it might be otherwise.

If gratitude calls for the benefactor's self-approbation, then how are we to conceive of the original benefiting call to which gratitude itself responds? On the kind of view Smith and Macnamara suggest, gratitude recognizes the merit of the benefiting act and calls for the benefactor's self-approbation and perhaps their approval of the beneficiary as a worthy recipient. But if gratitude itself responds to a call, what in the original benefaction can constitute such a call? On such a picture, it would seem as though the benevolence must seek to call attention to its and its agent's goodness and seek confirmation of this from its beneficiary.

So viewed, the relationship that gratitude presupposes and insinuates is something like a "mutual admiration society." This is no doubt a caricature, but it does highlight the way in which both Smith and Macnamara connect gratitude to approbation and esteem. To begin to see our way to an alternative view that maintains the second-personal reactive elements of Smith's and Macnamara's, it is worth pausing a moment over the phrase "you're welcome," which earlier I noted is an odd way to express self-approbation.

To welcome someone is to *receive* them welcomingly, and one can only receive what has been sent. So a welcome is itself a response that presupposes an earlier call, which may itself also be a response to a yet earlier call. If you welcome someone into your home when they have knocked on your door, then you invite them in and make them feel welcome. A welcoming presupposes some antecedent approach or attempt at personal relating, some effort to be received by the other.[8] And your welcoming consists in taking steps to make the other feel welcome, that is, pleased to be there with you and that you are pleased to be there with them (Darwall 2011). You succeed if, and only if, there is mutual pleasure in your mutual personal relating.

This suggests that gratitude welcomes a benefit; it implicitly communicates to a benefactor one's pleasure not just to have the benefit but also to have it as a result of the benefactor's giving it *to* one. But neither is it just any way of being pleased at being a beneficiary. I might be pleased by being a beneficiary of someone's will without feeling any gratitude, at least any gratitude toward *them*. Maybe the testator is my greatest enemy, and I regard having bamboozled them into leaving me something a final victory over them. Rather, I must be pleased with it, and pleasingly receive it, in the personal relational spirit in which I take it to have been given.

If a beneficiary says thanks, or feels grateful, to a benefactor, and the benefactor replies "you're welcome," as in Macnamara's example, the benefactor thereby makes clear to the beneficiary that they welcomingly receive the personal relating that the benefaction itself initiated and the expression of gratitude furthered. Both the thanks and the welcome reception it expresses are themselves welcomingly received by the benefactor, and "you're welcome" expresses this.

Welcomingly receiving someone's gift is a way of receiving *them*, and welcoming their gratitude is a way of receiving them as well. Both are forms of personal relation in the sense that through them we give and receive ourselves to one another. "Heart" is the metaphorical term we use to express the seat of personal relating. We give from our hearts, and if others express heartfelt thanks, then that is received as sent when it is received in a heartfelt way. This points in the direction of the kind of view I want to suggest: gratitude as a second-personal attitude of the heart.

5. To see why a view of this kind is on the right track, consider the much-discussed and experimentally confirmed relation between gratitude and

well-being. It is widely noted in popular as well as in academic circles that regularly experiencing and expressing gratitude carries very significant benefits for happiness or what psychologists call "subjective well-being."[9] The classic studies are by Emmons and McCullough, in which subjects who kept "gratitude diaries," in which they regularly recorded things they were thankful for, reported substantially greater subjective well-being than control groups (Emmons and McCullough 2002, 2003, see also Peterson and Seligman 2004: 524–526, and Seligman 2002: 74–75, 2011: 30–31).

Such a striking relation between gratitude and well-being would be puzzling if gratitude consisted entirely in the reactive responses hypothesized by Kant, Smith, and Macnamara. This is perhaps most obvious with Kant's view, on which gratitude consists in a complex state of respect for a benefactor who has placed one under obligation and for the greater relative merit they have thereby earned. Being regularly reminded of a debt, indeed one can never adequately repay, together with a level of merit one cannot hope to attain, hardly seems likely to cheer one up and make one feel good about one's life prospects. Hobbes's famous remark that having received benefits one cannot hope to requite puts one into a state of "extreme hatred" toward one's creditor, wishing that one "might never see" them again is perhaps extreme (Hobbes 1994: I.xi.7). But it seems closer to the mark than that it should lead to significant increases in well-being.

Or consider Smith's view that in feeling gratitude, we feel a desire to reward a benefactor and to make them feel both pleased with themselves and with their having chosen us to benefit (thereby confirming our worth). This does seem a likelier source of happy thoughts and increased well-being. But if this were all that gratitude involves, the strength and depth of the relation that psychologists and others have found between gratitude and subjective well-being would still be surprising. And this seems true also if we think of gratitude as Macnamara proposes, which in these respects is much the same as Smith's view. For Macnamara, as for Smith, gratitude expresses a kind of esteem for the benefactor and their giving that would hardly seem to have the heartwarming effects for our affective outlook that the psychological results report.

If, however, we see gratitude as a second-personal expression of the heart, as a heartfelt, appreciative *reception* of a gift as if from the benefactor's heart, then these results are hardly surprising. So understood, gratitude responds to the gift as an opening of the benefactor's heart—"how sweet of you"—to which it appreciatively opens the beneficiary's heart in return. It is of the nature of gratitude that it can complete and help to nurture an emotional connection. Having our hearts filled and warmed in a way that connects us to others seems exactly the kind of emotional benefit that would be likely to significantly positively impact our affective outlook.[10]

Also relevant here is the signal importance of the quality of personal relationships to health, well-being, and longevity. According to Robert Waldinger, the director of the Harvard Grant and Glueck Studies, "The clearest message that we get from this 75-year study is this: Good relationships keep us happier and healthier. Period."[11] Putting these results together suggests that at least part of the reason why gratitude is so strongly connected to well-being is its role in mediating emotionally deep and centering personal relationships.

6. An account that can be (creatively) read as pointing in the direction of my proposal, albeit in a Stoic key, is Seneca's discussion of gratitude in *On Benefits* (Seneca 2011).[12] "It is in the heart," Seneca writes, "that one seeks a friend, not in the vestibule; it is there that he must be welcomed, there retained and stored in one's affections. Teach this lesson: that is gratitude" (Seneca 2011: 160).

Seneca defines a "benefit" as "a well-intentioned action that confers joy and in so doing derives joy [*gaudio*]" (Seneca 2011: 24). The benefit itself "consists not in what is done or given but rather in the intention of the giver" (Seneca 2011: 24). "What is the intention of the person who gives a benefit?" (Seneca 2011: 54). Seneca replies:

> It is to be useful to the recipient and to give him pleasure. If he achieved this objective and if his intention got through to me and we felt mutual pleasure [*gaudio*], then he got what he was aiming at. (Seneca 2011: 54)

A benefactor's intention is to do something useful to a beneficiary, aiming thereby simultaneously to confer and derive joy, which consists in a "mutual pleasure" taken in the beneficial intention. For Seneca, then, "gratitude is [at least] accompanied by joy," and may be partly constituted by joy.[13]

Joy and its contraries, sadness, sorrow, and grief, are "affairs of the heart." They concern our affective outlooks, are naturally expressed interpersonally, and often find resonance in others' hearts when they do. They are expressed, as it were, "heart to heart." Adam Smith writes:

> Grief and joy . . . strongly expressed in the look and gestures of anyone, at once affect the spectator with some degree of a like painful or agreeable emotion. A smiling face is, to everybody that sees it, a cheerful object; as a sorrowful countenance, on the other hand, is a melancholy one. (Smith 1982: 11)

"The sight of a smiling countenance," Smith says, "elevates even the pensive . . . dispos[ing] him to sympathize with and share the joy which it expresses; and he feels his heart, which with thought and care was before that shrunk and depressed, instantly expanded and elated" (Smith 1982: 36).

Opening our hearts to others with joy and grief are ways of relating to them *personally*. We thereby let others into our hearts, where they can enter only by opening their hearts to us in return. Smith notes the different ways in which empathic personal relating affects joy and sorrow, respectively:

> The sympathy, which my friends express with my joy, might, indeed, give me pleasure by enlivening that joy: but that which they express with my grief could give me none, if it served only to enliven that grief. Sympathy, however, enlivens joy and alleviates grief. (Smith 1982: 14)

It is no accident that joy and sorrow are so naturally expressed in song. Smith counts both as "passions that are naturally musical" (Smith 1982: 37). We sing songs of joy or sadness "from the heart," whether "Oh, Happy Day" or the blues.[14]

My contention is that gratitude is, like joy and grief, an attitude of the heart. If we (again, creatively) read Seneca's "joy" in this way, then his view that gratitude consists in, or is at least intimately tied to, a beneficiary's joy in their benefactor's giving intention that helps to constitute a *mutual* joy, thereby connecting them together personally, is a view of gratitude of the kind I am proposing. It would make gratitude a second-personal attitude of the heart through which we relate to another *personally*.

Despite his remark that we seek friends "in the heart," however, Seneca would almost certainly not want to be understood in this way. On my proposal, gratitude is an attitude of heartfelt personal relating. But this is distinctly not the way in which Seneca's "joy" should be understood. "*Gaudio*" is Seneca's Latin for the Greek *chara*, which the Stoics used as a technical term for being properly pleased at something that is genuinely intrinsically good.[15] As a Stoic, Seneca holds that the only intrinsic goods are virtuous intentions and actions whose value is *impersonal* rather than personal, that is, not essentially *for* some individual or other. This means that the joy that a benefactor should wish to elicit in and share with his beneficiary is their shared appreciation of the benefactor's impersonally valuable virtuous intention.

If we understand "joy" in this Stoic way, then there is nothing personal about it. A beneficiary may be *epistemically* better situated to appreciate the goodness of their benefactor's intention, but its *value* has nothing *in particular* to do with them. The benefactor's intention neither relates to nor values the beneficiary *personally*; neither can the beneficiary's joy acknowledge and welcomingly receive such a personal valuing, thereby reciprocating with a personal valuing in return. There is no reason in principle, moreover, why an observer could not equally appreciate the benefactor's virtuous intention and so share the benefactor and beneficiary's joy. Nothing makes it distinctively *theirs*.

To be sure, a benefactor's benefiting some particular beneficiary may be virtuous and properly intended because the beneficiary has some specific relation to the benefactor that not just anyone can have. Perhaps it is a familial relation or one of friendship.[16] This, however, would not make the benefiting that relates the two one of personal valuing, that is, one that expresses the significance or value that the benefactor and beneficiary have *to* one another as the particular individuals they are. From the perspective of personal relations, this would still give benefactor and beneficiary "one thought too many," as Bernard Williams famously put it (Williams 1981: 18).

It is hard to see what such impersonal joy could have distinctively to do with the attitude of gratitude, as we normally understand it. Recognizing the value of a benefiting *as a virtuously intended act*, even one in the context of a personal relationship, is something with respect to which a beneficiary has, *at best*, a special *epistemic* standing. It is, however, of the nature of gratitude that it is from the perspective of the beneficiary. The beneficiary is grateful to the benefactor for having benefited *them* in particular.

7. We can capture this essential aspect of gratitude, and explain its signal connection to well-being, if we see it as a second-personal attitude of the heart that helps to mediate personal relationships. So viewed, it is an attitude that is felt within personal relating, expressing an appreciation of the significance and value the individuals have for one another as the particular individuals they are in relation to each other.

I have argued elsewhere that other second-personal attitudes of the heart include love (of the kind that seeks reciprocation) and (personal) trust (Darwall 2016a, 2017). Love that can be requited, whether between friends or lovers, is a Strawsonian reactive attitude (Strawson 1968: 75, Abramson and Leite 2011). But unlike juridical attitudes, like blame and guilt, it does not operate within the space of the deontic. Juridical attitudes give and receive *respect*, but love is not the sort of thing that can be demanded or arise from respect for a legitimate demand. We offer love to others in the *hope* they will offer theirs in return. They are certainly not accountable for doing so. If there is a reactive attitude that appropriately responds to unrequital, it is neither blame nor resentment, but what Strawson calls "hurt feelings," whose sting is felt in the heart.

Similarly trust, at least the "personal trust" we invest in personal relationships, is also a second-personal attitude of the heart. Like love, trust implicitly involves an emotional investment in the trusted that can only be invitational. Others have standing not to accept our trust, which can be felt as an imposition when it is not welcomingly received. Imagine, for example, a stranger telling you that you had let them down because they had trusted you, say, to exercise daily. In addition to being just plain weird, it would be presumptuous.

When we trust someone in a personal way, we implicitly invite them to welcome and accept our trust, in effect, to trust it and so us in return. As with love, this involves a mutual opening with shared emotional vulnerabilities. We put ourselves in one another's "hands," as Løgstrup puts it (Løgstrup 1997: 18). Although there are of course juridical examples when a violation or betrayal of trust is a fitting object of resentment or blame, when others fail to live up to personal trust (pure and simple), more personal feelings like personal disappointment or hurt or feeling "let down" or heartsick or saddened are more appropriate. Here the injury is to the heart. Outright violations and betrayals generally involve violations of legitimate expectations that extend beyond anything that results from simply trustingly placing ourselves in others' hands.

It may be clear enough that love and trust are attitudes of the heart, but why gratitude? Gratitude responds to a benefit as a *gift* meant *for one*. Feeling grateful or thankful for a gift presupposes an implied giver. There are cases, of course, like feeling grateful for a beautiful day, or even for life itself, where a grateful person may not believe that any relevant giving person exists, not even God. But thanking is uncontroversially a speech act that requires an addressee, however indeterminate or cosmic that might be. One might ruminate on one's thankfulness or gratitude and not be addressing anyone, even oneself. But gratitude or the feeling of being thankful itself has an implicit addressee just as much as do the juridical reactive attitudes of resentment or blame, again, however indeterminate or cosmic it might be.

So gratitude is felt as a reciprocating response to a benefactor. But neither is gratitude appropriate for just any intentional benefiting. To take an obvious case, if someone gives you something you desire solely to spite his enemy who had been eyeing it also, gratitude would hardly seem apt. Giving it to *you*, you might think, meant nothing to them except as a way to get back at a foe. You were just a variable in the equation; it wasn't really about you at all.

Here is a less obvious case. Someone takes it that he has a duty to do good but actually doesn't care about whom he benefits. I don't just mean that they don't care *which* people they benefit, but that they actually don't care about people and whether they are benefited at all, though they do care about doing their duty.[17] They pick you at random and benefit you. Here again, it seems obvious that gratitude is inapt.

You might agree but think that is because gratitude cannot be for what people are morally required to do or think they are. But suppose that this person thinks not that they have a moral duty to benefit, but that they accept a Moorean theory of impersonal intrinsic value and think that people benefiting is an intrinsically good state of affairs. Though they accept this as a philosophical proposition, and so care about people benefiting, they might not care at all about the people who benefit in the sense of not wanting this for *their* sake.[18]

Here again, I think, it would be odd for beneficiaries to feel gratitude, at least, *to the benefactor*. One might still be aptly grateful that one was benefited or that the person accepted the proposition they did rather than say some misanthropic doctrine. One could, as we say, "thank one's lucky stars." But feeling grateful *to the benefactor* in this case would still seem odd. Gratitude is a response to the benefactor on account of the concern *for the benefited* they have shown.

But need this be personal concern or imply or insinuate personal relationship? What about a case where one receives something that is not intended for, and cannot express any concern for, one *in particular*, but nonetheless expresses concern for individuals of a kind one instantiates. For example, I received a scholarship in college with funds donated by someone who knew nothing about me and presumably gave what they did with no antecedent desire to initiate any relationship with me. I was just the needy student the institution selected to receive the scholarship the donor had established for needy students. I remember feeling very grateful to have the scholarship and, with the college's encouragement, was happy to write to the donor to express my thanks.[19]

In feeling gratitude to the donor, I was assuming that they cared about not just, say, equal opportunity as an abstract proposition, but also about needy would-be students. My letter of thanks expressed my personal appreciation and what the scholarship, and so the donation, meant to me. I don't believe I received a reply, so I don't know how my letter was received, but my experience working with donors over the years leads me to believe that it is not unusual for them to be moved significantly by the heartfelt gratitude of their beneficiaries and the personal significance and value that donations have for them.

Gratitude thus mediates personal connection even if the relationship does not extend beyond the "call" of the benefaction and gratitude's "response." Even if it is unexpressed, gratitude implicitly responds to the benefiting call. Moreover, feeling thankful without expression is incomplete almost by definition. And a welcomingly received heartfelt expression of personal appreciation for a benefactor's personal concern connects beneficiary and benefactor in the heart.

Second-personal attitudes of the heart—gratitude, love, and trust—all involve heartfelt giving and receiving. Ultimately, we give and receive, as we say, our*selves* and those with whom we are in affective connection, respectively. Someone is said to be "giving," not because of tangible, or even indeed other intangible, benefits they bestow, but because of their affective openness to, and emotional investment in, those to whom they are connected, whether in ongoing personal relationships or in momentary interactions. They give of themselves. This is most obvious in the case of love, but also with trust. When we trust, we put *ourselves*, as Løgstrup says, "in others' hands" (Løgstrup 1997: 18). Similarly, when we feel gratitude, we manifest and implicitly reflect back the personal significance of the other's giving to us in our welcoming reception. In this way, attitudes of the heart are ways of personally valuing their objects; they express others' value to and significance for us.

Artistic performances—for example, music, drama, and dance—provide especially vivid examples of gratitude's heartfelt, second-personal structure. Arguably, all art is intended for some appreciative audience or other, if only for the artist themselves. Artistic *performance*, however, brings artworks into an audience's *presence*, thereby making possible simultaneous human exchange between performer and audience. It is common, for example, for actors or comedians to talk about feeding off an audience's "energy." Consider even a simple thing like performers' receiving an audience's applause. In showing their appreciation for a performance, an audience is, of course, expressing their esteem, their sense of its value as a performance. But this might be done in other ways. There might be a console at every seat where each member of the audience could rate the performance, and the results might be displayed so that everyone could see. It seems obvious that this would not begin to replace the psycho-social function of applause and its reception. I conjecture that this is because the applause acknowledges not just the excellence of a performance but personal appreciation for the way the performers put *themselves* into the performance. The applause expresses gratitude; it is the audience's appreciatively giving themselves back in return. That performers so perceive, and receive, it is shown by the way they often clasp their heart and bow in response. They are grateful for the audience's gratitude, and this completes a circle of mutually reciprocating gratitude.

In 1742, Lord Tweeddale, a Scottish peer in the House of Lords, rose to praise the British effort in the War of the Austrian Succession, saying that it "demand[s] our gratitude and applause" (Johnson 1825: 189). "Gratitude," he continued, "is always due to favorable intentions," even when these are frustrated, but "applause is often paid to success, even when it has merely been the effect of chance." In the instance before them, Tweeddale went on, "just measures have been happily executed" and "blessed with success." So this is cause for applause *and* gratitude. Despite political rivalry, applause, he believes, will be forthcoming, since "neither envy nor hatred will dare to refuse their acclamations." Gratitude, however, may not, since some from "the corruption of their hearts," may be "hinder[ed] from rejoicing" and be unable to feel the "love" that genuine gratitude involves (Johnson 1825: 189–190).

Unlike esteem, which we feel as if from an observer's third-person perspective, we feel gratitude from the perspective of implicit second-personal engagement with our gratitude's object.[20] And unlike the more usually cited examples of second-personal attitudes, juridical reactive attitudes, like blame, resentment, and guilt, which presuppose mutual accountability and respect, second-personal attitudes of the heart, like love, trust, and gratitude, open the heart to another heart we hope will be open to ours in return.

Both juridical attitudes and second-personal attitudes of the heart involve distinctive ways of valuing people. Juridical attitudes implicitly acknowledge an equal dignity, or second-personal authority, that is shared by all persons alike. Second-personal attitudes of the heart, like gratitude, on the other hand, value another *personally*; they indicate their object's personal significance *for us* and thereby help mediate personal relationship with them. Through juridical reactive attitudes, we relate to others and ourselves as *one person among others*. Through gratitude and other heartfelt attitudes, we open ourselves to others as the particular individuals they are.[21]

NOTES

1 Not always, of course. In gift economies, for example, what may be in play is something more like (public) socially constructed status. Here the question of what attitudes such actions actually express may be irrelevant.

2 As Coleen Macnamara points out in Macnamara 2013. Macnamara rightly criticizes my earlier writing on reactive attitudes in Darwall (2006, 2013a, 2013b) as assimilating all reactive attitudes to the juridical model. I attempt to correct that in Darwall (2016a, 2017), and in this chapter.

3 I have put "someone" where Strawson has "others'" because Strawson also includes guilt as a "self-reactive" reactive attitude (Strawson 1968: xxx).

4 I prefer "impartial" since "impersonal" suggests a third-person observer's perspective.

5 For this way of putting it, see Kukla and Lance (2009) and Macnamara (2013).

6 The full passage is: "The object, on the contrary, which resentment is chiefly intent upon, is not so much to make our enemy feel pain in his turn, as to make him conscious that he feels it upon account of his past conduct, to make him repent of that conduct, and to make him sensible, that the person whom he injured did not deserve to be treated in that manner." Thus, although "feel pain in his turn" might suggest something at least partly retaliatory, the relevant pain is that of repentance or guilt, that is, the painful appreciation that one has done wrong (and wronged a victim). This is an implicit feeling of (recognition) respect for the victim that is naturally expressed in (respectful) apology.

7 In Darwall (2013a: 18–19), I argue against Hume's account of justice (and in favor of the second-personal aspects of Smith's) on similar grounds.

8   The relating to which a welcoming is a response may itself be a response to a (prior) relating by the welcoming person. The person who knocks on your door may have come in response to your invitation. What if someone just walks through your unlocked door? Here you might welcome them also, but it seems that is because entering a house normally requires permission or an accepted request. What if, say, a homeless person is simply sleeping on the sidewalk outside your house? Assuming that people don't require the permission of the owner of a specific house, but rather suspension of something like a town ordinance, to sleep on a public sidewalk, it would seem that one could welcome the homeless person into one's house only if they accepted an invitation to enter. I am grateful to Robert Roberts for this example.

9   The Harvard Medical School has a mental health newsletter on the topic titled *In Praise of Gratitude* (Harvard Medical School 2011). Or consider a web page titled "The 20 Best TED Talks and Videos on the Power of Gratitude": https://positivepsy-chologyprogram.com/gratitude-ted-talks-videos/.

10   Scanlon emphasizes the deep relation between gratitude and relationship. Gratitude, he says, is "not just a positive emotion but also an awareness that one's relationship with a person has been altered by some action or attitude on the person's part" (Scanlon 2008: 151). So far, however, this seems more an observation about a relationship rather than a state of mind that is itself an essential part of the relationship, part of the connecting tissue with which the relational connection is forged.

11   https://www.inc.com/melanie-curtin/want-a-life-of-fulfillment-a-75-year-har vard-study-says-to-prioritize-this-one-t.html

12   My discussion of Seneca on gratitude is very much indebted to Jennifer Daigle. I have also benefited from discussion with Brad Inwood and Will Darwall.

13   As Jennifer Daigle suggests in Daigle unpublished.

14   https://en.wikipedia.org/wiki/Oh_Happy_Day.

15   See, for example, Graver 2007: 68. I am indebted here to Brad Inwood and to discussion with Will Darwall.

16   Here again, I am indebted to Brad Inwood and Will Darwall.

17   See Lawrence Blum's depiction of "Manny" in Blum (2009: 103–106).

18   For the distinction between caring about or wanting the state of affairs of someone's benefiting and wanting this for their sake, that is, out of concern *for them*, see Darwall (2002).

19   I am actually not sure whether I wrote to the donor, an investment banker named Mills MacPherson Fries, or to his widow, since Mr. Fries had died by 1970, and I entered college in 1964.

20   Cf. Hume's distinction between the "amiable" and the "awful" virtues: "The characters of *Caesar* and *Cato*, as drawn by *Sallust*, are both of them virtuous, in the strictest sense of the word; but in a different way: Nor are the sentiments entirely the same which arise from them. The one produces love; the other esteem: The one is amiable; the other awful: We could wish to meet with the one character in a friend; the other character we wou'd be ambitious of in ourselves" (Hume 1978: 3.3.4.2)

21   I am grateful to Robert Roberts and Daniel Telech for very helpful comments.

WORKS CITED

Abramson, Kate and Adam Leite (2011). "Love as a Reactive Emotion," *The Philosophical Quarterly* 61: 673–699.

Blum, Lawrence (2009). *Friendship, Altruism, and Morality*. Boston: Routledge Revivals.

Daigle, Jennifer (unpublished). "Gratitude, Joy, Benefits."

Darwall, Stephen (1977). "Two Kinds of Respect," *Ethics* 88: 36–49.

Darwall, Stephen (2002). *Welfare and Rational Care*. Princeton, NJ: Princeton University Press.

Darwall, Stephen (2004). "Equal Dignity in Adam Smith," *Adam Smith Review* 1.

Darwall, Stephen (2006). *The Second-Person Standpoint: Morality, Respect, and Accountability*. Cambridge, MA: Harvard University Press.

Darwall, Stephen (2011). "Being With," *The Southern Journal of Philosophy* 49: 4–24. Also in Darwall 2013b.

Darwall, Stephen (2012). "Bipolar Obligation," in *Oxford Studies in Metaethics*, v., vii, ed. Russ Shafer-Landau. Oxford: Oxford University Press. (Also in Darwall 2013a.)

Darwall, Stephen (2013a). *Morality, Authority, and Law: Essays in Second-Personal Ethics I*. Oxford: Oxford University Press.

Darwall, Stephen (2013b). *Honor, History, and Relationship: Essays in Second-Personal Ethics II*. Oxford: Oxford University Press.

Darwall, Stephen (2016a). "Love's Second-Personal Character: Holding, Beholding, and Upholding" in *Love, Reason, and Morality*, eds. Esther Kroeker and Katrien Schaubroeck. New York: Routledge.

Darwall, Stephen (2016b). "Making the 'Hard' Problem of Moral Normativity Easier," in *Weighing Reasons*, eds., Errol Lord and Barry Maguire. Oxford: Oxford University Press.

Darwall, Stephen (2017). "Trust as a Second-Personal Attitude (of the Heart)," in *The Philosophy of Trust*, Paul Faulkner and Thomas Simpson, eds. Oxford: Oxford University Press.

Darwall, Stephen (2018a). "Empathy and Reciprocating Attitudes," in *Forms of Fellow Feeling: Empathy, Sympathy, Concern, and Moral Agency*, eds., Neil Roughley and Thomas Schramme. Cambridge: Cambridge University Press.

Darwall, Stephen (2018b). "Contempt as an Other-Characterizing, 'Hierarchizing' Attitude," in *The Moral Psychology of Contempt*, ed. Michelle Mason. Lanham, MD: Rowman & Littlefield.

Emmons, Robert A. and Michael E. McCullough (2002). "The Grateful Disposition: A Conceptual and Empirical Topography. *Journal of Personality and Social Psychology* 82: 112–127.

Emmons, Robert A. and Michael E. McCullough (2003). "Counting Blessings versus Burdens: An Empirical Investigation of Gratitude and Well-Being in Daily Life," *Journal of Personality and Social Psychology* 84: 377–389.

Graver, Margaret (2007). *Stoicism and Emotion*. Chicago, IL: University of Chicago Press.

Harvard Medical School (2011). *Mental Health Newsletter: In Praise of Gratitude.*
https://www.health.harvard.edu/newsletter_article/in-praise-of-gratitude
Hobbes, Thomas (1994). *Leviathan*, ed. Edwin Curley. Indianapolis, IN: Hackett
Publishing Co., Inc. References to part, chapter, and paragraph number.
Hume, David (1978). *A Treatise of Human Nature*, ed L. A. Selby-Bigge, second edi-
tion, with rev. P. H. Nidditch. Oxford: Oxford University Press, 1978. References
are to book, part, section, and paragraph numbers.
Johnson, Samuel (1825). *The Works of Samuel Johnson in Nine Volumes.* Oxford:
Talbys and Wheeler.
Kant, Immanuel (1996). *Practical Philosophy*, trans. and ed. Mary J. Gregor. Cam-
bridge: Cambridge University Press. References are to page numbers of the Preus-
sische Akademie edition.
Kukla, Rebecca and Mark Lance (2009). *"Yo!" and "Lo!": The Pragmatic Topogra-
phy of the Space of Reasons.* Cambridge, MA: Harvard University Press.
Løgstrup, Knud Ejler (1997). *The Ethical Demand.* Notre Dame, IN: University of
Notre Dame Press.
Macnamara, Coleen (2013). "'Screw You!' and 'Thank You," *Philosophical Studies*
165: 893–914.
Peterson, Christopher and Martin E. P. Seligman (2004). *Character Strengths and
Virtues: A Handbook and Classification.* Oxford: Oxford University Press.
Roberts, Robert C. (1988). "What an Emotion Is: A Sketch," *The Philosophical
Review* 97: 193–209.
Scanlon, T. M. (2008). *Moral Dimensions.* Cambridge, MA: Harvard University
Press.
Seligman, Martin E. P. (2002). *Authentic Happiness.* New York: The Free Press.
Seligman, Martin E. P. (2011). *Flourish.* New York: The Free Press.
Seneca, Lucius Annaeus (2011). *On Benefits*, trans. Miriam Griffin and Brad Inwood.
Chicago: University of Chicago Press.
Strawson, P. F. (1968). "Freedom and Resentment," in *Studies in the Philosophy of
Thought and Action*, ed. P. F. Strawson. London: Oxford University Press.
Williams, Bernard (1981). *Moral Luck.* Cambridge: Cambridge University Press.

Chapter 8

Gratitude and Resentment: Some Asymmetries[1]

Justin Coates

A USEFULLY OPPOSED PAIR?

In "Freedom and Resentment," P. F. Strawson (2008) invites us to theorize about moral responsibility, not from the detached perspective of abstruse metaphysical speculation, but from the lived perspective of agents who are concerned with the quality of will that others display toward us (and toward others) in their actions. What's significant for moral responsibility, from this perspective, is the emotional responses to others' behavior, and to the quality of will that that behavior manifests—a set of responses Strawson calls the "reactive attitudes." Strawson himself focuses on the titular response of resentment, and on its vicarious and self-regarding analogs: indignation and guilt. But along the way he also suggests a set of positive reactive attitudes. Among these we can include emotions like gratitude, esteem, and pride; Strawson also mentions forgiveness and love, and some working in his wake have been quick to include trust as well.[2] But about these positive emotions, Strawson has little to say beyond the simple observation that gratitude and resentment, like praise and blame more generally, constitute "a usefully opposed pair," (2008, 7).

How useful is this pairing? There are surely some similarities, even deep similarities, between these emotions. Perhaps the most illuminating parallel that we can draw between these emotions—one that I've hinted at above—is that despite appearances, gratitude isn't a response to good deeds or benefits another has provided for us, and resentment isn't a response to the harms others have done us. Instead, each of these emotions is narrowly identifying a circumscribed set of benefits and harms and responding to those. In the case of gratitude, it's *beneficence that manifests goodwill* that makes the emotion fitting or deserved. After all, if someone unknowingly or accidentally helps you, then you probably won't feel grateful to them (nor should you), though perhaps some relief or vague sense of appreciation is fitting. Strawson puts it as follows:

> If someone's actions help me to some benefit I desire, then I am benefited in any case; but if he intended them so to benefit me because of his general goodwill towards me, I shall reasonably feel a gratitude which I should not feel at all if the benefit was an incidental consequence, unintended or even regretted by him, of some plan of action with a different aim (Strawson 2008, 6).

So too, in the case of resentment, it's *harms done with callous indifference or ill will* that makes the emotion fitting or deserved. If someone unknowingly or accidentally harms you, say, they trod on your foot when the subway jerked awkwardly, you'll feel quite different about that pain than if you see them bring about the pain intentionally *even if* the pain to your foot is qualitatively identical in these two cases. Strawson therefore seems clearly right to think that it's not benefits or harms per se that make gratitude and resentment fitting. In this key way, these emotions are *usefully* opposed to one another.

A second way in which these two emotions are usefully opposed is that they each seemed to be at least incipiently communicative. This point goes back at least to Adam Smith (1976). In his *Theory of Moral Sentiments*, he offered the following accounts of gratitude and resentment.

Gratitude

What gratitude chiefly desires is not only to make the benefactor feel *pleasure* in his turn, but to make him *conscious that he meets with this reward on account of his past conduct*, to make him pleased with that conduct, and to satisfy him that the person upon whom he bestowed his good offices was not unworthy of them.

Resentment

The object . . . which resentment is chiefly intent upon, is not so much to make our enemy feel *pain* in his turn, as to make him *conscious that he feels it upon account of his past conduct*, to make him repent of that conduct, and to make him sensible, that the person whom he injured did not deserve to be treated in that manner. (Smith, *TMS*, II.iii.10–11; emphases added)

Notice that on Smith's account, these emotions don't just seek to cause pleasure and pain in those to whom they are fittingly directed. They also seek to communicate something to that person: that their motives were appreciated (in the case of gratitude) or spurned (in the case of resentment).[3] So although the content gratitude and resentment aim at communicating are opposed to one another, the fact that each of these emotions aims at expressing our attitudes about the quality of others' will is another point of deep similarity.

Despite these two similarities, however, there are some significant differences in the emotions of gratitude and resentment. And if we acknowledge these differences, then what we'll find is that the role these emotions play in our lives as morally responsible agents is not equal but opposite. Gratitude and resentment are, in fact, asymmetrical in at least three key ways: in their fittingness conditions, in the norms that govern their expression, and in their value for human relationships. An adequate moral psychology of these emotions will therefore require us to move beyond superficial similarities in gratitude and resentment and instead attend to their deep differences.

ASYMMETRICAL RESPONSIBILITY

Theories of moral responsibility often identify it with deserving praise- and blame-manifesting attitudes like gratitude and resentment. Theories of moral responsibility also tend to treat the conditions under which agents deserve gratitude and resentment as being symmetrical. That is, theories of moral responsibility tend to hold that agents must be connected to their actions in just the same way so as to merit both gratitude and resentment. However, this is a mistake. The agential capacities that underwrite an agent's being deserving of praise-manifesting attitudes like gratitude are distinct from and not symmetrical to the agential capacities that underwrite an agent's being deserving of blame-manifesting attitudes like resentment. That is, the *fittingness* conditions of these two emotions differ in more than in the valence of their representational content.

This idea—that the conditions of moral responsibility are irreducibly asymmetrical—is not new. Susan Wolf's (1980) argument for this *asymmetry thesis* starts with the idea that an agent's status as morally responsible for her conduct is grounded in her ability to recognize and respond to what's "True" and "Good." In the case of a praiseworthy action—for example, one for which an agent would be deserving of gratitude—the agent responds to the True and the Good. And in the case of a blameworthy action—one for which an agent would be deserving of resentment—the agent fails to respond to the True and the Good. Yet, if an agent is genuinely *unable* to respond to the True and the Good, then, Wolf argues, her failure to do so does not redound to her in the way that actions must if an agent is to be morally responsible for that action. So in order to be deserving of resentment for transgressing moral norms, Wolf concludes, an agent must be able to do other than she actually does.

To this point, Wolf's story about the way an agent must be involved with her action doesn't look any different than other so-called leeway theorists, who also emphasize the ability to do otherwise as being necessary for moral responsibility. However, Wolf points out—rightly I think—that the intuition that agents must be able to do other than they actually do doesn't "stick" quite as hard in the case of praiseworthy action. Nor should it. After all, if an agent acts in a way so as to be deserving of praise-manifesting attitudes like gratitude, then she has *in fact* responded to the True and the Good. The ability to *fail* to do so, which is precisely what the ability to do otherwise secures in these circumstances, is simply the ability act contrary to the True and the Good. But surely *this* ability contributes nothing that serves to underwrite an agent's status as being morally responsible.[4] Consequently, Wolf reasons, although the ability to do otherwise is necessary for deserved resentment, it is not a necessary condition on being deserving of gratitude. The conditions under which agents are praise- and blame-worthy are thus conceptually distinct.

More recently, Dana K. Nelkin (2011) has also argued for the asymmetry thesis. Like Wolf, Nelkin also thinks that unless an agent is able to do otherwise, she cannot be deserving of blame-manifesting attitudes like resentment. So too, she thinks that this ability is not required for agents to be deserving of attitudes like gratitude. For Nelkin, however, the explanation of the asymmetry is different. Although she agrees with Wolf that the ability to do otherwise when you're able to get it right doesn't contribute to an agent's status as being morally responsible, she also goes deeper in explaining why this is so. The reason for the asymmetry, according to Nelkin, is connected to the idea that *ought implies can*—the thesis that an agent can't be obligated to perform some action unless she is able to do it. The contrary to this thesis thus holds that if an agent is unable to perform some action, then she is not obligated to do so. From there, it's a quick move to the thought that if an agent cannot perform an action, then she cannot be blameworthy for failing to do so. So if an agent who lacks the ability to do otherwise acts in a morally objectionable way, then she cannot be blameworthy for failing to act in a morally permissible way.

However, there's no similarly quick way to move from *ought implies can* to the idea that agents can be deserving of praise-manifesting attitudes like gratitude only if they are able to do otherwise. The principle *ought implies can* itself can't supply the link. But interestingly, Nelkin argues, none of the principles that *could* do so are independently motivated or plausible.[5] As a result, she concludes that an agent can be deserving of gratitude even if she lacks the ability to do otherwise. So she too arrives at the asymmetry thesis.

So far, so good. It looks like Wolf and Nelkin have given us good grounds for denying the symmetry between the conditions under which agents are deserving of gratitude and resentment, respectively. But this is perhaps too quick. After all, it's controversial that the ability to do otherwise is *ever* required for morally responsible agency—even in the case of blameworthy agency.[6] And if this is right, then the fact that Wolf and Nelkin have successfully argued that praise-manifesting attitudes like gratitude don't require the ability to do otherwise does nothing to show that gratitude and resentment aren't symmetrical in their fittingness conditions.[7] This suggests that Wolf and Nelkin have provided us with only a much weaker argument: *if* the ability to do otherwise is ever required for morally responsible agency, it's required only in the case of blameworthiness. If so, the importance of their defense of the asymmetry thesis looks diminished—it's something for "leeway" theorists to worry about, but not germane to the debate more generally.

Perhaps this is right, but it undersells Wolf's and Nelkin's insights. Even if it turns out that they're wrong to think the ability to do otherwise is sometimes required for morally responsible agency, their arguments might nevertheless point to a modified version of the asymmetry thesis that doesn't locate the difference between praise- and blame-worthiness in the ability to do otherwise. That is, Wolf and Nelkin might be right about the asymmetry thesis even if they're wrong about what explains why the conditions under which an agent deserves gratitude differ from the conditions under which an agent deserves resentment.

THE ASYMMETRY THESIS REFINED

The real asymmetry between the conditions under which agents can deserve praise-manifesting and blame-manifesting attitudes is not grounded in a distinct role that the ability to do otherwise plays in agents' blameworthiness. To discover where exactly it *is* located, consider the following cases of apparently altruistic helping behavior.

Broken Glass 1

Rob's thirsty, and he sees a glass across the room. Since she's closer to it than he is, Rob asks Pearl to hand him the glass so that he can pour himself some water. Pearl notices that the glass is broken, so she gets up and gets another glass that isn't broken and takes the unbroken one to Rob instead. Having a functional glass into which he can now pour water, Rob is genuinely grateful to Pearl and expresses his gratitude by telling her that he appreciates her help.

Crying Child 1

In a daycare filled with crying children, Julie sees Maggie crying and inconsolable. She brings Maggie her favorite toy and sits with her, gently touching her and waiting with her until she feels better. Cynthia sees this, and she is very appreciative that Julie took care of Maggie, since she's got two other crying children to deal with. Later, when she gets a free moment, Cynthia makes sure to thank Julie.

In these cases, it seems appropriate for Rob and Cynthia to feel and express gratitude toward Pearl and Julie, respectively. No doubt, there is some instrumental reason for this: by expressing their gratitude, Rob and Cynthia make it more likely that they are helped in the future. But I don't think this fully explains why gratitude is the fitting response in this case; independently of whether Rob and Cynthia stand to benefit from Pearl's and Julie's respective help in the future, there seems to be something *intrinsically* good about gratitude in these situations. In particular, it seems that Pearl and Julie *deserve* Rob's and Cynthia's gratitude, and giving people what they deserve is itself a good thing whether or not it leads to better future outcomes. (Of course, this final point leaves open whether you *should* all-things-considered give people what they deserve.) Now, because Pearl and Julie each seem to deserve Rob's and Cynthia's respective gratitude, it seems fair to conclude that they are each morally responsible for their respective actions. After all, only morally responsible agents can genuinely deserve praising attitudes like gratitude, appreciation, and esteem. And with no obvious excusing conditions present, barring something that (putatively) undercuts moral responsibility for all agents (e.g., causal determinism), who could doubt that Pearl and Julie are morally responsible for their action?[8]

Now consider the following two cases of disrespectful harming behavior.

Broken Glass 2

Rob's thirsty, and he sees a glass across the room. Since she's closer to it than he is, Rob asks Pearl to hand him the glass so that he can pour himself some water. Pearl notices that the glass is broken, but she simply doesn't care about that. And although she could have easily gotten a glass that wasn't broken, she just takes him the one he asked for instead. Once he sees that the glass is broken, Rob asks Pearl if she saw that it was broken and if so, why she didn't get him a functional one instead. She replies (bluntly, it seems to Rob) that she did see that it was broken but that that was the glass he asked for. Rob finds this annoying and is a bit resentful toward Pearl as a result.

Crying Child 2

In a daycare filled with crying children, Julie sees Maggie crying and inconsolable. She takes Maggie her favorite toy, but just as Maggie is about to grab it, Julie pulls it away and tells her that she can't have it. Cynthia sees this, and she is very upset that Julie made Maggie feel even worse. Later, when she gets a free moment, Cynthia makes sure to let Julie know that that kind of behavior is objectionable.

Here again we have two agents performing actions that we ordinarily regard as being blameworthy. In *BG2 and CC2*, Pearl and Julie act in ways that are apparently disrespectful, and since resentment is a response to interpersonal disrespect, it seems that it's fitting here. It seems, on its face, that Pearl and Julie *deserve* Rob's and Cynthia's respective resentment. This means that to the extent I've described them here, it seems that a perfectly symmetrical response is warranted in each of these two sets of cases.

But suppose now that you discover that Pearl and Julie in *BG1* and *CC1* are just toddlers whose behaviors are based on recent empirical work demonstrating young children to be quite capable of performing spontaneous helping behavior that is sensitive to the particulars of the context in a way that suggests the aid is not accidental but is instead motivated by an intention to help. Specifically, "Pearl" is a composite of three years old children discussed in Alia Martin and Kristina R. Olsen's (2013) work in developmental psychology, and "Julie" is a composite of even younger children discussed in Knafo, Zahn-Waxler, Hulle, Robinson, and Rhee's (2008) work.[9] Knowing this, do you still think that Pearl and Julie are morally responsible agents who are praiseworthy for their actions in *BG1* and *CC1* and blameworthy for their actions in *BG2* and *CC2*?

The dominant view in the philosophical literature is that young children, like Pearl and Julie, are exempt from moral responsibility and so not deserving of praise-manifesting attitudes in *BG1* or *CC1*. Nor are they deserving of blame-manifesting attitudes in *BG2* or *CC2*. The thought here, which (again) was first articulated by Strawson but which has been embraced widely in the interim, is simply that there is a suite of capacities that agents must possess if they are to be participants in our responsibility practices, and of course, all young children/toddlers lack these capacities. Consequently, they are not "in the ballpark" of morally responsible agency and so they are neither praiseworthy (or blameworthy) for what they do, nor they genuinely *deserve* gratitude or its expressions (or resentment and its expressions).

Although it's clear that Strawson takes youthfulness to be an exempting condition, he does appreciate that this is a complicated issue. He notes, for example, that thinking young children to be exempted from responsibility doesn't mean that we shouldn't respond to children's acts *as if* they were responsible for them. Such responses, he rightly claims, are the basis of their moral development and inculcation in the moral community:

> Parents of young children are dealing with creatures who are potentially and increasingly capable both of holding, and being objects of, the full range of human and moral attitudes, but are not yet truly capable of either. The treatment of such creatures must therefore represent a kind of compromise, constantly shifting in direction, between objectivity of attitude and developed human attitudes. Rehearsals insensibly modulate towards true performances. . . . In this matter of young children, it is essentially a borderline, penumbral area that we move in. (Strawson 2008, 20–21)

With young children, we rehearse and encourage them to act in this or that fashion as a way of teaching them about others' demand for goodwill or reasonable regard. These rehearsals, however, eventually become the "real deal," and so, from Strawson's point of view, the general practice of engaging with our children in this way might be ultimately justified. But although this all seems right, what's especially striking here is that while Strawson is sensitive to the possibility that young children's agency can be an "essentially a borderline" case of responsible agency, Strawson nevertheless insists that young children are not capable of being (appropriate) objects of the "human" attitudes (i.e., the reactive attitudes, which is a class of attitudes that includes gratitude, resentment, esteem, indignation, etc.).

There's a tension here, though. For if we take seriously Strawson's claim that young children are a borderline case, then it would seem plausible to think that even if they were not apt targets for the *full range* of human reactive attitudes, they could be apt targets of (at least) *some* of these attitudes. However, Strawson seems to ignore this possibility, and he just proceeds, despite his cursory acknowledgment of the complexities of these issues, as if being the appropriate object of these human attitudes is an all or nothing matter. This is evident in his subsequent claim that "the punishment of a child is both like and unlike the punishment of an adult" (Strawson 2008, 20). But again punishment, along with the punitive attitudes it expresses (e.g., resentment and indignation), is just one (rather extreme) feature of our moral responsibility practices. There is conceptual space, then, for thinking that an agent—yes, even a child—could be the proper (i.e., deserving) object of some of the human attitudes even if she is not deserving of all such attitudes.

This seems clear in the cases at hand. In *BG1* and *CC1*, Pearl and Julie do good things for good reasons, and in so doing, they show an incipient appreciation for others' moral significance. These are the very things that make gratitude a fitting response to another agent's behavior. It's true, of course, that as they grow up, Pearl and Julie will develop into much more sophisticated agents—agents who are much better able to recognize and respond to normatively significant considerations. But this doesn't mean that their very rudimentary understanding of what's important in these particular cases isn't a real achievement on their parts.

On the other hand, Pearl's and Julie's respective failures in *BG2* and *CC2* don't seem grounded in a degree of competence that's ordinarily presupposed for blame-manifesting emotions, in either moral or non-moral domains. This is because a full degree of competence in any domain requires more than some rudimentary skill and success in that domain. It requires that the person have the more general capacity to conform their conduct *consistently* to the standards that are normative within that domain. That is, something approaching full competency is required in order to deserve real blame for failures in a domain, and that requires a general capacity for consistent success within that domain. That's why, for example, we're prepared to praise a random, untrained bystander who saves another person's life at the scene of a car wreck, even though we wouldn't be as prone to blame her if she had failed. On the other hand, if the bystander were a trained doctor, although we'd praise her for any successes she had, we'd also be more disposed to blame her if she failed. And this is because we assume that medical professionals have a general capacity to recognize and act consistently in the ways that are required by the medical needs of their patient.

The lesson here is that it's something more basic than the ability to do otherwise that explains the asymmetry in the conditions under which agents can deserve praise- and blame-manifesting emotions, since this asymmetry will arise *even if* we assume that causal determinism is false and that our actions are undetermined by forces outside of our own control. What explains the asymmetry is simply that when one's action manifests an incipient competence in some domain, then one will be deserving of domain-specific forms of praise. In the moral domain, that regularly takes the form of gratitude. It's for this reason that Pearl and Julie genuinely deserve gratitude in the first set of vignettes. However to deserve domain-specific forms of blame, you must possess *more* than an incipient degree of competence in that domain: you must have a general capacity to recognize and be moved by the considerations that are relevant to that domain in a consistently successful way. Pearl and Julie (and indeed, all toddlers) lack that capacity, and so, they do cannot deserve moral blame, which paradigmatically takes the form of resentment.

Wolf and Nelkin had real insight: there is an asymmetry in the conditions of moral responsibility. That asymmetry is explained by different agential facts than the one that they take it to be explained by, but the take-home lesson is the same. The conditions under which agents are deserving of praise-manifesting emotions are not isomorphic to the conditions under which they are deserving of blame-manifesting emotions.

AN ASYMMETRY OF MORAL STANDING

Gratitude and resentment are also asymmetrical in their normative significance. In particular, the reasons to express gratitude are typically much less prone to defeat than the reasons to express resentment. What this means practically is that it will more frequently be true that we *should* all-things-considered express gratitude than that we *should* all-things-considered express resentment. Resentment is, I will argue, more rationally optional, and as a result, its reasons are more commonly defeated by nondesert-based considerations (e.g., generosity and mercy).

One clear difference here is that expressions of resentment generally require some kind of "moral standing" that expressions of gratitude do not. For example, if I've been late for our coffee meetings several times in the past, then it seems I have a reason not to be upset the one time you're late even if you have no good excuse for being late. Or, if I convinced you to grab a beer after work instead of going to the store to get the things your partner needed, then it seems I have a reason not to blame you for breaking your promise. In each of these cases, facts about me give me reason to refrain from expressing blame-manifesting emotions even though you apparently deserve them.

In addition to cases in which my own moral turpitude gives me reason to refrain from expressing blame-manifesting emotions, I might sometimes have reason to refrain from expressing those emotions if I'm not suitably related to you, say, in cases in which your transgression is none of my business. Alternately, I might be ignorant of whether you're really morally responsible for your action. For example, it might be unclear from your action whether you had a bad motive or whether you really knew what you were doing. In such cases, even if unbeknownst to me you were displaying ill will, it seems that I have a reason to refrain from expressing resentment—at the very least, I have reason to gather more information before criticizing or castigating you.[10]

Of course, these reasons might sometimes be outweighed, so that all things considered I should express my resentment toward you. If a lot is at stake in my failing to express my resentment—if, for example, you trust me a great deal, and it's only my rebuke that will get you to mend your ways—then the fact that I would be hypocritical in expressing blame-manifesting attitudes is itself outweighed. But these cases, it seems to me, aren't standard. Typically, when the hypocrite refrains from blaming, nothing of value is lost. In fact, I suspect that most of the time, when a hypocrite or someone who's complicit in wrongdoing refrains from blaming the wrongdoer, things are better off, since such blame frequently engenders a kind of defensiveness on the part of the wrongdoer that immunizes them from the truth of their moral failing. They get so vexed by the source of the criticism that they fail to appreciate its content. Yet even if such cases are more common than I take them to be, the more basic point I want to make stands: there are a range of *pro tanto* reasons to refrain from expressing blame-manifesting attitudes in cases of hypocrisy, complicity, ignorance, and so forth.

Notice that if there are reasons to refrain from expressing gratitude to someone who deserves it, the cases are not parallel. After all, what exactly would a reverse hypocrite be? Someone who freely benefits you and then turns around and expresses praise-manifesting attitudes toward you when you freely benefit them? *The nerve of some people!* Jokes aside, the fact that someone would be "reverse hypocritical" were they to express gratitude toward you is no reason at all for them to refrain from doing so. Indeed, the fact that we don't even have a name for such a "vice" already suggests that it is no such thing. So too, someone who is complicit in your good deeds has no reason to refrain from expressing gratitude when those good deeds have beneficial consequences for her. Nor do expressions of gratitude seem concerned with "its being your business."[11]

WEIGHTING GRATITUDE AND RESENTMENT

Expressions of gratitude either do not presume special standing in the way that expressions of resentment do, or, if they do presume standing, the scope of that presumption is different in the case of each emotion. The considerations that bear on the expressions of gratitude and resentment are thus distinct from one another.

The considerations that bear on expressions of gratitude are different than the reasons for resentment in another way as well. Imagine that someone has just harmed you and that they're morally responsible for doing so. In such a case, resentment is deserved. Additionally, this person might also deserve rebuke or criticism, which serve to manifest our resentment. But the fact that they deserve these expressions of resentment isn't sufficient to guarantee that you *must* rebuke or criticize them—that a failure to express your resentment would constitute a bit of wrongdoing on your part. We've already considered how lacking the standing to blame might provide you with a reason to *refrain* from blaming that would defeat desert-based reasons to have blame-manifesting emotions. But there might be other reasons to refrain from blame that have nothing to do with your own moral failings, or your lack of a standing relationship to the wrongdoer, or your ignorance. You might simply not be concerned with the harm in question. Or perhaps it leads you to pity the wrongdoer, who is acting from a place of pathetic insecurity. Here, you might decide to refrain from blaming *just because* that's how you feel. Or you might be tired or distracted or. . . . In such cases, one might take a more objective attitude towards a wrongdoer due to what P. F. Strawson aptly called "the strains of involvement" (Strawson 2008, 10).

In none of these cases, is it obvious at all that you've acted objectionably. A person who systematically fails to resent those who harm her may, of course, be servile, and this is perhaps objectionable. But she might also be generous or graceful, and these qualities are in no way objectionable. This tells us something important about the weight of reasons to resent (or to express resentment) those who deserve it: they aren't particularly weighty. Sure, they're weighty enough that you can't systemically ignore them on the grounds that you take your own value to be insignificant. So too, they're plausibly weighty enough that in cases in which you've suffered a great injustice, resentment might be best all-things-considered.[12] But beyond that, particularly in the vast majority of small-scale wrongs done to us (the minor indignities of dealing with bad customer service or a rude colleague or inconsiderate drivers or . . .), they don't seem to be decisive, such that it would be objectionable to refrain from resentment or its expressions. Indifference, boredom, distraction, exhaustion, and virtue might all give one reason to ignore reasons for resentment such that you wouldn't be subject to rational or moral criticism for failing to resent.

Yet this isn't true of gratitude. In fact, just the opposite is true: failing to be grateful or express gratitude when it is deserved is almost always a failing on the part of the ungrateful individual. There are, of course, cases in which it's not essential that one experiences gratitude or that one expresses it, even when gratitude would be deserved, but those cases are the exceptions rather than the rule. In particular, it seems that the "strains of involvement" no longer serve as an excuse or justification for failing to be grateful. A more objective attitude is *permissible* when resentment is deserved because to the extent that incurs harm, you are the one bearing it. However, in the typical case of deserved gratitude, taking an objective attitude involves you forcing your benefactor to lose out on what she deserves, and it's implausible that you, as the benefited party, have the standing to permissibly impact your benefactor in this way. What this means, then, is that reasons for gratitude are typically weightier than reasons for resentment; they cannot be so easily ignored or outweighed without fault.

It's worth pausing to note here that this point doesn't generalize to other blame-manifesting emotions. If one generally refuses to get indignant in the face of oppression, then the fact that one is tired or distracted or not particularly concerned with the wrongdoing does little or nothing to tell against the weight of reasons for indignation. So too, reasons for guilt are similarly weighty. The explanation for this is simple. It's by and large *my place* to decide how to best respond to wrongs done to me. This isn't always true, but in the case of ordinary wrongs of the sort that commonly occur, we have a great deal of latitude in how we respond. However, in the case of wrongs done to others, either by a third party or by ourselves, it's not our place to decide how best to respond. In cases in which a victim is present, she might direct us in how to do this. But this isn't generally true. And it seems we have reason to treat indignation and guilt as the default response for wrongs done to others in the absence of clear indication that some other form of response would better serve the situation. This perhaps means that the normative significance of resentment is idiosyncratic in a way that's belied by the vast majority of contemporary theorizing on praise- and blame-manifesting emotions suggests. The ease with which the strains of involvement serve to undercut its reasons' force indicates that we'd do well to shift our focus from it as a paradigm "reactive emotion" and turn instead toward emotions, like gratitude and indignation, that although not such a usefully opposed pair, seem to be the source of weightier reasons.

AN ASYMMETRY OF VALUE

Finally, I want briefly to suggest and consider a way in which the value of gratitude and the value of resentment do not track one another in any neat way. At first, this claim might seem surprising, since each of these emotions and their attendant expressions are *instrumentally* valuable. Gratitude and its expressions serve as the stitching that help to keep our social fabric free from rips and tears. Resentment and its expressions can serve to repair the social fabric by enjoining wrongdoers to recognize the badness of their conduct and repudiate the motives that lead them to act in that way. Both of these states of affairs are unquestionably good for our lives together.[13] So in this way, it seems like the value of gratitude and the value of resentment track one another fairly closely.

There is, however, an important difference in their value that we can see when we consider the role that these emotions play in relationships of the sort that we find most meaningful, say, close friendships. It's necessary for the possibility of a friendship that the parties to the friendship benefit one another out of genuine goodwill for the person and their good (and not exclusively because the other is *owed* that benefit). And it's also necessary for the possibility of a friendship that in the wake of such beneficence, a friend will regularly respond with warm gratitude. More simply, it's part of the normative ideal of friendship that we experience and express gratitude regularly with our friends.

This is not true of resentment. Resentment is made fitting by ill will, and while it's plausibly true that if your friend shows you ill will, you'll have reason to respond to her with resentment, there's nothing about the very ideal of friendship itself that involves parties to a friendship treating one another with ill will. It's a sad fact about us that we aren't always able to extend goodwill and warmth toward those we love, that sometimes we're indifferent toward them, callous, and even in some cases, unconscionably cruel. What this means, however, is that resentment is *only* instrumentally valuable within our most cherished relationships; it's at best a necessary evil that stands at watch in the event that we're not the friends that we could or should be.

But there is a further final value that attaches to gratitude and its expressions. Since gratitude and its expressions are in part constitutive of the ideal of friendship, they are an essential part of an organic unity that itself has a great deal of final value. That is, we ordinarily regard a friendship as something that is not only instrumentally valuable but also has final value. A friendship is a composite of many more basic things. Since gratitude and its expressions are essential members of the composite that serves as the normative ideal of friendship, they share in the value of friendship itself.

Even if this is true, it leaves open that gratitude in isolation is of no more final value than resentment. So to conclude, I'll supply an argument that the final value of gratitude is greater than the final value of resentment. First, let's suppose that A deserves resentment to the same degree that B deserves gratitude. Second, let's assume that there are both instrumental and non-instrumental (final) reasons for resenting A and being grateful to B. Let's also assume that the instrumental value of resenting A is identical to the instrumental value of being grateful to B. If resentment and gratitude have the same final value, then it would follow that, were we in a situation in which it was possible only to resent A or be grateful to B (but not both), we could be indifferent about how to respond and choose either option. But this seems implausible. A world with n instrumental goods and the good of being grateful to someone who genuinely deserves gratitude seems *better*—more worthy of actualization—than a world with n instrumental goods and the good of resenting someone who genuinely deserves resentment. Perhaps this is just because gratitude is non-contingently connected to pleasure, which has significant final value and resentment is non-contingently connected to suffering, which has significant disvalue. But perhaps it's also because being grateful when gratitude is deserved just is *better* than being resentful when resentment is deserved. In either case, it seems dubious that the final value of resenting someone who deserves it matches the final value of being grateful when gratitude is deserved.

CONCLUSION

The conditions under which gratitude and resentment are deserved are not symmetrical; the considerations that undercut one's standing to resent don't obviously bear on one's standing to be grateful; reasons for being grateful are apparently much less easily outweighed than reasons for resentment; and the final value of gratitude is, at least in part, grounded in considerations that do not apply to resentment. However useful it might be to treat these emotions as a pair in some contexts does not widely generalize. And given these significant asymmetries, I think we'd do well to theorize less programmatically—talking casually about the "reactive attitudes" as a neat set, where the only differences arise at the level of to whom they are responses. Instead we should consider each of these emotions on its own, even if that means that our preferred theories of responsible agency no longer fit so nicely together.

NOTES

1 For helpful feedback on these ideas, I'd like to thank Chris Franklin, Dana Gutierrez, Claire Katz, Ben Mitchell-Yellin, Garrett Pendergraft, Linda Radzik, Philip Swenson, Matt Talbert, and Neal Tognazzini. I'd also like to thank the other contributors to this volume for their comments on an early version of the chapter. And I especially want to thank the editors of this volume, Robert Roberts and Daniel Telech, who put a lot of work into giving me invaluable feedback on drafts of this chapter.

2 For example, Helm (2017).

3 In addition to Smith, many others have found these emotions to have some communicative aspect to them: Strawson (2008), Gary Watson (1987), Stephen Darwall (2006), Michael McKenna (2012), and Coleen Macnamara (2013).

4 It might be that the ability to act contrary to the True and the Good is valuable in the following way. If an agent is able to do otherwise and they are severely tempted to do so, then it seems that they are in some sense *more* praiseworthy for refraining from doing so than they would be had they not been able to do otherwise. This seems to follow from what Holly Smith (1991) has called the "battle citation" model of praise. So the ability do otherwise might not be relevant to *whether* you are praiseworthy for doing good for the right reasons, even if it is relevant to the *degree* to which you are praiseworthy for doing good for the right reasons.

5 This betrays the intricacy of Nelkin's powerful argument. For our purposes, however, it's enough to see that she's on the right track.

6 See Frankfurt (1969).

7 See Fischer and Ravizza (1998).

8 For the most thorough defense of desert-entailing moral responsibility skepticism, see Derk Pereboom (2001). However, despite the power of Pereboom's account, for the purposes of this chapter, I must simply take for granted that many human agents are responsible for at least some of their actions.

9 Pearl and Julie as described in *BG2* and *CC2* are simply meant to be parallel to their counterparts in *BG1* and *CC1*. *BG2* and *CC2* do not, however, come from relevantly similar cases in the developmental literature (though any parent of a toddler will be happy to supply you with cases of this general sort).

10 I argue for this in more detail in Coates (2016).

11 There might be an epistemic condition on gratitude that is similar to the epistemic condition on resentment and other forms of blame. One does perhaps have reason to refrain from expressing gratitude if it's unreasonable to think that the person in question deserves gratitude. So some of the considerations that constrain the expression of blame seem to similarly constrain expressions of gratitude. Thanks to Daniel Telech for helping me see this point.

12 Even here, though, we might want to preserve the possibility that someone could be saint-like in their ability to respond grave injustices done to their person with

generosity and grace. It's not clear to me that we all have reason to emulate such a person (or that we should want to), but neither is it clear to me that such a person is by virtue of her character open to rational or moral criticism. If not, then even when reasons of resentment are at their weightiest, it's not clear that they are ever decisive.

13 One may, of course, ask whether these two emotions serve these ends equally well. I doubt that they do, since resentment seems to invite defensiveness at least as frequently as it invites contrition. But since these issues are largely empirical, I leave it open that there may be an important symmetry here in the instrumental value of gratitude and resentment.

WORKS CITED

Coates, D. Justin. 2016. "The Epistemic Norm of Blame," *Ethical Theory and Moral Practice* 19.2: 457–473.

Darwall, Stephen. 2006. *The Second-Person Standpoint*. Cambridge, MA: Harvard University Press.

Fischer, John Martin and Mark Ravizza. 1998 *Responsibility and Control*. Cambridge: Cambridge University Press.

Frankfurt, Harry. 1969. "Alternate Possibilities and Moral Responsibility," *Journal of Philosophy* 66.23: 829–839.

Helm, Bennett W. 2017. *Communities of Respect: Grounding Responsibility, Authority, and Dignity*, New York: Oxford University Press.

Knafo, Ariel, Carolyn Zahn-Waxler, Carol Van Hulle, JoAnn L. Robinson, and Soo Hyun Rhee. 2008. "The Developmental Origins of a Disposition toward Empathy: Genetic and Environmental Contributions," *Emotion* 8.6: 737–752.

Macnamara, Coleen. 2015. "Reactive Attitudes as Communicative Entities," *Philosophy and Phenomenological Research* 90.3: 546–569.

Martin, Alia and Kristina R. Olsen. 2013. "When Kids Know Better: Paternalistic Helping in 3-Year-Old Children," *Developmental Psychology*, 49.11: 2071–2081.

McKenna, Michael. 2012. *Conversation and Responsibility*. New York: Oxford University Press.

Nelkin, Dana K. 2011. *Making Sense of Freedom and Responsibility*. New York: Oxford University Press.

Pereboom, Derk. 2001. *Living without Free Will*. New York: Cambridge University Press.

Smith, Adam. 1976. *Theory of Moral Sentiments*. Oxford: Oxford University Press.

Smith, Holly. 1991. "Varieties of Moral Worth and Moral Credit," *Ethics* 101.2: 279–303.

Strawson, P. F. 2008. "Freedom and Resentment," *Freedom and Resentment and Other Essays*, New York: Routledge.

Watson, Gary. 1987. "Responsibility and the Limits of Evil: Variations on a Strawsonian Theme," *Responsibility, Character, and Emotions*, ed. F. Schoeman. Oxford: Oxford University Press.

Wolf, Susan. 1980. "Asymmetrical Freedom," *Journal of Philosophy* 77:151–166.

Chapter 9

Gratitude and Norms:
On the Social Function of Gratitude

Bennett W. Helm[1]

Philosophical accounts of gratitude generally understand it to be a proper response to intentional (or even voluntary) and supererogatory actions of beneficence toward one.[2] Thus, first, the action to which gratitude is responsive must be performed *intentionally* rather than merely by accident: my stumbling and jostling the pickpocket about to take your wallet and thereby preventing the theft, while beneficial to you, is nonetheless not a fit object of gratitude because it was not something I did intentionally. (Some think in addition that the action must be *voluntary* rather than required or coerced: we do not feel gratitude toward someone who benefits us only because of a gun to her head [Simmons 1979]; I shall not press this case.) Second, the action, at least as intended (whether or not successfully carried out), must be one of *beneficence* in that it is performed so as to benefit you. There are two requirements here: that the action, if successful, does or would benefit you, and that it is done with the intention so to benefit you—that it is done with an attitude of *benevolence*. While gratitude may be warranted even if you are not in fact benefited, since someone who works long and hard to benefit you but fails through bad luck may nonetheless merit your gratitude, it also is generally thought that benevolent action on its own is inadequate in the absence of the intention to benefit: merely saying "good morning" to someone you pass on the street is not to act in a way that merits gratitude. Third, gratitude requires that the benefit received must be one that the beneficiary welcomes or at least does not reject. Finally, it is generally thought that the action to which one must be responsive must be *supererogatory*: actions one performs merely in the course of doing one's duty, such as a bank employee's processing your loan application, even when those actions benefit one and are done with good will, do not call for gratitude (Card 1988; Darwall 2006; Feinberg 1973, 1980; Heyd 1982; McAleer 2012; Roberts 2004; Walker 1980; Weiss 1985).

That gratitude must normally be a response to supererogatory acts is disputed (Walker 1988; Weiss 1985). Simmons (1979) argues that gratitude is merited toward a good Samaritan who acts on moral obligations; perhaps, then, what is required is that the benefactor sacrifice something or incur some liability in acting so as to benefit one. McConnell (2017) argues more strongly that whether gratitude is owed depends not simply on the action and attitude of the benefactor but as well on the overall social circumstances—on how people generally act and so on whether, in this context, the benefactor's action has "special moral significance":

> Even if displaying kindness is one way of fulfilling the imperfect duty of benefi-
> cence, it can generate an obligation of gratitude. Kindness in a sea of cruelty is
> clearly morally significant. (McConnell 2017, 289)

In claiming that beneficence is an "imperfect duty," McConnell has in mind that it is specifically a *wide imperfect duty*: something one must in general do, but which is not owed to any particular person and so which no one has a right to claim from one. Thus, we have some latitude in deciding how and when to uphold wide imperfect duties, for one can uphold a wide imperfect duty even though one fails to act accordingly on some occasions in which it might be appropriate to do so; however, only rarely to act in accordance with such a duty is not to uphold it. McConnell thus asks us to consider cases in which someone has an excuse not to act in accordance with the duty of beneficence—because, for example, of their upbringing (being taught that slaves are less than fully human) or the risks inherent in their social environment (being a guard at an army prison camp with a culture of brutality toward the prisoners). In such cases, McConnell argues that someone who acts beneficently in spite of having an excuse not to and whose actions thereby acquire a kind of moral significance even though they are not supererogatory—that such a person is owed gratitude by the recipient of the beneficence. Actions meriting gratitude therefore need not be supererogatory.

I agree with much of what McConnell says here. However, I am somewhat puzzled by the way he ends his discussion. McConnell considers an example in which Frederick Douglass expresses gratitude toward President Lincoln after meeting with him because "he treated me as a man; he did not let me feel for a moment that there was any difference in the color of our skins!" (Eaton and Mason 1907). McConnell goes on to claim that to feel gratitude

> merely because "he treated me as a man" seems to cheapen one's coin. Of
> course the President should have treated Frederick Douglass as a man. And it is
> hard to see that there were any major obstacles that would have prevented him
> from doing so. Gratitude is not called for here. (McConnell 2017, 292)

I think this is a mistake, one that arises from McConnell's too narrow focus on features of the benefactor's action, even if McConnell (rightly) thinks that action is one that must be understood in a broader social context. Why must the benefactor's action be difficult or involve some sacrifice for it to merit gratitude, lest such gratitude involve the beneficiary's devaluing themself? Why shouldn't the fact that Lincoln's recognition of Douglass's dignity as a person, given that it was something he did when far too few other people were willing to do likewise, be enough for gratitude, even if his doing that was his duty?[3] As I shall argue, to make sense of gratitude—at least the type of gratitude that is a reactive attitude—requires thinking more broadly about the social significance not only of the benefactor's actions but also of the gratitude itself, thereby revealing its broader social point. This in turn will lead me to question not merely whether gratitude requires supererogation or overcoming some obstacle but also whether it requires beneficence in addition to benevolence.

To begin to see this, consider a related example. My oldest child, Jaime, now in college, recently came out as gender non-binary. That is, Jaime identifies as neither male nor female and consequently prefers to use "they"/"them" pronouns rather than "he"/"him" or "she"/"her." Part of what Jaime did in the process of coming out was to go to their professors and indicate these preferences; their college has policies for its community members to recognize each other's gender and pronoun preferences, and Jaime's professors were open and accommodating in those initial conversations. Of course, old habits die hard, and in spite of good initial intentions, in the heat of class discussions, their professors forgot and used the wrong pronouns. Nonetheless, not too long into the semester, one professor, having used the wrong pronoun, had the presence of mind to correct herself. This was one of the first times this happened to Jaime—the first by a professor—and they were very excited and grateful to their professor.

This example of Jaime's gratitude toward their professor does not fit the mold of standard accounts of gratitude. First (and in line with McConnell's examples), the professor's action was in no way supererogatory, and even involved no liability or sacrifice on her part or even (contrary to the suggestion explicit in McConnell's Douglass–Lincoln example) any "major obstacles" to overcome beyond the minimal effort to overcome an ingrained habit of pronoun use. Second (and contrary to McConnell's claims), the professor's action involved no clear beneficence—and certainly not intentional beneficence—even if it was done benevolently. Moreover, whatever benevolence is involved here does not seem importantly different from that of merely acknowledging someone by saying "good morning" as you pass them on the street. After all, your using "he"/"him" pronouns to refer to me does not in any ordinary sense involve beneficence—it's just a matter of getting my gender right—and it would be odd for me to feel gratitude in return. Of course, the professor's use of correct pronouns toward someone who is non-binary was unusual and so stood out against the background of mis-identification that non-binary people typically have to put up with, but that alone doesn't seem to make it an act of beneficence. Nonetheless, as I shall argue, there is an important point to Jaime's feeling gratitude in that norms of transgender recognition are not clearly established within the community (as is evident in Jaime's everyday experience) so that in feeling gratitude, Jaime is simultaneously both recognizing and committing to such norms and calling on others in the community—including not just their professor—to do likewise. This social context makes the professor's action stand out as having "special significance" (albeit not necessarily special *moral* significance, as McConnell claims) and so makes this be a case of warranted gratitude: that action itself can be a way of taking a stand or at least can become that when Jaime's gratitude is taken up by the professor.[4]

One might object, as presumably McConnell would, that this merely shows that gratitude is not called for in this case. This seems to be McConnell's point in claiming that Douglass should not feel gratitude toward Lincoln for treating him "as a man" because that would be "to cheapen one's coin": treating a person as a person simply is what we ought to expect of each other, even if doing so is not typical in a particular society, and to do so without any special obstacle (as was the case for Lincoln) is not an act of beneficence meriting any special recognition. Indeed, to give it that recognition by feeling gratitude would be to "cheapen one's coin": to see the easy giving one what one is due as a benefit meriting special recognition and so to value oneself less than one ought. It is for this reason that gratitude is unwarranted in such a case. The same goes, McConnell might say, for Jaime's case: the professor's use of correct pronouns to refer to Jaime is simply what we ought to expect of each other, and there was no special obstacle to her doing so. Because the action provides no special benefit, it is not a fitting object of gratitude.

One person's *modus ponens* is another's *modus tollens*: I shall argue instead that because gratitude in this example is fitting, gratitude need not be a response to acts of beneficence nor to burdensome acts, as is commonly supposed. So what is there for Jaime to feel gratitude about if not beneficence directed their way? I'm not sure that is the right question to be asked, given its presupposition that the object of gratitude must be something "there" prior to and independent of the gratitude itself. Rather, I shall argue, gratitude is a response to notable instances of the upholding of social norms involving recognition respect, norms that themselves depend on and are partly instituted by the reactive attitudes, including gratitude itself. Making sense of this will require, as I already suggested, seeing gratitude as more broadly social than is commonly assumed; doing so will have the payoff of enabling us to get clearer both on the relationship between gratitude and the intentionality of the actions to which it is a response and on the sense in which one might owe a "debt" of gratitude.

To argue for this, I shall begin with a detour through an account of what it is to care about something. In large part, my claim will be that gratitude—at least the form of gratitude with which I shall be concerned here—is a reactive attitude and as such both presupposes and helps to constitute respect, a certain interpersonal form of caring. Consequently, to understand gratitude, we must understand its place as a reactive attitude in relation to respecting and to caring more generally. Thus, in section "Caring and Holism," I shall stipulate a background theory of how emotions constitute caring. In the section "Communities of Respect and the Reactive Attitudes," I shall extend this theory by again stipulating an account of reactive attitudes as constituting communities of respect, briefly drawing out the implications this has for gratitude as a reactive attitude. In the section "Understanding Gratitude," I shall test and elaborate this basic account of gratitude by discussing the implications it has for thinking about the connection between gratitude, duty, and obligation on the one hand and gratitude and intention on the other.

CARING AND HOLISM

As I have long argued (Helm 2001), what it is to *care* about something—what it is for that thing to have *import* to one—is for one to exhibit a projectable, rational pattern of emotions with that thing as a common focus. For example, my dog cares about going on walks insofar as he gets hopeful when I get up from my computer and head to the closet for my coat, excited when I mention going on a walk and pick up the leash, disappointed and frustrated when the phone rings and I answer it instead of going out the door with him, and joyous when I finally snap on the leash and we head out. This pattern of emotions is not merely *evidence* that he cares about going on a walk; it *constitutes* that caring, for each of these emotions is rationally connected to the others: given the dog's hopefulness and excitement, he rationally ought to be disappointed, frustrated, joyous, and so on. This requires some explanation.

Emotions are generally recognized to have both a *target* (that at which the emotion is directed, its "object") and a *formal object* (the evaluation of the target characteristic of the relevant emotion type). Thus, what my dog is frustrated at, the target of his frustration, is my answering the phone, and the formal object of his frustration is a hindrance or obstacle, for his frustration evaluates my answering the phone in these terms. In addition, I have argued that emotions also have a *focus*: a background object that the subject cares about that makes intelligible the evaluation implicit in the emotion of the target in terms of the formal object. Thus, my dog's evaluation, implicit in his frustration, of my answering the phone as a hindrance or obstacle can be explained in terms of his caring about going on a walk, which is the focus of his frustration. Given this, we can understand the pattern of the various emotions my dog has not in terms of their having a common target or formal object (they don't!) but in terms of their having a common focus: going on a walk. Moreover, as I have argued, each emotion is a commitment to the import of its focus and thereby to having other emotions with the same focus, and it is such "focal commitments" that explain the rational structure of this pattern. Finally, inasmuch as to care about something is to find it to be in some way a worthy object of attention and action, and given that such a rational pattern of emotions with a common focus is a way of finding that focus to be a worthy object of attention and action, we should understand *caring* itself to be a matter of exhibiting such patterns of emotions.

The basic account of caring just provided applies to persons and at least the higher mammals. Nonetheless, we persons are capable of other forms of caring, such as valuing, loving, and respecting, that I have argued we can understand in terms of patterns of distinctive types of emotions. Thus, valuing and loving can be understood in terms of rational patterns of what I call "person-focused emotions": emotions like pride and shame in terms of which we evaluate both certain things as elements in the kind of life worth living and, therefore, the persons who live those lives. And, as I shall claim in the section "Communities of Respect and the Reactive Attitudes," respecting can be understood in terms of rational patterns of reactive attitudes. This implies that particular emotion types and the conditions of their warrant are intelligible only in the context of these broader rational patterns constitutive of the import of their focuses. This methodological holism guides my approach to understanding emotions in general and, therefore, of gratitude in particular.

Such methodological holism is at odds with much work in the philosophy of emotions, including the apparent premise of this volume devoted to a single emotion. Partly through the influence of Davidson (1980), I think we should never lose sight of the way particular mental states are intelligible only in terms of their rational connections to other mental states and to actions. Considering single emotion types one-by-one thus risks missing or distorting important features of those emotion types. Moreover, many of the emotions that interest me most, including gratitude, are complex in a way that depends on a conceptual or cultural background; inasmuch as my central concern is with particular types of minds or agency more generally, I try to abstract away from particular emotions, instead focusing on overall structures of rationality constituting forms of caring, structures that I think hold cross-culturally in spite of variations in the particular emotions that constitute those structures. Hence, I am generally less concerned with particular emotions.

Nonetheless, this methodological holism can be taken too far, so that theory spins out of control, blinding one to the obvious facts on the ground that might falsify that theory. For this reason, I have argued in a previous work that understanding trust to be a reactive attitude (and hence to form rational patterns with other reactive attitudes) can illuminate various puzzling features of trust that alternative accounts struggle with (Helm 2014), a result that I take to be an important confirmation of the overall theory. I propose now to do the same with gratitude, arguing not merely for the relatively uncontroversial claim that gratitude can be a reactive attitude but also that the overall account I offer of the reactive attitudes—as constituting *our* respect for each other as fellow members of a community of respect in virtue of their *interpersonal* rational connections with each other's reactive attitudes—that this overall account can illuminate otherwise puzzling features of gratitude.

COMMUNITIES OF RESPECT AND THE REACTIVE ATTITUDES

How, then, should we understand the reactive attitudes and the rational patterns they form? What follows is a brief summary of my account (in Helm 2017) presented here without argument.

The *reactive attitudes* are emotions like resentment, indignation, and guilt, as well as gratitude, approbation, and self-approbation, whereby we hold each other responsible for his actions (Strawson 1962). If I elbow you out of the way as I jump into the buffet line, you ought to feel resentment, I ought to feel guilty, and others ought to feel disapprobation or even indignation. In feeling resentment, your concern in part is with a certain norm—one I have violated, a norm of taking turns, for example—and your resentment is a kind of commitment to that norm, one that partly constitutes your respecting it. Furthermore, your concern is also with me as having a certain *standing* as someone who is *bound* by this norm, as well as with yourself and others—certain witnesses—as having the *authority* to hold me responsible to it. In this way, your resentment is a kind of commitment to such standing and authority of yourself and others.

Central to the reactive attitudes, I claim, is that the concern they manifest is for the norms, standing, and authority as *communal* norms and as *communal* standing and authority, and the concern is not simply yours but *ours*. In feeling resentment (or other reactive attitudes), what you are committed to is the import of this norm as *our* norm, of this standing and authority as the standing and authority we each have *for us*. This explains why it is not simply coincidence that you feel resentment, I feel guilt, and they feel disapprobation in response to the same circumstances, for these reactive attitudes are all rationally connected insofar as your resentment *calls on* me to feel guilt and others to feel disapprobation and thereby to *(re)affirm* the import of these norms and of each as having such standing and authority. The same is true for my guilt and their disapprobation: each emotion *calls on* others to feel the appropriate coordinated reactive attitude. Of course, others may not take up this call, and in such a case, your resentment will be out of line, other things being equal. But when they do take up the call, the resulting interpersonal, rational interconnections among these reactive attitudes constitute not only these norms as *binding* on us but also the *standing* each has as bound by these norms and the *authority* we each have to hold others responsible to them.[5]

In constituting both the norms and the standing and authority of various people, these interpersonal, rational patterns of reactive attitudes also constitute a community whose norms these are and whose members have that standing and authority. After all, not everyone is bound by the norms of this community, but only its members; and not just anyone has the authority to hold its members responsible to these norms, but only other members. Such communities are what I call "communities of respect," for the recognition of and commitment to such standing and authority of others as one of us just is part of our *recognition respect* for our fellow members (Darwall 2006).[6] We must not forget that many (but not all!) of the norms of a community govern members' relations with each other, so that others will be potential victims of the violation of these norms. Consequently, respect for others as fellow members also requires *upholding* such norms—not merely in the sense of acting in accordance with the norm perhaps for ulterior motives but more strongly by doing so at least in part out of recognition for one's fellow members as meriting the sort of consideration these norms express. In this way, I claim, these interpersonal, rational patterns of reactive attitudes constitute our respect for each other and for the norms—all as a part of constituting us as a *community of respect*. As such, the call of the reactive attitudes is revealed to be in part a call for fellowship in a community of respect.[7]

Before applying this general picture to gratitude, it will be helpful to see more clearly how it applies to a related reactive attitude: resentment. For both resentment and gratitude are *backward-looking personal reactive attitudes*,[8] and as such are responses to the actions of another in relation to oneself, upholding or violating a communal norm. (Contrast this with *self-reactive attitudes* like guilt or self-approbation, which are responses to one's own actions upholding or violating a norm, and with *vicarious reactive attitudes* like approbation or indignation, which are responses to the actions of another upholding or violating a norm not involving oneself.) In particular, *resentment* is the recognition of both the relevant norm as binding on fellow members and the perpetrator as having standing and authority as a member of the relevant community of respect. The "recognition" here is a commitment to the import of that what is recognized—both of the standing and authority of the other as a fellow member and of the norms as binding on us. Resentment thus aims to hold the perpetrator responsible for notably violating the norm not merely through such a recognition but also through the call to others—the perpetrator and witnesses—likewise to recognize the standing and authority both of the perpetrator and victim and of the bindingness of the norm. Such a call is a call for mutual respect of both the norm and each other as members of a community of respect: it is a call for fellowship in that community.

How, then, does this apply to gratitude? Analogous to resentment, we can say that at least one form of gratitude—reactive gratitude—is a response to a notable upholding (or exceeding) of a norm governing the benefactor's relations to oneself.[9] Yet here it is important that in upholding the norm the benefactor's action is normally motivated at least in part by respect for the beneficiary as meriting consideration—by what I shall here call, in a technical sense, *"benevolence"*—for merely to act in accordance with the norm without being motivated at least in part by respect is not the same as to uphold it.[10] In feeling gratitude, the beneficiary recognizes this (apparent) benevolence in upholding the norm and calls on others, including the benefactor, to do so as well and thereby to affirm the norm and the standing and authority of both the benefactor and the beneficiary. By issuing this call for fellowship in a community of respect, gratitude thus aims to hold the benefactor responsible for their notable right doing.[11]

UNDERSTANDING GRATITUDE

Thus far I have presented an account of gratitude as a reactive attitude, an account that is embedded within a broader understanding of the reactive attitudes as essentially interpersonal emotions (via their "call") that, when connected within the appropriate rational patterns, constitute our respect for norms and for fellow members all as the norms and members of a community of respect. Yet why should we accept all of this theoretical baggage in providing an account of gratitude? How can locating gratitude within such a theoretical framework help us understand *gratitude* itself and the particular example of Jaime's gratitude toward their professor with which I began? Answering these questions will require thinking more carefully about the relationships between gratitude and duty or obligation, and between gratitude and the benefactor's intention in acting.

Gratitude and Obligation

As indicated earlier, most philosophical accounts of gratitude require that it be a response either to supererogatory actions or, on McConnell (2017)'s account, to actions that involve overcoming "major obstacles" to benefiting one. I have denied this partly through the example of Jaime's professor, who did no such thing. How does my background theory help illuminate this issue? On this account, gratitude as a reactive attitude is a response to situations in which the benefactor "notably upholds or exceeds" a communal norm, a standard of correctness in behavior for which we can be held responsible. What exactly does it mean "notably to uphold or exceed" a communal norm?

Start with an analogous case of resentment. It is warranted to feel a small degree of resentment toward someone who enters a building right in front of you but makes no attempt at all to hold the door for you; after all, failing to do so is bad manners. Of course, one can have an excuse for failing to hold the door for someone, as when one is carrying heavy packages,[12] but absent some special explanation, upholding this norm does seem to be an obligation: it is a way of exhibiting recognition respect for each other, and the failure to manifest that recognition respect at basically no cost explains the warrant of the resentment. In this way, resentment recognizes—and calls out—such a failure of recognition respect.

Likewise, it can also make sense to express gratitude to some small degree when someone holds the door for you—when they manifest recognition respect in upholding some norm. As with resentment, expressing such gratitude can itself be subject to certain norms, whereby the benefactor might justly feel resentment when their benevolence is not acknowledged, thereby holding the beneficiary responsible for that failure.[13] That we hold each other responsible in this way for expressions of gratitude indicates that there are norms for doing so, and clearly different communities can have different norms here: Americans expect expressions of gratitude more readily than Germans, for example. In our culture, the norms for the expression of gratitude depend on such factors as the magnitude of the benefit (if any), the degree of sacrifice the benefactor's action involves, and the centrality in the benefactor's motives for so acting of recognition respect and the intention to benefit (Berger 1975; Gulliford, Morgan, and Kristjánsson 2013). Nonetheless, we can readily imagine other cultures in which a positive, backward-looking reactive attitude serving very much the same social function as gratitude works differently. Moreover, such norms determine, more or less precisely, how the gratitude is expressed—its intensity and depth, for example.

Given this, just when a norm is "notably upheld or exceeded" depends on the community and its norms for expressing gratitude. Gratitude can thus be a response to benevolence—to actions motivated in part by recognition respect—even while not all instances of benevolence call for gratitude (i.e., saying "good morning" to a stranger I pass on the street). Moreover, this starts to make sense of the "special significance" of actions calling for gratitude,

for such actions are manifestations of recognition respect in upholding communal norms, and they are notable insofar as they are singled out by the norms for
feeling gratitude. Contra McConnell (2017), such significance is not necessarily a *moral* significance insofar as neither recognition respect nor these norms
need be moral in character (see note 7). (I shall have a bit more to say about
such significance in the section "Gratitude, Intention, and Indeterminacy.")

In short, gratitude involves two sets of norms: (a) norms of recognition
respect for the beneficiary that are notably upheld or exceeded by the benefactor and (b) norms governing the having and expressing of gratitude itself,
norms that apply to the beneficiary and that involve recognition respect for
the benefactor. In recognizing the norm upheld by the benefactor, the beneficiary thereby recognizes that, other things being equal,[14] this norm is binding
on them as well—that they also have an obligation (we might say a "duty,"
perhaps an imperfect duty) to uphold it. More than this, however, is that
feeling gratitude is a recognition of the benefactor's actions as an admirable
model for how, at least sometimes, to carry out that obligation, a model worthy of emulation. To feel gratitude is to feel, more or less strongly, a "debt"
of gratitude: to feel a commitment to the imperfect duty to exhibit recognition
respect for others in similar ways—a commitment, in essence, to "pay forward" that for which one is grateful when one is in a position to do likewise.
For such actions themselves to manifest gratitude to the benefactor, however,
they must be motivated not merely by this commitment to such an imperfect
duty but also by a recognition of the benefactor—out of recognition respect
for the benefactor. In this way, we might say, the feeling of gratitude is a
feeling of fellowship with the benefactor (see Darwall's essay, this volume).

Card (1988) is critical of the idea that there is a "debt" of gratitude, arguing that we should replace the "debt" metaphor with a metaphor of trust
and the more informal obligations being entrusted brings with it. I agree
that the "debt" metaphor can be taken too far and that the analogy to trust
is apt, but I think this is a point in favor of the account just given. For, first,
on my account, the "debt" is owed not only to the benefactor but also and
more fundamentally to the community at large. After all, insofar as in feeling
gratitude, you commit yourself to paying forward the benevolence, it is others, not in general simply the benefactor, who will be the recipients of your
future benevolence, and via the norms for having and expressing gratitude,
it is we community members who can hold you responsible for doing so.
Moreover, insofar as this commitment to pay forward the "debt" of gratitude
is an imperfect duty, it is not one that any particular person can claim from
you. (But see next paragraph for a weaker sense in which this "debt" is owed
to the benefactor.) Second, I have argued elsewhere that trust itself can be
a forward-looking reactive attitude and consequently calls on the trustee to
act as trusted in accordance with certain communal norms, thereby inviting

them into fellowship with one in the community of respect (Helm 2014) in a way that is analogous to my account of gratitude here. Indeed, Card (1988, 123) identifies such deepening and strengthening of ties with the truster or benefactor—such fellowship—as potentially "the most important difference between formal and informal obligations." (I shall argue in the section "Gratitude, Intention, and Indeterminacy" that the analogy between gratitude and trust runs much deeper.)

Understanding the "debt" of gratitude this way can help make sense of Hobbes's claim that it is a "law of nature"

> *that a man which receiveth Benefit from another of meer Grace, Endeavour*
> *that he which giveth it, have no reasonable cause to repent him of his good will.*
> (Hobbes 1651, 75)

The point here—and part of the point of talking about a "debt" of gratitude owed to the benefactor—is that the benevolent action and the uptake of this in gratitude establishes a special sort of relationship between the benefactor and the beneficiary. Normally, when someone acts well or poorly toward a third party, thereby upholding or violating a communal norm, one has reason to feel *vicarious* reactive attitudes such as approbation or indignation; other things being equal it would be odd to feel gratitude, resentment, or some other personal reactive attitude, since the perpetrator's actions did not benefit or harm one.[15] Yet earlier events, such as those involving trust, alter that relationship in such a way that the trustee's actions toward a third party can constitute a benefit or harm toward oneself. Consequently, when the trustee upholds or betrays that trust by acting well or poorly toward a third party, it is warranted for the truster to feel *personal* reactive attitudes—to feel gratitude or resentment (Helm 2014). We can now see that the same holds in cases of gratitude as well: when the benefactor's invitation is taken up in the beneficiary's gratitude, the beneficiary's subsequent actions toward third parties can gratify the benefactor, or can be cause of resentment or (reactive) disappointment in the beneficiary as insufficiently grateful. This means that we should not think of the benefactor's action as somehow mysteriously instituting all by itself a special sort of relationship with the beneficiary within which the benefactor comes to have newfound authority over the beneficiary to demand repayment of a debt of gratitude. Rather, whatever "debt" of gratitude the beneficiary may have is the result of their already being a fellow member with the benefactor in a community of respect that has existing norms for feeling and expressing gratitude—norms that may vary from community to community.[16]

Of course, the beneficiary may also reject the invitation implicit in the benefactor's action, rejecting that action as a model to be emulated and the new or extended norm as binding. In thereby refusing to take on a debt of gratitude, the beneficiary thus finds the benefactor's action to be unwelcome: not because it was not genuinely an action of goodwill toward, or even one that benefited, the beneficiary, but because it comes with social strings attached—certain normative expectations that we behave similarly in appropriate circumstances—that the beneficiary rejects. In this way, too, acts of benevolence can be like attitudes of trust: both can be unwelcome by the recipient, and unwelcome for the same reasons.

Gratitude, Intention, and Indeterminacy

It is almost universally accepted that gratitude requires the benefactor to act *with the intention* of benefiting someone. (An exception is Fitzgerald, who argues that "gratitude towards one's enemies . . . is a common ideal within Buddhism" [1998, 124]. However, it is not clear that the relevant response in this case is *gratitude* rather than a more general appreciation. Surely it is not *reactive* gratitude, for one does not thereby hold one's enemy responsible for upholding a norm.) Indeed, I have claimed that the benefactor must "normally" be motivated by recognition respect in following (rather than merely acting in accordance with) a communal norm. Yet, here, I think, we must be careful not to ignore abnormal cases that can show us something important about the social function of gratitude.

Consider what happens in related cases first. In the case of resentment, the perpetrator's norm violation normally involves the failure of recognition respect, and the resentment calls on the perpetrator to affirm the norm, show that respect, and take responsibility for that failure by owning it—feeling guilty, and making amends. Analogously, in cases of normal gratitude in which the benefactor acts benevolently, at least in part out of recognition respect, gratitude calls on the benefactor to affirm the norm, to recognize their upholding of it and respect for the beneficiary, and to take responsibility for that success by owning it—feeling pride or self-approbation. In abnormal cases of gratitude, in which the benefactor merely acts in accordance with the norm and without recognition respect—perhaps merely by accident as the side effect of other motives, or perhaps intending to benefit the beneficiary but for ulterior motives such as to impress a third party or to build a reputation or to infuriate someone else. In such cases, even when the beneficiary recognizes what the benefactor is up to, feeling gratitude—perhaps a "hopeful gratitude"—nonetheless calls on the benefactor to affirm the norm and hence the recognition respect toward the beneficiary the norm requires. While the benefactor may not initially have been motivated to act in accordance with the norm out of recognition respect, the call of gratitude is for the benefactor to respect the beneficiary *retroactively*. In the face of this call, the benefactor may accept it, (re)affirming the norm, potentially changing their motives in the future. When this happens, the beneficiary's gratitude will have "succeeded" in fulfilling a social function of gratitude.

Of course, to say that gratitude "succeeds" in such a case is not to say that it is *warranted*, for that implies that the circumstances to which gratitude responds are accurately portrayed by the gratitude itself—that the benefactor really did notably uphold a norm in a way that manifests recognition respect to the beneficiary; I will not here take a stand on whether determinate motives can be changed retroactively. More interesting, however, are cases in which the benefactor's motives are antecedently indeterminate.

The methodological holism I espouse (see the section "Caring and Holism"), when extended not just to emotions but to all mental capacities, suggests that what a person's motives are depends on how they fit in with a broad rational pattern of other attitudes and actions—attitudes and actions that can reveal even conscious intentions not to be the actual motives. This means in part that what someone is doing now may not be determinate until later, once the relevant rational pattern attains enough structure to rule out alternative possibilities. Interactions with others, therefore, can shape and define such patterns, prompting the agent subsequently to have certain attitudes or to act in certain ways, so as to make determinate what they were doing earlier. Gratitude through its call can be one such interaction when the benefactor takes up that call. (Trust is another.) In such a case, gratitude (or trust) is a warranted response to what turns out to have been benevolent (or trustworthy) action all along.

Thus far, gratitude's role in resolving indeterminacy has concerned the benefactor's motives and actions, and we have seen that the benefactor need not in advance intend to act benevolently in order for gratitude to be warranted. In other cases, gratitude can help resolve indeterminacy in communal norms or even institute new norms.

To see this, consider an analogy to trust. As I have argued elsewhere (Helm 2014), the call of trust can be an invitation to the trustee as well as others to take up a new norm—a new delineation of how it is appropriate for us to show recognition respect to each other in particular situations—and to respond accordingly. Thus, when I am injured and on crutches, I may trust my students and colleagues to help me carry books and papers to class and department meetings, thereby calling on them to respond accordingly. We may not have in advance a norm for how to respond respectfully to others in our community with this form of dependency, and my trust invites us to see how this might go. When this invitation is taken up by others by their upholding that trust not merely coincidentally but out of recognition respect for me, the community's norms are shaped and refined—made more determinate than they were antecedently.

Gratitude can work similarly to the taking up of trust. While in many cases, benefactors may simply uphold existing norms (of etiquette, say), in some cases, they may break new ground, where it may be indeterminate in advance whether the benefactor's action follows any existing norm. In feeling gratitude, the beneficiary thereby commits to a new norm or to a more determinate delineation of an existing norm, thereby inviting others, including the benefactor, to do likewise. For example, a dissertation adviser may meet with an advisee over lunch and pick up the check, much to the surprise and delight of the advisee; in feeling gratitude, the advisee thereby commits to this as a determination of the norms regulating interactions among graduate advisers and advisees, invites others to commit to this norm, and takes on a "debt" to be paid forward when in a position to do likewise.[17] Such a precisification of the norm succeeds when others pick up this call and so come to find acting in this way to be a part of the recognition respect they expect from each other.

This brings me back to the example of Jaime's gratitude toward their professor's calling them by the correct pronouns. Assume now that both kinds of indeterminacy are in play: that it is indeterminate whether our norms for recognizing each other's genders extend beyond the two genders commonly accepted in our culture, and that it is indeterminate what the professor's motives in using Jaime's preferred pronouns were—whether merely to follow college policy and avoid student complaints about her to the dean or a matter of recognition respect for Jaime. In this context, Jaime's excited response of gratitude interprets their professor's action as the manifestation of recognition respect and calls on her and others to accept this delineation of our norms of gender recognition. Once again, this call provides the professor with defeasible reasons to have subsequent attitudes and motives in line with that interpretation, potentially thereby making her earlier action more determinate. And, once again, this call provides the professor and others with defeasible reasons to commit to a clearer delineation of our norm and so of what is involved in recognition respect for each other.

Of course, Jaime's gratitude will not change things on its own. Others need to take up their call for the interpersonal rational pattern constituting the norms to change. And they may not, thereby undermining the warrant of that gratitude. Whether or not they do, we can nonetheless understand Jaime's gratitude to have the special significance of being a move toward clearer norms of transgender recognition and hence respect for others who are not cisgendered. The same can be said of Douglass's gratitude toward Lincoln: in the face of widespread disagreement about, and so indeterminacy in, what norms of the community of the United States apply to those with African ancestry, that gratitude has special significance as a move toward racial equality by calling on Lincoln and others in their reactive attitudes to commit to these norms thus understood.

CONCLUSION

Philosophical accounts of gratitude typically understand it to be normally a response to actions that are beneficent (and normally at some cost to the benefactor), supererogatory, and intentional. I have argued, however, that reactive gratitude only requires *benevolence*, understood as actions that express recognition respect, but not necessarily beneficence, and that the benefactor's actions need not come at any cost to the benefactor: Jaime's professor's use of correct pronouns was not a costly act, nor did it involve any clear bestowal of benefits on them. Moreover, I have argued that gratitude not only is consistent with the benefactor's acting out of duty—out of recognition respect—in following certain communal norms but also itself recognizes that obligation and potentially involves taking on a "debt" to pay forward that benevolence, for gratitude, involves commitment to the relevant norm and to the benefactor's actions as a way of upholding that norm that is worthy of emulation. Finally, I have argued that gratitude can be warranted even when the benefactor has no clear intention in advance to be benevolent, and that gratitude plays an important social role in calling on others to share in one's commitment to communal norms and to each other.

Fred Berger claims that

> the practices associated with gratitude are a manifestation of, and serve to strengthen, the bonds of moral community—the sharing of a common moral life based on respect for each person as having value in himself. (Berger 1975, 305)

This is right, but not because (as Berger thinks) gratitude is an acknowledgment of the other's sacrifice in bestowing beneficence on one (though Berger does correctly see the point of recognition respect). Rather, gratitude—like resentment—is a central and important part of the interpersonal rational patterns of reactive attitudes constituting a community of respect, its norms, and our fellowship within it.[18]

NOTES

1 Department of Philosophy, Franklin & Marshall College, Lancaster, PA. email: bennett.helm@fandm.edu.

2 We should distinguish between non-agential (or dyadic) and agential (or triadic) gratitude. *Non-agential gratitude* is generally understood to be an attitude of appreciation for certain features of the world or one's situation that benefit one—for natural beauty, for the good weather for one's planned outing, and so on. I will set this aside. Rather, my concern will be with *agential gratitude*: an attitude of appreciation

and, perhaps, indebtedness toward an agent on account of their actions toward one. It is agential gratitude that I intend in speaking of "gratitude" here.

3 Of course, McConnell allows that gratitude might be appropriate if there were obstacles preventing one's doing one's duty, and here one might wonder whether social pressures against such recognition would constitute such an obstacle. Fair enough, but it is clear from the passage just quoted that McConnell does not think that whatever obstacles there were in Lincoln's case were relevant here. Thanks to Daniel Telech for raising this point.

4 Thanks to Daniel Telech for help to clarify this point.

5 Many Strawsonians understand what I understand to be the "call" of the reactive attitudes to be a matter of one's making *demands* on others for a certain kind of treatment. (See, for example, Strawson [1962, 200]; this is echoed in Wallace [1994] and Darwall [2006].) This, I believe, is too strong in general: it does not make sense of positive reactive attitudes nor of self-reactive attitudes. Other Strawsonians understand this "call" to be a matter of the reactive attitudes having the function of getting the recipient to take up its representational content concerning someone's morally significant action (Macnamara 2015). This is too weak, insofar as it seems to omit the way reactive attitudes are forms of praise or blame, thereby holding someone responsible for their actions. My attempt to understand the "call" of the reactive attitudes in terms of the interpersonal affirmation of certain communal norms they thereby constitute is an attempt to find middle ground here. (For details, see Helm [2017, Chapter 3]. Thanks to Daniel Telech for prodding me to clarify this point.)

6 As Darwall (2006) understands it, recognition respect is a matter of recognizing (and being committed to) the standing and authority of others; it is distinct from appraisal respect, which is a positive evaluation of someone as worthy of esteem.

7 As I understand them, there are many overlapping and nested communities of respect to which we each belong, each with its own distinctive norms and members constituted by distinct interpersonal patterns of reactive attitudes. While I suspect the moral community is also a community of respect, namely the community of all persons, the smaller communities of respect with which I am primarily concerned here are not the moral community, and hence the sort of respect they involve is not moral respect.

8 Not all reactive attitudes are backward-looking; we must recognize various forms of trust and distrust as forward-looking reactive attitudes (Helm 2014), though I shall not argue this here.

9 There are other forms of gratitude. In general, gratitude is a response to actions that involve a certain kind of care or concern for the beneficiary; likewise, the response that gratitude is involves a similar concern for the benefactor. However, there can be different sorts of concern involved here, at least two of which are personal love (involving person-focused emotions) and respect (involving the reactive attitudes), which implies that there are at least two forms of gratitude: personal and reactive. What makes these both be types of *gratitude* is that they have the same formal object, even while they differ in what type of focus they have and so the patterns of what type of other emotions they form. (This is analogous to there being both personal and reactive forms of shame [Helm 2017, Chapter 7].) I shall not argue this point further here.

10   I shall qualify this blanket statement about gratitude—clarifying what I mean by "normally"—in the section "Gratitude, Intention, and Indeterminacy."

11   This understanding of gratitude merely in terms of benevolence might seem too thin; after all, it ignores the thought, central to the English concept of gratitude, that gratitude is a response specifically to kindness or generosity (see Chappell's contribution to this volume). Something like this is surely right about our concept of gratitude, though we can imagine that other cultures may have concepts of positive, backward-looking reactive attitudes reasonably close to gratitude that are specified in somewhat different terms—that have somewhat different formal objects. In understanding gratitude broadly as I have described it here, I aim to include such variants. (Thanks to Agnes Callard, Sophie Grace Chappell, and Terry McConnell for helpful discussion on this point.)

12   For an account of excuses consistent with this account of gratitude, see Helm (2018).

13   For further discussion of failures of gratitude, see Manela's contribution to this volume.

14   Other things may not be equal when, for example, the norm applies only to those occupying a certain social role, which the beneficiary does not.

15   Other things will not be equal, for example, when one identifies with the beneficiary as a part of loving them.

16   Thanks to Agnes Callard and Adrienne Martin for pushing me to clarify this point.

17   While it is possible to construe this example as a case of personal gratitude, it is important for present purposes that it be construed as an instance of reactive gratitude instead. Thus, the assumption is that the benefactor acts out of recognition respect within a community of philosophers and the beneficiary likewise holds the benefactor responsible through a commitment to a communal norm.

18   Thanks to Bob Roberts and Daniel Telech for many deep and insightful comments on this chapter, many of which, unfortunately, get into topics too complex to be addressed here. Thanks as well to participants in the University of Chicago's Workshop on the Moral Psychology of Gratitude for further helpful comments and criticisms, and to Agnes Callard and especially to Daniel Telech for their hard work organizing that workshop.

REFERENCES

Berger, Fred R. 1975. "Gratitude." *Ethics* 85 (4): 298–309. doi:10.1086/291969.

Card, Claudia. 1988. "Gratitude and Obligation." *American Philosophical Quarterly* 25 (2): 115–27.

Darwall, Stephen L. 2006. *The Second-Person Standpoint: Morality, Respect, and Accountability*. Cambridge, MA: Harvard University Press.

Davidson, Donald. 1980. *Essays on Actions and Events*. New York, NY: Clarendon Press.

Eaton, John, and Ethel Osgood Mason. 1907. *Grant, Lincoln, and the Freedmen: Reminiscences of the Civil War with Special Reference to the Work for the*

Contrabands and Freedmen of the Mississippi Valley. New York: Longmans, Green, & Co.

Feinberg, Joel. 1973. *Social Philosophy.* Englewood Cliffs, NJ: Prentice-Hall.

———. 1980. *Rights, Justice, and the Bounds of Liberty: Essays in Social Philosophy.* Princeton, NJ: Princeton University Press.

Fitzgerald, Patrick. 1998. "Gratitude and Justice." *Ethics* 109 (1). Chicago: The University of Chicago Press: 119–53.

Gulliford, Liz, Blaire Morgan, and Kristján Kristjánsson. 2013. "Recent Work on the Concept of Gratitude in Philosophy and Psychology." *The Journal of Value Inquiry* 47 (3): 285–317.

Helm, Bennett W. 2001. *Emotional Reason: Deliberation, Motivation, and the Nature of Value.* Cambridge: Cambridge University Press.

———. 2014. "Trust as a Reactive Attitude." In *Oxford Studies in Agency and Responsibility:* Freedom and Resentment *at Fifty,* edited by David Shoemaker and Neal Tognazzini, 2:187–215. Oxford: Oxford University Press.

———. 2017. *Communities of Respect: Persons, Dignity, and the Reactive Attitudes.* Oxford: Oxford University Press.

———. 2018. "Personal Relationships and Blame: Scanlon and the Reactive Attitudes." In *Social Dimensions of Responsibility,* edited by Katrina Hutchison, Catriona Mackenzie, and Marina Oshana. Oxford: Oxford University Press.

Heyd, David. 1982. *Supererogation: Its Status in Ethical Theory.* Cambridge: Cambridge University Press.

Hobbes, Thomas. 1651. *Leviathan, or the Matter, Forme, & Power of a Common-Wealth Ecclesiasticall and Civill.* London: Andrew Crooke.

Macnamara, Coleen. 2015. "Reactive Attitudes as Communicative Entities." *Philosophy & Phenomenological Research* 90 (3): 546–69.

McAleer, Sean. 2012. "Propositional Gratitude." *American Philosophical Quarterly* 49 (1): 55–66.

McConnell, Terrance C. 2017. "Gratitude, Rights, and Moral Standouts." *Ethical Theory and Moral Practice* 20 (2): 279–93.

Roberts, Robert C. 2004. "The Blessings of Gratitude: A Conceptual Analysis." In *The Psychology of Gratitude,* edited by Robert A. Emmons and Michael E. McCullough, 58–78. Oxford: Oxford University Press.

Simmons, A. John. 1979. *Moral Principles and Political Obligations.* Princeton, NJ: Princeton University Press.

Strawson, Peter F. 1962. "Freedom and Resentment." *Proceedings of the British Academy* 48: 187–211.

Walker, A. D. M. 1980. "Gratefulness and Gratitude." *Proceedings of the Aristotelian Society* 81: 39–55.

———. 1988. "Political Obligation and the Argument from Gratitude." *Philosophy & Public Affairs* 17 (3): 191–211.

Wallace, R. Jay. 1994. *Responsibility and the Moral Sentiments.* Cambridge, MA: Harvard University Press.

Weiss, Roslyn. 1985. "The Moral and Social Dimensions of Gratitude." *Southern Journal of Philosophy* 23 (4): 491–501.

Part IV

AUTHENTIC SELVES AND BRAINS

Chapter 10

Neural Perspectives on Gratitude

Christina Karns

Imagine that it's your birthday and you come home to see an envelope tucked under your doormat. Excitedly, you tear open the envelope and two tickets flutter to the ground. You pick them up and see that they are for a sold-out performance of your favorite band. Who could have left such a gift? They are probably from your best friend, who attended a show with you last weekend. The two of you had talked about the upcoming performance. But it's such an expensive gift and you know your friend has been out of a job recently.

You pull the card from the envelope and open it to see the signature. The tickets are actually from a coworker who has asked you out a few times, but you aren't interested in pursuing a romantic relationship. What do you do with the tickets?

If you put yourself in the aforementioned scenario, you might feel a range of emotions as you accumulate information about the unfolding events. Curiosity when you see the envelope, excitement about having tickets to the performance, nascent gratitude when you imagine the gift is from your friend, guilt when you think that the cost may be too great, and finally when the identity of the benefactor is revealed, the awkward realization that you now need to graciously handle an unwanted overture.

Suppose an alternative ending.

You look inside the envelope and a note from your friend that explains that the tickets were a prize from a radio contest. Your friend wants you to have them. You feel a wave of gratitude in recognition that your friend knows what you enjoy, and of course, you invite your friend to attend with you.

I hope this simple vignette illustrates the complexity of the social and moral evaluations that undergird an experience of gratitude. At its most basic, we could define gratitude as a rewarding emotion resulting from receiving a tangible or non-tangible benefit, but surely the earlier given example illustrates that gratitude is a complex state consisting of several distinguishable and interacting social and cognitive attributes. The identity of the benefactor transforms a benefit to a burden.

Gratitude is a positive emotional response and a motivation to express thanks. In contrast guilt, another emotion that can be associated with receiving a benefit, is a negative emotion and a motivation to make amends. A mature body of research suggests that gratitude, as a trait or as a state, can lead to beneficial mental, health, and behavioral outcomes. For example, interventions that promote gratitude increase positive affect and decrease negative affect (Emmons & McCullough, 2003; Froh et al., 2008; Sheldon & Lyubomirsky, 2006). Gratitude increases well-being (Wood et al., 2010). Gratitude improves mental and physical health (Cheng et al., 2015; Lambert et al., 2012; Mills et al., 2015; Ng & Wong, 2013; Otto et al., 2016; Shao et al., 2016; Van Dusen et al., 2015; Wong et al., 2016). Nonetheless, research on the underlying brain mechanisms supporting the experience of gratitude is still in its infancy.

My aim in this chapter is to illuminate ways in which research can provide an understanding of how neural systems may work together to support an experience of gratitude and how the plastic and changeable nature of the brain might be used to promote gratitude. In the section "Gratitude as a Multifaceted Construct—A Gateway Model," I first give an overview of my conceptual model of gratitude, called the gateway model in which I describe various interdependent components supporting the experience of gratitude. The goal is to provide a scaffold to generate testable hypotheses about the neural underpinnings of gratitude, as well as to evaluate current research to determine which aspects of gratitude are being tested in various experimental contexts. In section "Neural Studies of Gratitude," I review the new and very few studies that directly investigate the neural basis of gratitude and evaluate them in light of the conceptual framework outlined in the section "Gratitude as a Multifaceted Construct—A Gateway Model." In addition, I draw connections to other more established research domains like reward processing, decision-making, empathy, and social neuroscience. In section "The Future of Brain Research on Gratitude," I posit that the study of gratitude provides a rich opportunity to understand how multiple neural and biological systems contribute to understanding complex social and moral emotions that individuals or society may wish to cultivate.

GRATITUDE AS A MULTIFACETED CONSTRUCT: A GATEWAY MODEL

As in the previous example, the situations that elicit feelings of pleasant gratitude versus unpleasant or guilty indebtedness or even outright entitlement require complex social evaluations. If a beneficiary decides that a gift comes with "strings attached" or appraises a gift as too costly, that may lead the recipient to feel indebted (Tsang, 2006; Watkins et al., 2006). A reciprocal act is then necessary—and perhaps expected by the benefactor—to restore a social balance. Suppose a roommate reluctantly offers to lend you his new car for the day so that you can get to work. You need and appreciate the favor, but his reluctance indicates that a big return favor is necessary to restore goodwill; failing to offer tit-for-tat payback could lead to his resentment. Other benefits might simply be expected or considered the duty of the benefactor; benefits are received in the absence of gratitude. For example, if you are a student and your parents are well off, you might expect them to pay your tuition bill for college. It is a benefit to which you feel entitled given the social norms of your family and you may feel indignant if this benefit is withheld. In contrast, in gratitude, the benefit is seen as grace.

Now imagine you are struggling financially and a relative unexpectedly sends you a check. A note explains that someone once helped her when she fell on hard times. This might elicit a feeling of sincere gratitude. It is these scenarios that illustrate the many ways in which a simple transfer of goods or a benefit to the self does not automatically elicit gratitude.

Precursors to Gratitude: Recognition and Evaluation

Figure 10.1 depicts my working conceptual model of gratitude. Similar to other views (e.g., McCullough et al., 2001), I posit that the emotional experience of gratitude consists of multiple affective and cognitive processing stages. The model relies upon several sequential processing modules, gateways that lead toward a full experience of gratitude, though of course, these processes are best represented as networks with both feed-forward and feedback mechanisms. First, a benefit must be recognized through a rewarding emotion and cognitive appreciation, components that are potentially separable across different neural systems. "This is a good thing" our brain tells us. If a benefit is not recognized, it cannot lead to gratitude.

The recognition of the benefit draws attention to or highlights the potential role of a benefactor. "Where did the good thing come from?" A social agent could already exist in our awareness, but the gateway is the attribution that the social agent is responsible for the benefit that has just been recognized. In this view, recognition is followed by a social evaluation of whether a social agent, a benefactor, is responsible. "Someone intended this to benefit me," our brain tells us. Without some perceived agency of the benefactor acting on our behalf, there would be no gratitude.

Here, I must point out that popular conceptions of gratitude often diverge from theoretical accounts of gratitude. In popular renditions, we are urged to

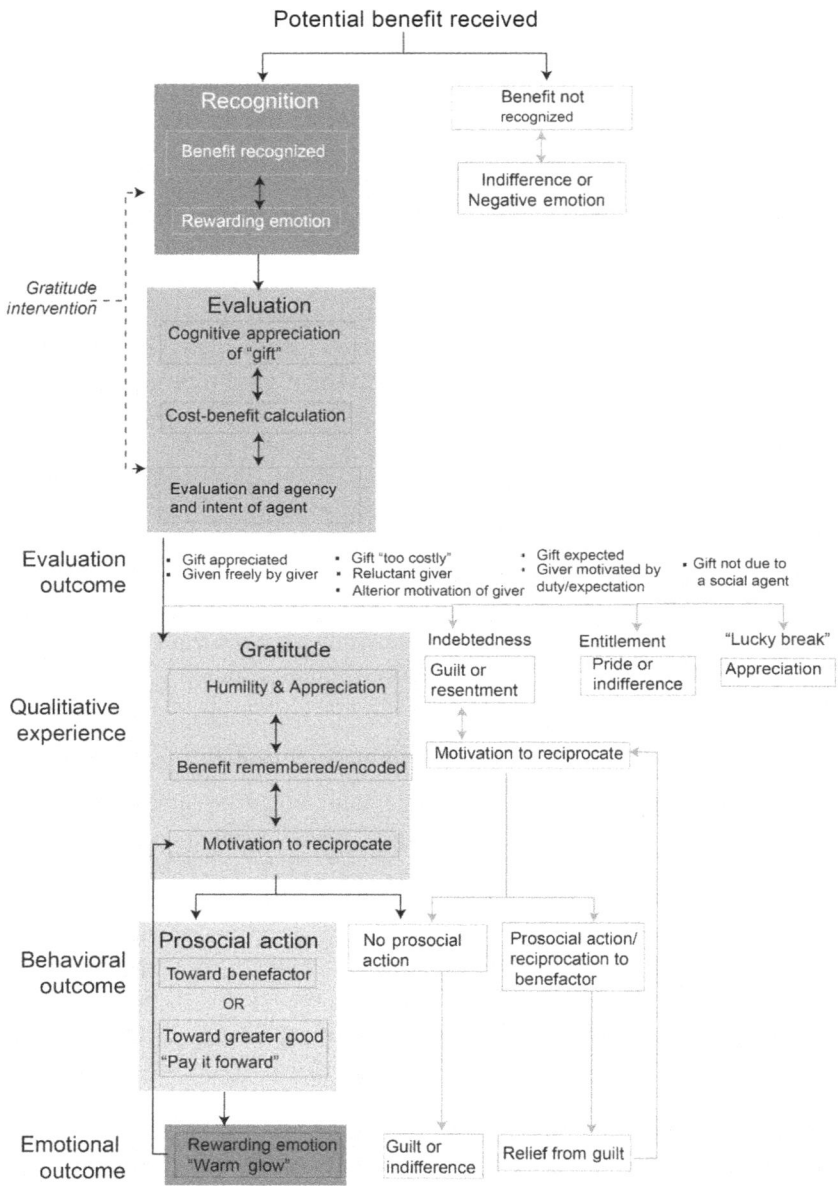

Figure 10.1 Depicts the Gateway Model, a working conceptual model of gratitude. The emotional experience of gratitude consists of multiple affective and cognitive processing stages. The model relies upon several sequential processing modules, gateways that lead toward a full experience of gratitude, though of course, these processes are best represented as networks with both feed-forward and feedback mechanisms. In this model, gratitude is represented as a qualitative experience with behavioral and emotional outcomes that include prosocial action toward the benefactor or the grater good. A typical gratitude intervention would target recognition of a benefit or its evaluation.

be grateful for a beautiful spring day, for our health, or to direct our positive feelings toward other benefits we might take for granted. But, this appreciation of some "lucky break" like winning the lottery or of having good health is not necessarily gratitude (see Ehrenreich, 2015 for a critique). Instead, gratitude theorists have been stressing that gratitude is distinct from happiness, appreciation, or gladness, because rather than simply noticing or being attuned to existence of something positive, gratitude involves a social component of recognizing the role of benefactors (Carr, 2013; Gulliford et al., 2013). The attribution of social agency is a key component to experience the moral emotion of gratitude. In fact, it may be that the popular confusion around gratitude versus *gratification* occurs because when one appreciates health or good weather, there is an attribution of social agency to one's conception of God or a benevolent universe, which could still lead to the qualitative experience of gratitude. These social attributions could be explicit or perhaps unconscious. To make headway on ways to improve well-being by promoting gratitude, we need to be clear about what the key definitional aspects of gratitude are and use appropriately specific terminology.

Even if a social agent is responsible for a gift, gratitude is still not obligatory. In the gateway model, this attribution simply allows for gratitude to be one of several potential experiences. The recognition of a social agent as a benefactor leads to an evaluation of the cost to the benefactor, the benefit to self, and the cost-benefit of the gift being accepted or received. This involves inference about the intent of the benefactor and gratiude results when we determine that the benefactor cares about our well-being. The gift, while potentially costly, is given freely.

The neural underpinnings of these complex social evaluations require hypotheses to be rooted in the burgeoning field of social neuroscience. For example, inferences about intent require social perspective-taking, a form of empathy that is related to theory of mind. Figure 10.2 depicts three distinct brain networks that we would expect to be involved in different domains of gratitude: the reward network responds when a benefit is received; a network for cognitive and social perspective-taking is recruited to determine the intent of the benefactor; and a network recruited with empathy for pain may be involved in evaluating the cost to the benefactor.

The brain's reward network consists of subcortical brain regions such as the ventral tegmentum and nucleus accumbens along with midline cortical regions such as the ventromedial prefrontal cortex (VMPFC) and orbital frontal cortex. These regions are responsive to tangible rewards like pleasurable food as well more abstract rewards like money (Clithero et al., 2014). The brain's cognitive and social perspective-taking network includes the more caudal and anterior medial prefrontal cortex, the superior temporal sulcus, temporal pole, and temporal-parietal junction. This network is recruited

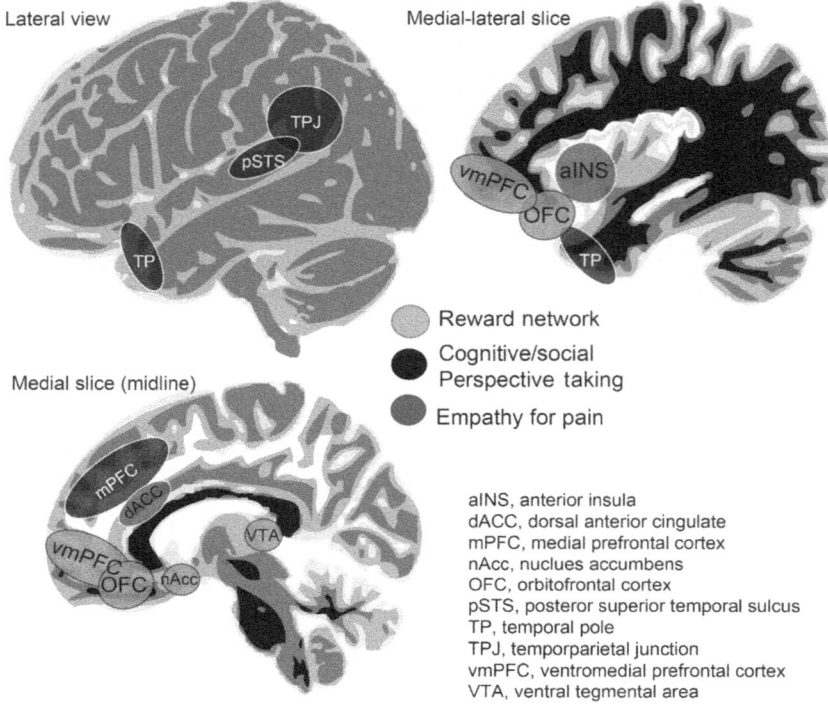

Figure 10.2 As a complex social and cognitive emotion, gratitude is likely to be rooted in multiple brain systems. The reward network responds when a benefit is received (VTA, nAcc, OFC, vmPFC); a network for cognitive and social perspective-taking is recruited to determine the intent of the benefactor (TPJ, pSTS, TP, mPFC); and a network recruited with empathy for pain may be involved in evaluating the cost to the benefactor (aINS, dACC).

when we reason about other people's minds (Decety & Lamm, 2007; Saxe et al., 2003; Young et al., 2010) with abstract social values likely represented along the superior temporal sulcus (REFS Zahn Moll). This network, related to cognitive and social processes, should not be confused with networks that are often reported in research on empathy, research that typically employs observing pain in others to elicit empathy. Empathy for pain recruits the anterior insula and dorsal anterior cingulate cortex, regions that are involved in directly experienced pain (Hein et al., 2008).

Different contexts that elicit gratitude may differentially engage these networks and potentially other networks. A benefactor may be responding with empathy to a beneficiary's pain—the perspective-taking and empathy-for-pain network becoming coupled as the benefactor acts to benefit us. Meanwhile, as discussed more in the next section, the beneficiary perceives the high or painful cost of a gift to the benefactor, which could recruit empathy for pain networks within the beneficiary.

The Qualitative Experience of Gratitude

So far I have described two groups of potential precursors to the experience of gratitude that could be considered gateways that allow for gratitude: first, the recognition of a benefit accompanied by a rewarding emotion, and second, the evaluation of social agency, intent of the benefactor, cost to the benefactor, and cost-benefits of accepting the gift or offer of help. Both recognition and evaluation are necessary, but not sufficient for gratitude. As depicted in figure 10.1, distinct emotions could still result, such as indebtedness, entitlement, or appreciation of a lucky break. Research supports the view that the qualitative experience of gratitude is positive, unlike guilt, for example (Watkins et al., 2006), but it also involves humility and appreciation (Kruse et al., 2014). There is more to gratitude than an undifferentiated positive emotion. Importantly, the experience of gratitude involves a moral motivation to express gratitude or to reciprocate by returning a favor or deepening social ties to the benefactor (Gordon et al., 2012; McCullough et al., 2001). The target of this reciprocity can also be a non-benefactor, manifesting as a prosocial desire to "give back" to others—to *be* a benefactor or pay it forward (Bartlett & De Steno, 2006; De Steno et al., 2010; Nowak et al., 2007).

In contrast to the social evaluations that precede gratitude, the neural underpinnings of these motivational aspects of gratitude may be best investigated through experiments analogous to those in neuroeconomics and other studies of motivation and emotion. Several neuroimaging studies of gratitude have used neuroeconomic paradigms to simulate a direct experience of gratitude (Kini et al., 2015; Yu et al., 2016). Both of these studies found that responses in the ventral medial prefrontal cortex correlated with self-report measures of experienced gratitude. These brain regions are important for complex evaluations of reward and cost and are deeply integrated into motivational systems in the brain.

The moral motivational component of experienced gratitude is not pure economics. It certainly has a social component. Gratitude has been categorized as an "other-praising" emotion akin to elevation and admiration (Algoe & Haight, 2009). Elevation is a warm feeling elicited by witnessing unusual virtue accompanied by a desire to emulate it. Admiration of a skilled or talented individual can induce a desire to work harder or to praise the other. Gratitude focuses on the relationship between benefactor and beneficiary. When someone goes out of his way to help you, he may be showing extraordinary virtue, but when the actions of the admirable person benefit you directly, the stakes of the social attribution of intent are higher. The benefactor's virtuous actions may reflect a high level of care for your well-being. In this sense, gratitude can also be humbling and can broaden and build relationship-seeking behaviors (Algoe & Haight, 2009).

In terms of motivation, it should be noted that motivation and reward are not synonymous. Brain mechanisms that support motivation such as a nucleus accumbens are responsive to both gains and losses (Carter, 2009), perhaps reflecting a more general motivation engaged in seeking a delayed reward. When we are motivated to do well on an exam or meet a deadline, we might bypass a short-term reward, skipping a movie or time with friends to study or write.

Behavioral Outcomes of Gratitude

The motivational component of gratitude should lead to some form of behavioral expression (see figure 10.1). The behavioral expression of gratitude can look like simple reciprocity such as giving back to the benefactor or saying "thank you." You could buy a friend dinner to express your gratitude that she volunteered to help you move, but this has a certain tit-for-tat quality, and the behavior alone does not illustrate whether gratitude was experienced. Perhaps the gesture to return the favor was more about restoring balance to a social relationship or restore justice in an unfair exchange. Say a relative helps out with a check in a time of need—the gift was motivated by a previous act of kindness the relative had received—this might induce a different kind of expression rather than tit-for-tat behaviors. The recipient of such a generous gift might express his gratitude by turning around and helping others who are in need rather than offering to reciprocate directly to the relative. When paying a benefit forward (as in DeSteno et al., 2010), he may be motivated by a heightened sense of thankfulness and humility about benefits received (Exline & Hill, 2012). Rather than seeking relief from guilt (Chang et al., 2011), or seeking to restore a social balance between the recipient and the benefactor (Watkins et al., 2006), prosocial acts of gratitude may be motivated by a desire to be rewarded by the act of giving and the resulting social connection (Algoe & Haight, 2009). Indeed, prosocial actions toward a non-benefactor may best distinguish gratitude from indebtedness at the level of observable behavior. After all, rewarding your helpful roommate with dinner could be done because you feel guilty or because you do not want to be seen as a freeloader. When experiencing gratitude, you would be motivated by a warm prosocial emotion of appreciation, humility, and openness to increased social bonds. Helping someone else in need, or "paying it forward," implies a purer grateful motivation. It is interesting to note how the term "give back" is often used in our society to encourage donations to charity or community volunteering—highlighting the idea that prosocial acts can be motivated by a sense of gratitude for the benefits we have received through the acts of others.

Summary

So far, I have described how gratitude involves multiple cognitive and emotional stages. First, a beneficiary has to recognize a benefit to experience gratitude. Gratitude has a strong social component. So second, the experience of gratitude requires positive attributions of agency to a benefactor, with the benefactor motivated by the beneficiary's well-being.[1] Finally, prosocial actions or behaviors are the result of the moral motivation generated as part of the qualitative experience of gratitude. Importantly, gratitude, though it can be humbling, is a positive emotion, in contrast to guilt or indebtedness. In this model, both benefit-recognition and a social agent are precursors to gratitude, and are necessary but not sufficient for a qualitative experience of gratitude.

This conceptual model is but one possible approach to systemizing gratitude as a higher-order social and moral emotion. For example, McCullough and colleagues describe gratitude as a moral barometer, a moral motivation, and a moral reinforcer (McCullough et al., 2001). The analogy of the moral barometer illustrates the recognition that a benefit has been received and also that a moral act, a beneficiary bestowing a gift, has taken place. The moral motivation component involves the beneficiary feeling motivated to express his gratitude. This expression could take several forms, be they verbal, overtures to increase social closeness, offers or acts of reciprocity, or paying one's gratitude forward to benefit the greater good. The final component of the model proposed by McCullough and colleagues is that there is a reinforcing aspect of gratitude: when a benefactor receives the grateful expression of the beneficiary, her prosocial actions are further reinforced. Given that gratitude is so multifaceted, I suspect that the neural understanding of gratitude will be advanced only if researchers address distinguishable domains of gratitude in a targeted fashion and clearly communicate which aspects of gratitude are being tested in an experimental design.

NEURAL STUDIES OF GRATITUDE

While there are numerous behavioral studies investigating various aspects of gratitude, relatively little neuroscience research has been devoted specifically to the study of gratitude. A critical challenge for the developing neuroscience studies of gratitude is the ecological validity of the experimental stimuli, since the practicalities of neuroimaging research require tasks to be readily implemented in a laboratory setting, such as an MRI machine. The experiments I review here instantiate gratitude in different ways in varied laboratory settings, but all involve fMRI neuroimaging. In the following section,

I discuss which domains of gratitude are investigated in these studies and review potential disparities and similarities across studies with the aim of providing an analytical framework for future work.

Narrative Studies of Gratitude: Who Did What

Several studies have taken a narrative approach to instantiating gratitude in the lab. It is convenient to have participants read a scenario in the lab and imagine their experiences. This approach has the advantage of being able to simulate a fairly rich social context to the experience of being in an MRI scanner. Any avid reader knows the ease with which we can experience an imagined world through words on a page. The ecological validity of the approach depends on the extent that participants can elicit a genuine grateful feeling from the text.

In one early study of gratitude, using a narrative technique, participants listened to simple sentences designed to involve four moral emotions: gratitude, pride, guilt, and indignation (Zahn et al., 2008). The name of the participant's actual best friend was used to evoke gratitude with simple sentences such as "Paul was kind to you." Pride was evoked by inverting the agency of the participant, "You were kind to Paul." Indignation was evoked by changing the positive word to a negative, "Paul was rude to you," and guilt evoked by "You were rude to Paul." All of these moral emotions, both positive and negative, elicited increased task-correlated activity in the anterior temporal pole (see figure 10.2), a region that has been implicated in perspective-taking in non-moral domains as well (e.g., Decety & Lamm, 2007; Saxe et al., 2003; Zahn et al., 2007). This result led the authors to conclude that the anterior temporal pole is involved generally in abstract conceptual representations of social values. Meanwhile, the positive moral-emotions, both pride and gratitude, evoked mesolimbic and basal forebrain reward-system responses. Other analyses were designed to highlight which regions of the brain differentiated these four moral emotions from each other. Only the hypothalamus/ventral tegmental area, a region implicated in reward processing, was associated with higher individual frequency of gratitude, perhaps due to its role in affiliative social bonding (Zahn et al., 2008). This study relates broadly to the precursors in the gateway model of gratitude; recognition and evaluation; and the potential experience of gratitude as it compares to pride, guilt, and indignation. This study does focus on the motivational component of gratitude and does not focus on the role of agency in the experience of gratitude; a social agent, either the self or the best friend, was always present in the stimuli.

Another study using narratives to evoke gratitude is one in which participants read stories describing events that occurred during the Holocaust, subsequently rating how much gratitude they felt (Fox et al., 2015). For example: "Farmer provides refuge for your family on a cold winter night. The next day, Germans storm his house, force your family out of hiding, and burn his farmland." As highlighted by this story, a beneficial intent is not always met with beneficial results in the presence of hostile outside forces, and this can affect levels of gratitude. So here, participant ratings of gratitude after reading the story were used as correlates for the neural activity across trials. The gratitude ratings correlated with increased medial prefrontal activity and anterior cingulate activity during the reflection period following the story. These are key brain regions for reward processing and value judgments (Clithero & Rangel, 2014) as well as self-referential processing (Jankowski et al., 2014; Moore et al., 2014). The more dorsal anterior cingulate region is also involved in perception of pain and cognitive control (Hein & Singer, 2008). A strength of the study is that the stories used are highly evocative and were drawn from real-life reports from a horrifying period of history, but a weakness is that the stories are well outside the everyday events through which most people experience gratitude, leaving the ecological and external validity in question. In terms of the gateway model outlined in the previous section, this instantiation of gratitude potentially relies upon the cost of the gift and whether the intended benefit was realized.

In a recent study (Karns, 2017), I used short narrative vignettes based on everyday stressful situations in which the participant might need help, such as searching for a parking spot or missing an exam. The need is either met or not met and a positive or negative outcome results. In these vignettes, I varied whether the outcome was determined by a social agent such as a friend, colleague, or stranger, or whether it was simply good or bad fortune. The overall goal was to dissociate the reward of simply receiving a positive benefit—such as finding an empty parking spot when you really need it—from that of a positive benefit bestowed from another person—such as a person waving you ahead into a parking spot they were waiting for. The first question was to determine which brain regions were sensitive to the interaction of valence and agency, candidates for integration of the recognition of a benefit, and the evaluation of the intent of the agent. Here, once again, the ventromedial prefrontal cortex (VMPFC) was implicated along with a region of the precuneus, the posterior cingulate cortex, that frequently coactivates with the VMPFC (Clithero et al., 2014). Social agency alone (as a main effect) elicited a robust response across the medial prefrontal cortex, precuneus, superior temporal sulcus, and temporo-parietal junction. The posterior superior temporal sulcus, the same region highlighted by a perspective-taking (theory of mind) localizer task run in the same participants, was sensitive to the interaction of valence and agency. All these regions showed a differential response for the positive result due to a social agent with little difference between the negative outcomes and positive outcomes without social agency.

The next question was to determine whether an independent measure of trait gratitude related to differences in these brain regions. I used a self-report questionnaire that assesses the frequency with which a participant experiences gratitude (GQ-6; McCullough et al., 2002). I hypothesized that frequent experiences of gratitude would predict a larger neural interaction for emotional valence and the presence or absence of social agency. It did, and did so most robustly in the VMPFC and bilateral posterior superior temporal sulcus, providing evidence that these regions relate to gratitude that occurs outside of the laboratory environment. In terms of the gateway model, this instantiation of gratitude probes the evaluation component of gratitude, controlling for the actual benefit received (i.e., you get the parking spot whether or not a benefactor was responsible) highlighting the role a social agent plays in magnifying a positive outcome.

Across these three studies, the narrative stimuli ranged from fairly straightforward (Zahn et al., 2008) to highly evocative (Fox et al., 2015), but all capitalized on the utility of language and imagination to simulate social stimuli. Narratives have been successfully used in other domains of social neuroscience as well (Dodell-Feder et al., 2011). Looking ahead, I expect future studies will use other forms of narrative such as video or film to capture the precursors to and qualitative experience of gratitude.

Neuroeconomic Studies of Gratitude, Exchanges, and Helping

As described earlier, narrative studies offer a straightforward means of simulating gratitude in the laboratory. However, they suffer in one respect. They rely on the power of the participant's imagination to translate the words into an actual experience. The narratives used vary in terms of how relatable they are to participants' lived experiences. An alternative approach has capitalized on approaches used by neuroeconomics researchers to simulate real-time exchanges of benefits to the participants in clever ways. These actual exchanges can more clearly home in on aspects of gratitude that occur later in the gateway model (figure 10.1), motivation and prosocial behavior.

In one recent study, the exchange of goods was literally tangible. Participants were subjected to a painful shock, but the intensity of the shock could be reduced if another person, a confederate of the experimenter, took on some of the shock on the participant's behalf. The experimenters manipulated whether the shock was shared as well as whether the reduction in shock was attributed to the social agent or to a non-agent, the computer. They found that the interaction between agency and sharing in the VMPFC predicted the interaction in allocation—participants could choose to bestow a surprise payment upon their benefactor—but this was mediated, or explained, by the interaction in gratitude ratings. The researchers went a step further, comparing the relationship of the neural interaction to both gratitude ratings and trait gratitude ratings (GQ-6). The measures overlapped in the precuneus and posterior cingulate cortex, a region frequently implicated in studies of reward and social processing. Specifically querying the septum and ventral tegmentum as well as the VMPFC, they found that only the septum accurately distinguished the condition where the social agent chose to share the participant's painful shock. This region was also implicated in the narrative study by Zahn and colleagues, which was the only region unique to gratitude among the four social values examined (Zahn et al., 2008). In the context of this experiment, from the participant's point of view, a real benefit is being bestowed by a stranger introduced to them before the experiment. Participants reciprocate behaviorally by giving a monetary gift to their benefactor, who they are told is not aware that the gift will be given. Thus, this experiment demonstrates a link between the social agency, the qualitative experience of gratitude, and the behavioral outcome, in this case, reciprocity.

In another study, gratitude was simulated in a "pay it forward" task (Kini et al., 2015). Participants received an allocation of money from a person depicted in an image (who, they are told, is a real person). Then they are asked to donate some of the money to a charity to the extent that they feel grateful for the gift. At the time of the decision to donate, regions related to motor preparation and motivation were associated with the amount of money participants paid forward (though the medial prefrontal cortex showed the opposite pattern). When the researchers examined the relationship of two self-report measures of gratitude (GAC-3, Watkins; GQ-6, McCullough), they found that the GQ-6 was related to regions related to the desire to help while the GAC-3 was related to regions related to the amount donated. These findings seem to highlight that self-report measures of trait gratitude are not all alike, and also highlight the importance of clearly describing which aspects of gratitude (evaluation, experience, and behavior) are associated with particular brain regions. However, some aspects of the task may be problematic, for example, the extent to which participants believe the benefactors are real people, and whether the pay-it-forward donations are motivated by gratitude or other factors, such as guilt (though this was rated by the participants and modeled by the experimenters), social signaling of generosity (to the experimenters), or the warm glow associated with choosing to give a donation.

My colleagues and I have also used neuroeconomic approaches to investigate gratitude, using a specific measure of altruism that controls for some of these concerns (Karns et al., 2017). In this task, participants are assigned $20 to their "account" and then are presented with transfers of different amounts from their account to that of a local charity. Some of the transfers are voluntary (participants can accept or reject the transfer) while most are mandatory (resembling taxation). Some transfers are costly to the participant (reducing the amount in their account), while others are a simple allocation of money to either the participant or to the charity. The measure of importance here is the neural response to the mandatory simple allocation to the participant versus the mandatory simple allocation to the charity. In line with previous work (Harbaugh et al., 2007; Hubbard et al., 2016), we consider this a neural measure of pure altruism, which cannot be attributed to impure motivations (see Andreoni, 1990) such as reciprocity because the donation goes to a charity that cannot reciprocate. Impure, warm glow related to a participant's decision is also controlled because the transfers are mandatory. Social signaling to the experimenter is controlled because great care was taken to ensure that the participants understood that the experimenter is not aware of their choices and that the transfers are real.

We found that a self-report measure of the frequency of experienced gratitude (GQ-6) predicted the neural measure of pure altruism and it did so particularly in the VMPFC. We also found that a more general benevolent disposition that also included social values toward care for others (principles of care; Bekkers and Wilhelm, 2016; Wilhelm and Bekkers, 2010) and satisfaction ratings with costly transfers predicted neural pure altruism in reward-related brain regions. This result aligns with the others, indicating that trait gratitude is related to prosocial motivations and may lead to behaviors that benefit others versus the self, providing a potential neural substrate for the behavioral and motivational domains outlined in the gateway model.

THE FUTURE OF BRAIN RESEARCH ON GRATITUDE

As a neuroscientist investigating gratitude, I am often called upon to explain to other neuroscientists why I have devoted time and resources to its study. I point out that gratitude, with its complex social and emotional structure, represents the kind of emotion that we can really study only in human beings, and that neuroimaging technology has reached a point where we can and should start applying it to understand complex emotions. I point out that while we have devoted many resources to the study of depression, anxiety, and other mental health disorders, we have devoted comparatively little to the study of the prosocial positive emotions that seem to help us build strong relationships, contribute to society, and thrive as human beings. As the fields of social neuroscience and prevention science have grown, it has become easier to bolster my argument that positive moral emotions should matter and merit careful research, but still, those eyebrows raise.

As a neuroscientist working at the intersection of neuroscience and philosophy, I am often called upon to explain to philosophers why the time and resources the neuroscience research requires should matter for a moral emotion as complex as gratitude. Why should it matter whether we understand how the brain builds gratitude? Does that help us understand the nature of gratitude? Does it help us to answer questions about the nuances of gratitude that philosophers have pondered for ages? As a scientist, I think it does. I am interested in understanding a phenomenon through a testable and falsifiable model that allows predictions to be made. These models, however flawed they are at the outset, can be honed through careful cumulative research. Models can also help us clarify our terms, serving as a Rosetta stone to translate ideas between fields. But beyond these academic pursuits, brain-based models can be used to build more efficient interventions to promote gratitude in the real-world. The field of "translational neuroscience" is growing rapidly, and has repeatedly demonstrated that understanding neurobiological effects of experiences can provide insight into specific and effective interventions (see Fisher and Skowron, 2017).

Given that some of the studies reviewed used trait measures of gratitude to query relationships with neural measures, a key question seems to be, can neural responses related to gratitude be changed by a gratitude intervention? There are early signs that the answer is yes. For example, in one study of people seeking treatment for anxiety or depression, Kini and colleagues randomly assigned people seeking treatment for anxiety or depression to one of two groups: therapy as usual or therapy plus gratitude exercises (2015). Three months later, the gratitude group showed an increased response in the VMPFC to gratitude ratings during a pay-it-forward task. In our study of pure altruism (Karns et al., 2017), we also tested how the brain responded to a gratitude intervention. The results I described in the previous section—the association between the trait gratitude and the VMPFC—were from the first MRI session prior to random assignment to one of two groups: neutral journaling or gratitude journaling. The second MRI session was performed after three weeks of daily journaling. Relative to pre-test levels, gratitude journaling increased "trait" gratitude and increased the neural pure altruism response in the VMPFC. Thus, while trait effects predict altruistic neural responses, these responses can be altered with practice. Here the neuroimaging gives us a more specific understanding of precisely what is altered by the intervention and avoids the many problems with self-report measures. While there are uncountable questions that studies like this do not, and perhaps cannot, answer, certainly they do offer clarity, perhaps appeasing some critics of a scientific approach to moral emotions.

As the field develops, I am enthusiastic about what neuroscience can bring to the study of gratitude. New directions will likely include more robust and ecologically valid manipulations as well as more precise measures and advanced analyses (Skorburg et al., forthcoming). For example, one recent study brings the temporal precision of event-related potentials to a gratitude intervention study (Patalano et al., 2018). Another recent study uses advanced computational approaches to fMRI analysis to decompose neural components of gratitude into those related to the benefit to self and cost to benefactor (Yu et al., 2018), an approach that maps nicely onto the Gateway Model of Gratitude presented here. As neuroscience continues to encroach on territory long occupied by philosophers, interdisciplinary collaborations and conflicts may prove particularly fruitful to advance our understanding of this parent of all virtues.

NOTE

1 A social agent can certainly be recognized prior to the recognition of a benefit. For example, the friend exists as a social agent before she gives you the concert tickets. What the gateway model explains is that there is an evaluation of social agency attached to a particular benefit. The receipt of the tickets would trigger a cascade of processing that leads to an evaluation of which social agent, if any, is responsible for a benefit.

REFERENCES

Algoe, Sara B., and Jonathan Haidt. 2009. "Witnessing excellence in action: The 'other-praising' emotions of elevation, gratitude, and admiration." *The Journal of Positive Psychology* 4(2): 105–127.

Andreoni, James. 1990. "Impure altruism and donations to public goods: A theory of warm-glow giving." *The Economic Journal* 100(401): 464–477.

Bartlett, Monica Y., and David DeSteno. 2006. "Gratitude and prosocial behavior: Helping when it costs you." *Psychological Science* 17(4): 319–325.

Bekkers, René, and Mark Ottoni-Wilhelm. 2016. "Principle of care and giving to help people in need." *European Journal of Personality* 30(3): 240–257.

Carr, David. 2013. "Varieties of gratitude." *The Journal of Value Inquiry* 47(1–2): 17–28.

Carter, R. McKell, Jeff J. MacInnes, Scott A. Huettel, and R. Alison Adcock. 2009. "Activation in the VTA and nucleus accumbens increases in anticipation of both gains and losses." *Frontiers in Behavioral Neuroscience* 3: 21.

Chang, Luke J., Alec Smith, Martin Dufwenberg, and Alan G. Sanfey. 2011. "Triangulating the neural, psychological, and economic bases of guilt aversion." *Neuron* 70(3): 560–572.

Cheng, Sheung-Tak, Pui Ki Tsui, and John HM Lam. 2015. "Improving mental health in health care practitioners: Randomized controlled trial of a gratitude intervention." *Journal of Consulting and Clinical Psychology* 83(1): 177.

Clithero, John A., and Antonio Rangel. 2013. "Informatic parcellation of the network involved in the computation of subjective value." *Social Cognitive and Affective Neuroscience* 9(9): 1289–1302.

Decety, Jean, and Claus Lamm. 2007. "The role of the right temporoparietal junction in social interaction: how low-level computational processes contribute to meta-cognition." *The Neuroscientist* 13(6): 580–593.

DeSteno, David, Monica Y. Bartlett, Jolie Baumann, Lisa A. Williams, and Leah Dickens. 2010. "Gratitude as moral sentiment: emotion-guided cooperation in economic exchange." *Emotion* 10(2): 289.

Dodell-Feder, David, Jorie Koster-Hale, Marina Bedny, and Rebecca Saxe. 2011. "fMRI item analysis in a theory of mind task." *Neuroimage* 55(2): 705–712.

Ehrenreich, Barbara. "The Selfish Side of Gratitude." *The New York Times*, December 31, 2015.

Emmons, Robert A., and Michael E. McCullough. 2003. "Counting blessings versus burdens: an experimental investigation of gratitude and subjective well-being in daily life." *Journal of Personality and Social Psychology* 84(2): 377.

Exline, Julie J., and Peter C. Hill. 2012. "Humility: A consistent and robust predictor of generosity." *The Journal of Positive Psychology* 7(3): 208–218.

Fisher, Philip A., and Elizabeth A. Skowron. 2017. "Social-learning parenting intervention research in the era of translational neuroscience." *Current Opinion in Psychology* 15: 168–173.

Fox, Glenn R., Jonas Kaplan, Hanna Damasio, and Antonio Damasio. 2015. "Neural correlates of gratitude." *Frontiers in Psychology* 6: 1491.

Froh, Jeffrey J., William J. Sefick, and Robert A. Emmons. 2008. "Counting blessings in early adolescents: An experimental study of gratitude and subjective well-being." *Journal of School Psychology* 46(2): 213–233.

Gordon, Amie M., Emily A. Impett, Aleksandr Kogan, Christopher Oveis, and Dacher Keltner. 2012. "To have and to hold: Gratitude promotes relationship maintenance in intimate bonds." *Journal of Personality and Social Psychology* 103(2): 257–74.

Gulliford, Liz, Blaire Morgan, and Kristján Kristjánsson. 2013. "Recent work on the concept of gratitude in philosophy and psychology." *The Journal of Value Inquiry* 47(3): 285–317.

Harbaugh, William T., Ulrich Mayr, and Daniel R. Burghart. 2007. "Neural responses to taxation and voluntary giving reveal motives for charitable donations." *Science* 316(5831): 1622–1625.

Hein, Grit, and Tania Singer. 2008. "I feel how you feel but not always: the empathic brain and its modulation." *Current Opinion in Neurobiology* 18(2): 153–158.

Hubbard, Jason, William T. Harbaugh, Sanjay Srivastava, David Degras, and Ulrich Mayr. 2016. "A general benevolence dimension that links neural, psychological, economic, and life-span data on altruistic tendencies." *Journal of Experimental Psychology: General* 145(10): 1351–1358.

Jankowski, Kathryn F., William E. Moore, Junaid S. Merchant, Lauren E. Kahn, and Jennifer H. Pfeifer. 2014. "But do you think I'm cool?: Developmental differences in striatal recruitment during direct and reflected social self-evaluations." *Developmental Cognitive Neuroscience* 8: 40–54.

Karns, Christina M. 2017. "It's the thought that counts: The neural interaction of person and valence in everyday social and non- social scenarios that elicit gratitude or distress." In *Proceedings of the 10th Annual Social Affective Neuroscience Society Meeting, Los Angeles, CA.* p. 97 http://www.socialaffectiveneuro.org/SANS%20 2017%20full%20program.pdf

Karns, Christina M., William E. Moore III, and Ulrich Mayr. 2017. "The cultivation of pure altruism via gratitude: a functional MRI study of change with gratitude practice." *Frontiers in Human Neuroscience* 11:599.

Kini, Prathik, Joel Wong, Sydney McInnis, Nicole Gabana, and Joshua W. Brown. 2016. "The effects of gratitude expression on neural activity." *NeuroImage* 128: 1–10.

Kruse, Elliott, Joseph Chancellor, Peter M. Ruberton, and Sonja Lyubomirsky. 2014. "An upward spiral between gratitude and humility." *Social Psychological and Personality Science* 5(7): 805–814.

Lambert, Nathaniel M., Frank D. Fincham, and Tyler F. Stillman. 2012. "Gratitude and depressive symptoms: The role of positive reframing and positive emotion." *Cognition & Emotion* 26(4): 615–633.

McCullough, Michael E., Robert A. Emmons, and Jo-Ann Tsang. 2002. "The grateful disposition: a conceptual and empirical topography." *Journal of Personality and Social Psychology* 82(1): 112.

McCullough, Michael E., Shelley D. Kilpatrick, Robert A. Emmons, and David B. Larson. 2001. "Is gratitude a moral affect?." *Psychological Bulletin* 127(2): 249–66.

Mills, Paul J., Laura Redwine, Kathleen Wilson, Meredith A. Pung, Kelly Chinh, Barry H. Greenberg, Ottar Lunde et al. 2015. "The role of gratitude in spiritual well-being in asymptomatic heart failure patients." *Spirituality in Clinical Practice* 2(1): 5–17.

Moll, J., R. De Oliveira-Souza, and R. Zahn. 2008. "The neural basis of moral cognition: sentiments, concepts, and values." *Annals of the New York Academy of Sciences* 1124: 161–180.

Moore III, William E., Junaid S. Merchant, Lauren E. Kahn, and Jennifer H. Pfeifer. 2013. "'Like me?': ventromedial prefrontal cortex is sensitive to both personal relevance and self-similarity during social comparisons." *Social Cognitive and Affective Neuroscience* 9(4): 421–426.

Ng, Mei-Yee, and Wing-Sze Wong. 2013. "The differential effects of gratitude and sleep on psychological distress in patients with chronic pain." *Journal of Health Psychology* 18(2): 263–271.

Nowak, Martin A., and Sébastien Roch. 2007. "Upstream reciprocity and the evolution of gratitude." *Proceedings of the Royal Society of London B: Biological Sciences* 274(1610): 605–610.

Otto, Amy K., Elana C. Szczesny, Emily C. Soriano, Jean-Philippe Laurenceau, and Scott D. Siegel. 2016. "Effects of a randomized gratitude intervention on death-related fear of recurrence in breast cancer survivors." *Health Psychology* 35(12): 1320–1328.

Patalano, Andrea L., Sydney L. Lolli, and Charles A. Sanislow. 2018. "Gratitude intervention modulates P3 amplitude in a temporal discounting task." *International Journal of Psychophysiology* 133): 202–210.

Saxe, Rebecca, and Nancy Kanwisher. 2003. "People thinking about thinking people: the role of the temporo-parietal junction in "theory of mind"." *Neuroimage* 19(4): 1835–1842.

Shao, Di, Wen Gao, and Feng-Lin Cao. 2016. "Brief psychological intervention in patients with cervical cancer: A randomized controlled trial." *Health Psychology* 35(12): 1383–1391.

Sheldon, Kennon M., and Sonja Lyubomirsky. 2006. "How to increase and sustain positive emotion: The effects of expressing gratitude and visualizing best possible selves." *The Journal of Positive Psychology* 1(2): 73–82.

Skorburg, Joshua-August, Mark Alfano, Christina, M. Karns (forthcoming). "Moral thinking, more and less quickly." https://philpapers.org/rec/ALFMTM

Tsang, Jo-Ann. 2006. "Gratitude and prosocial behaviour: An experimental test of gratitude." *Cognition & Emotion* 20(1): 138–148.

Van Dusen, John P., Mojisola F. Tiamiyu, Todd B. Kashdan, and Jon D. Elhai. 2015. "Gratitude, depression and PTSD: Assessment of structural relationships." *Psychiatry research* 230(3): 867–870.

Watkins, Philip, Jason Scheer, Melinda Ovnicek, and Russell Kolts. 2006. "The debt of gratitude: Dissociating gratitude and indebtedness." *Cognition & Emotion* 20(2): 217–241.

Wilhelm, Mark Ottoni, and René Bekkers. 2010. "Helping behavior, dispositional empathic concern, and the principle of care." *Social Psychology Quarterly* 73(1): 11–32.

Wong, Y. Joel, Jesse Owen, Nicole T. Gabana, Joshua W. Brown, Sydney McInnis, Paul Toth, and Lynn Gilman. 2018. "Does gratitude writing improve the mental health of psychotherapy clients? Evidence from a randomized controlled trial." *Psychotherapy Research* 28(2): 192–202.

Young, Liane, David Dodell-Feder, and Rebecca Saxe. 2010. "What gets the attention of the temporo-parietal junction? An fMRI investigation of attention and theory of mind." *Neuropsychologia* 48(9): 2658–2664.

Yu, Hongbo, Qiang Cai, Bo Shen, Xiaoxue Gao, and Xiaolin Zhou. 2017. "Neural substrates and social consequences of interpersonal gratitude: Intention matters." *Emotion* 17(4): 589–601.

Yu, Hongbo, Xiaoxue Gao, Yuanyuan Zhou, and Xiaolin Zhou. 2018. "Decomposing gratitude: representation and integration of cognitive antecedents of gratitude in the brain." *Journal of Neuroscience* 38(21): 2944–17.

Zahn, Roland, Jorge Moll, Mirella Paiva, Griselda Garrido, Frank Krueger, Edward D. Huey, and Jordan Grafman. 2008. "The neural basis of human social values: evidence from functional MRI." *Cerebral Cortex* 19(2): 276–283.

Zahn, Roland, Jorge Moll, Frank Krueger, Edward D. Huey, Griselda Garrido, and Jordan Grafman. 2007. "Social concepts are represented in the superior anterior temporal cortex." *Proceedings of the National Academy of Sciences* 104(15): 6430–6435.

Chapter 11

Gratitude, Authenticity, and Self-Authorship

Jack J. Bauer and Colin Shanahan

I was 26. I moved to [location]. I stayed with my cousin but she moved [away] after only three months. I ended up being completely alone for six months and it turned out to be the best six months of my life. I was able to go deep within myself and cater to my wants and needs. I became very grateful [and] learned to depend on me. I matured and blossomed into the woman that was within.

—Research participant, age forty-two, describing a
"turning point in life"

It's the truth of who I am [. . .] all the peace and joy, and harmony and gratitude that I seek in my life is within me. It is who I am.

—Research participant, age forty-three, describing her
"religious or spiritual beliefs"

These excerpts come from two studies of autobiographical life stories (Bauer & DesAutels, 2017; Bauer, Graham, Lauber, & Lynch, 2017) and illustrate how gratitude and authenticity can arise together in the developmental process of self-authorship. However, these brief passages hardly convey the range and depth of the phenomena at hand. In this chapter, we approach gratitude and authenticity as forms of meaning-making, as qualities of a good life, as characteristics of personality and self-identity, and as developing skills for thinking about the self and others.

As a form of meaning-making, the virtue of gratitude has at its root the ideal of cooperative human relationships. The grateful individual is routinely aware of and acknowledges others' beneficence, which in turn motivates others and oneself toward good works in the future. Gratitude helps make communal endeavors worthwhile and meaningful.

217

As a form of meaning-making, the virtue of authenticity has at its root the ideal of freedom. The authentic individual acts and maps out a life according to an internal compass pointing to a magnetic north that is oneself, which in turn motivates the individual person to be more than just a cog in the social machine. Authenticity helps make agentic endeavors worthwhile and meaningful.

Living thankfully and authentically are hallmarks of a good life. Where gratitude and authenticity have been studied together, they correlate (Wood, Linley, Maltby, Baliousis, & Joseph, 2008). Yet gratitude and authenticity have received little joint attention in either theory or empirical research, perhaps because the two virtues seem to be so different. Gratitude is about giving thanks, whereas authenticity is about being true to oneself. Expressions of gratitude are readily recognizable (Emmons, 2004), whereas expressions of authenticity are subtler, made known only in light of one's interior life. Gratitude appears to be necessary for human reciprocity and social relations (and perhaps the survival of our species [Bonnie & de Waal, 2004]), whereas authenticity (at least in its existential sense) is a more refined virtue, hardly necessary for survival and reproduction. Gratitude, even as measured in various ways, routinely correlates with measures of subjective or psychological well-being (for a review, see Wood, Froh, & Geraghty, 2010), whereas high levels of authenticity correlate with either high levels of well-being (Kernis, 2003) or low levels of well-being (Shimai, Otake, Park, Peterson, & Seligman, 2006), depending on how authenticity is measured. It might seem as though the only connection between gratitude and authenticity is that they appear as two virtues on a list of character strengths (e.g., Shimai et al., 2006).

However, gratitude and authenticity converge in a way that is central to the development of a good life, particularly when viewed through the lens of self-authorship. In authoring or narrating one's self-identity, the person values and positions the self and others relative to each other—a process that informs and is informed by the experiencing and expressing of both gratitude and authenticity. In this chapter, we examine how gratitude, authenticity, and self-authorship jointly facilitate the individual's developing capacity to understand the interdependent nature of both personal experience and a good life. The result is a mutually increasing capacity for *authentic gratitude* and *grateful authenticity*.

GRATITUDE

Gratitude is a complex phenomenon and has been approached as a situation-based emotion (e.g., DeSteno, Bartlett, Baumann, Williams, & Dickens, 2010; McCullough, Kilpatrick, Emmons, & Larson, 2001), a motivation (e.g., Froh,

Bono, & Emmons, 2010), a moral barometer (McCullough & Tsang, 2004), a cause of well-being (Emmons & McCullough, 2003), a facilitator of relationships (Algoe, Haidt, & Gable, 2008; Algoe, Frederickson, & Gable, 2013), a duty or rule that cultures universally encourage their members to express (Emmons & Crumpler, 2000), and a spiritual or transcendent experience (e.g., McCullough, Tsang, & Emmons, 2004). These features play important roles in the present chapter, but all through the lens of the development of gratitude as a virtuous personality characteristic—that is, as a feature of a good life.

For gratitude to serve as a feature of a good life, gratitude must be expressed and experienced routinely in a person's life—a characteristic of one's thoughts, feelings, and behaviors (McCullough et al., 2004). McCullough and Tsang (2004) review support for Cicero's claim that gratitude is the "parent of the virtues." We take this position, arguing from a developmental perspective that the *expression* of gratitude represents one of the earliest virtues we teach young children to exercise, from which later in childhood develops a more genuine (in other words, more authentic) *experience* of gratitude, with increasingly deeper experiences of gratitude as authenticity develops in one's narrative self-identity.

As a parent of other moral virtues, gratitude involves certain minimum requirements for thinking and acting virtuously. Gratitude is among the primary or basic motivators of moral behavior (McCullough & Tsang, 2004). Gratitude involves one of the more primitive features of conventional definitions of moral reasoning: attributing intentionality of the good to another person (McCullough et al., 2001). We are not specifically grateful to someone if we believe they *had* to help us (i.e., it was their duty) or if we believe their helping us was by accident or a byproduct (Roberts, 2004). Furthermore, the fact that we know others might be grateful serves as an additional motivation to do good.

Gratitude may well serve to facilitate social reciprocity, raising the question of gratitude's evolutionary function in humans and other primates (Bonnie & de Waal, 2004). Reciprocal social arrangements, in which one organism repays another organism for bestowing some good, is common in the animal world. However, gratitude is relatively uncommon among species, as it requires a mental capacity for making attributions of agency that further facilitate reciprocal behaviors. This ability for "calculated reciprocity" is largely restricted to humans, chimpanzees, and possibly other primates (Bonnie & de Waal, p. 220). However, the bar is high: merely "attitudinal reciprocity" (p. 220), or mirroring the other's attitude, is not enough to be considered gratitude. Bonnie and de Waal emphasize the cognitive complexity required for such reciprocal interactions to be called gratitude.

The concept of genuine gratitude or authentic gratitude can be defined by the capacity not only to express gratitude as a social script but also to *experience* the emotion of gratitude (Froh, Miller, & Snyder, 2007). The difference here is between knowing when to say "thank you" and knowing why gratitude is appropriate, the latter of which facilitates feeling grateful. Such authentic gratitude seems to develop as a routine characteristic of personality sometime in later childhood (more on this later). Yet the authentic gratitude of the child is not the authentic gratitude of the adult, who has considerably heightened capacities for living authentically, the topic to which we turn next, before eventually considering how authentic gratitude (and grateful authenticity) develops as a function of an increasingly more humane and interdependent self-authorship.

AUTHENTICITY

Gratitude may require more cognitive complexity than almost any other species can muster, but compared to other human virtues, gratitude falls on the simpler side of the scale. Whereas gratitude lays a simple foundation for other moral virtues, authenticity functions as one of the more complex, developmentally advanced forms of virtue. Gratitude is a requirement of a good life; authenticity is an aspiration of it.

Or so it would seem to philosophers of ethics and virtue. But at least one model of authenticity in psychological science and in folk psychology claims that authenticity does not require a moral consideration of others' welfare.

Essentialist versus Existentialist Authenticity

Generally speaking, authenticity is being true to yourself. But is it better to be what you were born to be, rather than what you want to be? Or is it better to be what you want to be, rather than what you were born to be? The two questions presuppose two important definitions of authenticity that are often pitted against each other: essentialist authenticity and existentialist authenticity (Bauer, in press). We describe each of them further, but we first wish to emphasize that essentialism and existentialism are two philosophical positions that make both ontological and ethical claims about the source and functioning of the self and personhood. As forms of authenticity, essentialist and existentialist authenticity represent two models that are studied by researchers in psychology and that are held intuitively in folk psychology (although only recently have these models been framed as *essentialist* and *existentialist*; Bauer, in press).

These two positions are not mutually exclusive but rather are contrasted by *developmental capacities*. The capacity to be authentic from an essentialist perspective develops prior to the capacity for existentialist authenticity.

The qualities of existentialist authenticity include some of the qualities of essentialist authenticity but are not bound to them. Existentialist authenticity is characterized by capacities that build on those of essentialist authenticity but in addition include capacities that develop later.

Essentialist authenticity. Essentialist authenticity means being *true to your traits*, especially the most deeply embedded of your traits—"what you were born to be" or "what you were brought up to be." The term "essentialist authenticity" refers to the belief that one's true self already exists in oneself— the core traits that, left to their own devices, would (and should) govern one's behavior (e.g., McGregor, McAdams, & Little, 2006). Not only that, but these core traits do not necessarily require much self-discovery or psychological unearthing; these traits may well be readily observed, like extraversion or even aggression. Essentialist authenticity asks the person to live out those core personality characteristics that are considered to be implanted or embedded within us—that is, shaped by nature (i.e., one's genetically predisposed traits), nurture (i.e., one's socially ingrained traits), or some supernatural force (e.g., one's god-given soul). Whereas the attempt to enact one's essence may involve intense efforts toward self-discovery, the goal of essentialist authenticity may also be simpler to conceptualize, such as the attempt to enact those traits that one believes to be factually and *inherently who we are*. To some degree, concern for others' welfare may be beside the point. Let's say Donald routinely disparages others. If Donald is a belligerent soul (i.e., belligerent in essence), then not only is he justified in disparaging others but he also *should* do so, because then he is being authentic: "It's just Donald being Donald."

Existentialist authenticity. Existentialist authenticity means being *true to our values*, or being "what you want to be." The term *existentialist authenticity* refers to the belief of existentialist philosophers that the person *constructs* a self-identity based on virtues that one chooses and that carry responsibilities for the welfare of others (Sartre, 1943). However, the "choosing" that we have in mind is not radically constructivist. It is constructivist to the degree that psychosocial development in practice will allow (Erikson, 1950; McAdams, Diamond, de St. Aubin, & Mansfield, 1997): the narrative construction of a self-identity is rooted in certain biological and social affordances that limit choices as well as the person's capacity to conceptualize and enact those choices (Taylor, 1989). Thus, by *existentialist authenticity*, we mean a eudaimonic, existentialist authenticity (Bauer, in press). This constructing and choosing does not mean that the person can simply choose some particular virtue and that this choosing makes the person virtuous. Something of essentialism obtains: We in fact are born and bred to have particular characteristics, some of which are virtuous, which limits the degrees to which we can enact various virtues. Existentialist authenticity, then, is part self-discovery and part self-creation (May, 1969). Of those particular virtues (and vices) that we discover "within" us and that we can cultivate like skills (Annas, 2011), we choose some and not others. To the degree that we—after critical examination of our ethical roles and responsibilities in a world of others—cultivate and enact virtues that we value or identify with, we live more authentically from an existentialist perspective.

These virtues are typically subtle and are not easily articulated, even if they might fall under categories like "wisdom" or "love." The person who enacts these authentic virtues routinely recognizes the formidable forces, both external and internal, that often seem to conspire against pursuing wisdom or love. Enacting existentialist authenticity, generally speaking, requires decades of development, self-examination, testing one's idealized virtues in real-life contexts, and modifying or reconstructing one's (narrative) self-identity in light of the outcomes and one's evolving ideals. This development over decades leads the individual to recognize not only how to enact one's own configurations of virtues and abilities but also how deeply and pervasively dependent one's life and self-identity are on other people. Such understandings and processes are critical to the developmental processes of Maslow's (1968) self-actualization, Rogers's (1961) fully functioning person, and Jung's (1959) individuation.

Essence of what? The notion that essentialist authenticity might not involve a concern for morality might sound strange, because eudaimonists (e.g., Flanagan, 2007; Haybron, 2008; Waterman, 2013) generally posit an ingrained essence that depends on ethical reasoning. However, essentialist authenticity focuses on the essence of one's *personality, not of ethics* or living a good life. For the person who believes in essentialist authenticity, authenticity is a matter of living according to one's core personality characteristics, which may or may not have anything to do with ethics. In contrast, existentialist authenticity focuses on the *ethical essence* of one's personality—those personality characteristics that facilitate the living of a morally *good* life. Whereas Sartrean existentialism emphasizes the radical primacy of choice and free will, existentialist perspectives can also include a position of choice within the limits of one's deeply embedded characteristics (given by genes or social environments), such that one's understanding of self and others is a matter of biologically, psychologically, and socially contextualized meaning-making (particularly in narrative forms—e.g., Guignon [2004] and Ricoeur [1985]).

The role of gratitude. Gratitude plays different roles in these two definitions of authenticity. Essentialist authenticity as a broad class of authenticity requires no gratitude at all. However, essentialism in virtue ethics more broadly is found in the eudaimonic tradition, which emphasizes the essence *of* the person and requires dependence-related virtues like gratitude, compassion, and generosity (Chappell, this volume; MacIntyre, 2001). Of course, individuals who hold an essentialist view of authenticity may well feel and express gratitude to those they believe to have contributed to their formation. Individuals might be thankful to their parents, their god, or any number of other people or forces that created their inner essence. But gratitude is not necessary for essentialist beliefs in authenticity. Only enacting one's inner essence, whether morally virtuous or not, is necessary.

However, gratitude plays a critical role for existentialist authenticity, which is inherently moral. "Authenticity requires something more than making a decision to identify with something, where *what* we identify with is irrelevant" (Guignon, 2004, p. 155). "Instead, we need to see that our identity-conferring identifications are drawn from, and are answerable to, the shared historical commitments and ideals that make up our communal life-world." Existentialist authenticity involves an awareness of the causes, constitution, and effects of personhood as inherently embedded in a world of others. Such an awareness of oneself would seem to lead naturally to an appreciation for and gratitude toward other people and forces. We call this *existentially authentic gratitude*.

Self-Discovery: Essentialist or Existentialist Authenticity?

Existentialist authenticity in the eudaimonic tradition also involves a searching for or otherwise trying to discover and enact a true self that is buried deep within. This process of self-discovery might look like an essentialist belief (and to some degree it is), but three factors steer this process in the existential direction.

First, whereas essentialist authenticity may involve a process of self-discovery, self-discovery involves not merely acting in accord with the many characteristics that one discovers in the process of self-searching but also an acknowledgment of one's *choosing* from them—choices that rest on which personal characteristics one values and does not value. Existentialist authenticity does not ignore the fact that certain characteristics are deeply embedded by nature and nurture. Essentialist authenticity involves a belief that nature and nurture are all that matter for authenticity. As it turns out, individuals who strive to match their chosen personal values with their inborn traits were found to have especially high levels of psychological health and well-being (Sheldon, Ryan, Rawsthorne, & Ilardi, 1997). (However, we note that subjective well-being is not a requisite of existentialist authenticity.) In any case, for the existentialist, "Self-discovery requires *poēsis*, making" (Taylor, 1991, p. 62). Recently we found that people who hold essentialist beliefs in authenticity value discovery but not creation metaphors of the "true self," whereas people who hold existentialist beliefs in authenticity value both discovery and creation metaphors of the "true self" (Shanahan & Bauer, 2018).

Second, whereas a belief in essentialist authenticity need not accept the idea that one's true self must have something to do with morality, ethics, or concern for others' welfare, a belief in existentialist authenticity claims that authenticity is inherently a moral concern. The active pursuit of self-discovery is ultimately about choosing to become more virtuous (i.e., to enact virtues more routinely). Recently, we found that people who hold existentialist beliefs in authenticity score higher on measures of identifying with ethical concerns—gratitude and generativity specifically, and morality in general—whereas people who hold essentialist beliefs in authenticity do not (Shanahan & Bauer, 2018).

Third, the sense of interdependence is central to existential authenticity. Consonant with an existentialist perspective on authenticity, Charles Taylor (1991, p. 41) writes, "Authenticity is not the enemy of demands that emanate from beyond the self; it *supposes* such demands" (emphasis added). We add that, given the maturity of authenticity that we explain later, these demands are not viewed as exclusively burdensome but rather as a natural extension of human interdependence. It would seem that gratitude would logically and naturally follow from an awareness of such an interdependent reliance on others. However, gratitude is scarcely mentioned in either the philosophy or psychology of authenticity (e.g., Guignon, 2004; Sartre, 1943). Indeed, one of the three dimensions of a prominent self-report measure of authenticity (Wood et al., 2008) casts "accepting external influence" as *antithetical* to authenticity.[1] We note that the self-report items that measure "accepting external influence" are especially conformist in nature. In contrast, existential authenticity as a moral virtue requires a post-conformist capacity to think about the necessarily interdependent relation between self and others (see the developmental section next on the role of the conformist mindset in gratitude and authenticity)—and requires, it seems to us, an experience of gratitude.

As an example of this grateful kind of authenticity, Abraham Maslow (1968) notes that the self-actualizing person, whose central characteristics feature authenticity, experiences deep gratitude toward other people or a transcendent entity. Experiences of existential enlightenment (Maslow's "peak experiences" included), which are in many ways acute experiences of authenticity, are notable for profound experiences of gratitude (James, 1902). As a personality characteristic, existential authenticity involves a deep sense of gratitude, which we explain later, after first explaining how the development of self-authorship serves to bridge gratitude and authenticity.

SELF-AUTHORSHIP

Gratitude and authenticity are not merely virtuous characteristics that can be used to *describe* a person who routinely enacts those virtues. These are also virtues with which some people *identify* and routinely *strive* to enact. For such people, gratitude or authenticity is a personally meaningful value. These people *believe in* the virtue of gratitude or authenticity. When people strive to live gratefully and authentically, these virtues become personally meaningful features of their self-identity.

People create a self-identity—that is, their personally meaningful understanding of themselves over time—in the stories they construct and tell about their lives (McAdams, 2008). In creating a *narrative self-identity*, the person attempts to make sense of the myriad aspects of her life (of oneself as a whole, particular characteristics of oneself, other individuals and groups as wholes and in particular events, specific actions, things, etc.). The idea that a life story is *an attempt* raises the question: What are people trying to do in constructing a life story, in making sense of themselves and their lives? In a nutshell, people are trying to create a good life—and they do so by trying to create a *good life story* (Bauer, 2016). For people who identify with the virtues of gratitude and authenticity, these virtues surface as themes in people's life stories—themes on which a good life story is based.

Cultural Master Narratives of Gratitude and Authenticity

Individuals are not left on their own to create a good life story, nor need they reinvent the wheel. Cultures provide individuals with models of virtues and even stories of virtues by which to live. Such stories are known as *cultural master narratives* (Hammack, 2011; McAdams, 2006). Cultural master narratives are stories that a culture treasures for the virtues those stories extol. These stories and virtues pervade a culture. They are found across forms of publishing and cultural discourse that are produced by social institutions. Cultural master narratives are found in literature, film, music, religion, politics, education, government, commerce, media, and advertising. Cultural master narratives present models for individuals on what a good life is—and on how to construct (and live out) a good life story (Bauer, 2016). Individuals borrow from cultural master narratives to interpret and plan their actual lives.

Enter gratitude and authenticity: individuals draw on cultural master narratives that feature the virtues of gratitude and authenticity. The stories and mythology of all major religions and cultures around the world emphasize the virtue of gratitude (e.g., Emmons, 2004; Roberts, 2004; Steindl-Rast, 2004). In these stories, individuals are reminded and encouraged to express and experience thanks to friends, parents, authority figures, legendary sages, social institutions, belief systems, animals, natural or supernatural forces, and even one's enemies. In religious contexts, expressions of gratitude toward a central religious figure (e.g., the Abrahamic religions' God, the Buddha) are often offered as part of prayer, religious rituals, and everyday rituals like meals. Cultural master narratives of origin myths (in which the universe is created by a god in human form, animal form, an egg, etc.) emphasize the importance of gratitude toward the creator or creation itself (Campbell, 1988).

Similarly, stories in (especially Westernized, industrialized) cultures emphasize the virtue of authenticity—the ideal of being oneself, being true to oneself, and being the genuine article. From commercial advertising to literature and film, individuals are advised from a young age to "be yourself." The ideal of authenticity as a cultural master narrative is found in perhaps its most crystallized form in the *Bildungsroman* genre of literature, featuring coming-of-age and character-development stories (Bauer, 2016). Generally speaking, the *Bildungsroman* protagonist rejects mainstream life and values, sets off on a course of personal adventure, receives training from a master (e.g., in the arts or spirituality), is tested by evil forces (generally symbolizing features of mainstream life), masters them, and returns to society to help or transform it—all the while developing an increasingly authentic understanding of one-self (Jeffers, 2005).

Narrative Tools of Self-Authorship

Individuals identify with cultural master narratives of gratitude and authenticity in an attempt to live out these virtues and to construct a good life story—a life story of a good life. But individuals do not simply buy into cultural master narratives wholesale. Individuals do not simply try to turn their lives into an exact replica of a cultural master narrative. Instead, individuals treat cultural master narratives like a buffet, ingesting only the features of those stories that the individual finds palatable. Cultures do shape what most individuals will find palatable, but individuals' tastes also vary widely. In drawing on cultural master narratives, individuals select this value, that image, this script, that character prototype, and so on, thereby creating a relatively unique life story, somewhat like a plate in a buffet (if only it were that easy, or that tasty).

Let's switch metaphors from a buffet to the construction of a building. To construct meaning in her life story, the person relies on the same narrative tools that writers of cultural master narratives use—tools like narrative tones, imagery, themes, structure, scripts, and character prototypes. Two narrative tools that are especially relevant to the present topic are narrative *theme* and narrative *structure*. (Importantly for research, all these tools of self-authorship can be measured by first asking people to tell or to write personal narratives and then by identifying systematically the degree to which these tools—tones, themes, structures—are featured in the narratives, and finally by describing those features either quantitatively or qualitatively.)

Themes of Gratitude and Authenticity

Narrative themes tell us why a person or event is important. Themes reveal what the narrator or various characters in a story value, want, and are motivated by. Narrative theme is a tool for harnessing abstract values and motives onto the concrete events and people in a story. Agency and communion are two of life's greatest themes, encompassing a range of values and motives, such as (respectively) power and love, independence and dependence, and mastery and nurturance (McAdams, 1993). Themes serve as a character's or narrator's meaningful basis of interpretation and reasons, justifications, and purposes of action. Virtues, like other types of value, serve as themes in life stories (Bauer, 2016). The virtues of gratitude and authenticity serve as themes in the life stories of people who identify with those virtues. People convey their valuing and identifying with virtues in personal narratives that feature the person possessing, seeking, or otherwise being motivated by those virtues (Bauer & DesAutels, in press). Gratitude or authenticity can be said to characterize a person's narrative self-identity when themes of gratitude or authenticity surface in many of the episodes of that person's life story.

Themes of virtuous growth. A third great theme of life stories is growth—and more particularly, eudaimonic growth (Bauer, 2016). Whereas themes of agency and communion deal with orientations toward the individual person and others (respectively), which might be thought of as orientations in psychosocial space, the theme of growth deals with an orientation toward psychosocial *time*. Growth themes can come in the form of or overlap with either agentic or communal themes. More important for the study of gratitude and authenticity, however, is the *humanistic* (rather than materialistic, egoistic, or economistic) value orientation of growth themes (Bauer, McAdams, & Pals, 2008). Narrative growth themes focus on humanistic concerns of cultivating deeper personal experiences via personally meaningful activities and relationships, rather than materialistic or egoistic concerns for social status, self-image, physical appearance, approval-seeking or approval-gaining, and other concerns that reflect an economistic view of personhood. Humanistic values and narrative themes facilitate virtuous development and well-being years later (Bauer & McAdams, 2010; Kasser, Koestner, & Lekes, 2002; Kasser & Ryan, 1996). While economistic concerns are also important to consider in navigating the pragmatics of life, humanistic concerns are more directly tied to the development of virtues like gratitude and authenticity (e.g., Froh, Emmons, Card, Bono, & Wilson, 2011; Kernis, 2003; Wood et al., 2010).

The theme of gratitude. The expression of gratitude is relatively easy to detect in a narrative: statements of thanks or appreciation for others generally indicate a valuing of others' help. Gratitude involves an attribution of beneficent agency to the other (McCullough & Tsang, 2004), which is to say, a *valuing* of a particular person and a particular kind of action. The valuing of a particular kind of action is what makes gratitude a theme in narratives: gratitude in a narrative reveals the narrator's valuing of helpful behavior.

On the topic of helpful behavior itself, we note that helping oneself is not a virtue of gratitude. But expressions of genuine gratitude are not selfish, even if they serve the self in a relationship of reciprocal social exchange (DeSteno et al., 2010). Expressions of gratitude reflect an acknowledgment of the moral good of helping (Emmons, 2004). Consider the converse: when a personal narrative describes how the narrator cared for others, the narrative has a communal theme, expressing a personal valuing of caring (McAdams, 1993). Narratives that express personal contributions to the welfare of future generations have themes of generativity (McAdams & Guo, 2015), a developmentally salient theme that we examine later. Thus, expressions of gratitude—even in their simplest forms (see section on narrative structure)—reflect a personal value orientation toward the virtue of helping.

Furthermore, themes of gratitude in a narrative, as expressions of genuine gratitude, are *self-reflections, not social-exchange paybacks*. The expression of gratitude in a life story or a personal narrative is not the same as the expression of gratitude in real time, when individuals say or otherwise express thanks for what others have given to oneself. Narrated gratitude is a *reflection* on a past event in which the narrator is conveying to the listener—and to oneself—the importance of expressing thanks for benefits received. Again, the expression of gratitude in a personal narrative, which is more reflective than expressing gratitude in situ, reveals that the person *values* gratitude—or at the very least recognizes the personal benefit of expressing gratitude.

The theme of authenticity. Authenticity is more difficult than gratitude to detect in a life story (from the researcher's perspective). This difficulty reflects how much more difficult it is to live authentically and to articulate doing so than it is to experience and express gratitude (from the narrator's perspective). Authenticity as a theme in a narrative comes in both essentialist and existentialist forms, as distinguished earlier.

To give some examples of what authenticity sounds like from essentialist and existentialist perspectives, the following excerpts come from a self-report questionnaire, the Essentialist and Existentialist Authenticity Scale (EEAS; Shanahan & Bauer, in preparation). Themes of essentialist authenticity convey the value of acting in accord with personality characteristics that are deeply embedded, whether by nature or nurture. These themes come in forms like "my true self is who I was meant to be, as defined by my divinely created soul," "my true self is who I was born to be, as defined by my genetics," and "my soul or inner essence is unchanging. It is the foundation of my authentic self." Themes of existentialist authenticity come in forms like "my true self is who I want myself to be, as defined by careful reflection that I have done," "my self-identity and beliefs are evolving. They are the foundation of my authentic self," and "an authentic person builds on their best traits while working on changing their worst traits." Now, these excerpts are generic abstractions of specific themes in people's life stories, but they convey the kinds of concerns that emerge in people's life stories as themes. Again, themes of existentialist authenticity also involve an emphasis on self-discovery, for example, "I've worked hard for years to discover who I really am." As noted earlier, even though the idea of self-discovery assumes an essentialist belief in an inner essence, self-discovery also involves a personal *choice* not to cultivate unvirtuous personality tendencies—while accepting them as part of one's personhood—in favor of pursuing other tendencies that one deems more virtuous. Beliefs in authenticity that emphasize the essentialism of personality (e.g., McGregor et al., 2006) eschew the notion that authenticity necessarily has anything to do with morality and virtue.

Narrative Structure of Gratitude and Authenticity

Narrative structure is how the content in a story (notably themes) is organized, most prominently by degrees of complexity and coherence (e.g., Habermas & de Silveira, 2008; Suedfeld & Bluck, 1993). Some stories are simple, such as children's stories in which each character has a single theme (e.g., courage). Other stories are complex, and thus more compelling to adults, as when each character has multiple and conflicting themes (e.g., motives for power and love, and major life decisions that hang in the balance). Similarly, some stories are incoherent and fragmented, whereas other stories are coherent and integrated. Fragmented stories can be simple or complex, just as coherent stories can be.

Any one meaningful event in a life story can be interpreted (and communicated) simplistically or complexly—as can the virtues of gratitude or authenticity. Gratitude can be expressed in a narrative with a simple "I'm really thankful that . . ." or else complexly by elaborating on the reasons and ways in which the narrator is grateful. Similarly, authenticity can be expressed in a narrative with a simple "I've always been true to myself" or else complexly by elaborating on the reasons and ways in which the narrator believes himself to be (or to have been) authentic.

Narrative structure lies at the heart of an entire branch of the study of self-identity development that is informed by Piaget (1970). Neo-Piagetian theories of self-identity development (e.g., Damon & Hart, 1988; Kegan, 1982; Loevinger, 1976) shed light on the dynamic development of gratitude, authenticity, and self-authorship.

THE DEVELOPMENT OF GRATITUDE, AUTHENTICITY, AND SELF-AUTHORSHIP

As self-authorship develops, so does the individual's understanding and experience of gratitude and authenticity. The development of these two virtues unfolds according to developments in the narrative themes and structure of one's self-authorship. In addition, gratitude, authenticity, and self-authorship scaffold the development of each other toward an increasingly interdependent, humanistic, and complex understanding of personal experience and a good life. In this section, we consider the development of gratitude and authenticity as they unfold at different stages of self-authorship. We pay particular attention to the development of authentic gratitude and grateful authenticity.

Before We Start: Enacting Virtue versus Narrating Virtue

To be clear, in this section, we focus on the development of the *self-authorship of* gratitude and authenticity, which is not quite the same as the development of gratitude itself and authenticity itself. As mentioned earlier, it is one thing to express gratitude in situ; it is another thing to use gratitude as a theme in one's life story. The former demands little reflection, as when a child says "thank you" by rote; the latter demands self-reflection on the importance of giving thanks in one's life. As for authenticity, it is one thing to live authentically and another to articulate the importance of authenticity in one's life story.

The capacity to enact gratitude develops earlier than the capacity to enact authenticity, as will be explained in this section. Gratitude is akin to the foundation for constructing a good life (and thus built into social norms), whereas authenticity is more like the architectural ornament of a good life (and thus more a refinement than a necessity). Not to diminish the importance of authenticity: just as architecture gives a building its distinct character and a particular measure of excellence (as in Aristotelian *arete* in a good life), authenticity is a hallmark of excellence in a good life story (Guignon, 2004; Taylor, 1991).

Furthermore, the differences between *enacting* gratitude and authenticity and *narrating* gratitude and authenticity are asymmetric. Whereas gratitude is easier to enact than to narrate, authenticity is easier to narrate than to enact. The expression of gratitude (saying "thank you") can be learned earlier in life than one's genuine experience of it. The development of expressing and even experiencing gratitude probably does *not* demand that one use themes of gratitude in one's life story; many more people say "thank you" in situ than express thanks in their life stories (McAdams & Bauer, 2004). In contrast, the development of expressing and experiencing authenticity probably *does* demand that one use themes of authenticity in one's life story; authenticity requires a relatively coherent narrative self-identity that corresponds to one's actions. In other words, we can probably be routinely grateful without identifying especially with efforts toward gratitude, whereas we probably cannot be routinely authentic without identifying with efforts toward authenticity. Existential authenticity is too difficult to enact in one's life without personally meaningful efforts to do so.

THE DEVELOPMENT OF NARRATIVE THEMES AND NARRATIVE STRUCTURE

Narrative themes and narrative structure both develop interactively. Narrative structure organizes narrative themes in their degrees of complexity and coherence, just as narrative themes orient narrative structure (which alone is content- and value-free) toward the lived values and experiences of actual lives.

Yet theme and structure also develop independently. For instance, a theme of gratitude may remain a constant feature of self-authorship throughout a person's life, but the structure of that theme is likely to change drastically. For example, the gratitude of a child is egoistic and self-protective (saying "thank you" because one was told to do so or to get praise from an authority figure), whereas the gratitude of an adolescent or adult is more likely to be authentic (saying "thank you" because one experiences another's beneficence and wants to make the other experience good feelings for helping).

In the following sections, we present the development of gratitude, authenticity, and self-authorship according to age-based life periods, which is admittedly clunky (e.g., age is a crude guide for psychological maturity). For gratitude, we focus on the development of the expression and the experience of gratitude, where authentic gratitude requires an experience of gratitude. For authenticity, we focus on existentialist (not essentialist) authenticity, which is largely a non-issue before adolescence and the development of a relatively coherent and comprehensive life story (McAdams, 1993; McLean et al., 2007).

Childhood: The Emergence of Authentic Gratitude

No one is born grateful. However, infants develop capacities that seem necessary for the expression and experience of gratitude, such as empathy and making inferences of intentionality in others. For instance, infants exhibit "social smiling"—that is, smiling as a socially coordinated response to another person's smile rather than smiling as merely a reflex to physical pleasure—reliably by two months of age (Messinger & Fogel, 2007). Yet social smiling is surely not gratitude, even though we might infer the seeds of gratitude there. As a cognitively more advanced phenomenon, empathy seems to develop in infancy and certainly by toddlerhood (Eisenberg, 2000). Inferring intentionality (i.e., recognizing that others intend certain behaviors, such as those that benefit oneself) also seems to develop in infancy (Gergely, Nádasdy, Csibra, & Bíró, 1995), and to the point of detecting false beliefs and a theory of others' minds by the preschool ages (Wellman, Cross, & Watson, 2001)—developmental capacities that seem to be required for gratitude (McAdams & Bauer, 2004). Preschool children can be taught to express gratitude routinely (saying "thank you" in appropriate situations), but the likelihood of their doing so has been shown to quadruple by later childhood (Gleason & Weintraub, 1976).

The experience of gratitude—which is to say, genuine or authentic gratitude—is also learned, but probably not until middle or late childhood, in the wake of learning to express gratitude, which is enhanced by parental or others' encouragement to take the perspective of the benefactor (Froh et al., 2007). Thematically, then, children develop the capacity to *value* gratitude around this time. Structurally, children around the ages eight to ten start to narrate the self and others in terms of the *individuality* of personhood, revealing their understanding that others have routine, distinct personality characteristics, and intentions, just as they themselves do (Damon & Hart, 1988). The perspective-taking required for such complexity of thought likely enhances the child's capacity for appreciating another's beneficent acts—the experience of gratitude. By the middle-school years, gratitude serves as a moral motive and a predictor of social integration (Froh et al., 2010), suggesting both themes of group identification that mark a transition from the egoistic stages of self-identity structure to more groupish and conformist stages (e.g., Loevinger, 1976).

So older children seem to develop a capacity for "authentic gratitude" and for identifying with the idea of gratitude as a moral good. From there gratitude develops as one comes to think more deeply and complexly—and authentically—about the self and others.

Adolescence-Plus: Proto-Authenticity and Principled Gratitude

Adolescence and emerging adulthood—the term for roughly ages eighteen to twenty-five that serves as an extended adolescence in modern, industrialized cultures (Arnett, 2000)—is a time for figuring out one's definition and place in the world. Erik Erikson's (1950) label for this stage of development is "identity versus role confusion." Identity refers to one's understanding of who one is, particularly in terms of values or personally meaningful concerns, where that understanding emerges in the wake of both considerable exploration of alternative values, and commitment to a set of values of one's own. To self-author an identity in this sense, one must know where one stands in society, relative to others; one must not only know the social roles that one plays in life but also have a relatively solid sense of the underlying values of those roles in one's culture. In their narrative self-identity, if all goes well by Eriksonian standards, adolescents and emerging adults are searching for and selecting themes of values and virtues that will anchor their developing life stories. Lacking such themes with which to identify amounts to being confused with regard to one's role in society.

Structurally, the commitment to a set of self-examined values amounts to thematic coherence in one's life story. The lack of committed values expresses itself in a lower degree of thematic coherence. But commitment and coherence can be either simplistic or complex. Structural complexity develops with the differentiation of perspectives on values and persons, as when adolescents try to break free of the limited perspectives of their upbringing—the perspectives engendered by their parents, their schools, their religion, and other authoritative persons and institutions. In adolescence, if self-authorship continues to develop structurally, one moves from a more conformist positioning of the self and others toward a more conscientious positioning that is driven by critical thinking (Loevinger, 1976). Self-authorship shifts from valuing the self by others' standards (e.g., hinging one's self-worth on what others say) to valuing the self in terms of critically examined, systematic beliefs, plans, and principles (Damon & Hart, 1988). Critical reasoning simply requires greater perspective-taking than does conformity, and the person who comes to exercise (and identify with) critical reasoning rather than conformist reasoning comes to self-author an identity with greater complexity, with implications for gratitude and authenticity.

Adolescent gratitude. Gratitude at this stage involves an appreciation, both experienced and expressed, of other people for their having helped oneself to become oneself. At this stage, one's capacity for gratitude has a self-focused quality that is characteristic of adolescent thinking: The notion of being grateful is *still routinely rooted in social exchange*, where individuals come in contact with each other and may decide to help each other. While adolescents may have glimpses of gratitude for being part of something larger than themselves (as with peak, mystical, or transcendent experiences), *gratitude at this stage is still about the individualistically defined self who receives goods from other individualistically defined persons*. For example, perceptions that a partner has expressed gratitude correlates with perceptions that "my partner saw the 'real' me" (Algoe et al., 2013). While gratitude at this stage is genuine (as in later childhood), it is limited by the adolescent's capacity to be genuine or authentic in the first place (see further).

Despite these limitations, gratitude is likely to have become more principled with the thematic and structural development of self-authorship in adolescence. As one comes to identify with particular values (i.e., to self-author with particular themes), one comes to be grateful in a more concentrated way for the people and forces that facilitate those values. As self-authorship develops toward greater structural complexity, one comes to identify with abstract principles and underlying causes and processes—including those that facilitate gratitude. One's understanding of gratitude becomes more principled, where gratitude is not just something important to express interpersonally but is also integral to social cohesion on a larger scale.

Adolescent authenticity. Authenticity is a matter of being true to oneself, so authenticity serves as an ideal or guiding principle for the entire project of identity development, particularly in Erikson's seminal sense of the term. However, authenticity at this stage of development is not the authenticity of the psychosocially mature person. Perhaps we would better frame the underlying phenomenon as "autonomy." For the adolescent, autonomy means independence, whereas for the mature adult, autonomy means something more like existential authenticity (Bauer, in press). In adolescence and emerging adulthood, one's sense of autonomy is defined by one's independence from parents and other authority figures, cast largely in terms of finances, being told what to do, and choosing one's social roles. Attaining these freedoms is a monumental task, and not coincidentally these capacities emerge around the time that self-authorship proper—that is, narrative self-identity—develops into its relatively adult form (McAdams, 1993; McLean et al., 2007). This is not to say that adolescents cannot be authentic; of course they can. Adolescents can certainly take stands and follow paths of their own in ways that resonate with deeply held and even self-examined beliefs. But the adolescent's understanding of self as an individual is—compared to the mature adult's self-identity—too shallow, too inexperienced, too lacking in perspectivity (see next section on structural development), and importantly too lacking in an embedded sense of interdependence to be consonant with what is known as existential authenticity (e.g., Guignon, 2004). So the existential authenticity at this stage is more like a proto-authenticity than authenticity proper.

Then again, we can see the seeds of interdependent thinking in the structural complexity and principled nature of thinking that is possible at this stage. (We note that the term "interdependent" in a developmental sense refers to a view of self and others that is post-conformist, and even post-independent via critical-thinking. Interdependence refers to a model of personhood that values both individuality and its social embeddedness, that is, interindividuality—Kegan, 1982.) Thinking at this stage is not yet interdependent (e.g., Kegan; Loevinger, 1976), so while we can find authentic gratitude here, gratitude as a principle is more idealistic than contextualized, much like the life stories of adolescents in general (McAdams, 1993).

Adulthood: Existentialist Authenticity and Deep Gratitude

Adulthood encompasses a range of expectable themes for self-authorship and levels of structural development. As a source of narrative themes, Erikson's theory provides three values or motives around which young, midlife, and older adults tend to anchor the meaning of their life stories, respectively: intimacy, generativity, and ego integrity. Structurally, based on measures of Loevinger's (1976) ego development, self-authorship spans from routinely self-protective and egoistic perspectives to strictly conformist, a combination of conformist and conscientious, conscientious (i.e., the routinely critical-thinking stage mentioned earlier that develops at the earliest in late adolescence or emerging adulthood), and three advanced stages that identify with interdependent views of personhood that were mentioned earlier. In this section, we consider the implications of Erikson's and Loevinger's theories of development on the development of gratitude and authenticity—and on authentic gratitude and grateful authenticity—in adulthood.

Intimacy and interpersonal interdependence. In Erikson's (1950) theory, young adulthood is the period in life (again, in modern, Western cultures at this time in history) that individuals work on establishing intimacy in their lives. Intimacy refers to a mature, reciprocal relationship with another person. Isolation is the lack of such a connection (the stage is called "intimacy versus isolation"). From Erikson's point of view, intimacy is not merely about having a committed relationship but rather about the development of a genuinely mutual relationship. At this point, the abstract, adolescent ideal of interdependence develops into a more lived, experienced interdependence in the context of mutually intimate relationships, as one values and acts upon an understanding (however intuitive) of one's interpersonal interdependence.

An early sense of existential authenticity proper seems capable of emerging around this period of development. Indeed, we argue that the development of existential authenticity underlies Erikson's placing the intimacy stage after the identity stage: intimacy in Erikson's sense can develop only after one has established a relatively authentic understanding of oneself (for empirical support, see Beyers & Seiffge-Krenke, 2010). A sense of one's own self-examined values (from the earlier stage) deepens with more years of experience in trying to enact those values in real-life contexts. Intimate relationships test that enactment. A nascent existential authenticity hedges against the possibility that one either too readily imposes one's beliefs on others or too readily capitulates to the other's beliefs. Such are the hazards of committing to a relationship before one has established a set of self-examined values. In addition, in the stage of intimacy, if all goes well, the person can give and want to give "autonomy support," the phenomenon of supporting another's autonomy without risk of forfeiting one's own autonomy (and indeed facilitating it—Deci, 1995). Self-identity becomes known to oneself as a dialogical process, with two individuals developing in their own autonomous ways in conjunction, with the mutual relationship as a valued good in itself—an interpersonal interdependence.

Gratitude in the sense of intimacy is not merely a matter of being thankful that the other person helps one to become oneself. As with stages in most developmental theories, the person does not simply discard any concerns or abilities from previous stages upon reaching a later stage. Rather, the person *adds* concerns and abilities to the previous stages' concerns and abilities. Stages are cumulative, not substitutive. Thus, in addition to more commonly understood notions of gratitude—thankfulness to another person or supernatural force for a particular good bestowed—the person at the present stage develops the capacity to be thankful for what is at least an inherently interdependent facet of one's life. Gratitude takes on a mutually shared meaning, compatible with the structural complexity of Loevinger's (1976) individualistic stage (at least in relationship contexts). This stage involves a recognition of gratitude (and its opposite, blame) as an emotion that affects the person not in the abstract, but in the personal context of intersubjective relations (Labouvie-Vief & Medler, 2002) between the self and others. An intimate relationship has not only emotions and values but their development over time at its core (Loevinger, 1976). Especially at higher stages of development, one can be thankful *for* the authentically mutual relationship itself (in addition to the actual persons in that relationship) and thankful *to* the relationship itself. Similarly, one can be thankful to or for one's family and to or for the universe or cosmos (see Chappell, this volume), even though one is part of one's family and of the cosmos.

As suggested in the section on adolescence, neither Erikson nor we are claiming that adolescents cannot experience gratitude toward relations (or groups or abstract principles). Of course they do (e.g., gratitude toward their families, their country, their god). Instead, we are pointing to differences in the self-identification of those things not merely as abstract ideas but as lived experiences (see Beyers & Seiffge-Krenke, 2010). Adolescents typically express thankfulness to their boyfriends and girlfriends, but that thankfulness is for gifts such as "helping me be myself" and "loving me for who I am" (good things to be sure), rather than for gifts such as a mutually constructed life space and other mutually planned-and-lived phenomena that color broad spans of one's activities for years. Few adolescents can understand, articulate, or enact such a phenomenon—or thus feel grateful for it.

Generativity and organismic interdependence. In midlife, life stories more commonly take on themes of generativity (McAdams & Guo, 2015;

Peterson, 2002), the Eriksonian concern for and commitment to fostering the welfare of future generations of society—and even of the species. Having such concerns and acting on them, Erikson says, is an integral part of psychological health and well-being for adults in midlife. Not to have such concerns or not to act on them leads the person toward a sense of stagnation, a sense of not contributing to something larger than oneself. Generative actions come in many forms, including the more obvious instances like parenting, teaching, coaching, and mentoring. These actions can have multiple motives. What matters for generativity as a theme of self-authorship is the individual's motive to care for others, society, and humanity (de St. Aubin, 2013). While an overarching concern for generativity is not necessary for gratitude, generative concern deepens gratitude, extending it beyond the interpersonal realm, toward society or even humanity and its future generations (McAdams & Bauer, 2004).

In contrast to the sense of autonomy as independence in adolescence and emerging adulthood, the sense of autonomy can more likely emerge as existential authenticity—in its fuller, ethically framed sense—at the present stage of development. Midlife has afforded the individual decades of experience in trying to enact her values and ideals. By trial and error, if all goes well, the individual has developed the capacity to understand how those values and ideals actually pan out in the varied contexts and vicissitudes of everyday life—a life with other individuals, groups, institutions, and perhaps cultures and a sense of history. At this point in development, one's understanding of interdependence moves beyond the interpersonal to become dynamic, systemic, and organismic (Bauer, in press)—an understanding of persons as self-organizing systems within broader systems of persons—and then in a lived, concrete sense rather than merely the idealistic sense of adolescence.

If one has continued to develop psychosocially, the person has honed his values and ideals to reflect what is possible, given the restraints of life—as Tiberius (2008) puts it, "living wisely within our limits." Such thinking corresponds to the advanced individualistic or early autonomous stage of ego development (Loevinger, 1976) and to the interindividual stage of self-development (Kegan, 1982). Self-authorship positions the self and others in an interdependent relation. This interdependence functions not just in relationships (as in Erikson's stage of intimacy) but also in *all* relations, from interpersonal to collective, as a pervasive quality of personhood.

Existentially authentic gratitude. Gratitude takes shape accordingly. Generativity is to no small degree a monumental expression of gratitude to society or even the world (McAdams & Bauer, 2004; on cosmic gratitude, see Chappell, this volume). At this point, one identifies not just with him- or herself, set with or against other individuals (as in Erikson's stage of identity), and not just as merged with another person (as in the intimacy stage), but now one identifies with future generations of society, even the species. Gratitude becomes similarly multifaceted, expressed at interpersonal, mutually relational, and multiplicatively relational forms. As mentioned earlier, we are not claiming that adolescents or young adults cannot experience gratitude for society and other abstract phenomena as just that—abstract phenomena. Youth certainly express concerns for generativity, as when they wish to do volunteer work to help children or society. Such generative concern among young adolescents and young adults has been shown to correlate with a sense of gratitude (Froh et al., 2010; Sandage, Hill, & Vaubel, 2010). However, we are claiming that youth are, on average, limited by their fewer experiences in life and in their understanding of the intricacies of what it means to live in a society, permeated as it is by political, religious, socioeconomic, and other cultural values that either support or suppress one's own values. Those growing up in conditions of poverty or other forms of oppression (e.g., racial, ethnic, and gendered) come to understand the perils of interdependent personhood (e.g., Bhatia, 2007; Hammack, 2011; Nussbaum, 2000). In any case, the structural development of interdependent self-authorship emerges from decades of experience in trying to live out one's values in real-life contexts and recognizing palpably the difficulty of doing so.

Grateful authenticity. Authenticity can emerge in its full existential force, with *grateful* authenticity as a natural extension of perceiving personhood as a nexus of interdependent experience. Gratitude reaches a level of depth that is not merely principled and idealistic but also contextualized, with the appreciation of virtues enacted despite both external and internal hurdles. Authentic gratitude, which first emerged in late childhood, becomes existentially authentic gratitude.

NOTE

1 The other two dimensions are "authentic living" and another antithetical dimension, self-alienation; antithetical scores are reversed and then added to authentic-living scores.

REFERENCES

Algoe, S., Fredrickson, B., & Gable, S. (2013). The social functions of the emotion of gratitude via expression. *Emotion, 13*(4), 605–609. http://dx.doi.org/10.1037/a0032701

Algoe, S., Haidt, J., & Gable, S. (2008). Beyond reciprocity: Gratitude and relationships in everyday life. *Emotion, 8*(3), 425–429. http://dx.doi.org/10.1037/1528-3542.8.3.425

Arnett, J. J. (2000). Emerging adulthood: A theory of development from the late teens through the twenties. *American Psychologist, 55*(5), 469.

Bauer, J. J. (2016). Eudaimonic growth: The development of the goods in personhood (or: cultivating a good life story). In J. Vittersø (Ed.), *Handbook of Eudaimonic well-being* (pp. 147–174). Cham, Switzerland: Springer.

Bauer, J. J., (in press). *The transformative self: Identity, growth, and a good life story.* New York: Oxford University.

Bauer, J. J., & DesAutels, P. (in press). When life gets in the way: Virtuous self-development along non-idealized paths in women's lives. *Journal of Moral Education.*

Bauer, J. J., Graham, L. E., Lauber, E. A., & Lynch, B. P. (2017). What growth sounds like: How redemption, recovery, self-improvement, and eudaimonic growth in narratives of different life events relate to well-being, motives, and traits. Manuscript under review.

Bauer, J. J., & McAdams, D. P. (2010). Eudaimonic growth: Narrative growth goals predict increases in ego development and subjective well-being three years later. *Developmental Psychology, 46*, 761–772.

Bauer, J. J., McAdams, D. P., & Pals, J. L. (2008). Narrative identity and eudaimonic well-being. *Journal of Happiness Studies, 9*(1), 81–104.

Beyers, W., & Seiffge-Krenke, I. (2010). Does identity precede intimacy? Testing Erikson's theory on romantic development in emerging adults of the 21st century. *Journal of Adolescent Research, 25*(3), 387–415.

Bhatia, S. (2007). *American karma: Race, culture, and identity in the Indian diaspora.* New York: New York University.

Bonnie, K., & de Waal, F. (2004). Primate social reciprocity and the origin of gratitude. In R. A. Emmons & M. E. McCullough (Eds.), *The psychology of gratitude* (pp. 213–229). New York, NY: Oxford University Press.

Campbell, J. (1949). *The hero with a thousand faces.* Princeton, NJ: Princeton University.

Campbell, J. (1988). *Myths to live by.* New York: Viking.

Cramer, P. (1999). Ego functions and ego development: Defense mechanisms and intelligence as predictors of ego level. *Journal of Personality, 67*, 735–760.

Damon, W., & Hart, D. (1988). *Self-understanding in childhood and adolescence.* Cambridge, UK: Cambridge University.

de St. Aubin, E. (2013). Generativity and the meaning of life. In J. A. Hicks & C. Routledge (Eds.), *The experience of meaning in life.* New York: Springer.

DeSteno, D., Bartlett, M., Baumann, J., Williams, L., & Dickens, L. (2010). Gratitude as moral sentiment: Emotion-guided cooperation in economic exchange. *Emotion, 10*(2), 289–293. http://dx.doi.org/10.1037/a0017883

Deci, E. L. (1995). *Why we do what we do.* New York: Penguin.

Eisenberg, N. (2000). Emotion, regulation, and moral development. *Annual review of psychology, 51*(1), 665–697.

Emmons, R. A. (2004). The psychology of gratitude: An introduction. In R. A. Emmons & M. E. McCullough (Eds.), *The psychology of gratitude* (pp. 3–18). New York, NY: Oxford University Press.

Emmons, R. A., & Crumpler, C. A. (2000). Gratitude as a human strength: Appraising the evidence. *Journal of Social and Clinical Psychology, 19*(1), 56–69.

Emmons, R. A., & McCullough, M. E. (2003). Counting blessings versus burdens: An experimental investigation of gratitude and subjective well-being in daily life. *Journal of Personality & Social Psychology, 84*(2), 377–389.

Erikson, E. H. (1950/1994). *Childhood and society*. New York: Norton.

Froh, J., Bono, G., & Emmons, R. (2010). Being grateful is beyond good manners: Gratitude and motivation to contribute to society among early adolescents. *Motivation and Emotion, 34*(2), 144–157. http://dx.doi.org/10.1007/s11031-010-9163-z

Froh, J., Emmons, R., Card, N., Bono, G., & Wilson, J. (2011). Gratitude and the reduced costs of materialism in adolescents. *Journal of Happiness Studies, 12*(2), 289–302. http://dx.doi.org/10.1007/s10902-010-9195-9

Froh, J., Miller, D., & Snyder, S. (2007). Gratitude in children and adolescents: Development, assessment, and school-based intervention. *School Psychology Forum: Research in Practice, 2*(1), 1–13.

Gergely, G., Nádasdy, Z., Csibra, G., & Bíró, S. (1995). Taking the intentional stance at 12 months of age. *Cognition, 56*(2), 165–193.

Gleason, J. B., & Weintraub, S. (1976). The acquisition of routines in child language. *Language in Society, 5*(2), 129–136.

Guignon, C. B. (2004). *On being authentic*. London: Routledge.

Habermas, T., & de Silveira, C. (2008). The development of global coherence in life narratives across adolescence: Temporal, causal, and thematic aspects. *Developmental Psychology, 44*, 707–721.

Hammack, P. L. (2011). *Narrative and the politics of identity: The cultural psychology of Israeli and Palestinian youth*. New York: Oxford University.

James, W. (1902). *The varieties of religious experience*. New York: Library of America.

Jeffers, T. L. (2005). *Apprenticeships: The Bildungsroman from Goethe to Santayana*. New York: Palgrave Macmillan.

Jung, C. G. (1959). *Aion: Researches into the phenomenology of the self*. (Trans. by R. F. C. Hull.) Princeton, NJ: Princeton University.

Kasser, T., Koestner, R., & Lekes, N. (2002). Early family experiences and adult values: A 26-year, prospective longitudinal study. *Personality and Social Psychology Bulletin, 28*, 826–835.

Kasser, T., & Ryan, R. M. (1996). Further examining the American dream: Well-being correlates of intrinsic and extrinsic goals. *Personality and Social Psychology Bulletin, 22*, 281–288.

Kegan, R. (1982). *The evolving self: Problem and process in human development*. Cambridge, MA: Harvard University Press.

Kernis, M. H. (2003). Optimal self-esteem and authenticity: Separating fantasy from reality. *Psychological Inquiry, 14*(1), 83–89. doi:10.1207/s15327965pli1401_03

Labouvie-Vief, G., & Medler, M. (2002). Affect optimization and affect complexity: Modes and styles of regulation in adulthood. *Psychology and Aging, 17*(4), 571.

Loevinger, J. (1976). *Ego development*. San Francisco, CA: Jossey-Bass.

Maslow, A. (1968). *Toward a psychology of being*. New York, NY: Van Nostrand Reinhold.

MacIntyre, A. (2001). *Dependent rational animals: Why human beings need the virtues*. Peru, IL: Open Court.

May, R. (1969/2007). *Love and will*. New York: Norton.

McAdams, D. P. (1993). *The stories we live by: Personal myths and the making of the self*. New York, NY: Guilford Press.

McAdams, D. P. (2006). *The redemptive self: Stories Americans live by*. New York: Oxford University.

McAdams, D. P. (2008). Personal narratives and the life story. In O. P. John, R. R. Robins, & L. O. Pervin (Eds.), *Handbook of personality*, 3rd edition (pp. 241–261). New York: Guilford.

McAdams, D., & Bauer, J. (2004). Gratitude in modern life: Its manifestations and development. In R. A. Emmons & M. E. McCullough (Eds.), *The psychology of gratitude* (pp. 81–99). New York, NY: Oxford University Press.

McAdams, D. P., & Guo, J. (2015). Narrating the generative life. *Psychological Science, 26*, 475–483.

McAdams, D. P., Diamond, A., de St. Aubin, E., & Mansfield, E. D. (1997). Stories of commitment: The psychosocial construction of generative lives. *Journal of Personality and Social Psychology, 72*, 678–694.

McCrae, R. R., & Costa Jr., P. T. (1980). Openness to experience and ego level in Loevinger's Sentence Completion Test: Dispositional contributions to developmental models of personality. *Journal of Personality and Social Psychology, 39*, 1179–1190.

McCullough, M., Kilpatrick, S., Emmons, R., & Larson, D. (2001). Is gratitude a moral affect? *Psychological Bulletin, 127*(2), 249–266. http://dx.doi.org/10.1037/0033-2909.127.2.249

McCullough, M., & Tsang, J. (2004). Parent of the virtues? The prosocial contours of gratitude. In R. A. Emmons & M. E. McCullough (Eds.), *The psychology of gratitude* (pp. 123–144). New York, NY: Oxford University Press.

McCullough, M., Tsang, J., & Emmons, R. (2004). Gratitude in intermediate affective terrain: Links of grateful moods to individual differences and daily emotional experience. *Journal of Personality and Social Psychology, 86*(2), 295–309. http://dx.doi.org/10.1037/0022-3514.86.2.295

McGregor, I., McAdams, D. P., & Little, B. R. (2006). Personal projects, life stories, and happiness: On being true to traits. *Journal of Research in Personality, 40*(5), 551–572.

McLean, K. C., Pasupathi, M., & Pals, J. L. (2007). Selves creating stories creating selves: A process model of self-development. *Personality and Social Psychology Review, 11*(3), 262–278.

Messinger, D., & Fogel, A. (2007). The interactive development of social smiling. *Advances in Child Development and Behaviour, 35*, 328–366.

Nussbaum, M. C. (2000). *Women and human development: The capabilities approach*. Cambridge, UK: Cambridge University.

Peterson, B. E. (2002). Longitudinal analysis of midlife generativity, intergenerational roles, and caregiving. *Psychology and Aging, 17*, 161–168.

Piaget, J. (1970). Piaget's theory. In P. Mussen (Ed.), *Carmichael's manual of child psychology* (pp. 703–732). New York, NY: John Wiley.

Roberts, R. C. (2004). The blessings of gratitude: A conceptual analysis. In R. A. Emmons & M. E. McCullough (Eds.), *The psychology of gratitude* (pp. 58–80). New York, NY: Oxford University Press.

Rogers, C. R. (1961). *On becoming a person.* Boston, MA: Houghton Mifflin.

Sandage, S. J., Hill, P. C., & Vaubel, D. C. (2011). Generativity, relational spirituality, gratitude, and mental health: Relationships and pathways. *International Journal for the Psychology of Religion, 21*(1), 1–16.

Schimmel, S. (2004). Gratitude in Judaism. In R. A. Emmons & M. E. McCullough (Eds.), *The psychology of gratitude* (pp. 37–57). New York, NY: Oxford University Press.

Shanahan, C., & Bauer, J. J. (2018). *The Essentialist and Existentialist Authenticity Scale: Being true to your traits or to your values.* Manuscript in preparation.

Sheldon, K. M., Ryan, R. M., Rawsthorne, L. J., & Ilardi, B. (1997). Trait self and true self: Cross-role variation in the Big-Five personality traits and its relations with psychological authenticity and subjective well-being. *Journal of Personality and Social Psychology, 73*(6), 1380.

Shimai, S., Otake, K., Park, N., Peterson, C., & Seligman, M. (2006). Convergence of character strengths in American and Japanese young adults. *Journal of Happiness Studies, 7*(3), 311–322. http://dx.doi.org/10.1007/s10902-005-3647-7.

Steindl-Rast, D. (2004). Gratitude as thankfulness and as gratefulness. In R. A. Emmons & M. E. McCullough (Eds.), *The psychology of gratitude* (pp. 282–290). New York, NY: Oxford University Press.

Suedfeld, P., & Bluck, S. (1993). Changes in integrative complexity accompanying significant life events: Historical evidence. *Journal of Personality and Social Psychology, 64*, 124–130.

Taylor, C. (1991). *The ethics of authenticity.* Cambridge, MA: Harvard University.

Tiberius, V. (2008). *The reflective life: Living wisely with our limits.* New York, NY: Oxford University Press.

Trulock, J. E., & Courtenay, B. C. (2002). Ego development and the influence of gender, age, and educational levels among older adults. *Educational Gerontology, 28*, 325–336.

Wellman, H. M., Cross, D., & Watson, J. (2001). Metaanalysis of theory of mind development: The truth about false belief. *Child Development, 72*(3), 655–684.

Westenberg, P. M., & Gjerde, P. F. (1999). Ego development during the transition from adolescence to young adulthood: A 9-year longitudinal study. *Journal of Research in Personality, 33*(2), 233–252.

Wood, A., Froh, J., & Geraghty, A. (2010). Gratitude and well-being: A review and theoretical integration. *Clinical Psychology Review, 30*(7), 890–905. http://dx.doi.org/10.1016/j.cpr.2010.03.005

Wood, A., Linley, P., Maltby, J., Baliousis, M., & Joseph, S. (2008). The authentic personality: A theoretical and empirical conceptualization and the development of the authenticity scale. *Journal of Counseling Psychology, 55*(3), 385–399. doi:10.1037/0022-0167.55.3.385

Part V

GRATITUDE AND VIRTUE

Chapter 12

Gratitude as a Virtue

Sophie Grace Chappell

I

All ethical virtues are directed at good/right response. "Good/right response" can mean both feeling and action; maybe other things too, but I focus on those two kinds of response here. So here is a distinction among the ethical virtues that we should make more of (I don't know that anyone anywhere *has* made much of it, till now): some ethical virtues are directed *more* at good/right action (e.g., the canonized "cardinal virtues" justice, temperance, courage, practical wisdom), some *more* at good/right feeling (e.g., relatively neglected virtues such as forgivingness, joyfulness, friendliness, intellectual curiosity, love, and humor). My thesis here is that gratitude is an ethical virtue of this latter sort: a virtue primarily of feeling rather than of action. That doesn't mean it's irrelevant to action, of course. It just means that gratitude is *about* feelings and emotions, connected with feelings/emotions, with a closeness and intimacy that does not apply to, say, justice or practical wisdom.

However, philosophers dispute whether gratitude is a feeling or an emotion or a reactive attitude or a disposition or a virtue. (See the *Stanford Encyclopedia of Philosophy* article on gratitude for some of the references.) This dispute is unnecessary. For we can just say that gratitude is *all* of these things, and maybe some other things too; a language game or a speech-act, for instance.

Gratitude-phenomena occur across a range of psychological and philosophical categories; for the sake of clarifying these phenomena, I shall spend a little time exploring this range. For instance, there is, occupying an important place among the small-scale ceremonial norms of our human form of life, the paradigmatic speech-act of gratitude: "Thank you very much," a phrase with multiple variants in English, and with equivalents in every human language known to me. Perhaps this is the first gratitude-phenomenon that small children typically encounter. In learning the little ceremony of say-ing "Thank you" when they are given something nice, they learn something important about their place in the world, and about what it is to occupy any place in the world; about their relationships to others, and what relationships are; and about the notion of being benefited by someone—in particular about the socially central transactions of gift-giving and gift-receiving. Perhaps say-ing "Thank you" has something like equivalents in some animal languages, or pre-languages (as MacIntyre calls them in *Dependent Rational Animals*), as well. Anyone who lives with dogs will find it easy to agree that they are capable of expressing gratitude; at least to humans, though it is an interesting question whether they can be grateful *to each other*. Given all these consid-erations, it seems quite intelligible to suggest that the category that gratitude belongs in is not virtue, but *speech-act*: that the language-game of receiving a favor and responding to it with the speech-act of thanking is what gratitude *is*. This isn't my own suggestion; but I do think it's an intelligible one.

There again, something worth calling gratitude belongs in the category of *feeling*. Every normal person has experienced the feeling of gratitude—an impulse of *allegria*, an often-sudden raising of the spirits, rather like a sense of relief or release, or a flash of joy. Perhaps "the Christmassy feeling," in some of its forms and manifestations, is, or involves, one culturally specific modification of this feeling.

There is too, distinct from the *feeling* of gratitude, the *emotion* of gratitude. This (I propose) is, roughly speaking, the feeling plus a conceptual framework that gives the reasons for the feeling. As a matter of first-person report: quite generally, it is possible for me, introspecting, to see that I have some feeling, and ask myself why. So in particular, I can notice that I am feeling grateful, and ask myself why I have this feeling. When I see (say) that I am feeling grateful to my wife for buying me some pretty earrings for my birthday, we contextualize my *feeling* of gratefulness in a way that shows its place within the more complex and more cognitive configuration of the *emotion* of gratitude. (We can feel both feel-ings and emotions; but emotions have an intentional structure that makes them more than just feelings.) Maybe, then, gratitude goes in the category of emotion.

Notice, by the way, that the reasons that we give, when we trace out the sort of contextualizing that gets us from feelings to emotions, are not solely causal, nor solely rationalizing, nor solely constitutive. They are all three. It's true that my feeling of gratitude has my wife's gift as its cause: her giving me the lovely earrings is what's brought about this lovely feeling in me. And it's true that my gratefulness is rationalized by her gift. If there's been some mix-up, and in fact she has *not* given me the earrings for my birthday (she meant them for herself, and I have mistaken her intentions), then my feeling of gratitude, if it persists after I realize the mix-up, ceases to make sense. But it's also true that my emotion of gratitude is *constituted* by the reasons for which I have the feeling. My *feeling* of gratitude can be, probably will be, the very same feeling in all sorts of different contexts. But my *emotion* of gratitude is, essentially, my gratefulness *to my wife for this gift now*. Subtract or modify that context (probably a purely hypothetical possibility, but bear with me) and you will have the very same *feeling*, but a different *emotion*.

We can also distinguish a sense in which gratitude is neither a feeling nor an emotion nor a move in a language-game, but what I shall call a reactive attitude. (I should stress that I am using this term in my own way. My use of it is as it is partly in tribute to Peter Strawson, but my use is narrower than his.) On my use of the term, then, a reactive attitude is, roughly, an emotion minus the element of feeling. It is the conceptual framework on its own, with or without the affective underpinning, and taken as something less episodic and longer-term; as a disposition to judge or appraise in a given way. Feelings come and go—to a great extent. And emotions come and go—to a considerable extent, though to a lesser extent than feelings. Compared with feelings, we are more inclined to view emotions as standing propensities; compared with emotions, we are more inclined to view reactive attitudes that way. Reactive attitudes (as I mean the phrase) are less episodic, more dispositional, more part of the structure of my character, than either feelings or emotions. They are also more cognitive, and so—at least potentially—more rational: my reactive attitude is a *stance* of gratitude toward my wife for buying me the earrings. It is an *appraisal* of her as to-be-thanked-for-this-generosity. It may or may not be accompanied, at particular times, by episodic feelings of gratitude, or, over longer spans of time, by an intelligent disposition to feel such feelings, that is, by an emotion of gratitude.

II

One thing a reactive attitude characteristically does is rekindle its affective analogues, when that attitude returns to the focus of conscious attention. Thinking again about my wife's generosity with the earrings, I feel a new rush of gratitude toward her; or I am reminded of the dispositional and habitual backup to this rush of gratitude, which is in part my longer-term emotion of gratitude toward her for all sorts of things; most fundamentally, no doubt, for being my wife. Still, in itself the reactive attitude can persist with or without the corresponding feeling(s) or emotion(s). For the reactive attitude is not so much a feeling as a *judgment*. The emotion of gratitude combines the cognitive and the affective, whereas the feeling of gratitude and the reactive attitude of gratitude separate them out again: the feeling is the affective all on its own, the reactive attitude is the cognitive all on its own. But the fact that it is possible to separate them out in these ways does not show that the cognitive and the affective do not belong together here. The opposite is true. Any realistic human psychology will be crowded with spectrum-blurs of such things. My neat philosopher's categorizations feeling/emotion/reactive attitude will apply to real psychologies all right. But not necessarily, in fact necessarily not, in ways that are at all clear-edged.

Moreover, in an emotion, it is not just that the cognitive and the affective *blur* into each other, statically and unmovingly; they also *bleed* into one another, changingly and dynamically. This can happen in both directions. Going from the affective to the cognitive, it can be like this: to start with I have a sense of dread about some situation. Then I decide to take this dread seriously as a potential source of information: "Why do I feel this dread?" I ask myself. And in answering that question, I come to see that I have (or alternatively don't have) good reason to feel it. This can happen through my remembering, or recalling to attention, dread-worthy things that I already know about my situation, but which I have either forgotten or stopped focusing on: that I am about to give a half-baked philosophy paper to a devastatingly intelligent and rabidly hostile audience, say, or that Donald Trump has just put Godzilla in charge of US foreign policy.

It can also happen because the feeling of dread that I find myself having in some situation prompts me, not just to retrieve, or look again at, information I already have, but actually to focus my attention in a way that brings me to learn something new from the feeling. I feel unease as I walk down an unlit street, the unease makes me listen more carefully, and listening more carefully, I realize that I can hear someone following me. When I notice that sound I don't just retrieve or recall a reason I already have to feel uneasy, I acquire a new one. This sort of "trusting our feelings" can, of course, be a surrender to magical thinking, or to vague dependence on something woollily called instinct or intuition; it can often be composed of thoroughly irrational elements like wishfulness ("I want to walk this road, therefore this road is safe") or irrelevant association ("It's Friday the 13th, so I must be extra cautious"). But it can also, in the right circumstances, be a way of understanding our situation better. So, for example, in mountaineering, it is very easy to kid yourself that a sérac or an avalanche-prone slope will be safe simply because "you have a good feeling" about it. On the other hand, over time, you *do* get better at making safety calls in the mountains, and very often—because you have to make a lot of them—you make these calls inarticulately and subconsciously; so the way they show up in your consciousness very often *is* simply as a good feeling, or a bad one.

Going in the other direction, from the cognitive to the affective, my judgment can serve as a critical influence on my feeling. Spiders cause scary feelings in many, and so even *look* scary to them—while their judgment tells them plainly that, this being Britain, no spider is genuinely a fit object of fear. Over time, this judgment can diminish or remove their fear of the spider. *Can* do so; sometimes it does, sometimes it doesn't. In the well-known cases of "recalcitrant emotion," on the usual story, the fear of the spider remains even though the fearer judges quite consciously that the spider is nothing to be afraid of. It is obvious from experience that this *can* happen. When it does, many argue that what it shows is that emotions don't contain judgments, because "*the* judgment" in the case is that the spider is *not* dangerous. This doesn't follow. The presupposition is that the fearer must have just one judgment about the spider. But that's false: it is perfectly psychologically possible for her to hold contradictory judgments at one and the same time.

Anyway, there are other possibilities besides the fear being rationally removed by the judgment that the spider isn't dangerous, and the fear being irrationally recalcitrant to that judgment. Another thing that can also happen is that the *fear* of the spider—that is, the emotion involving the judgment that the spider is *dangerous*—gets transmuted into something better described as a *phobic response* to the spider, a feeling of horror or disgust (or an emotion with the content that the spider is horrifying and disgusting). Talking to friends who actually are arachnophobes suggests that what they often feel is not so much fear *of the spider*, with the accompanying judgment "This spider is dangerous," as fear of their phobic response to the spider. They know that seeing a spider will induce an extremely unpleasant reaction in them (one arachnophobe friend reports an actual physical response, a gagging reflex). Really they are afraid, not so much of the spider, as of experiencing this reaction. And given its unpleasantness, quite reasonably and non-recalcitrantly so.

This kind of description, I suspect, will be applicable to at least some of the cases typically treated as examples of recalcitrant emotion. My analysis of emotions as "organic compounds" of feelings and reactive attitudes helps here: it helps us to see how many descriptions that differ significantly in detail can hide behind a single name, such as "recalcitrant emotion," that is often, apparently, supposed to be a unitary phenomenon, all cases of which fall the same way to philosophical analysis.

III

Other cases besides gratitude can illustrate how the affective and the cognitive can blur or bleed into one another along the spectrum from feelings, via emotions, to reactive attitudes. I have been using the example of fear, and in particular arachnophobia, partly because of its familiarity from the already-existing literature, and in particular because of its prevalence as an example of "recalcitrant emotion." These claims apply to gratitude as well. For instance, I've already noted earlier how, with gratitude, there can be a move from the cognitive to the affective, as when the reactive attitude of gratitude characteristically kindles, or rekindles, its affective analogues (the case of the earrings). It's also true with gratitude that there can be a move in the opposite direction, from the affective to the cognitive. One move of this sort is entirely commonplace in intimate relationships: it begins when I feel a vague and unfocused gratitude toward my partner, and attempt to focus this positive attitude, for example, by saying "How am I grateful to you? Let me count the ways," and so recollecting—or just collecting—the reasons why I feel that vague sense of gratitude.

Pursuing the analogy a little further, can there also be "recalcitrant" gratitude—gratitude that I go on feeling when, rationally speaking, I shouldn't? There certainly can, and such an emotion is likely to have an important place in, for instance, the moral psychology of a number of kinds of abusive power-relationships. "Stockholm syndrome" is one such case (at least if it involves gratitude, as certainly seems possible); many psychologically abused wives' feelings toward their manipulative and domineering husbands are another; perhaps Tom Pinch's attitude to his master, in Dickens' *Martin Chuzzlewit*, is a third. A can owe B no gratitude *whatever*, and know it perfectly well—and yet have feelings of gratitude toward B despite his own better judgment. This is recalcitrant gratitude, and it is closely parallel to the recalcitrant fear that the arachnophobe feels, not least because this too is typically a result of some kind of pathology.

For another example of an emotion with the same structure, consider what is in some ways the exact opposite of gratitude, namely Strawson's Exhibit One in his most famous essay: resentment. (Strawson focuses on resentment, Sartre focuses on shame and disgust and boredom—why are philosophical examples so often such *downers*? Maybe thinking about something positive like gratitude will help us to lighten up a bit. Anyway.) Resentment too can traverse the spectrum from the affective *feeling* of grudge, via the recall or discovery of a context of reasons for this feeling, which gets us to the emotion of resentment, to the cognitive judgment or appraisal that someone is indeed to-be-resented. Or resentment can go back in the other direction, from the purely cognitive to the affective as well. I remember that you stole my pet rabbit, and that cognitive remembering, calm though it is when it first appears in my consciousness, quickly "rekindles," as I put it above, my active feelings of resentment toward you over the rabbit-episode. Finally resentment too can all too easily be *recalcitrant* resentment: one familiar instance is how hard forgiveness can be—I know I've forgiven you, you've apologized profusely and returned the bunny, and I've decided not to resent what you did, but residual hard feelings remain. Or again, there is this near-comical thing that can and does happen between people (I've had it happen to me): you are resentful at me for allegedly doing something ("You've blocked me in with your rubbish parking"); I show quite clearly that in fact I didn't do X ("But that's not my car"); and your response is not to *abandon* your resentment but to *abate* it ("Hmmph. Well, just don't do it again, that's all"). Such residual resentment, if you realize how unreasonable you're being in harboring it, and nonetheless go on harboring it—as you might—will be recalcitrant in the fullest sense.

This completes my sketch of a moral psychology of feelings, emotions, and reactive attitudes. It is a sketch that can be right without applying to *every single emotion without exception*. Though actually, off the cuff, I can't think of any counter-examples. The sketch does look promising for application as a general analysis; it also looks likely to work, in particular, for fear, resentment, and gratitude.

So where does the ethical virtue of feeling, that I say gratitude is, fit into this moral psychology? The quick answer is that a virtue is among other things a disposition to *get it right* about reactive attitudes, emotions, and feelings. So there will be a virtue of gratitude simply on this condition: if and only if there is such a thing as being disposed to take up *correct* reactive attitudes, having *the right* emotions, and feeling *appropriate* feelings, with respect to gratitude. The virtue of gratitude will also involve being disposed to have gratitude-feelings and making gratitude-appraisals and engaging in speech-acts of thanking at the right times, to the right agents, to the right degree, and so on; and it will have plenty of other implications for action too.

Here we may still want to press the straightforward normative question: "What *are* the right/appropriate/correct responses in the case of gratitude?" We might also want some more information on the structure and nature of gratitude. I give more information of that sort in section IV, which offers what I'll call a *Foot-analysis* of gratitude. And I address the straightforward normative question in section V.

IV

A Foot-analysis of a concept is a philosophical grammar of it. Foot herself, in her classic papers "Moral Arguments," "Moral Beliefs," and "Approval and Disapproval," famously presents Foot-analyses of *pride, fear, dismay, danger, warning*, and other normatively loaded concepts. We cannot make sense of pride or fear or dismay unless we can see it as connected in the right way to something appropriate in the context. The utterance "I am proud of Ursa Minor" is not something I can come out with just whenever I will to, or prefer to. To be intelligible, it needs a background in descriptions of the world around me—and for such an odd claim as this one, they need to be fairly unusual descriptions. What I can be proud of must *as a matter of logic* be my own achievement, or my property, or in some way connected to my practical identity and my intentional agency; but the constellation Ursa Minor doesn't have these connections to anyone's achievement, property, or agency.

(Except perhaps God's; maybe the quickest way to bring intelligibility to the utterance "I am proud of Ursa Minor" is to imagine God saying it, rather as Slartibartfast, in the *Hitchhiker's Guide To The Galaxy*, is proud of the fjords of Norway, because he made them.) Again, "I'm afraid I've won the Nobel Prize" needs supplementation by an account of why the speaker doesn't want, as people usually do, to win the Nobel Prize. (Perhaps the speaker lives in Minnesota, and can't be bothered to travel to Sweden.) And "To my dismay, he accepted me when I proposed marriage to him" needs supplementation by an account of why the speaker was proposing marriage to someone *without* wanting him, as people usually do, to accept the offer. (P. G. Wodehouse has plenty of possible suggestions about this.) Concepts have their intelligibility-conditions necessarily; and those intelligibility-conditions relate not to anyone's *bare wanting* but to the descriptive conditions on what it is intelligible to want. To attempt to use a concept without observing these conditions is not to make a mighty effort of will in the direction of an unusual or reforming use of the concept. It is to fail to use the concept at all.

So what is the Foot-analysis of gratitude? I propose this:

> Gratitude is a positive emotion, feeling, reactive attitude, or disposition, directed toward someone in recognition of something received from them that is taken to be positive (typically past and/or present, but sometimes also future), that they are taken to be responsible for, and that is taken to display their generosity.

Let's take this bit by bit. For my purposes, it has five bits.

1. *Gratitude is an emotion, feeling, reactive attitude, or disposition*: see the arguments of sections II–III.
2. *Gratitude is a positive emotion (or feeling or reactive attitude or disposition)*. So I can be grateful to X for A despite negative *feelings* about A, and X, because in spite of those feelings my reactive attitude is positive. Conversely, I can be grateful to X for A despite a negative *reactive attitude* about A, and X, because in spite of that reactive attitude my feelings are positive. Either of these is possible, but what can't happen—logically can't happen, by the nature of the concept—is gratitude with *no* positive element.
3. *Gratitude is in recognition of something taken to be positive*. It doesn't have to *be* positive, but the grateful one does have to *see* it as positive. Whatever else may be wrong with "My father beat me twice a day for twenty years, and I'm grateful; made me the man I am," there is nothing *conceptually* awry about its deployment of gratitude: the last clause gives a clear reason for the gratitude, by citing a supposed positive effect of all those beatings. The same cannot be said for "My father beat me twice a

day for twenty years, and I'm grateful; it was an irredeemably wretched, hateful experience all the way through." To this speaker, we want to say "But then, why and in what sense are you *grateful*?" For nothing in his words explains his gratitude. The word "irredeemably" even suggests that there is no explanation.

4. *Gratitude is typically past- or present-directed.* Gratitude is always *for* something that someone has done, or been; and that means, for something already present. Some philosophers, especially consequentialists, are apt to assume that all reasons are prospective (forward-looking, future-based). Some familiar philosophical difficulties cannot even be set up without this assumption. So, for instance, the "paradox of deontology" says that my reason for refusing, say, to murder one to prevent four being murdered must be either that I want to bring about a world where there are fewer murders than otherwise (in which case my calculation of consequences is poor) or else that I want to bring about a world where there are fewer *murders-by-me* than otherwise (in which case I have a value, the avoidance of murders by me, which seems irrationally egocentric). But this dilemma has bite only if my reason to refuse to commit a murder cannot be, say, antecedent respect for the individual whom I would be murdering: the individual is there, as an already-existing fact, and my reason not to murder that individual arises from her existence. This is a past-based reason for action—it arises from something that is and has been already the case, not from some future consequence of the action proposed. The existence of such counter-examples shows that the assumption that all reasons must be future based is false. And gratitude is another such counter-example—as are resentment, and regret, and remorse, and repentance, and retributiveness, and presumably most other *reactive* attitudes—given that to react is by definition to respond to something past. Our reasons for gratitude typically lie in *what has happened in the past*, not in whatever future benefit there may be to be had from gratitude, or from the appearance of gratitude. In general, we are not grateful *in order to obtain a future good*, but *in response to a past good already obtained*. More strongly, in fact, it is not even coherent to attempt to be grateful *solely in order to achieve the good consequences* of gratitude. You might have your eye on good consequences *as well*, of course; but essentially, gratitude is a response to generosity, and anything that is not such a response simply is not gratitude at all.

"Typically" and "in general": of course the object of my gratitude can be present right now, so that sometimes my reason for gratitude is present based—for example, the gift that you are handing me right now. There can even be cases where I am grateful now for something that you *will* do; when you promise to look after my rabbit while I'm on holiday, this makes me grateful *now* for what you will do *in the next fortnight*. (It isn't just that I'm grateful now that you've now promised to do this, though I am that too.) In these cases, my gratitude *is* future based (at least in part). But even here gratitude is a responsive attitude, not an acquisitive one. I am grateful *in response to* what you do, not in order, say, to make you agreeable to doing it again.

And finally:

5. *Gratitude is (a) to someone who (b) is taken to have acted generously.*

   (a) Gratitude is, constitutively, an interpersonal attitude; the key words of gratitude are, as we have seen, "Thank *you*." In gratitude, I give thanks *for* something *to* someone. If either of these components of gratitude is missing, we have something else and not gratitude. Respectively, perhaps, we have pleasure that something has happened, and goodwill toward a person; but we do not have gratitude.

   (b) Gratitude is, characteristically, *a response to generosity*. To say this is not quite the same as saying two other things that are often said: first that gratitude is necessarily for the supererogatory, and second that gratitude is necessarily a response to intentional action. I think neither of those claims is quite right, and that the target which both aim at, but don't quite hit, is the claim about generosity.[1]

The familiar claim that gratitude necessarily responds to intentional action is not quite right, because I can be grateful for lots of things that are not intentional actions at all (though they are certainly characteristics of intentional agency). For example, I can be grateful that you love me, or that you refuse to suspect me of a crime for which I seem the obvious suspect. Again, I can be grateful to you for something that you do that—while still characteristic of intentional agency—is itself *un*intentional action; I can even be grateful precisely *because* you act unintentionally. Example: I am black and live in a white, racist society; I walk into the room and everyone else flinches and looks away, but you, without even realizing you're doing it, smile welcomingly at me, and so far from flinching, move up on the bench to make room for me next to you. Gratitude does not necessarily respond to intentional *action*; but it does necessarily respond to intentional *agency*.

The oft-repeated claim that gratitude necessarily responds to the supererogatory is not quite right either, because it too faces counter-examples. For instance, it is an A & E doctor's job to perform emergency life-saving procedures on acutely injured patients. Doing so is both in his employment contract, and his professional obligation: it would still be the other of these two, even if it were not the one of them. So the doctor does nothing supererogatory if in the course of his regular duties, during normal working hours, he saves *my* life. Nonetheless, it makes perfectly good sense for me to feel grateful to the doctor for saving my life. What I feel here really is *gratitude*, and not some kindred emotion. And my gratitude is not "really" directed somewhere else, at some aspect of the doctor's deed that *is* supererogatory. For instance, I am not "really" grateful just that he does his duty and saves my life willingly and with a cheerful smile, when he could have been grumpy and reluctant about it (perhaps, like the doctor played by Hugh Laurie in *House*, he *is* grumpy and reluctant, but I can still be grateful); nor just that he chose this life-saving profession of emergency surgery, within which he is now doing his duty, when, maybe, he could have been a merchant banker or a professional surfer instead. Nor am I "really" grateful just that we still have in Britain—despite successive governments' best efforts—a National Health Service (NHS) that so to speak *institutionalises* supererogation, by making it a routine thing and a matter of obligation that doctors should have it as their duty to do the kind of work that my A & E doctor does in saving my life—work much of which, without an NHS, would either be actually supererogatory, or at the very least much less clearly obligatory. All of these facts represent aspects of the case for which I can perfectly reasonably be grateful *too*. Their presence neither explains away, nor even derogates from, the central fact about the case, which is that I am grateful to the doctor for saving my life, because what he does in saving me is generous, even though it is his obligation. Gratitude therefore responds to *generous*, not as such to *supererogatory*, intentional agency.

(Of course, there are possible cases where the doctor saves my life but is *not* an instance of generous agency—not even a grumpy one like Hugh Laurie. Maybe the doctor only saves my life because his superior intervenes forcefully when he wants to leave me to die and go off for a round of golf: she points a gun at him and *forces* him to save me. If I know that to be the case, I can't be grateful to the doctor; though perhaps I can to his superior, depending on *her* motives. Thanks to Robert Roberts for the case.)

This completes my Foot-analysis of gratitude.

VI

How much, then, should we be grateful? How much gratitude is appropriate in life?

I want to respond to this question in two opposite ways. First, in this section, I want to explore the possibility of a case against gratitude: a case for thinking that we should be a lot less grateful than we typically actually are, and maybe, never grateful at all. I see no chance at all of making out such a case; but there are things to be learned from trying—in particular, things about Aristotle, and about ideology.

Then second, I want to explore the opposite case—a case for thinking that we should be a lot *more* grateful than we actually are, and maybe, grateful the whole time. This case—call it the case for *cosmic gratitude*—I think deserves to be taken much more seriously. I'll turn to it in section VII.

So first, the case against gratitude. To begin with, clearly not *all* gratitude is a good thing. Take misplaced gratitude. Someone treats me atrociously but I am grateful to her anyway, either because her atrocious behavior involved going behind my back, or because I know about it but mistakenly view it as not atrocious but admirable; or maybe she is an abusive parent who has trained me to thank her for abusing me. Or take extorted gratitude. Suppose some manipulative person deliberately puts me in a situation where I find myself very much in his debt. I am unaware of his mind-games, and so I feel grateful, when really it would be much better for me to be on my guard against him. With situations like these, the fact that I am grateful in them can plausibly be said to make them worse than they would otherwise be. Or again, consider the gratitude of a wretched beggar in a grossly unequal society when I give him alms. Here, it is probably better that the beggar be grateful than ungrateful. Yet it would be better than either if the beggar had no *occasion* to be grateful to me, because the beggar did not need to beg, because our society was not grossly unequal. Here not just the beggar but the whole situation is wretched. More generally, gratitude can be institutionalized as part of a thoroughly unjust and oppressive social order, correlative to what is rightly decried as the ideology of "charity." *Oliver Twist* is a study of both these ideologies in Victorian England; Seneca's eight books *de Beneficiis* ("On favors bestowed") are, among other things, an exposition of the ideology of patron-client relations in Julio-Claudian Rome; Aristotle's *megalopsychos* is a third case, which I'll consider further.

Still, we can find cases of *genuine* generosity, untainted by the grimy background ideology of the society it occurs in, and *genuine* gratitude responding to that generosity, in both Seneca and *Oliver Twist*. Faced with examples of bad gratitude like the last paragraph's, we can respond that they are not *central*. Gratitude per se is not ideological but innocent; *paradigmatic* gratitude (not necessarily the statistical majority of cases) is not bad but good. In a typical case, you, being someone of good will who is appropriately placed to show me generosity, make a gift to me of your generosity, and I respond with gratitude; for example, we go to the bar after my talk, and you buy me a drink. In cases like this, it is proper for you to be grateful to me for my talk (assuming it is any good) and for me to be grateful to you for the drink (on the same condition). It is a good thing if each of us is grateful, and a bad and improper thing if either of us is ungrateful. No manipulation or mind-games here; if there is an ideological background to this little exchange, it is either inert or actually helpful. Of course the possibility of such cases implies the further possibility of a thousand and one ways of abusing the conventions of generosity and gratitude, and indeed of paper-giving and academic hospitality. But *abusus non tollit usum*, as we say in Milton Keynes: the possibility of misuse does not undermine the possibility of correct use. In fact, typically such abuses of gratitude *presuppose* the existence of correct uses of gratitude, indeed of a whole set of conventions and social practices about gratitude: what we might call the language-game of generosity and gratitude, and are often structurally parasitic upon the correct uses. And as I say, the existence of this language-game of giving and receiving, of doing things with which it goes to say "Here you are" and "Thank you," and the existence of the feeling of gratitude as a part of this practice, is so manifestly a good thing that it will occur to very few non-philosophers even to question its goodness.

In the light of all this, consider Aristotle's *megalopsychos*:

> The *megalopsychos* is ashamed to receive benefits, because it is a mark of a superior to confer benefits, of an inferior to receive them. He returns benefits with more besides, because this will put his original benefactor in *his* debt, and make *him* the benefactor. The great-souled are reckoned to have a good memory for their own benefactions, but not for cases where they have been the beneficiary; for the beneficiary is inferior to the benefactor, but the great-souled man wants to be the superior. He likes to hear of the benefits he has bestowed, but not of those that has received. . . . It is characteristic of the great-souled man not to ask for help, or only reluctantly, but to help others most willingly. (NE 1124b9–19)

Cp. NE 1120a33 (from the account of the virtue of liberality): "The liberal man would not be the one who asks others for a lot, for it is not part of what it is to be a benefactor to others, to find it easy to bear to be a beneficiary." And 1167b17: "Those who bestow benefits seem to love their beneficiaries more than those who receive the benefits love those who bestow them. People ask why this is so, taking it to be unreasonable. But as most people agree, it is because the one side are debtors, the other side creditors."

For Aristotle, on the evidence of these passages, generosity is noble, gratitude servile. The etymology of our English word "generous" in the Latin *generosus*, and of its Greek near-equivalent *eleutheros*, is relevant here: the generous man is the man of good family (*genus*), the *eleutheros*—the "liberal" person, the man of liberality—is free-born. Apparently Aristotle thinks that generosity, in the external sense of benefits conferred (a sense also visible in Cicero), is a virtue that aristocrats show to their social inferiors. That is why he says here that there is something demeaning about being on the receiving end of generosity, and thinks that the right response to generosity is either to repay it—with interest—or to feel ashamed if you can't; but does not say that in either case anyone ought to feel gratitude.

Alasdair MacIntyre's comment on this network of attitudes is to condemn the whole lot:

> To [the] virtues of giving must be added virtues of receiving: such virtues as those of knowing how to exhibit gratitude, without allowing that gratitude to be a burden, courtesy towards the graceless giver, and forbearance towards the inadequate giver. The exercise of these latter virtues always involves a truthful acknowledgement of dependence. And they are therefore virtues bound to be lacking in those whose forgetfulness of their dependence is expressed in an unwillingness to remember benefits conferred by others. One outstanding example, even perhaps *the* outstanding example of this type of bad character and also of a failure to recognise its badness is Aristotle's *megalopsychos.* . . . We recognise here an illusion of self-sufficiency, an illusion apparently shared by Aristotle, that is all too characteristic of the rich and powerful in many times and places, an illusion that plays its part in excluding them from certain types of communal relationship. For like virtues of giving, those of receiving are needed in order to sustain just those types of communal relationship through which the exercise of those virtues first has to be learned. (DRA 126–27)

Now I am not a true believer in the actual Aristotle's actual ethics. I don't think it simply impossible for the actual Aristotle ever to be wrong about anything, as some contemporary commentators apparently do. Perhaps they transfer to Aristotle a habit of implausibly charitable exegesis originally developed through evangelical readings of the knottier bits of, say, 1 Corinthians and Leviticus. But in fact, like the actual St. Paul and the actual author(s) of Leviticus, the actual Aristotle is patently wrong about plenty of things, and not just the stock examples, slavery, and women.

Nonetheless, I think MacIntyre is overreacting here. The first thing to bear in mind about what Aristotle says in these passages is the sociological background of client/patron relations in Aristotle's Athens.[2] It is obvious to any reader of Dickens how, in a society like his, someone might develop a decidedly jaded attitude to the whole idea of "charity," given the way that moral idea was systematically warped, distorted, abused, and exploited for their own ends by the rich and powerful in Victorian England, as yet another ideological weapon in their tireless war against the poor and marginalized. Can we really not see how, in parallel with this, the correlated notions of generosity and gratitude could have become ideologically infected by the power-structures that dominated Aristotle's society? Such infection would not of course be a reason to disbelieve in the reality or the possibility of genuine and untainted gratitude and generosity; any more—as Dickens himself constantly insists—than the existence of men like Squeers or Bumble the beadle would be a reason to believe that there could never be genuine charity. But it would be a reason to be *suspicious*, and to want to distance ourselves from some of our society's most characteristic, and most infected, manifestations of the ideology under criticism. Aristotle's *megalopsychos*—whatever else may be true of him—perhaps has at least this in his favor: that he is in this sense duly *suspicious* of his own society's ideology of dependence, and the place that carefully calculated acts of generosity, and indeed gratitude, played in sustaining and perpetuating that ideology.

How else might we moderate this surprisingly fierce disagreement between Aristotle and MacIntyre? In at least two other ways, both of them more directly about the text of Aristotle itself, and less about the implicit social background to that text. The first is to protest that MacIntyre is not taking due account of all the evidence for Aristotle's views about independence, dependence, and interdependence. There certainly are passages in the *Ethics*, and in the *Politics* too, where Aristotle makes unconvincingly strong claims about the importance of *autarkeia*, independence; the ones that prompt MacIntyre's attack, as quoted earlier, are among them. But these short passages need to be balanced against some obvious and important points about the overall tenor of Aristotle's practical philosophy as a whole. For one thing, Aristotle spends a whole chapter of the NE (IX, 9) arguing in detail that no individual alone can achieve *eudaimonia*, and that for full *eudaimonia*, each of us needs friends: "to the serious man by nature, a friend who is serious is something he has reason to choose" (NE 1170a13–15).

That point might lead us to think that Aristotle's point about *autarkeia* can at most be that it is not the solitary individual, but a small *hetairia* of friends, who are *together* self-sufficient. But after all the whole aim of Aristotle's *Politics*, and of the prolegomenon to it that we call Aristotle's *Ethics*, is to describe and display the indefinitely many ways in which humans are a species of animal for which the natural life is life in a *polis*, a social community of conspecifics. That is bound to mean that it is not just our friends with whom we are interdependent. As Aristotle himself insists at the very beginning of the *Politics,* it is the entire political community.

Another way in which we might defend Aristotle's approach to this topic from MacIntyre's criticisms is to note the differences between different *forms* of generosity and gratitude: generosity *with what*, and gratitude *for what*, and about exchanges *between whom*? These questions of detail are not raised either by MacIntyre or by Aristotle in the very short discussion of gratitude (or rather of being a beneficiary) in Book IV of the *Nicomachean Ethics* that MacIntyre quotes. But Aristotle does get a little closer to raising them in at least one important other place.

The place I have in mind is *Rhetoric* 2.7, a passage that has perplexed translators for centuries. The main problem with it, as David Konstan has recently argued (David Konstan, "*Kharin Ekhein,*" in David Mirhady, *Influences on Peripatetic Rhetoric: Essays in Honor of William W. Fortenbaugh,*

Leiden: Brill 2007), is simply that most translators have not understood the Greek idiom *kharin ekhein*. Literally, the phrase means "to hold [a] grace," that is, to have received a free favor; hence it comes to mean "feel gratitude," *kharis* to mean "an act of generosity," and *kharin hypourgein* to mean "bestow a (generous) benefit on." As Konstan argues, these understandings of the key terms in *Rhetoric* 2.7 give sense to Aristotle's discussion—in fact, clarify what it is a discussion *of*—in a way that no other linguistically possible understanding of them could. The point of the whole discussion is, as we would expect in the *Rhetoric*, to give instruction to the orator. Specifically, the passage tells the orator how to get it across to a jury that they, as citizens, have reason to be grateful to someone who appears before the court: such reasons include that the benefactor acted in the citizens' interest and not his own, that he responded to urgent need, that his benefactions were great and difficult to give, that he gave what he gave at the right times, or that he was the only one to give it, or the first, or the most generous (dAR 1385a22–26).

Conversely, there being one science of opposite things, Aristotle goes on to advise his class of aspiring orators on how to *undermine* a jury's sense of gratitude toward someone who appears before them:

> So it is also obvious how it is possible to *remove* gratitude and make [the jurors] ungrateful (*akharistous*): either the benefactors were acting or are acting for their own sake—so there was no generosity (*kharis*); or their "generosity" was mere chance, or they showed it under compulsion; or they were just repaying what they owed anyway—whether or not they realised this, for either way their action is merely *quid pro quo*, so that in neither case does it count as generosity. Again, we should look through all the categories: all generosity will be such either because of *what*, or *how much*, or *quality*, or *time*, or *place* [and so on; Aristotle omits the other five of the *Categories'* categories]. And it is significant, if people have not helped in a smaller way [that there is something suspect about their motivation for helping in the larger way]. Likewise [it is significant], if they have given our enemies too just the same benefit, or something equal to it, or something even greater; for in that case it is clear that they did not give us the benefit *for our sake*. Or [it is significant] if they knowingly gave us something paltry; for no one admits to needing what is paltry. (dAR 1385a42–b11)

Here once again, as so often in the *Rhetoric*, Aristotle's advice to budding orators about how to work persuasively on their audiences can only be understood against the background of the rich and detailed phenomenology of the emotions and reactive attitudes of their shared society that Aristotle presupposes. In this phenomenology, it is indeed important to note the various conditions attendant on acts of generosity that Aristotle details, in order to understand what level of gratitude, if any, is appropriate—and so, what arguments to stimulate gratitude, or to quench it, are likely to work for an orator.

The cases of gratitude that Aristotle and the pupils in his rhetoric class are considering here are, of course, cases where the benefactor and the beneficiaries are, usually, going to be importantly unequal. The benefactor who is the person before the court—whether accuser or accused—is being considered as a benefactor *to the city* or *to the people*. He is therefore either an aristocrat, or a rich man, or both. The jurors who sit in the court, on the other hand, are—or at least the vast majority of them are—the ordinary people of Athens whom Plato and Aristotle scornfully labeled the *hoi polloi*. Now the gratitude that such low-born jurors are likely to feel to their privileged benefactors is, of course, a very particular kind of gratitude; it is also peculiarly easy for it to swell into frenzied mob-adulation, or curdle into spiteful mob-envy. Difficulties of these particular kinds appear very easily in relations of gratitude and generosity between unequals. But this is a point that Aristotle himself recognizes, and gives a great deal of space to in NE VIII–IX. He tells us again and again in those two books that it is essential to friendship to wish well, and act for the benefit of, one's friend; he also tells us, with no less emphasis and repetition, that relations of friendship hold most naturally and easily *between equals* (e.g., see 1163b31).

Aristotle then takes it as a matter of course—as something so obvious that he feels no need to state explicitly—that the focal cases of generosity and gratitude are going to occur within friendships, and in particular within the virtue-friendships of equals. The cases of gratitude discussed in *Rhetoric* 2.7 are therefore untypical and nonfocal, for Aristotle, *as cases of gratitude*; what is important about them is how clearly these atypically public and political cases show up the obstacles that inequality puts in the way of gratitude and generosity.

Something similar comes out when we consider the other (and of course related) factor that can skew the ideal operations of gratitude and generosity, namely money. If I receive, say, a beautiful oil painting of Donegal as a birthday present from my sister or an old friend, then for me to feel *ashamed* at or *belittled* by this gift is just as absurd and reprehensible as MacIntyre thinks. But suppose I am young and poor, and you are my rich old next-door neighbor; we are passing acquaintances only, and I've never discussed my money problems with you nor asked for your help; but you are not blind, and you have a soft spot for me, and you like to think of yourself as benevolent; so one day I find a cheque for £20,000, made out to me on your account, in a plain envelope on my doormat. Should I be grateful, or ashamed, or a bit of both? Should I perhaps actually feel *insulted*? Should I even take the money, or would it be more dignified for me to return it to you with a note saying "A kind thought—thank you, I'm touched; but I really can't accept this"?

The answers to these questions will depend on the very large number of ways in which we might further specify my, as it stands, rather thinly described case. But a large class of those further specifications are clearly going to fall Aristotle's way not MacIntyre's. We can grant to MacIntyre that it is—at the level of complete generality—folly and pride for humans to refuse to admit their necessary interdependence. Certainly; but there are plenty of more specific levels that are worth thinking about. And it is at these levels that Aristotle's reservations about relations of generosity and gratitude have most point.

For as a matter of social fact, there really are a lot of cases where generosity, or attempted generosity, naturally and reasonably leads not to gratitude but to awkwardness or worse. As I say, many of the most obvious of these involve generosity with money. And as Aristotle says or at least implies, at least part of the reason *why* money seems to be such a problematic gift is, very often, a reason that brings us directly back to equality: because giving it can so easily seem to be a kind of power-play. In our own society, we have the word "patronizing," which is a signpost to some of the problems. And even where we aren't in a society dominated by client-patron relations in the way that Seneca's or Aristotle's was, and even where a monetary gift is not a conscious *assertion* of class superiority or other economic superiority, it can all too easily still be an *expression*, even if an unintended one, of that superiority. Even without the Schlegels' egregious blunderings in *Howards End*, this would still be Leonard Bast's reasonable complaint against them; it is also what Mr. Doolittle rather garrulously complains about to Professor Higgins in *Pygmalion*.

Money gifts are liable to be or seem disrespectful not only because of their tendency to look like a power-play but also for a second reason: because of their impersonality. A gift in kind, at least where it is carefully chosen, expresses a particular form of benevolence, directed personally at some specific aspect of the recipient's character, especially one that has been of particular relevance to our relationship: as it might be, I give you paints and canvas because I know you like painting, and because in the past you have painted *me*. By comparison, a monetary gift can tend to look like a sign of uninterest in the recipient, especially if bestowed without consultation. Conversely—I speak here from decades of Christmas and birthday experience—a recipient who insists on money-gifts only is apt to seem grasping, or insufficiently interested in the particularities of his benefactors, or both.[3]

Mutual respect is then a necessary condition of both generosity and gratitude, if these two things are not to misfire. This is one correct point that we may, I think, extract from what Aristotle says about gratitude at NE 1124b9 ff. MacIntyre is right to object that at least some of that discussion overdoes the advantages of maximal independence from other people. However, as I have pointed out, we have to take account of the social background to what Aristotle says. As I have also pointed out, there is actually far more in Aristotle about interdependence than about independence. Moreover, an important part of what Aristotle thinks about gratitude is (unfortunately) simply left *implicit*: Aristotle simply takes it for granted that generosity and gratitude are good things, and especially, though not exclusively, among equals. Finally, the mutual respect requirement on generosity and gratitude that we can quarry out of NE 1124b is correct, important, and also, of course, perfectly consistent with MacIntyre's own insistence on recognizing our mutual dependence. There is, no doubt, a balance to be struck between them—or a mean to be found.

Aristotle does not, then—*pace* MacIntyre—reject the idea that gratitude is a positive feature of character; the idea that he radically *opposes* gratitude is just a mistake, and even the idea that he is seriously neglectful of it by comparison with a Christian author such as Aquinas is a questionable one. On the contrary, as is particularly clear from his treatise on friendship in NE VIII–IX, and from his discussion of how orators should deal with the *topos* of gratitude and benefaction in dAR 2.7, he takes the notions of gratitude, and of its correlative generosity, for granted. If we want to find a philosopher who is simply a *foe* of gratitude, we will have to look to someone other than Aristotle. And who that someone else might be, I have no idea. (It is certainly not Nietzsche, for instance, for whom a capacity for gratitude is clearly an important part of living life affirmingly.)

VII

So much for the case against gratitude; now for the case for, and for *cosmic* gratitude. What I want to denote by that name is the possibility that we should be grateful more frequently than we actually are. Maybe *far* more frequently. Maybe, even, our attitude should be the attitude that St. Paul recommends: "Give thanks in *every* circumstance" (ἐν παντὶ εὐχαριστεῖτε, 1 Thessalonians 5.18).

This is, be it noted, no isolated saying of St. Paul's. The idea of giving thanks to God is central to the entire Judaeo-Christian tradition, from the 3,000-year-old thanksgiving of the Psalms to the contemporary North American late-autumn festival, now largely secular, of the same name. The center point of Christian worship is the eucharist, and the name means "the thankyou." On this outlook—which is no local or occasional eccentricity, but the (or at least a) dominant outlook of our entire culture over the last two thousand years—gratitude is not just a virtue to display from time to time, as and when other people do nice things for us in the ordinary course of life. Gratitude should be the keynote of our entire lives, and we should be grateful in everything, maybe even (a stronger claim) *for* everything; our universal outlook should be what we might call *cosmic* gratitude.

I am attracted by this outlook. (I would be. I'm a Christian.) I would mount a full-scale, all-out, ground-up defense of it, if only I knew how. I'm not sure I do. Still, I will try and say something briefly in support of St. Paul's injunction, and of the broader idea of cosmic gratitude.

Here we face a conflict between two obvious and important thoughts. One is that gratitude is good for us; the other is that gratitude needs to be truth-tracking. The conflict between them arises, well, from the state of the world. Of course it would be great—people are likely to say—if we *could* be "grateful in everything" as St. Paul urges, and as various websites do as well; maybe even grateful *for* everything. Consider this, from a Japanese Buddhist self-help/DIY therapy website that was the first return when I googled "gratitude" just now:

> Thank you so much for this article about complaining and gratitude. . . . I have been practising not complaining. It took me about three weeks before I had a day with no complaints! The reason I started was because I thought, "Oh, this is going to be easy; I hardly ever complain." I found out differently. Then I discovered that by evening I almost every day forgot what I had complained about that day, so I decided to keep a journal about it, nothing very long or drawn out, just a little something to keep me focused. Later I wrote one day that I was grateful I hadn't complained that day. Now I always add something I am grateful for. (http://www.todoinstitute.org/gratitude.html)

Yet it needs no Buddhist self-help website, nor Syrian last apostle, to tell us about the psychological benefits of living our lives in a mind-set of celebration and gratitude and thankfulness. (Provided, of course, that our unceasing and indefatigable cheerfulness does not drive everyone around us to reckless thoughts of homicide.) As a matter of mental health, such warm and fluffy feelings are all to the good, if only we can achieve them, given their obvious good consequences. But as I insisted earlier, it is incoherent to try and get these good feelings simply for their consequences. Unless these positive emotions are grounded in the truth, in responsiveness to how things are, we cannot reasonably value them *except* for their mental-health benefits. Beneficial illusions may be beneficial, but are nonetheless illusions; moreover, understanding their illusory nature destabilizes their power to benefit. Cosmic gratitude is gratitude *for* everything, *to* God. But the non-theist doubts that God is there to be the recipient of this gratitude; she also doubts that gratitude is an appropriate or a possible or even a tasteful response to a very great deal indeed of what goes on in this sad old world of ours. (No one is, or should be, grateful for the Holocaust or the Ebola virus, nor for Donald Trump or Brexit.)

This is not the place—you will be relieved to hear—for an all-out argument for the existence of God or the goodness of the world. But it might be the place for me to say something to render at least intelligible the mind-set of the believer in cosmic gratitude. I have five thoughts to offer about this, with which I close this paper. But I repeat: I am not trying to *argue for* this mind-set, to prove it correct, against anyone who does not share it. I am merely trying to *describe* it, with a view, I hope, to make it at least intelligible to such non-sharers.

First and least ambitiously, then, we can remind ourselves that gratitude, like many other virtues, is a corrective virtue. If we think it important (as we should) that our responses to value in the world around us should be truth-tracking—should capture the value that is actually there—and if we accept the plausible suggestion that we have some natural tendencies (whinging, negativity, self-centredness) that tend to blind us to the values around us, then we should agree that making an effort to be more grateful than we feel inclined to be is not necessarily an exercise in well-meaning, Pollyannaish self-deception. It may actually be a way of improving our responsiveness to value.

Second, and connected: despite the obviously all-embracing implications of the phrase *cosmic* gratitude, we should bear in mind how much of our mental life necessarily involves selective attention, where the direction of our attention is a matter of our own choice (conscious or otherwise). A lot of the time we *choose* what to focus on. Where there are both negatives and positives that we *could* focus on in this way, it is neither more nor less truth-tracking to focus on the positive than it is to focus on the negative.

But more than this (thirdly), what we dwell on mentally, what we choose to focus on, is a kind of psychic food to us. Our spirits need the nutrition of the beautiful and the good, the joyous and the pleasant, and become poisoned and starved and unable to endure or go on without it. To dwell, in delight and celebration, upon the good things that have been given to us (as the theist takes it), or at any rate that have come our way (as anyone can agree), is not just a selection choice about what to make central to our thoughts. It is a way of nourishing our minds.

Anyway (fourthly), the believer in cosmic gratitude doesn't have to say that gratitude is the *only* warranted response to the world in general. Of course, other attitudes can and will be warranted too, and they may be attitudes that in some sense or other are in tension with gratitude: sorrow at losses, for example, or anger at injustices. As already noted, St. Paul said, "Be thankful *in* every circumstance," not "*for* every circumstance."

However—fifthly—what the believer in cosmic gratitude must say is that there is something fundamentally right about gratitude as a response to the world, as such, and as a response to my existence in it, as such. The idea is that at the deepest level, gratitude is the *right* response, in a way that sorrow, or anger, or indifference, would not be right. And what makes it right? The theist's basic idea, I think, is that the mere existence of the world, and my own mere existence, are themselves good things: good things in themselves, already, before any further qualities or qualifications are added.

Of course, once the world exists, and once I exist, pain and tragedy and disaster can supervene on existence—and so can delight and redemption and triumph. But—according to the mind-set of cosmic gratitude—that doesn't mean that, as modern ethicists usually assume without argument, existence itself is merely neutral. Still less does it mean, as Sophocles, Thomas Hardy, and David Benatar dolefully declare, that it would have been better never to exist at all. The fundamental idea of cosmic gratitude is that whatever else may come *after*, it is at any rate good for the world, and for me (and you), to be. These things would be good in themselves even if they had *just happened*. But the outlook of cosmic gratitude says, further, that the world's existence and my own existence are not just good things but good gifts—and that God is the one who gives them.

Remember: I'm not claiming to have proved this outlook, by ground-up argument all the way from a priori or otherwise obvious premises to the conclusion that cosmic gratitude is right. But if it *is* right, then it enables the believer in cosmic gratitude to explain how an attitude of gratitude for everything can also be a truth-tracking response to value. If the mere existence of the world, if my own mere existence, really is a good thing in itself, and if God stands behind my own existence and the world's as the creator of both, then there will indeed always be something for which gratitude is appropriate. And then, gratitude, thankfulness, will indeed be a virtue that it is right to allow to color and seep through every other experience that the world affords us.

> There is at the back of all our lives an abyss of light, more blinding and unfathomable than any abyss of darkness; and it is the abyss of actuality, of existence, of the fact that things truly are, and that we ourselves are incredibly and sometimes almost incredulously real. It is the fundamental fact of being, as against not being; it is unthinkable, yet we cannot unthink it, though we may sometimes be unthinking about it; unthinking and especially unthanking. For he who has realized this reality knows that it does outweigh, literally to infinity, all lesser regrets or arguments for negation, and that under all our grumblings there is a subconscious substance of gratitude. (G.K. Chesterton, *Chaucer* (London: Faber, 1932, pp. 36–37)

NOTES

1 For an extended discussion of the interplay between gratitude and generosity in Dickens's *Bleak House*, see the chapter by Roberts (this volume).

2 Historical caveat: we know a good deal less about patrons and clients in classical Athens than in classical Rome. To some extent this merely reflects the fact that we know a good deal less about *everything* in classical Athens than in classical Rome; but it does seem undeniable that the patron-client relation was far less heavily systematised and ideologised in classical Athens than it was in Rome. ("*Amicitia* was a weapon of politics, not a sentiment based on congeniality": Ronald Syme, *The Roman Revolution,* p. 12.) Nonetheless, it can be argued that "a similar phenomenon to Roman patronage, though by no means identical, did indeed exist in classical Athenian society": see Rachel Zelnick-Abramovitz, "Did Patronage Exist in Classical Athens?" L'antiquité classique 69 (2000), 1, pp. 65–80, at p. 69. (It is particularly interesting to note Zelnick-Abramovitz's point that the Greeks' *words* for "patron" and "client" were, on both sides of this assymetrical relationship, *philos*: this remark sheds revealing and novel light on Aristotle's discussion of "political" and "economic" *philia* in NE VIII–IX.)

3 Seneca, *de Beneficiis* 1.14.1: Licet ita largiri, ut unusquisque, etiam si cum multis accepit, in populo se esse non putet—"So the right way to be beneficent is to do it so that each particular beneficiary—even if he is benefited along with lots of others—does not think of himself as just one of a multitude."

Chapter 13

Gratitude, Truth, and Lies

David Carr

GRATITUDE AND DECEITFUL BENEFIT

Much recent literature has emphasized the positive contribution of gratitude to human psychological, social, and moral good or flourishing (for useful survey of recent work on gratitude, see Gulliford et al. 2013; also Carr 2013). Given this, what should we think of the following case? In Graham Greene's novel *Brighton Rock* (Greene, 1983), the psychopathic central character Pinkie Brown marries the rather pathetic waitress Rose to prevent her from testifying against him for the murder of his fellow gangster Spicer. At one point in this narrative, Rose persuades him to make a recording affirming his love for her (presumably as a kind of wedding present). In the novel, the spiteful Pinkie agrees but records the following message: "God damn you, you little bitch, why can't you go back home forever and leave me be?" (Greene, p. 177). However, the classic 1947 movie version of the novel (directed by John Boulting and starring the distinguished British actor Sir Richard Attenborough) gives this episode an intriguing twist by having Pinkie record: "What you want me to say is, 'I love you. Well I don't. I hate you, you little slut.'" After Pinkie's violent death in flight from the police (following a failed attempt to arrange his wife's death), Rose attempts to play the record back—which, now damaged, sticks after the first sentence, repeating the words "I love you" over and over again. Rose is therefore left in a state of happiness for what she takes to be Pinkie's assurance that he did really love her and might even feel grateful to him for (what she takes to be) his affirmation of love.

If so, in line with much recent work on the topic, Rose's possible gratitude might count as conducive to her welfare: it is personally comforting and keeps her going. That said, one may well anticipate objections to this example—not least about the use of such terms as "virtue" and "flourishing" with respect to it. Still, perhaps the most obvious objection is that the good will presupposed to any genuine expression of gratitude is just absent from this example: Pinkie is simply not benevolent, he means Rose no good whatsoever (quite the opposite), and the words "I love you" are a fragment of a larger sentence primarily intended to offend and wound her. So, while Rose might feel grateful for a (wrongly) perceived benefit, any such gratitude could only rest on a mistake, and therefore—from a logical viewpoint—be quite unwarranted and uncalled for.

What, however, if we change the example? Adam and Eve are happily and lovingly married with a grown up soldier son. In the course of recent military action, the son has met his death—though only Adam knows this. Adam convinces his wife—who is only too ready to believe him—that their son is simply missing in "fairly safe" action and will eventually turn up unharmed. He says this because he knows that Eve will otherwise go to pieces and perhaps take her own life: he lies in the interests of her flourishing or well-being, and—since she may seem to have benefited from the deceit in terms of continued functioning, she might feel comforted by Adam's reassurance. Of course, Eve might not consider herself benefited or appreciative if she was subsequently told the truth. She might then wish she had never been told the truth and forever resent or hate Adam for shattering her comfortable illusion. From this viewpoint, to be sure, we might judge that Eve *should* not continue to feel benefited in the light of the truth. But we might equally ask not only whether it is not right of Eve to feel benefited in her deceived state but also whether it is not more conducive to her flourishing to continue in that state rather than learn the truth. Still, the main present trouble is that while Eve may or may not consider herself benefited, any actual or possible benefaction in this case is not clearly something that calls for her *gratitude* as such—since she is not presently well placed to see herself as a beneficiary of anything. To be sure, there is a looser sense of gratitude whereby we might judge Eve to be grateful for her husband's reassurance: it is in this sense that one might be grateful that one missed the bus that crashed or that it did not rain on today's parade. But this sense—according to which an agent is not aware that there is any benefactor to whom it is appropriate or required to be grateful—is really just a generalized sense of appreciation, whereby we might equally say (without much loss of sense) that we are relieved we missed the bus, glad that it did not rain, or that Eve was comforted by her husband's reassurance (see Carr 2013; Fagley 2015).

Let us, therefore, try a further example. Dawn is convinced that her husband Derek is having an affair. She therefore asks her close friend Jennifer to spy on him with a view to gaining evidence about Derek that might explain his suspicious behavior. As Jennifer works closely with Derek, she has access to information that Jane has not—about, for example, whether he is actually going to the overseas conferences that he says he is. In fact, Jennifer quickly discovers that Derek is having an affair with a young office secretary but judges that this is likely to be short-lived, and that Dawn—who is pregnant—is in too fragile state to be told the truth. When asked to report back, Jennifer therefore lies to Jane, assuring her that Derek is above suspicion. Dawn is consequently not only happily reassured but positioned to be grateful to Jennifer whom she takes to have gone out of the way to do her a favor— which she also duly acknowledges with a present of flowers and chocolates. Thus, unlike Rose for whom any gratitude would lack a benevolent agent, or Eve who is not well placed to appreciate benefaction, Dawn would seem genuinely grateful for something from which she does appear to benefit—a friend's lie to her—which is indeed aimed at her benefit. On the one hand, then, all commonly accepted conditions for gratitude seem to be in place. On the other hand, however, if gratitude is held to be a kind of moral good or virtue, it may be troubling that it is here implicated—at both the benefaction and beneficiary ends of this transaction—in intentional falsehood or untruth, which may raise questions about the moral status of gratitude and its role in human flourishing that do not seem to have received much previous attention.

GRATITUDE AS A VIRTUE

As recent work and aforementioned remarks have suggested, the received terminology and grammar of gratitude discourse is complex and suggestive of different and divergent concepts or senses of such key terms as "grateful" and "thankful." At the most basic level, many expressions of thanks for some service or benefit are hardly more than casual or habitual social courtesies involving little real thought, feeling, or meaning. For expressions of gratitude to have greater meaning or substance, however, they would probably be held to require the presence of some real feeling or sentiment of appreciation for benefits received. It is just such "sincere" expressions of gratitude that have been regarded by psychologists and other social scientists as contributory not only to personal health and well-being but also to positive interpersonal and social associations and relationships (see, for example, essays in Emmons and McCullough 2004).

Still, it has also been pointed out—mainly by philosophers—that gratitude has a significant normative or moral dimension, according to which genuine expressions of this sentiment may be judged inappropriate if some or other of the basic logical conditions for its exercise are absent or otherwise questionable. Insofar as warranted gratitude would seem to require the presence of a genuine benefactor, something worth regarding as a genuine benefit and someone in a position to appreciate both benefit and benefaction, it may not be due in the absence of these conditions: so, as seen, while Rose lacks a benefactor, Eve is not much in a position to recognize either benefit or benefaction. However, other conditions that may undermine gratitude are cases of real enough benefaction in which benefactors have ulterior motives or their benefits are little more than means to manipulation or exploitation of beneficiaries, or (perhaps)—in cases of the kind under consideration—where benefits bestowed on beneficiaries are deceitful or dishonest. It is to this issue that we shall shortly return.

To be sure, while appreciating the normative or moral dimensions and implications of gratitude is imperative—not least to the end of an "educated" or discriminating gratitude that is capable of distinguishing appropriate from inappropriate occasions for its expression—it is arguable that this does not adequately capture all that is involved in truly grateful agency. Indeed, one evident problem is that agents may well be able to appreciate the difference between appropriate and inappropriate gratitude, recognize that gratitude is due in their circumstances and even express gratitude in their conduct, yet precisely lack the grateful feelings or sentiments mentioned earlier. So, while such grateful feelings or sentiments may not be sufficient for any fully developed sense or response of gratitude, they would nevertheless seem necessary. It would be difficult to describe those who appear to act gratefully, but without appropriate feeling, as truly grateful persons. From this viewpoint, it has lately been customary to regard *genuine* gratitude—along the lines of such other normatively ordered sentiments as honesty, justice, self-control, courage, and compassion—as a *virtue*.

Indeed, while diverse conceptions of virtue are available in contemporary ethics, the currently most common approach derives primarily from Aristotle (1941), who takes virtues to be acquired and settled states of character governed by a rational capacity to which he gave the name *phronesis* or "practical wisdom." For present purposes, the key question is that of the standards or criteria whereby virtue in general or virtues in particular need to be ordered in order to qualify as such. Here, it is important to appreciate that while Aristotle clearly identifies *phronesis* or practical wisdom as an "intellectual virtue," he no less clearly distinguishes this from the truth-seeking concerns of other intellectual virtues: hence, unlike his "epistemic virtues," practical wisdom is not primarily, if at all, concerned with discovering theoretical or scientific knowledge of the world, but rather with the regulation of natural human feelings, sentiments, and appetites for the formation of good character (and agency), to the ultimate end of what he calls *eudaimonia* or flourishing (sometimes more loosely rendered as "happiness"). From this viewpoint, while correct discernment of the facts of any given circumstance of action is important for practical wisdom, the acquisition of knowledge or information of this or any other kind is less important than cultivating the character and capacities conducive to effective agency.

We should here note the strong influence that this Aristotelian emphasis on the *practical* concerns of the intellectual virtue of *phronesis* has had on more recent neo-Aristotelian or virtue ethical thinking. Generally, even the very best of contemporary virtue ethicists (e.g., Annas 2011) have been much drawn to Aristotle's explicit comparison between the cultivation of virtues and the acquisition of practical skills—though Aristotle himself stressed the limits of this analogy in other parts of the *Nicomachean Ethics* (e.g., Aristotle Book 5, Chapter 6). There can be little doubt, however, that insofar as recent virtue ethics has given much attention to the epistemic dimensions of Aristotle's *phronesis*, it has been strongly inclined to construe the knowledge of practical wisdom in terms of the "know-how" of skill more than the "knowing that" of theoretical enquiry (for the classic modern account of this distinction, see Ryle 2000). Thus, on recent "eudaimonistic" accounts of virtue (e.g., Besser-Jones 2014), what matters more for the cultivation of such qualities as courage, temperance, or modesty is the practical effects of deliberation about the ends of such virtues on human personal or social well-being—largely regardless of concerns with knowledge and truth as such. To this extent, the main aim of practical deliberation is to make us more courageous, temperate, or modest rather than to gain knowledge of the world—and this is to be achieved by avoidance of the defects and excesses of feeling, passion, and appetite that Aristotle associates with two kinds of unhelpful departure from virtue. But in one recent virtue ethical account of the virtue of modesty (Driver 1989, 2001), this can only be achieved by some *ignorance* of our merits, since a person could not offer a true estimate of these (at any rate, if they are evidently superior to those of others) without seeming or being immodest. While this view seems objectionable on several counts (see, for example, Flanagan 1990; Sandler 2005), it does show the extent to which the idea of virtuous deliberation has become untethered from any stricter epistemic concern with knowledge, truth, and honesty in recent virtue ethics.

LIES AND DECEIT IN GRATITUDE

Still, enough may now have been said to begin to assess the logical and psychological status of gratitude and benefaction in the cases so far considered in this chapter. As so far observed, Rose (logically or normatively) owes Pinkie no gratitude, since he is simply not a benefactor, and—while Adam *is* a benefactor—Eve is not well placed to recognize him as such. That said, Rose could still have (misplaced) prepositional gratitude toward Pinkie, and Eve might still feel gratitude in the general appreciative ("propositional" or grateful "that" or "for") sense; and, of course, Dawn may experience gratitude in either of these senses. Insofar as the more sentimental or appreciative aspects of gratitude are often extolled in the psychological literature as precisely conducive—irrespective of normative warrant—to both personal (subjective) well-being and social flourishing, they may also be considered, as in these examples, sources of psychological support for all three women of our narratives. To this extent, their gratitude is also consistent with eudaimonistic virtue ethical accounts that place prime emphasis on the contribution of virtues to effective human functioning and well-being. However, to the extent that their responses are void of the critical discrimination or evaluation that might secure appropriate normative warrant, our heroines could not be in and of themselves considered grateful in the more robust moral or virtue ethical senses of these terms. That said, aside from Eve who has no actual reason to feel "moral" gratitude, we might still credit Rose and Dawn with some discriminating gratitude, since Rose has the "evidence" of the recording and Dawn has the testimony of her friend Jennifer. The trouble is, of course, that both of these grounds for genuine gratitude are *false*. So one thing we might want to say here is that while the gratitude of Rose and Dawn is not inconsistent with moral or virtuous gratitude, it is also not rationally warranted to the extent that they are both mistaken about what they are grateful for.

However, while this is clearly apparent in the case of Rose, it is less so in that of Dawn: For was not she the recipient of a real and kind enough benefit—from a no less well-meaning beneficiary? Certainly, we need not doubt that Jennifer lied to her friend—just as Adam lied to Eve—because she thought that it was in the best interests of Dawn not to know the truth and that the lie would therefore be of benefit to her. But we might now question this so-called benefit on several counts. First, is it really appropriate to regard a lie as a benefit? While the example rules out that Dawn is in a position both to regard Jennifer's lie as a benefit and to know the truth, we may still ask (counterfactually) whether she would still regard it as a benefit if she were in a position to know the truth: after all, what she asked Jennifer to ascertain for her was precisely the truth. Second, there would seem something anyway generally suspect about regarding an instance of falsehood or deceit as a benefit—precisely because we would intuitively regard a benefit as a kind of *good*, and untruth and deceit certainly seem morally untoward. But third, by much the same token, there would seem to be something especially morally questionable about Jennifer's lie to Dawn, given their closeness as friends and the key role and importance of trust in friendship. Dawn has specifically asked her friend to tell her the truth in this situation and Jennifer's lie would therefore appear to involve some betrayal of their friendship.

On the other hand, it also seems that Dawn *does* derive some benefit from the lie: she is able to keep going without falling into depression or undergoing a troubled pregnancy and is also able to preserve her marriage. Perhaps we may also suppose that Jennifer threatens Derek that she will reveal the truth to Dawn if he continues to misbehave—and he proceeds to mend his ways in this light. So everyone—mother, baby, cradle and all—seems to benefit in this situation. Dawn does precisely appear to have something to be thankful for and someone to be grateful to in this circumstance. From an ethical viewpoint, perhaps we might also justify Jennifer's lie on the utilitarian grounds that it is by far the lesser of two possible evils. Or, if one is unhappy with utilitarianism, one may on more virtue ethical grounds justify her actions by appreciating that even in the case of virtuous (or near virtuous) agents, there are inevitable, unavoidable, and often tragic tensions or conflicts between virtues such that it may be quite impossible to be (for example) both honest and compassionate in some circumstances (see Carr 2003). Jennifer is by nature and nurture both a compassionate and honest person: far from believing, like utilitarians, that the positive outcome of her lie makes it morally right or good, she is seriously disturbed and upset by it. At the same time, her feelings for Dawn are such that she believes lying to be the best (moral) option in her friend's current predicament.

GRATITUDE, VIRTUE, AND MORAL VIRTUE

All the same, in the light of recent points about the inherent moral dubiety of falsehood and lying and the importance of veracity and truthfulness in friendship, one may yet be uneasy about the ethical status of Jennifer's decision. One way of putting this might be to say that while she no doubt acted virtuously, it is less obvious that she acted with *moral* virtue. To be sure, this may at first sight seem an odd or counterintuitive suggestion: for, one might ask, how could there be conduct that is at once virtuous, but not moral? However, as I have elsewhere argued (Carr 2015), any philosophical unease regarding this matter may turn on a common contemporary conflation of virtue with *morality*—or, more precisely, on supposing that all virtues are moral virtues or conducive to moral ends. But, as is readily apparent from commonplace examples, this seems far from so. For the Greeks in general, and Aristotle in particular, the term *arête* (later rendered, via the Latin *virtus*, as "virtue") meant "excellence" and was used to refer to a range of acquired or cultivated qualities or capacities from which human (or other) agents or their social groups might benefit, prosper, or flourish. While such qualities could be considered goods of real benefit to individuals or their communities, such benefit might fall well short of anything that we would nowadays regard as morally commendable. Indeed, it is clear even in contemporary Anglophone usage that many of the qualities commonly regarded as virtues—such as courage, temperance, and loyalty—may be exercised in the service of aims and goals that are immoral, criminal, or otherwise ethically untoward. There can evidently be brave, loyal, and self-controlled bank robbers and terrorists, no less than saints or war heroes.

While there may also be exceptions to this general rule (it could be, for example, that justice—at least in modern post-Christian or post-Kantian senses of impartial universal respect—is inherently moral), it should be clear with regard to present concerns that neither compassion nor gratitude is so. On the one hand, one can easily conceive acts or benefits that are—as, arguably, in Jennifer's case—motivated by genuine compassion and informed by responsible (Aristotelian) deliberations about what is conducive in the circumstances to local well-being, that we might nevertheless regard as morally questionable. But gratitude can also be sincerely and responsibly expressed for favors or benefits that fall somewhat short of moral propriety. For example, a mobster might well be grateful to another for "bumping off" the rival gangster who was attempting to kill him. While the life-saving action may be morally deplorable, insofar as the mobster at least takes himself to have benefited from the killing, it is clearly an occasion for gratitude and his failure to be grateful would therefore seem to be a form of (vicious) ingratitude. So while it is common to regard failure to thank those from whom one has benefited as morally deficient (though it is also not clear that this is always so: see Carr 2015), it does not follow that gratitude is as such necessarily moral or directed to moral ends—despite the fact that it may yet comply with the conditions of virtue required for other virtues. But now, just as we might distinguish the virtuous courage or self-control that is exercised in pursuit of bad or evil ends from the morally virtuous self-control or courage that is employed in pursuit of good or just ends, we may also distinguish virtuous from *morally* virtuous compassion or gratitude. If so, this point may have significant implications—to which we shall shortly turn—not only for the moral status of Jennifer's compassion, and the "beneficial" deception through which this is expressed, but also for Dawn's gratitude.

At this point, however, it may be worth saying something about the grounds upon which any such distinction between virtue and moral virtue might be made. So while there may be virtuous self-control or courage that is not moral, insofar as it is directed toward immoral ends, what would make it morally virtuous self-control or courage? One possible answer—to which neo-Aristotelians might well be drawn (perhaps in the name of some degree of virtue unity)—is that such courage or self-control would have to be in the service of justice. But this response seems problematic in Aristotelian terms. For while Aristotle certainly has a substantial conception of justice as a virtue, this is also a culturally local one that is certainly at some odds with any modern egalitarian view of justice. Indeed, even to express the objection in this way might seem offensively understated. For, insofar as Aristotle's conception of justice would regard women and slaves (for example) as inferior to other human beings, we might rather want to say that it hardly qualifies as any *morally* defensible conception of justice. But if Aristotle's account of justice fails to provide moral grounds for virtue, where else might we look?

Arguably, one useful ancient perspective on this problem is available in the work of Aristotle's illustrious philosophical predecessor Plato. Early in the *Nicomachean Ethics*, Aristotle (1941) rejects what he takes to be Plato's search for a "universal" idea or ideal of the good or justice on the grounds that this is insufficiently practical, and it is upon this basis that he builds his case for a special practical wisdom of *phronesis*—which he also subsequently distinguishes from other more theoretical or knowledge-seeking virtues. However, while Aristotle himself seems less than clear on the precise relationship of practical wisdom to epistemic virtues of honesty and truth, we have also seen that this has certainly encouraged latter day eudaimonistic conceptions of virtuous deliberation as a kind of practical knowledge in which considerations of truth are not of prime concern. In this regard, it is arguable that while the Platonic search for a universal conception of justice seems to have been of itself less than successful, it may yet have been onto something of considerable ethical importance. Indeed, insofar as it appears to reflect some appreciation—apparent in Plato's "divided line" epistemology—of a level of normative reasoning that transcends the kind of naturalistic or empirical enquiry that evidently underpins Aristotelian virtue ethics, it might well have presaged the modern deontology pioneered in the eighteenth century by Rousseau (1977) and Kant (1967), which also defends a non-natural universal conception of moral regard.

Be that as it may, Plato's search for a non-empirical account of moral good or justice seems even more basically rooted in a profound Socratic distrust of sense experience as a source of moral insight. In this regard, it is well known that Socrates regarded virtue as a kind of wisdom grounded in knowledge. However, as the Socratic dialogues also make clear, such wisdom is not to be understood as the acquired academic or practical knowledge of professional expertise, but more as a kind of liberation from the cave of illusion, vanity, and self-deceit into which human agents are born and bound by sensory experience. Faithful to his teacher, Plato fairly consistently holds—from such Socratic dialogues as the *Symposium* through to such later non-Socratic dialogues as the *Laws*—that human moral error and wrongdoing has its basic source in egotistic human attachments to vain and selfish desires and ambitions from which it is the goal of philosophical enquiry to release the soul (Plato 1961). In philosophical thinking nearer our own day, it is this self-same liberation from personal and social vanity and self-delusion that is the prime focus of Rousseau's own Plato-indebted work (1977) and which—in an even more directly Platonic vein—has been the major theme of the writings of Iris Murdoch (1970, 1993). The key idea is that the main source of moral error is a kind of misperception of the world (see also, McDowell 1997) aided and abetted by human egotism. On this view, it would seem that there can be no genuine moral virtue or response that is inconsistent with honesty and truth and that (for example) Driver's suggestion that there might be "virtues of ignorance" may only be regarded as morally objectionable. In short, while Socrates may (perhaps) have been mistaken to regard knowledge as sufficient for moral virtue, it would certainly seem—at least to the best of human capacity— to be necessary for it (Carr 2016).

TRUTH AND HONESTY IN MORAL BENEFIT AND GRATITUDE

While more would need to be said in defense of this large claim than present space permits, there seems enough basis here for a post-Aristotelian distinction between virtue and moral virtue and for its useful application to the cases so far considered in this chapter. To begin first, then, with the benefaction and benefit for which deceived beneficiaries might be expected to be grateful. In this regard, we need not doubt that both Jennifer and Adam are clearly acting with the best interests of (respectively) Dawn and Eve at heart. It is also undeniable that there is a real enough respect in which those they deceive do genuinely benefit from the lies they are told: they are able to keep going and avoid falling apart. Hence, insofar as Adam and Jennifer act with genuine compassion in the light of careful practical deliberation toward what they consider to be personally beneficial outcomes, there is no reason why we should not consider their actions to be—in the full Aristotelian sense— virtuous or at least consistent with virtue. On the other hand, however, their alleged benefits are deliberate false comforts. Both Jennifer and Adam are also involved in close personal relationships of friendship and marriage with those they deceive, regarding which trust and trustworthiness ought to be morally constitutive features. Indeed, Dawn has particularly asked Jennifer to discover and tell her the truth about her husband and her gratitude is a direct response to the lie that Jennifer has told her. Hence, despite her good will and best intentions, Jennifer's lie might still be considered a significant personal betrayal. At best, irrespective of her genuine desire to protect her friend, Jennifer's deceit might be held to fail the test of true and morally mature friendship. In this light, the no-doubt-compassionate Jennifer may appear much in the position of the truly self-controlled or courageous who dedicate themselves with knowing commitment to morally dubious ends: she is virtuous but not morally so.

Moreover, finally parting company with Eve—who has no reason to suppose she owes any gratitude to Adam—we are left with a last awkward question about Dawn's gratitude to Jennifer. First, we might generally ask whether Dawn *should* (normatively) be grateful to Jennifer? On the face of it, it may here seem reasonable to reply both "no" and "yes": while she should clearly not be grateful for the deceit, she might still feel grateful for Jennifer's sincere concern for her health and feelings. However, in the light of previous considerations about deceit as a betrayal of friendship, it might be that Dawn would or should want to say—if, as the example precludes, she were positioned to do so—that she does *not* (at least unambivalently) feel gratitude for Jennifer's "benefit" as expressed in the narrative example.

To be sure, by way of thought experiment, we might suppose that Dawn dies and goes to heaven only to learn post-mortally of Jennifer's deceit. We might now imagine Dawn responding in various ways: with gratitude toward her friend for having saved her life, with some resentment at her deceitful betrayal of their friendship—or, perhaps, with some ambivalent mixture of the two. Actually, this conjecture is neither entirely fanciful nor ethically frivolous. For while Dawn of the example may not have been in a position to know the truth, she *might* be the kind of person (of whom there may be no small number) to whom veracity is not a prime psychological or moral concern, and who—though she suspects in her heart that Jennifer is not being honest with her—prefers false consolation to hard truth. So, to be sure, if Dawn's gratitude of the narrative *was* based on honest and considered confidence that Jennifer would never do other than tell her the truth, then it could—though here misplaced—nevertheless count as virtuous or even morally virtuous. But if Dawn would have in any event personally *preferred* a lie to the truth, while she might well have had sincere and genuine feelings of gratitude to Jennifer on the occasion, these might not be considered moral virtues—or, perhaps, as any kind of virtues whatsoever.

REFERENCES

Annas, J. (2011) *Intelligent Virtue*, Oxford: Oxford University Press.

Aristotle (1941) Nicomachean ethics. In R. McKeon (Ed.) *The Basic Works of Aristotle*, New York: Random House, 1941, pp. 935–111.

Besser-Jones, L. (2014) *Eudaimonic Ethics: The Philosophy and Psychology of Living Well*, New York: Routledge.

Carr, D. (2003) Character and moral choice in the cultivation of virtue, *Philosophy*, 78 (2) 219–232.

Carr, D. (2013) Varieties of gratitude, *Journal of Value Inquiry*, 47 (1/2) 17–28.

Carr, D. (2015) Is gratitude a moral virtue? *Philosophical Studies*, 172 (6), 1475–1484.

Carr, D. (2016) Virtue and knowledge, *Philosophy*, 91 (357): 375–390.

Driver, J. (1989) The virtues of ignorance, *Journal of Philosophy*, 86 (7): 373–384.

Driver, J. (2001) *Uneasy Virtue*, Cambridge: Cambridge University Press.

Emmons, R. A. and McCullough M. E. (Eds.) (2004) *The Psychology of Gratitude*, Oxford: Oxford University Press.

Fagley, N. (2016) The construct of appreciation: it is so much more than gratitude. In D. Carr (Ed.) *Perspectives on Gratitude: An Interdisciplinary Approach*, London and New York: Routledge.

Flanagan, O. (1990) Virtue and ignorance, *Journal of Philosophy*, 87 (8): 420–428.

Greene, G. (1983). *Brighton Rock*, Harmonsworth: Penguin Classics.

Gulliford, L., Morgan, B. and Kristjansson, K. (2013) Recent work on the concept of gratitude in philosophy and psychology, *Journal of Value Inquiry*, 47, 285–317.

Kant, I. (1967) *The Critique of Practical Reasoning and Other Works on the Theory of Ethics*, translated by T.K. Abbott, London: Longmans.

McDowell, J. (1997) Virtue and reason, in R. Crisp and M. Slote (eds.) (1992) *Virtue Ethics*. Oxford: Oxford University Press.

Murdoch, I. (1970). *The Sovereignty of the Good*, London: Routledge and Kegan Paul.

Murdoch, I. (1993) *Metaphysics as a Guide to Morals*, Harmondsworth: Penguin.

Plato (1961) Symposium, republic and laws. In E. Hamilton and H. Cairns (Eds.) *Plato: The Collected Dialogues*, Princeton, NJ: Princeton University Press.

Rousseau, J-J. (1977) *The Social Contract and Other Discourse*, London: Dent Everyman.

Ryle, G. (2000) *The Concept of Mind*, Harmondsworth Penguin.

Sandler, R. (2005) Ignorance and virtue, *Philosophical Papers*, 34 (2): 261–272.

Chapter 14

Cross-Pollination in the Gardens of Virtue

Liz Gulliford

THE CROSS-POLLINATION OF VIRTUE: A RATIONALE

This chapter focuses on how spiritual and self-examination practices promote a number of virtues simultaneously, and demonstrates how there can be cross-pollination from one virtue to another within a person's character. The chapter covers both conceptual and practical ground, beginning by elucidating the theory behind the idea of cross-pollination, and then turning to two examples of this at work. The chapter will close with some suggestions as to how psychological interventions to promote strengths of character might be enriched by fostering mutually reinforcing strengths, rather than targeting virtues individually.

A recently published paper examines the rationale for why one might expect some virtues of character to be mutually reinforcing, and scrutinizes existing psychological work that provides a degree of empirical support for this theorizing (Gulliford & Roberts, 2018). The main contention of the chapter is that virtues of character come in clusters. Virtues *within* the same cluster share family resemblances that distinguish them from virtues in other clusters. Gulliford and Roberts (2018) focus specifically on five virtues they label "the allocentric quintet." This cluster consists of generosity, gratitude, forgiveness, compassion, and humility. The common ground shared by these virtues and their unifying feature is benevolence and, as the label "allocentric" indicates, this benevolence manifests in an "others-focused" well-wishing and well-doing.[1]

The authors explain how virtues within the "allocentric quintet" reinforce one another. For example, compassion and humility are ingredients in forgiveness, and the experience of having been forgiven could be expected to give rise to gratitude, which one would expect to promote further instances

280

of forgiveness of others in the future (see also Gulliford, 2017b, p. 72).[2] The benevolent regard for others is what characterizes the virtues of the "allo-centric quintet," whereas virtues of willpower (such as perseverance) are, in contrast, unified by powers of self-management that can be motivated by both moral and non-moral concerns.

The relation of virtues to each other could be elucidated by means of the metaphor of a symphony orchestra, which is made up of different sections: strings, percussion, woodwind, and brass. Each of the instruments in each of the sections is more similar to the instruments within its own section than the others. However, all sections consist of kinds of instrument, and often all four sections play as one to produce harmonious music. Thus, the metaphor of the orchestra captures both the special sympathies some virtues have with one another and the overall unity of the virtues.[3]

The thesis of the "unity of the virtues" goes back, in various permutations, to antiquity (see Gulliford and Roberts, 2018 for a sketch). The proposal is that all virtues are so integrated with one another that one cannot have one virtue without having them all. For Aristotle, the "unity of the virtues" inhered in the virtue of practical wisdom (*phronesis*). When an individual possesses this fundamental excellence of character, he has all the other virtues by extension (1985, p. 171 [1145a1–2]). Since *each* virtue incorporates a kind of knowledge (practical wisdom), it is this knowledge that is essentially uni-fied and common to all virtues. Thus, all human excellences share common ground by virtue of *phronesis*. Returning to the metaphor of the orchestra, *phronesis* (for Aristotle) could be likened to the conductor (see Gulliford, 2017a).

The thesis of the "unity of the virtues" has not gone unchallenged. In a well-known paper, Badhwar contests the notion of the fundamental unity of the virtues, and puts forward a modification which she calls the "limited unity of the virtues" (LUV) thesis (Badhwar, 1996). She suggests that the virtues are disunited across different domains but united *within* domains. For Badh-war, "domains" refers to different spheres of human relationships. Her point is that "a person (P) could be kind towards her friends and colleagues without being kind (or virtuous in any other way) towards acquaintances or strangers" (1996, p. 308). She argues that practical wisdom almost always is exhibited in *only some* domains of an individual's life (1996, p. 308, my italics).

While Badhwar (1996) proposes a thesis of the limited unity of the virtues based on their manifestation in specific domains of life, Gulliford and Rob-erts (2018) propose a modification of thesis of the "unity of the virtues" that is based on virtue *types*. While the overarching thesis of the unity of all virtues may be a stretch, there do seem to be "unities of allied virtues." For example, the virtues of "intelligent caring," including justice, compassion, and truthful-ness, are unified by perceptive benevolence toward others, whereas "virtues of willpower" (e.g. perseverance, self-control and patience) are those capacities concerned with the management of impulses. The commonality between virtues within a cluster makes for particularly mutually reinforcing relationships ("cross-pollination") between these associated virtues. This is not to say that *only* virtues within a cluster reinforce one another; virtues between clusters also interact with each other. A moral dilemma might call for the exercise of virtues from more than one cluster. However, there are special sympathies between virtues within a cluster that make cross-pollination between these virtues especially likely.

Having offered a theoretical rationale for the unities of allied virtues ("virtue clustering"), Gulliford and Roberts (2018) review a number of empirical studies that, to some extent, substantiate their reasoning about the mutually reinforcing nature of the virtues of the "allocentric quintet."[4] For instance, Bartlett and DeSteno (2006) showed that a laboratory-induced state of gratitude led participants to help a person who had previously helped them (even when doing so was costly), demonstrating the mutually reinforcing nature of gratitude and generosity. For a close conceptual examination of the bond between the virtues of generosity and gratitude, illustrated by a novel by Charles Dickens, see Roberts (this volume). Karremans, Van Lange, and Holland (2005) reported that reflecting on past actions of forgiving others increased the probability of participants donating to and volunteering for charity, suggesting that forgiveness promotes generosity. Similarly, Exline and Hill (2012) found humility to be a robust predictor of generous behavior, showing that humility may promote the virtue of generosity.[5] For the full analysis of how generosity connects to each of the other virtues of the "allocentric quintet," see Gulliford and Roberts (2018, pp. 208–226).

Within the context of spiritual disciplines, the idea of pollinating one virtue from another has deep and well-established roots. In this chapter, the practice of *lojong* (from the Tibetan Buddhist tradition) and the exercises making up Twelve Step programs will be discussed to examine how they might be said to promote cross-fertilization of virtues.

CROSS-POLLINATION OF VIRTUES IN TWELVE STEP PROGRAMS: THE PLACE OF HUMILITY

An example of the cross-pollination of virtues is Twelve Step recovery programs where the virtue of humility seeds the development of other strengths of character targeted at later stages of recovery. The key role played by humility is at first more implicitly assumed within the program, though it rises to prominence more explicitly as the program progresses in Steps 5, 6, and 7.

Post, Pagano, Lee, and Johnson (2016) describe Twelve Step programs as "one of the twentieth century's most successful social experiments in applied spirituality" (p. 10). As such, the program is valuable to both addicts and non-addicts, for it is above all concerned with the development of good character, principally achieved by deflating the ego and substituting other-focused willingness for self-centered willfulness—a problem that can hardly be said to be unique to addicts!

Having said this, few people today seem to be aware of the potential relevance of Twelve Step programs to their own lives, seeing the advice contained therein as specific to people with "addictive personalities." This has not always been the case. Indeed, in the foreword to the *Twelve Steps and Twelve Traditions* (1952), the relevance of the program to non-members of Alcoholics Anonymous (AA) was unambiguously highlighted:

> Though the essays which follow were written mainly for members, it is thought by many of AA's friends that these pieces might arouse interest and find application outside AA itself. Many people, nonalcoholics, report that as a result of the practice of AA's Twelve Steps, they have been able to meet other difficulties of life. They think that the Twelve Steps can mean more than sobriety for problem drinkers. They see in them a way to happy and effective living for many, alcoholic or not. (*Twelve Steps and Twelve Traditions*, foreword, pp. 15–16)

It is the often misunderstood virtue of humility that is placed at the forefront of Twelve Step programs and is identified by Post et al. (2016) as a "cardinal virtue" in AA. A close reading of the Twelve Steps shows that humility catalyzes a change in terms of the relation of the self to others, potentiating a spiritual chain of events that leads to growth in other virtues, such as forgiveness, compassion, gratitude, generosity, and service.

But what is humility? Humility involves a certain way of seeing oneself in relation to others. Humble persons do not place themselves at the center of their world and do not deem themselves to be more significant than they really are. The etymological root of humility is *humus* (Latin), meaning ground or earth. While the comparison of a humble person with the earth suggests lowness, it also suggests being "down to earth" and not claiming undue importance or loftiness.

Erik Wielenberg (forthcoming) conceives of humility as having two core elements. On the one hand, humility consists of the ready acknowledgment of flaws and limitations shared by fellow human beings. These flaws include helplessness (being subject to forces outside one's control), fallibility (being subject to ignorance and error), and moral imperfection. From a Christian point of view, this moral imperfection would be labeled "sin," though clearly the understanding that human persons are not morally perfect is not limited to religions.

The other broad aspect of humility lies in "recognising one's relative insignificance in comparison with some aspect of reality distinct from oneself" (Wielenberg, forthcoming, p. 7). From a theistic point of view, this relative insignificance is perceived in relation to God, but God's place could be taken in a secular context by anything deemed a "higher power" or, as Wielenberg argues, could be inspired by the feeling of awe for the natural world (Wielenberg, forthcoming, pp. 7–8).

Humility (like purity) can be understood primarily as an absence. Whereas purity is characterized by the absence of contaminants, humility represents the absence of the moral pollutants of vanity, arrogance, and other vices of pride (Roberts, 2016; Roberts & Wood, 2007). These vices are all ways of being concerned about a misconceived kind of personal "importance," a point echoed by Wielenberg; "Misplaced pride can lead to an unwarranted belief that one deserves special treatment from others; when such special treatment is not forthcoming, indignation and anger can result" (Wielenberg, forthcoming, p. 4). This distorted (and vicious) species of hubristic pride can be contrasted with an authentic and healthy pride in one's genuine achievements. As psychologists Carver, Sinclair, and Johnson (2010) point out, authentic pride "arises from a self-evaluation of 'doing,' whereas hubristic pride arises from a self-evaluation of being" (Carver, Sinclair & Johnson, 2010, p. 698).[6]

Post et al. (2016) note that there are two predominant views of humility in Western thought (broadly Roman Catholic and Protestant), both of which have influenced the understanding of humility in Twelve Step programs (see Lobdell, 2004). The Catholic interpretation, dating back to Aquinas (which itself owes much to Aristotle's notion of the "Mean"), takes humility to be keeping oneself within appropriate bounds, avoiding both excessive *and deficient* self-esteem (see ST II-II, Q. 161). This kind of understanding seems to be in mind in the following:

> If temperamentally we are on the depressive side, we are apt to be swamped with guilt and self-loathing. We wallow in this messy bog, often getting a misshapen and painful pleasure out of it. As we morbidly pursue this melancholy activity, we may sink to such a point of despair that nothing but oblivion looks possible as a solution. Here, of course, we have lost all perspective, and therefore all genuine humility. For this is pride in reverse. (*Twelve Steps and Twelve Traditions*, Step Four, p. 46)

Thus, the absence of humility can manifest in self-pity and unworthiness, as well as in grandiosity and vanity.

On the other hand, the Protestant understanding of humility going back to Martin Luther is voluntarist—that is to say that it foregrounds the will (rather than the intellect) in human conduct. For Luther, humility is submission to the divine will, which supplants one's own self-will: "Thy will, not my will, be done." This understanding of humility seems particularly prominent in the earlier steps of the program, though it remains a thread through to Step Twelve, as we shall see. These two understandings of humility (the intellectual more "Catholic" strand, and the voluntaristic interpretation Post et al. [2016] label "Protestant") map onto the two core features of humility identified by Wielenberg (forthcoming). Understanding one's flaws and limitations incorporates the *intellectual* element of humility, whereas acknowledging one's relative insignificance before a "higher power" (however that might be conceived) serves as a recognition of the limits of the *will*.

Steps 1–3 are characterized by Post et al. (2016) as "Humility as complete defeat before a Higher Power." In these stages, the Twelve Stepper must accept that life impelled by self-will has failed and he must turn his will over to God. Post et al. (2016) note that this "modulation" of humility in Twelve Step programs (they identify three other such modulations or "forms" of humility in recovery) "verges on the *humiliation* of realizing that reliance on self in overcoming addiction has totally failed. . . . Yet it is a necessary first step to radically reduce an inflated self-perception" (p. 6, my italics). A more palatable take on these initial steps might be described by the term "letting go," as this conveys a sense of acceptance without the overtones of capitulation and dishonor inherent in humiliation.

In contrast, the more Catholic understanding of humility predominates in Steps 4–7, which are characterized by Post et al. (2016) as "Humility as accurate self-appraisal." This second modulation of humility sees the person in recovery dealing with the damage they have caused others. For that purpose, Twelve Steppers need to develop as truthful and undistorted a view about themselves as possible. At Step 4, the person in recovery conducts a "searching and fearless moral inventory," which tackles the question of character flaws head-on.

Twelve Step programs devote *most* of their time to the development of virtue and good character, recognizing that it is not possible to proceed in this process until an addict has stopped using. Step One directly concerns the grip of addiction. The following steps describe a "moral metamorphosis" that cannot begin *until* the Twelve Stepper is sober and clear-headed. Undergirded by an accurate sense of one's self and its limitations that is "sensible, tactful, considerate and humble without being servile or scraping" (AA, 1939/2001, p. 83), the person in recovery admits his defects to another person (Step Five), a stage which leads toward *forgiveness*—of others and oneself.

> This vital step was also the means by which we began to get the feeling that we could be forgiven, no matter what we had thought or done. Often it was while working on this step with our sponsors or spiritual advisors that we first felt

truly able to forgive others, no matter how deeply we felt they had wronged us. Our moral inventory had persuaded us that all-round forgiveness was desirable, but it was only when we resolutely tackled Step Five that we inwardly knew we'd be able to receive forgiveness and give it, too. (*Twelve Steps and Twelve Traditions*, 1952, Step Five, p. 59)

Confiding one's defects in another trusted person engenders humility, which in turn lights the way to forgiveness and the possibility of a remedy for human failings: "our first practical move toward humility must consist of recognising our deficiencies. No defect can be corrected unless we clearly see what it is" (*Twelve Steps and Twelve Traditions*, 1952, p. 59). Thus, both receiving forgiveness oneself and extending forgiveness to others is made possible by first implanting the virtue of humility (see Worthington, Jr. [1998]). In this connection, in one correlational study, Powers, Nam, Rowatt, and Hill (2007) found that self-reported humility and a quality they called "spiritual transcendence" correlated with the self-reported tendencies to forgive.

Step Seven is unequivocal about the central importance of humility in recovery. It focuses specifically on fostering this virtue, offering its most thorough treatment of all the steps of the program. This is not the species of humility-as-submission encountered in Steps One to Three:

Where humility had formerly stood for a forced feeding on humble pie, it now begins to mean the nourishing ingredient which can give us serenity. This improved perception of humility starts another revolutionary change in our outlook. Our eyes begin to open to the immense values which have come straight out of ego-puncturing. (*Twelve Steps and Twelve Traditions*, Step Seven, pp. 75–76)

Humility seems to seed the first fruit of change within a person's values and character, though this humility needs to be accompanied by a searing *honesty* about oneself and one's faults. It might be argued that it is impossible to have genuine humility *without* honesty. The close tie between the virtues of humility and honesty is implicitly acknowledged in Lee and Ashton's (2004) HEXACO model of personality, wherein "honesty-humility" constitutes one of six overarching personality factors alongside emotionality, extraversion, agreeableness, conscientiousness, and openness to experience. Moreover, in order for a humble person to have a truly *accurate* assessment of their worth, humility would need to be seasoned with honesty as Flanagan (1990) contends against Driver (1989, 2001).

Forgiveness is one of the values to emerge from this deflation of the ego. The virtue of humility, however, remains a constant and appears to be the taproot of self-transformation and spiritual growth as it is conceived within Twelve Step programs:

We should pause here to consider what humility is and what the practice of it can mean to us. Indeed, the attainment of greater humility is the foundation principle of each of AA's Twelve Steps. For without some degree of humility, no alcoholic can stay sober at all. Nearly all AA's have found, too, that unless they develop much more of this precious quality than may be required just for sobriety, they still haven't much chance of becoming truly happy. (*Twelve Steps and Twelve Traditions*, Step Seven, p. 71)

The voluntaristic view of humility as submission of the will, necessary for an addict to admit her powerlessness over addiction, is "required for sobriety." However, it is acknowledged that there is a humility that is somehow beyond this that is essential to happiness ("the attainment of *greater* humility," my italics). The non-addict does not require the species of humility that submits to powerlessness over addiction *in particular*, but she must accept the limits of her existence in other more general respects.

The idea and associations of submission and dependence sit uncomfortably with a great many of us. They compromise our sense of personal agency and autonomy. However, there are adaptive and maladaptive forms of dependence. One clearly maladaptive form is the dependence of substance abuse, but another equally pernicious one is evident in the adult child who has been unable to separate himself from his parents, and is incapable of making key life decisions on his own or who is still inappropriately financially dependent on others. This latter species of pernicious dependence, coupled with the complete absence of humility, is epitomized by the character of Harold Skimpole in Dickens's novel, *Bleak House* (see Roberts, this volume). This particularly vicious manifestation of dependence is an extreme type, though there are plenty of individuals who, to a lesser degree, seem to believe other people can (and should) solve their problems for them—financial or otherwise.

In contrast, there is an appropriate sense of dependence on others that recognizes that since we are all vulnerable to life's ups and downs, we can trust and rely on other people to be there for us when the going gets tough, without assuming our own helplessness in the matter. We could call this adaptive kind of dependence "interdependence" in recognition of the fact that it is based on mutual aid, rather than in an imbalanced or co-dependent type of helping behavior, which sees one side providing all the help for another (e.g., the parents of the dependent adult child). It should be acknowledged, however, that the ideal balance of being interdependent could be severely disrupted by early life experiences—and heavily influenced by caregivers whose own patterns of behavior fell to either one or other side of this ideal.

The privileging of autonomy over an appropriate sense of dependence on others could be labeled "hyper-autonomy." This tendency conceives of the human person as independent and autonomous, minimizing an appropriate degree of dependence on others. Virtues are construed as privatized "inner resources" rather than being sustained in participation with others (Gulliford, 2011). For instance, forgiveness, while it has been identified as a virtue in

Peterson and Seligman's Values in Action (VIA) taxonomy (2004), seems to be interpreted in a way that emphasizes the autonomous individual forgiving in the strength of his own resources. In addition, the focus is very much on what forgiving other people does for *one's own well-being.* This has led to forgiveness being construed as something that is primarily "dispensed" to others—a capacity that people possess (or do not). There is no sense of mutuality and participation in a power in which individuals are caught up interdependently as *both givers and receivers* (Gulliford, 2011, p. 59).

Similarly, positive psychological approaches to the virtue of hope locate the ground of confidence in individuals' self-control and self-belief (Gulliford, 2011, p. 169). Yet, our most fundamental sense of hope is kindled by *other people.* The developmental psychologist and psychoanalyst Erik Erikson proposed that the first stage of psychosocial development in infancy is to negotiate the conflict between basic trust and basic mistrust. Hope ultimately stems from trust that an infant can *depend* on his caregivers to meet basic needs. Thus, hope can be sustained where a person has been able to learn that he can *depend* on others. The psychoanalyst and priest William Lynch (1974) observed that hope is kindled *between* people—for instance, in the alliance between patient and therapist—or between sponsor and sponsored in AA. Bressan, Iacoponi, Candidi de Assis, and Shergill (2017) acknowledge that hope may be one of the most powerful therapeutic aspects of the doctor-patient relationship.

The limits of the individual will to solve our deepest problems is readily recognized within the AA literature; "By now, though, the chances are that he has become convinced that he has more problems than alcohol, and that some of these refuse to be solved by all the sheer personal determination and courage he can muster" (*Twelve Steps and Twelve Traditions,* Step Three, p. 40). Through the transformative virtue of humility and its acceptance of an *appropriate* human dependence, a person begins a spiritual transformation, which potentiates growth in the virtues of forgiveness, compassion, gratitude, and service.

Steps Eight and Nine are characterized by reflecting on how one has harmed other people and on making amends. Being able to confront one's own moral failings in a spirit of humility inevitably leads one to reflect on the failings of others and the possibility of forgiveness:

> We shall want to hold ourselves to the course of admitting things we have done, meanwhile forgiving the wrongs done to us. (*Twelve Steps and Twelve Traditions,* Step Eight, p. 84)

What is clearly discernible in all the steps is an emphasis on ongoing character development and the cultivation of virtues that are intrinsic to a flourishing life. "'Self-searching" needs to become a regular habit (p. 90). The steps implicitly acknowledge that many people may begin to address character flaws only as a result of facing up to substance abuse. "Seldom did we look at character-building as something desirable in itself" (Step 7, p. 73). Only after the fog has begun to lift do "we reluctantly come to grips with those serious character flaws that made problem drinkers of us in the first place" (Step 7, p. 74).

As a result of a journey through the steps, beginning with the humility to accept powerlessness over addiction, people experience "a spiritual awakening" (Step Twelve, p. 109), which reaches a recurring end in service to others (Step Twelve, p. 128):

> We heard story after story of how humility had brought strength out of weakness.[7] (*Twelve Steps and Twelve Traditions*, Step Seven, p. 75)

Certainly, Post et al. (2016) cast humility in this foundational role, though it would be interesting to see how this relates to Twelve Steppers' own experience. Some individuals may feel a different virtue flowered first for them, with other virtues coming into bloom later in the day.[8] Another form of spiritual transformation that sees virtues being potentiated by other virtues is the Buddhist practice of *lojong*, to which attention is now turned.

CROSS-POLLINATION OF VIRTUES IN THE PRACTICE OF *LOJONG*: CREATING INTERDEPENDENCE THROUGH GRATITUDE

Lojong is a Tibetan Buddhist mind training practice that was developed between 900 and 1200 CE. The originator is thought to be Atisa (982–1054 CE), though the aphorisms in their current form were composed by Chekawa Yeshe Dorje (1101–1175 CE). The basic meaning of *lojong* is "thought transformation" or "mind training" (*lo* translates as mind and *jong* as transformation). The kind of change promoted by the practice is radical and profound and brings about a complete "transformation of subjectivity" (Ozawa-de Silva, Dodson-Lavelle, Raison & Negi, 2012). Its overarching goal is a complete reorientation from self-centeredness to other-centeredness—a completely new way of seeing oneself in relation to other persons.

The practice has recently been incorporated into cognitively based compassion training (CBCT) programs (see Ozawa de Silva & Dodson-Lavelle, 2011; Reddy et al., 2013; Dodds et al., 2015). This form of mind training establishes preconditions for the cultivation of compassion by foregrounding the virtue of gratitude. Just as the virtue of humility pollinates other virtues within Twelve Step programs, this more ancient spiritual exercise uses reflection on the kindness of other people (to promote gratitude) as a means of propagating compassion for all beings.

The premise of *lojong* is that in the natural and normal (unenlightened) state, individuals are capable only of a biased form of compassion that does not extend to all people equally. In order to cultivate a universal form of compassion, practitioners are instructed to recollect the kindness of other people, beginning with a reflection on all the benefits bestowed on them by their mother. Having generated gratitude and loving kindness toward their mother, practitioners reflect on the kindness of their father and other relatives, then strangers and finally enemies (see Ozawa-de Silva, 2003, p. 116). The thinking behind the process is that all beings have been kind to oneself and are fundamentally involved in creating a fully interdependent life. Reflecting on these benefits in gratitude offers a magnifying lens through which to behold one's interconnectedness with other beings.

While the original *lojong* practice envisages the mother as the matrix from which a sense of gratitude emerges, secularized meditation practices (e.g., CBCT) that are inspired by *lojong* may not include this specific meditation, though they distil its central insight that compassion can be kindled by gratitude. There could be good psychological reasons for this; first, it cannot be assumed that all people enjoy an unproblematic relationship with their mother! If not, this specific reflection advocated in *lojong* may be unhelpful and fundamentally unconducive to growth. Nonetheless, gratitude (toward other people) can be used to promote compassion, an insight that has found its way into modern forms of meditative practice like CBCT.

CBCT is a secular practice developed at Emory University in 2004 by Geshe Lobsang Tenzin Negi. It is informed by both the *lam rim*[9] and *lojong* traditions of Tibetan Buddhism (see Ozawa-de Silva & Dodson-Lavelle, 2011). CBCT has been used in a range of contexts including schools and prisons and also incorporates mindfulness techniques and social and emotional learning skills. The CBCT program consists of eight sessions focusing on eight topics, which are presented sequentially. After meditative preliminaries to foster the ability to attend to one's inner states, the fifth stage is the point in the program's path where appreciation and gratitude are developed to engender a sense of interdependence; the recognition that we are all, to a *healthy* extent, dependent on others. This in turn promotes affection for those others and empathy. Practitioners come to appreciate how they have received a host of benefits from other people, which stimulates them to wish to repay these benefits. Thus, the practices of *lojong* also help individuals come to an awareness that, in the words of the poet John Donne, "no man is an island entire of itself."

One exercise used to promote gratitude and interconnection is reflecting on all the people who have had a hand in creating one's clothes or other objects.

Participants in CBCT interventions are encouraged to reflect on all the beings that contributed toward producing the item; "Practitioners begin to see that directly and indirectly, consciously or inadvertently, these other beings contributed something of benefit to each CBCT participant" (Parrish Florian, 2014, p. 17; Ozawa-de Silva & Dodson-Lavelle, 2011, pp. 1–3). This exercise helps to break down the "hyper-autonomous" view of selfhood we encountered in the previous section; "Our default modes of thinking mistakenly assume a level of personal independence that is not borne out by the kind of cognitive analysis taught in Week 5 of CBCT" (Parrish Florian, 2014, p. 16).

The recognition of an appropriate degree of dependence on others as the natural state of humanity is therefore just as crucial to spiritual growth in CBCT (and *lojong*, upon which it is based) as it is in AA. Whereas in AA, a healthy degree of dependence on others is realized by foregrounding the cardinal virtue of humility, in CBCT (and *lojong*), this interdependence is brought about by means of gratitude. However, the recognition of human (inter)dependence is not the end-point of either AA or CBCT. The goal of both practices is a spiritual transformation, which heightens feeling for and promotes service to others:

> CBCT teaches concepts such as interdependence and gratitude to foster a sense of connectedness and equality with others that then yields cognitive changes which allow a more encompassing and more powerful sense of love and compassion for others. (Ozawa-de Silva & Dodson-Levelle, 2011, p. 12)

We have seen how certain spiritual practices presuppose that the development or intentional foregrounding of one virtue can have powerful "ripple effects" on other virtues. While it might, in principle, be possible to isolate and target individual virtues for promotion, it seems that some virtues might be better cultivated "indirectly" by fostering allied character strengths.

The spiritual exercises we have been examining are clearly predicated on the understanding that related virtues prepare or reinforce one another; "a key feature of CBCT . . . is its analytical, logical flow. Each step of the sequence—equanimity, gratitude, affection, love/compassion, resolve—is profoundly *primed* by what precedes it and foundational for what follows" (Parrish-Florian, 2012, p. 75, my italics). Similarly, in AA, cultivating the virtue of humility makes it possible to deflate the ego sufficiently to allow space for other virtues of character to be promoted.

CROSS-POLLINATING VIRTUES IN EDUCATIONAL AND THERAPEUTIC INTERVENTIONS

In recent years, there has been a flowering of interest in strengths and virtues brought about by the resurgence of virtue ethics in philosophy and by the increasing popularity of positive psychology. As a result of the theoretical turn toward examining positive aspects of human functioning, psychologists have taken practical steps to promote strengths and virtues, such as resilience, optimism, forgiveness, and gratitude and have devised interventions in both educational and therapeutic contexts to cultivate these desirable strengths of character.

Much of this research has examined strengths in relative isolation from one another, and while schools and other establishments may take an additive approach and target a number of virtues in turn, very few of the methods that have been devised capitalize on the insights illuminated by the two sets of practices we have been examining here—namely, that virtues might more fruitfully be developed simultaneously, since there are theoretical and empirical grounds that support the view that certain strengths of character reinforce one another. This may be particularly true of strengths that build up an appreciation of our human interconnectedness with, and benevolent regard for, one another. The virtues of the "allocentric quintet," consisting of generosity, gratitude, forgiveness, and compassion are unified by an "other-focused" well-wishing and well-doing. Cultivating any of the virtues in this cluster strengthens this common core and helps other virtues within the cluster to flower as a result.

From a practical point of view, current positive psychological interventions to promote strengths and virtues would benefit from the insights these disciplines bring to light. Such studies could be used to test further the hypothesis of the mutually reinforcing nature of virtue clusters. For instance, in a recent neuroscientific study, Karns, Moore III, and Mayr (2017) found evidence to support the association between gratitude and altruistic (generous) motivations, and showed that the practice of keeping a gratitude journal for three weeks increased neural measures of pure altruism recorded in the ventromedial prefrontal cortex relative to controls. This sort of empirical work serves to corroborate what many of the world's spiritual practices have implicitly understood—namely, that the "flowering" of virtue proceeds by a process of cross-pollination among allied character strengths.

NOTES

1 The authors describe humility as a "guest virtue" of the "allocentric quintet." "Humility is not itself allocentric, but because the 'other'-orientation of the properly allocentric virtues *requires* some degree of humility, and because the allocentric virtues tend to promote humility, we include it as an honorary member of the quintet" (Gulliford and Roberts, 2018, p. 217).

2 A number of chapters in this volume bear witness to the way gratitude gives rise to—or motivates—other virtues, such as generosity to one's own benefactors (see

McConnell and Fenton, this volume) and to other people. Both Karns' and Callard's chapters address the latter kind of generosity, commonly referred to as "paying it forward."

3 Gulliford and Roberts (2018) use the analogy of a healthy body consisting of many parts to elucidate the relationship of the virtues to one another.

4 The review incorporates a critique of the limitations to which such techniques may be subject. For instance, Gulliford and Roberts (2018) recognize that laboratory-induced experiments may be poor imitators of real life.

5 A degree of caution is required in interpreting studies where temporarily induced states are used to substantiate claims about enduring personal qualities.

6 Daniel Telech, one of the editors of this volume, points out, however, that there could be healthy forms of non-agential pride (ways of being proud for "being" in a way that is not hubristic). He suggests that a person might be proud, in a non-arrogant way, of their heritage. Furthermore, an individual might suffer from hubristic pride arising from a self-evaluation of doing if they suppose that they deserve special treatment as a result of their accomplishments.

7 The idea of "strength from weakness" is redolent of a passage from St. Paul's second letter to the Corinthians (2 Cor. 12:9). The apostle reports that the Lord said to him: "My grace is sufficient for you, for my power is made perfect in weakness." Twelve Step programs have Christian roots (Pittman, 1988). Although the interpretation of the "Higher Power" is not restricted to a theistic one—many Twelve Steppers might interpret this as the power of the group itself—there can be no doubt that the program has been heavily influenced by the Christian worldview underlying it. As such, it is not surprising that the virtues of forgiveness, gratitude, and humility that are all central to the cultivation of Christian character in the New Testament are foundational to the personal transformation envisaged in the program.

8 A cautionary note ought perhaps to be sounded about the overall success of Twelve Step Programmes. Peer-reviewed studies place the success rate at between 5% and 10% (Dodes & Dodes, 2015) though this contrasts markedly with AA's own internal surveys.

9 *Lam rim* (literally "graduated path") is a textual form for presenting the stages of the path to enlightenment.

REFERENCES

Alcoholics Anonymous. (1952). *Twelve Steps and Twelve Traditions*. New York, NY: AA World Services.

Alcoholics Anonymous. (2001). *Alcoholics Anonymous*. New York, NY: AA World Services. (Original work published 1939).

Aristotle (1985). *The Nicomachean Ethics* (T. Irwin, Trans.). Indianapolis: Hackett.

Aquinas, Thomas (1947). *Summa Theologica*. New York: Benziger Brothers Inc.

Badhwar, N. K. (1996). The limited unity of virtue. *Nous, 30*, 306–329.

Bartlett, M. Y. & DeSteno, D. (2006). Gratitude and prosocial behaviour: Helping when it costs you. *Psychological Science, 17*, 319–325.

Bressan, R. A., Iacoponi, E. Candido de Assis, J. & Shergill, S. S. (2017). Hope is a therapeutic tool. *The British Medical Journal, Christmas 2017*, 1–2.

Carver, C. S., Sinclair, S. & Johnson, S. (2010). Authentic and hubristic pride: Differential relations to aspects of goal regulation, affect, and self-control. *Journal of Research in Personality, 44*, 698–703.

Dodds, S. E., Pace, T.W. W., Bell, M.L. Fiero, M. et al. (2015). Feasibility of cognitively-based compassion training (CBCT) for breast cancer survivors: A randomized, wait list controlled pilot study. *Support Care in Cancer, 23*, 3599–3608.

Dodes, L. & Dodes, Z. (2015). *The Sober Truth*. Boston: Beacon Press.

Driver, J. (1989) The virtues of ignorance. *Journal of Philosophy*, 86, 373–384.

Driver, J. (2001) *Uneasy Virtue*, Cambridge: Cambridge University Press.

Exline, J. J. & Hill, P.C. (2012). Humility: A consistent and robust predictor of generosity. *Journal of Positive Psychology, 7*, 208–218.

Flanagan, O. (1990) Virtue and ignorance. *Journal of Philosophy*, 87, 420–428.

Gulliford, L. (2011). *An interdisciplinary evaluation and theological enrichment of positive psychology*. Unpublished PhD Thesis, University of Cambridge, UK.

Gulliford, L. (2017a). *Phronesis and the integration of the virtues*. Unpublished conference paper for the 5th Annual Jubilee Centre for Character and Virtues conference, Oriel College, Oxford University, January 2017.

Gulliford, L. (2017b). Strengths and virtues: An integrated approach. In M. White, G.R. Slemp & S. Murray (Eds.), *Future Directions in Wellbeing: Education, Organisations and Policy*. Cham: Springer International Publishing.

Gulliford, L. & Roberts, R. C. (2018). Exploring the "unity" of the virtues: The case of an allocentric quintet. *Theory and Psychology, 28*, 208–226.

Karns, C. M., Moore III, W. E. & Mayr, U. (2017). The cultivation of pure altruism via gratitude: A functional MRI study of change with gratitude practice. *Frontiers in Human Neuroscience, 11, (599)*, 1–14. doi: 10.3389/fnhum.2017.00599.

Karremans, J. C., Van Lange, P. A. M. & Holland, R. W. (2005). Forgiveness and its associations with prosocial thinking, feeling, and doing beyond the relationship with the offender. *Personality and Social Psychology Bulletin, 31*, 1315–1326.

Lee, K. & Ashton, M. C. Psychometric properties of the HEXACO personality inventory. *Multivariate Behavioral Research, 39*, 329–358.

Lobdell, J.C. (2004). *This Strange Illness: Alcoholism and Bill W*. New York, NY: Aldine de Gruyter.

Ozawa-de Silva, B. R. (2003). *Becoming the wish-fulfilling tree: Compassion and the transformation of ethical subjectivity in the Lojong tradition of Tibetan Buddhism*. Unpublished D. Phil. University of Oxford, UK.

Ozawa-de Silva, B. R. & Dodson-Levelle, B. (2011). An education of heart and mind: Practical and theoretical issues in teaching cognitive-based compassion training to children. *Practical Matters, Spring 2011 (4)*, 1–28.

Ozawa-de Silva, B. R. Dodson-Lavelle, B., Raison, C. L. & Negi, L. T. (2012). Compassion and ethics: Scientific and practical approaches to the cultivation of compassion as a foundation for ethical subjectivity and well-being. *Journal of Healthcare, Science and the Humanities, 2*, 145–161.

Parrish Florian, M. (2014). *Cognitively based compassion training: Buddhist-inflected meditation in a secular mode*. Unpublished thesis submitted to the Faculty of the Candler School of Theology in partial fulfilment of the requirements for the degree of Master of Theological Studies, Atlanta, GA.

Peterson, C. & Seligman, M. E. P. (2004). *Character Strengths and Virtues: A Classification and Handbook*. Washington, DC: American Psychological Association.

Pittman, B. (1988). *AA, The Way It Began*. Seattle: Glen Abbey Books.

Post, S. G., Pagano, M.E., Lee, M.T. & Johnson, B.R. (2016). Humility and 12-step recovery: A prolegomenon for the empirical investigation of a cardinal virtue in alcoholics anonymous. *Alcoholism Treatment Quarterly, 34 (3)*, 262–273.

Powers, C. Nam, R.K., Rowatt, W.C. & Hill, P.C. (2007). Associations between humility, spiritual transcendence and forgiveness. *Research in the Social Scientific Study of Religion, 18*, 75–94.

Reddy, S. D., Negi, L. T., Dodson-Lavelle, B., Ozawa-de Silva, B. R. et al. (2013). Cognitive-based compassion training: A promising prevention strategy for at-risk adolescents. *Journal of Child and Family Studies, 22*, 219–230.

Roberts, R. C. (2016). Learning intellectual humility. In J. Baehr (Ed.), *Intellectual Virtues and Education: Essays in Applied Virtue Epistemology* (pp. 184–201). London, UK: Routledge.

Roberts, R. C. & Wood, W. J. (2007). *Intellectual Virtues: An Essay in Regulative Epistemology*. Oxford, UK: Oxford University Press.

Wielenberg, E. (forthcoming). Secular humility. In J. Cole Wright (Ed.), *Humility: Reflections on Its Nature and Function*. Oxford: Oxford University Press.

Worthington, E. L. Jr. (1998). An empathy-humility-commitment model of forgiveness applied within family dyads. *Journal of Family Therapy, 20*, 59–76.

Chapter 15

The Virtue of Gratitude and Its Associated Vices

Tony Manela

It is common and natural to conceptualize gratitude as a virtuous character trait a person might possess. On one plausible understanding of character traits, a grateful person is one who is consistently disposed to respond with the proper degree of grateful behavior and feelings in situations that call for gratitude, and one person is more grateful than another when the former is disposed to come closer to this ideal degree than the latter. When people think of the virtue of gratitude in this way, they typically think of one vice associated with it—ingratitude—which is understood as a shortfall in certain grateful feelings and behaviors vis-à-vis those which a situation calls for. This understanding of gratitude as a virtue and ingratitude as its sole associated vice has two implications: (1) that there is a scale along which gratitude as a character trait can be quantified and (2) that falling short along this scale, when gratitude is called for, is the only way a person can fail to be properly or virtuously grateful. I believe the first implication is misleadingly simplistic, and the second implication is patently false. My goal in this chapter is to show why those implications are mistaken by developing an account of the virtue of gratitude that reveals the rich variety of ways a person can fail to be properly grateful.

In the first two sections of this chapter I sketch an account of *response-gratitude*: what it means for a beneficiary to be grateful to his benefactor in response to a particular act of benevolence she performs.[1] I argue that for a beneficiary to be grateful to a benefactor for an act of benevolence is essentially for the beneficiary to be disposed to think, feel and behave in certain ways concerning his benefactor, and so response-gratitude is properly understood as a complex of cognitive, affective, and behavioral dispositions. In the third section, I define the *virtue of gratitude* as the general disposition to form these particular dispositions toward the right (and only the right) benefactors at the right times to the right degrees. With this account of the virtue of gratitude on the table, In the fourth section I turn to an exploration of the ways a person can fail to possess this virtue, and I articulate the senses in which those failures can constitute *vices*—morally bad character traits. My analysis will reveal a surprising richness in the kinds of vices constituted by tendencies to respond improperly to benevolence or apparent benevolence. I conclude, in the fifth section, by suggesting several implications this richness in gratitude-associated vices has for moral education and for certain common generalizations about ingratitude that have been put forward by philosophers.

RESPONSE-GRATITUDE AND APPRECIATION

Gratitude as a virtue is rightly (if vaguely) analyzed as the disposition to manifest the right kind and degree of gratitude in all (and only) situations in which it is called for. In order to understand the virtue of gratitude, then, we first need to understand the circumstances that call for gratitude and what it means for a beneficiary to be properly grateful in any given circumstance of that kind. In doing so, we must be careful not to let ordinary usage of gratitude terms lead us astray, because ordinary usage belies an important conceptual distinction.[2] We sometimes use gratitude terms ("grateful," "thankful," etc.) to convey or describe *appreciation*, as is typically done when such terms are followed by the word *that* and a proposition. Utterances like "I am grateful that the weather was beautiful on my wedding day," "I am grateful that the police officer was distracted as I sped by her cruiser," and "I am grateful that my mother's cancer went into remission" all express appreciation. Appreciation is properly a response to beneficial states of affairs or states of affairs one finds valuable, and this response is constituted by certain cognitive elements (a recognition of the value of the thing being appreciated) and certain affective elements (a tendency to take pleasure or enjoy the state of affairs being appreciated). Part of what it is to be grateful that my mother's cancer went into remission, for instance, is to recognize the goodness and the rarity of that event, to refuse to take it for granted, and to take joy in the additional life and health such a state of affairs allows my mother. Appreciation is not fundamentally an interpersonal or inter-agential phenomenon, and though it is a mode of valuing, it does not necessarily entail any kind of care or concern, on the part of the beneficiary, for the well-being of its object. My gratitude that the weather was beautiful on my wedding day, for instance, certainly does not entail a care or concern on my part for the well-being of the weather.

We express a different kind of attitude when we use gratitude terms followed by the preposition *to*, as we do in utterances like "I am grateful to a stranger for coming to my rescue," "I am grateful to my mentor for all her time and attention," and "I am grateful to my parents." In contrast to gratitude *that* (or appreciation), gratitude *to* is properly a response not to good states of affairs, but to the benevolent attitudes and actions of our benefactors. My gratitude toward my mentor is fitting or called for so long (and only so long) as she seems to have been motivated by a genuine intrinsic desire to see me flourish. If it turned out my mentor was mentoring me only because she was afraid she might not receive tenure otherwise, that might very well render my gratitude to her unwarranted (though it may still be reasonable to be grateful *that* she mentored me, insofar as I found her mentorship beneficial). By the same token, if the police officer who let me speed by without ticketing me had actually seen me and, out of kindheartedness, allowed me to get away without being ticketed, it seems I should be grateful *to* her, and not just grateful *that* I escaped without getting a ticket.

Gratitude *to* differs from gratitude *that* (or appreciation) in that the former entails a kind of concern or care for the object of the attitude. This concern or care manifests in several ways. Perhaps most notably, it manifests in certain feelings—namely, feelings of *goodwill* toward the benefactor.[3] It would ring false, after all, for me to claim to be grateful to my mentor for giving me so much time and attention if I find myself with no additional goodwill toward her—no hope that she fares well, no tendency to be happy when I hear things are going well for her, no tendency to be sad when I learn that things are going poorly for her. Gratitude *to* also entails certain behaviors or behavioral dispositions. It involves, for instance, a disposition to reciprocate favors a benefactor has done for me, a disposition to help her should I find her in distress in the future, and a disposition to avoid harming her myself.[4] If I find out that a stranger who once came to my rescue is now in need of similar rescuing, and I can rescue her with little risk to myself, then it seems false to say I am grateful to her if I have no motivation to help her, even if I bear her feelings of goodwill. Gratitude *to*, then, includes certain behavioral dispositions, which, together with feelings of goodwill, are a fundamental part of what distinguishes gratitude *to* from gratitude *that*, or appreciation.

In this chapter, I will be primarily concerned with the virtue associated with gratitude *to* (which, from this point on, I will call simply "gratitude"). Though I will occasionally mention gratitude *that* for the sake of contrasting it with gratitude *to*, I will not be primarily concerned here with the virtue corresponding to gratitude *that*, or appreciation (a virtue which I will call *appreciativeness*).

AN ELEMENTAL ANALYSIS OF RESPONSE-GRATITUDE

Gratitude, I will take it, is properly a response to benevolence. What are the elements of the grateful response?—that is, what are the components of the response a beneficiary must have to an instance of benevolence in order to count as fully or properly grateful for it? It seems to me that the grateful response can be resolved into three more or less distinct but closely interconnected kinds of elements: cognitive elements, affective elements, and behavioral elements. I will consider each of these in turn.

Cognitive elements. As a response to acts of benevolence, gratitude requires at the very least an accurate judgment or private recognition on the part of the beneficiary that an act of benevolence has occurred.[5] It seems impossible, after all, that I could be grateful to my mentor for all her attention and advice if I am unaware or incredulous that she bore me some benevolence that motivated that attention and advice (though I could of course be grateful *that* she gave me her attention and advice without recognizing anything about her mental states). We would be hard pressed to call such a beneficiary grateful because, at the very least, a beneficiary who failed to judge that an act of benevolence had been performed would be unlikely to have the feelings or exhibit the behaviors a grateful person ought to have and perform. Such feelings and behaviors, after all, do not arise ex nihilo in normal people, so without accurate beliefs about an instance of benevolence, we would expect them not to arise.

To count as properly grateful for a particular instance of benevolence, a beneficiary must recognize not only *that* benevolence has been demonstrated; he must also be sensitive to the *magnitude* and the *scope* of the benevolence being demonstrated (i.e., roughly, which interests of the beneficiary the benefactor had an intrinsic desire to advance and how strong that desire was). This means that a grateful beneficiary will be properly attuned to evidence of such benevolence—will recognize such evidence, give it the weight it warrants in his deliberation, and come to reasonable conclusions about how much and what kind of benevolence a benefactor had for him. A properly grateful beneficiary will, for instance, tend to recognize the difference between a wealthy person who gives him a certain amount of money and a poorer person who gives him the same sum of money. He will also tend to recognize the difference between someone who drops money in his lap accidentally and someone who intentionally and thoughtfully gives him money. He will tend to recognize the difference between the mentor who mentors him because she genuinely cares about his philosophical and professional development and the mentor who mentors him only because she worries about receiving tenure. A beneficiary who did not make such distinctions, it seems, would often thereby fail to respond to the former and latter parties with different degrees of gratitude, as a properly grateful person should. Being properly grateful to a benefactor, then, consists in part of a tendency to apprehend the benefactor's benevolence and infer its magnitude and scope correctly.[6]

Affective elements. As I noted in distinguishing gratitude from appreciation, an essential part of what it is for a beneficiary to be grateful *to* is to have certain feelings vis-à-vis the benefactor that he wouldn't have if not for her benevolence. Some philosophers believe there is a single feeling of gratitude, and that what it is to be grateful to someone is to have this feeling concerning them and their benevolence.[7] This, however, is a mistake. It is true that often when we first become aware of someone's benevolence toward us, we experience a positive feeling; but this positive feeling is more accurately understood as part of *appreciating* the fact that someone has benefited us. This pleasant feeling is not always called for in response to acts of benevolence *qua* acts of benevolence.[8] And indeed, it seems plausible that being grateful in a particular moment need not entail having any feelings at all toward a benefactor in that moment. I am, for example, grateful to people for things they did for me years ago, even though there are long stretches of time during which I do not have any feelings regarding them. What makes me grateful during such stretches is my *disposition* to feel certain things regarding them when I am reminded of them. In particular, part of what makes me grateful to past benefactors is that when I hear of them and learn they are doing well, I experience positive feelings of joy or satisfaction, and when I hear that they are doing poorly, I experience negative feelings of sadness or grief. When it comes to feelings, what it means to be grateful is to be disposed to be happy when things go well for a benefactor and disposed to be upset or sad when things go poorly for her. This is the affective disposition I referred to as *goodwill* in the previous section.

As with the cognitive elements of the grateful response, the affective elements should be proportional to the benevolence shown to the beneficiary by the benefactor. That is, the magnitude, intensity, and duration of the feelings of goodwill I am disposed to experience vis-à-vis a benefactor of mine should be proportional to the benevolence my benefactor has shown me. A properly grateful beneficiary should, all else equal, experience stronger feelings of happiness when he hears of the flourishing of a benefactor who showed him a great deal of benevolence than when he hears of the flourishing of a benefactor who showed him only a mild amount of benevolence. And if a beneficiary discovers evidence that his benefactor was more benevolent toward him than he originally believed, this realization should result in an increase in the amount of pleasure he takes in learning of her flourishing. So too, *mutatis mutandis*, for the feelings of grief or upset he would experience upon learning of such benefactors' misfortunes.

Behavioral elements. As I noted in the previous section, it seems that certain behaviors or behavioral dispositions are also an essential part of the grateful response. After all, a beneficiary who recognized his benefactor's benevolence and developed an affective disposition of goodwill toward her would still seem to fall short of gratitude if he found himself, despite those beliefs and feelings, completely unmotivated to return a favor or help her out in some way. Typically, the sorts of behaviors we expect to see from a grateful beneficiary include returning a favor, coming to the aid of the benefactor if she is in trouble (especially if she requests help), taking care to avoid harming her,[9] and using the gift or benefit she conferred in a way that is consistent with her reasonable hopes for how it should be used.[10] This is not to say that all or even any of these behaviors is necessary for gratitude. After all, a beneficiary may be grateful but never have the opportunity to carry out any of these behaviors. What would make the difference between a grateful beneficiary and an ungrateful one in such cases, it seems, is whether the beneficiary has the *disposition* to do these things should the opportunity arise. As far as grateful behaviors go, then, we can say that gratitude entails not certain behaviors but certain behavioral dispositions concerning the benefactor. Specifically, it entails grateful beneficence (a heightened disposition to benefit a benefactor) and grateful nonmaleficence (a heightened disposition to avoid harming a benefactor).

As with the cognitive and affective elements of the grateful response, the behavioral elements of the grateful response should be proportional to the benevolence shown to the beneficiary by the benefactor. That is, the degree to which a beneficiary is disposed to exert effort, expend resources, incur risk, and suffer harm to benefit a benefactor should be proportional to the benevolence the benefactor showed him. A properly grateful beneficiary should, all else equal, be willing to do more to help or return a favor to a benefactor who showed great benevolence than one who showed only minor benevolence. And if a beneficiary discovers evidence that his benefactor was more benevolent toward him than he originally believed, this realization should result in an increase in what he would be willing to do to help or refrain from harming her.

To count as properly grateful, a beneficiary must not only be disposed to act in the proper beneficent and nonmaleficent ways, but he must be disposed to do so for the right reasons as well. After all, a beneficiary who is disposed to help a benefactor but only for prudential reasons (e.g., to keep her benevolence flowing or to avoid getting a bad reputation) seems to fall short of gratitude.[11] Grateful beneficiaries must be motivated by the ultimate goal of seeing their benefactors fare well. They should take the fact that some action will benefit a benefactor to be, more or less by itself, a good reason to act in such a way, and they should be motivated to act in light of such reasons.

Thanking. A final aspect of gratitude worth noting is the practice of thanking. Thanking is clearly a crucial part of a grateful response, in the sense that a beneficiary who fails to thank a benefactor might very well be the clearest instance of an ingrate. Interestingly, thanking cannot be easily classified as one of the three kinds of elements (cognitive, affective or behavioral) I have outlined earlier. Some might be tempted to classify thanking as a kind of cognitive element, especially when thanking is understood to serve the function of reporting a beneficiary's belief that a benevolent act has occurred. And indeed, in order to be sincere, it seems that a beneficiary's thanking must be backed by the right beliefs. But thanking is clearly more than merely forming (or even reporting) a private judgment. After all, even when a beneficiary knows that his benefactor knows he's grateful, it seems he still ought to express his gratitude to her by thanking her. Some might be tempted to see thanking as a manifestation of the affective elements of gratitude, insofar as thanking often takes the form of a spontaneous expressive outpouring of the feelings of gratitude a grateful beneficiary should have. But thanking seems at least sometimes to be something other than an expressive outpouring of feelings. Indeed, there are times thanking seems called for, reasonable and sincere when a beneficiary is not experiencing any of the typical feelings of gratitude. This may happen, for instance, if a beneficiary receives a benevolent gift at a moment when he is preoccupied with other stronger thoughts and feelings that temporarily preclude him from experiencing feelings of gratitude. In such cases, thanking might still be sincere if it is understood as a commitment to take up the behavioral and affective dispositions gratitude entails.[12] It might be thought, finally, that thanking is a manifestation of beneficent behavioral tendencies a beneficiary should have. After all, a benefactor often has an interest in knowing whether her act of benevolence was received, recognized, and appreciated by her beneficiary, and letting her know these things (by thanking her) might count as the sort of return-beneficence a grateful beneficiary should be disposed to perform. But while thanking might sometimes count as a kind of benefit for the benefactor, this isn't true of thanking in all cases. There are times, for instance, when benefactors do not want or enjoy or have an interest in being thanked, and times when benefactors might come to know from third parties all they might want to know about how their benevolence was received; yet even in such cases, thanking seems called for.[13]

One possible explanation for all this is that thanking is its own element, distinct from the cognitive, affective, and behavioral elements of the grateful response I have outlined. Another possibility, though, and one I find more plausible, is that thanking can play a variety of roles, any one of which can be reduced to the three elements I detailed earlier. If this were true, a beneficiary's failure to thank could always be traced back to a shortfall in one of these three elements. And that seems plausible enough. After all, it is difficult to imagine a beneficiary who shows the proper cognitive, affective, and behavioral responses toward a benevolent benefactor but nevertheless reprehensibly fails to thank her. This entails that there is no need to posit thanking as a fourth distinct element of the grateful response and that the grateful response can be fully specified in terms of cognitive, affective, and behavioral elements. Though a full argument for this position is outside the scope of this chapter, I will proceed on the premise that although thanking (or at least a disposition to thank) is necessary for being grateful, thanking is not a distinct element of the grateful response.

The grateful response, then, is a complex of interrelated cognitive, affective, and behavioral elements. More specifically, a grateful beneficiary is one who, in response to an act of benevolence from a benefactor, forms certain beliefs about that benefactor and her benevolence, forms an affective disposition of goodwill toward her, and forms dispositions of grateful beneficence and nonmaleficence toward her. Out of these dispositions, he should also be disposed to thank his benefactor.

THE VIRTUE OF GRATITUDE

As my analysis of response-gratitude shows, gratitude to a benefactor for something she's done is best understood not as a feeling or as an emotional episode or as a behavior, but as a set of interconnected cognitive, affective, and behavioral dispositions. If the *virtue* of gratitude is the disposition to consistently form properly grateful responses to acts of benevolence, and the properly grateful response to an act of benevolence is a complex of dispositions, then the virtue of gratitude is what we might call a meta-disposition: a disposition to consistently form the right cognitive, behavioral, and affective dispositions in response to the right kinds of events (instances of benevolence), at the right times, to the right degrees. A grateful person, then, is one who is attuned to evidence of benevolence being shown toward him, reliably recognizes this benevolence, and consequently forms dispositions to think and feel and behave in properly grateful ways regarding his benefactors.

This account of the virtue of gratitude has several features worth noting. In the first place, it is compatible with the possibility of obligations of gratitude.[14] To say that there are obligations of gratitude is to say that certain called-for grateful behaviors or refrainings, like returning a favor or rescuing a benefactor or going out of one's way to refrain from harming a benefactor, are moral obligations. To say they are moral obligations is to say that such behaviors or refrainings are justified by moral reasons of a certain priority and stringency, that the beneficiary has little or no latitude in deciding to behave in such ways on certain occasions, and that failing to behave in such ways on those occasions without excuse is not just lousy or non-ideal but morally wrong.[15] If there are obligations of gratitude, then a grateful beneficiary should recognize all those features of such obligatory grateful actions and refrainings and be inclined to act or refrain from acting in light of them. On my view, a virtuous beneficiary is someone who is disposed to do just that. A virtuously grateful beneficiary is one who is disposed, in practical reasoning, to take the fact that an action of his will benefit or protect a benefactor to constitute a reason to perform that action. If such an action is obligatory, then an ideal and virtuous beneficiary will be disposed to perceive the strength, priority, and stringency of that reason accurately. Of course, a grateful beneficiary usually will benefit or avoid harming a benefactor spontaneously, from natural inclination, without any conscious deliberation. This is because a grateful beneficiary will also wish his benefactor well, and this affective component of his gratitude may tend to motivate grateful beneficence and nonmaleficence prior to any deliberation.[16] But in circumstances when this natural inclination is overwhelmed (e.g., in cases where coming to a benefactor's aid will be difficult or unpleasant or will conflict with another of the beneficiary's commitments or moral obligations), a virtuously grateful beneficiary will still be disposed to recognize and acknowledge that helping or refraining from harming a benefactor is sometimes something he in some sense *must* do. And in these circumstances, this disposition is what will lead a virtuous beneficiary to act gratefully—perhaps not spontaneously, but from a sense of duty.

The second feature of my account worth noting is that it can be adapted to describe what it means to be grateful in contexts of varying degrees of specificity. A person who is grateful *to his parents*, for instance, is one who is inclined to recognize and respond with the appropriate dispositions to benevolence from his parents, but not necessarily from other benefactors. A person described as grateful *to strangers* is one who is inclined to recognize and respond with the appropriate dispositions to benevolence from strangers, but not necessarily to benevolence from those he knows well. A person described as grateful *for advice* is one who is inclined to recognize the benevolence implied by the giving of thoughtful advice, but not necessarily other manifestations of benevolence. In these and other ways, my account of the virtue of gratitude can be adapted to describe not only the global character trait of gratitude but more local, fine-grained grateful dispositions as well.

Finally, my account of the virtue of gratitude can serve as a basis for a systematic exploration of the ways in which beneficiaries can fail to be grateful to benefactors and the vices these failures might constitute. It is to that exploration I now turn.

WAYS TO FAIL TO BE GRATEFUL

There are three kinds of ways a beneficiary can fail to be properly grateful for an act of benevolence: he can fail to be properly attuned to evidence that an act of benevolence has occurred; he can fail to establish the proper grateful dispositions when gratitude is called for; and he can fail to preserve those dispositions for a proper or reasonable amount of time after the initial act of benevolence. I will consider each of these kinds of failure in turn.

Failures of attunement. Beneficiaries can fall short of gratitude, in the first place, by failing to notice whether gratitude is called for in a certain situation. We can imagine a beneficiary who believes that benevolence should be met with gratitude and who typically reacts with thanks, goodwill, and beneficent dispositions when he perceives that benevolence has been shown to him, but who nonetheless often fails to notice such evidence, even in conditions when he should notice it. When people benefit him, he is all too rarely left with the impression that they did so benevolently. Because he sometimes overlooks evidence of benevolence, such a person will not always respond with the proper grateful dispositions when gratitude is called for, and so he fails to qualify as fully or properly grateful. A person who displays such a failing once in a while is guilty of what we might call *ungrateful insensitivity*. When insensitivity is a recurring aspect of a person's character, we can say such a person manifests the *vice* of ungrateful insensitivity.[17]

We can view the vice of ungrateful insensitivity as a kind of deficiency— a shortfall in the sort of sensitivity necessary to count as fully and properly grateful. If just the right amount of this sensitivity is a component of the virtue of gratitude, and a deficiency in this sensitivity is a vice, what should we make of an *excess* of this sort of sensitivity? A person who demonstrates this excess—what we might call *oversensitivity*—is a person who either exaggerates the significance of evidence of benevolence so as to perceive more benevolence from a benefactor than is likely really there, or, in the extreme case, mistakenly takes certain features of a situation as evidence of benevolence when there is no benevolence at all. An oversensitive person might, for instance, be left with the impression that a coworker cares more about him than she really does when she gives him a mundane gift during a mandatory holiday gift exchange. Oversensitivity might also be ascribed to someone who is left with the impression that an apple tree bears him benevolence when an apple falls into his lap as he sits under the tree.

Is such oversensitivity a vice? Some might argue that it is simply on the grounds that oversensitivity is more than—and therefore, different from—the right amount of sensitivity we would expect from a grateful person.[18] And oversensitivity also seems, almost by definition, to render someone confused or "foolish."[19] But there are several reasons to think that oversensitivity is vicious or morally problematic in a deeper sense. The first is that an oversensitive person is liable, in virtue of that oversensitivity, to be distracted by morally insignificant, gratitude-irrelevant features of situations, and will therefore be less likely to notice gratitude-relevant features of situations that are important to recognize. An illustrative parallel can be found in the virtue of hospitality. A genuinely hospitable person is one who is properly sensitive to evidence of his guests' discomfort. To be insensitive to such evidence obviously makes one an imperfect host, since such insensitivity would lead to a lack of hospitable feelings and behavior when those are called for. But oversensitivity in this case is also a problem for a host, since it might lead him to be so distracted by minor or false signs of guest discomfort that he misses substantial genuine signs that he should note and act on. By the same token, an oversensitive beneficiary might get so distracted or overwhelmed attending to irrelevant features of a situation that he may sometimes overlook genuine evidence of benevolence. That will make it less likely that he will establish the beliefs and behavioral and affective dispositions that constitute gratitude toward those who genuinely deserve it.

Grateful oversensitivity may also be morally problematic to the extent that it leads a beneficiary to establish settled beliefs, affective dispositions, and behavioral dispositions vis-à-vis a benefactor that are out of proportion to what that benefactor actually warrants. This is a possibility I will return to shortly.

Failure to establish proper dispositions: deficiencies. Even if a beneficiary is properly attuned to evidence of benevolence (and especially if he is not), he can fall short of gratitude if he fails to form settled beliefs and establish long-term properly grateful dispositions in response to such benevolence. Some might think that the establishment of settled beliefs and long-lasting affective and behavioral dispositions that constitute a virtuous response to some stimulus follows necessarily from proper sensitivity to that stimulus. But this isn't necessarily true. The existence of manipulative psychopaths, for instance, seems to show that it is possible to be highly attuned to evidence that others are suffering without actually experiencing genuine compassion. And many non-psychopaths are properly sensitive to evidence of suffering, in that they recognize it and respond in the moment with virtuous-seeming reactions, even though those reactions fail to endure for more than a few moments. It is not uncommon, for instance, for television viewers to be momentarily captivated by images of abused and neglected animals in a commercial and then forget those animals moments later, thus never forming the longer-term dispositions to feel for and help such animals that a genuinely compassionate person should have. By the same token, a beneficiary might be properly attuned to evidence of benevolence, and thereby get the accurate impression that gratitude is called for in a particular instance, but fail to see that initial impression solidify into the settled, long-term beliefs and lasting affective and behavioral dispositions constitutive of genuine gratitude.

The most obvious form this failure can take is *ingratitude*—a failure to establish one or more of the elements of the grateful response to a sufficient magnitude when a grateful response is called for.[20] Typically, a beneficiary who is ungrateful to a benefactor is one who fails to form a settled belief that the benefactor was as benevolent and deserving of gratitude as the evidence available to him should lead him to believe. He is someone who does not form a settled disposition to wish his benefactor well with sufficient intensity, someone who fails to form a settled disposition to be sufficiently motivated to benefit his benefactor in the future. Typically, because the cognitive, affective, and behavioral elements of the grateful response are interconnected, someone who is ungrateful will show a shortfall in all three kinds of elements. But it is worth noting that a beneficiary can, at least theoretically, be guilty of ingratitude vis-à-vis certain elements of the grateful response but not others. We could imagine, for instance, a beneficiary who forms settled accurate beliefs about how much benevolence his benefactor showed and forms a settled proportional affective disposition of goodwill, but finds himself not sufficiently motivated to come to his benefactor's aide when the situation calls for it. Such a person, we might say, is guilty of *motivational* or *behavioral* ingratitude, but not *total* ingratitude. In any event, when a person's settled beliefs and dispositions fall short along at least one of these dimensions, he is guilty of ingratitude; and when such a person *habitually* falls short along at least one of these dimensions, he manifests the *vice* of ingratitude.

Three categories of ingratitude are worth distinguishing.[21] The first kind of ingratitude occurs when a beneficiary responds with some settled belief in a benefactor's benevolence, some enduring affective disposition of goodwill, and some lasting increase in beneficent tendencies toward the benefactor, but the magnitude of these elements falls short of what would be justified by the benefactor's benevolence. We can call this stripe of ingratitude *subgratitude*. Another kind of ingratitude is one in which a beneficiary notices that benevolence has been done but finds himself completely indifferent; he shows no increase at all in affective goodwill or grateful beneficence toward the benefactor, and perhaps forms no intermediate- or long-term memory of his benefactor's benevolence. We can call this kind of ingratitude *nongratitude*. A third kind of ingratitude involves cases in which a beneficiary responds to evidence of a benefactor's benevolence with resentment, ill will, and hostility. We can imagine, for instance, a beneficiary who accurately perceives a benefactor's benevolence and, because he envies that benefactor's moral goodness, comes to resent her—comes to hope she fares poorly in the future, rejoices in her suffering to some degree, and perhaps even goes out of his way to set back her interests. We can call this especially devilish form of ingratitude *anti-gratitude*. Again, each of these species of ingratitude could theoretically manifest in only one or two elements of the grateful response, and any one of these species of ingratitude, should it become habitual or regular for a beneficiary, would qualify as a vice—the vice of sub-gratitude, the vice of non-gratitude, and the vice of anti-gratitude, respectively.

Failure to establish proper dispositions: excesses. Just as a beneficiary's response to benevolence can fall short of what an act of benevolence calls for, a beneficiary's response can also *exceed* that which an act of benevolence calls for.[22] The cognitive element of such an excessive response would be an unjustified belief that the benefactor bears more benevolence toward the beneficiary—that she is more willing to sacrifice for the beneficiary, that she cares more about the beneficiary—than she actually does. The affective element of an excessive response would be an outsized affective disposition of goodwill toward her—a disposition to be too ecstatic when things go well for the benefactor and too upset or devastated when things go poorly for her relative to what her benevolence justifies. The behavioral element of an excessive response would be an outsized tendency to benefit or refrain from harming the benefactor—a willingness or tendency to sacrifice too much for a benefactor relative to her own initial benevolence. Such an excessive response will also typically be associated with overly enthusiastic or extravagant thanking. As with oversensitivity, overgratitude can occur when a person responds gratefully toward something that is incapable of benevolence—such as an apple tree. As with ingratitude, overgratitude can theoretically manifest in only one or two of the elements of the grateful response. A beneficiary could, for example, overestimate how much the benefactor cared about him, but then coincidentally respond with just the right amount of affective goodwill and beneficence. But in reality, because the cognitive, affective, and behavioral aspects of gratitude are interconnected, most beneficiaries will likely show excesses along all or none of the elements of the grateful response, at least in any given instance of a particular response to a particular moment of benevolence from a benefactor. When a beneficiary reacts with an excess in one or more of the elements of the grateful response, we can say he was *overgrateful* to the benefactor for that benefit. And a person who is habitually or regularly overgrateful, we can say, manifests the trait of *overgratitude*.[23]

In what sense, if any, is overgratitude a vice? Like oversensitivity, overgratitude is vicious in the formal sense that it is a failure to achieve just the right amount of a virtuous disposition. Some think these excesses, though perhaps "foolish," are not moral shortcomings in the sense that makes their bearer a less-than-ideal moral agent.[24] There are several reasons, however, to believe that overgratitude can be morally problematic, not merely foolish. For example, overgratitude, especially when fueled by grateful oversensitivity, can lead to an inaccurate sense of self-worth. This can happen in several ways. Imagine a person who goes around the world perceiving evidence of benevolence toward him far more often than is warranted. Over time, such a person would come to believe that he was cared-about and wished-well far more widely than he actually was. Such a person might come to develop the morally problematic belief that he is more special and more to-be-cared-about than he really is, and this condition comes very close to the definition of arrogance.[25]

Under other circumstances, overgratitude can lead a person to a kind of servility—the very opposite of arrogance. Imagine a beneficiary who habitually believes that his benefactors' benevolence toward him is more than it really is, or more than he has any evidence to believe it is. If he judges his own benevolence accurately, such a beneficiary might systematically underestimate his own benevolence vis-à-vis that of others. Insofar as it is morally good and praiseworthy to be benevolent, then, and insofar as self-appraisal is in some ways tied to comparisons with others, an overgrateful beneficiary might wind up with a lower appraisal of his character and actions than he ought to have.

Overgrateful beliefs can lead to servility within intimate relationships as well. Imagine an overgrateful person in an abusive relationship who, despite frequently being treated with disregard or contempt, comes to believe his partner bears him great benevolence.[26] Despite a scarcity of evidence, he persuades himself that the cruel things his partner says to him are intended to benefit him, are said and done out of care for him. Such a person is likely to think better of his partner and remain in such a relationship longer than he should—and longer than any virtuously self-respecting person would—at least in part because of the benevolence he mistakenly attributes to his partner.

Judgments aside, overgrateful affective and behavioral responses could also amount to a kind of servility when they lead a beneficiary to commit more emotional and behavioral resources to others than they deserve. An overgrateful beneficiary is one who spends more time worrying about others—more time feeling upset and sad when they suffer, for instance—than he should. He is also someone who spends more time and energy going out of his way to benefit his benefactors than he should. And the more time he spends worrying about others, and the more time and resources he spends doing things to benefit others, the less time, energy, and resources he has to dedicate to himself and his own projects. A sufficiently overgrateful beneficiary will not have enough time or resources to treat his own interests with the care and attention proper self-respect would require, and, in that sense, overgratitude can amount to a vice.

Overgratitude is also morally dangerous for another reason: it can lead a person to incorrectly rank his moral priorities. This can happen if a beneficiary is prone to show *differential overgratitude*—that is, overgratitude to certain entities but properly proportioned gratitude to others. A person who mistakenly believes he owes gratitude to an apple tree for giving him its apples when he was starving, for instance, might be more inclined to protect that tree or come to its aid than to help a human benefactor who intentionally and benevolently provided him with a benefit of lesser value; and if such a beneficiary finds himself in a position where he has to choose between helping the tree and helping his human benefactor, his overgratitude would lead him to make the wrong choice. Overgratitude can thus lead to problems with ordinal gratitude judgments and actions. It can also lead to problems prioritizing moral actions more generally. Consider again an overgrateful person who has an outsized motivation to protect an apple tree he thinks showed him benevolence. If his motivation to protect the tree on a particular occasion conflicts with his motivation to keep a promise, he might be inclined to protect the tree rather than keep the promise, and, in that way, his overgratitude would keep him from acting as he morally should.

Failures of duration. A final category of gratitude-associated vices comes to light when we note that even if a beneficiary accurately perceives benevolence and establishes the proper cognitive, affective, and behavioral dispositions, those dispositions might nonetheless fail to endure as long as they should. The beneficiary of a monumental act of benevolence might, for instance, recognize a benefactor's benevolence and thank her and form accurate judgments and proportional affective and behavioral dispositions but forget about the act of benevolence after a few days. Alternatively, he may remember the benevolence but may find that his motivation to come to his benefactor's aid or his feelings in wishing his benefactor well wane too quickly over time. Insofar as the grateful disposition should endure for some period of time, such a beneficiary falls short of gratitude, and he thereby manifests what we might call *evanescent gratitude*. When a beneficiary is habitually evanescently grateful, we can say he manifests the vice of *gratitude evanescence*.

If we take evanescent gratitude to be a deficiency (a deficiency in the durability of the grateful dispositions), we might wonder whether there is an associated excess: a grateful disposition that endures too long. One might think that an ideally grateful person will remember an act of benevolence and be disposed to respond with the right feelings and behaviors *indefinitely*, even if this is a psychological impossibility for any actual human beneficiary.[27] But perhaps it is ideal that our memories of benevolence and our affective and behavioral dispositions concerning our benefactors' welfare fade somewhat over time. This fading may mirror the changes our benefactors go through over time, changes that eventually make them different people from the ones who earned our gratitude in the first place. Imagine a benefactor who showed someone genuine benevolence when she was twenty, but then over subsequent decades became hardhearted and uncaring to the point where she would no longer perform the same kind of act of benevolence for the same person under the same circumstances. When her beneficiary encounters her fifty years later, there seems to be a sense in which the benefactor as she is at seventy no longer deserves the gratitude she did when she was twenty. For the beneficiary to show her now exactly the same gratitude he owed her decades ago for things she decades ago did might thus seem to be a sort of misfiring, not unlike grateful oversensitivity or overgratitude. Insofar as grateful dispositions can persist too long, we can think of them as constituting *overpersistent gratitude*, and a person whose gratitude is habitually overpersistent we might say suffers from the vice of *gratitude overpersistence*.

CONCLUSION

My goal in this chapter has been to sketch an account of the virtue of gratitude and to explore the range of vices associated with that virtue. On my account, the virtue of gratitude is best understood as the disposition to form and sustain a properly grateful response to the right people at the right times and to the right degree. The grateful response itself is at its core a complex of dispositions that includes beliefs about the benefactor, an affective disposition of goodwill, and behavioral dispositions of grateful beneficence and nonmaleficence. Gratitude as a virtue, then, is essentially a meta-disposition: specifically, the disposition to perceive benevolence and to form the proper grateful beliefs and affective and behavioral dispositions vis-à-vis the source of that benevolence. If this is the right way to construe the virtue of gratitude, I argued, then there are three kinds of ways a beneficiary can fail to be properly grateful: he can fail to be properly sensitive to evidence of benevolence (failures of attunement); he can fail to establish the proper beliefs and dispositions when gratitude is called for (failures of establishment); and he can fail to preserve those beliefs and dispositions for a proper or reasonable amount of time (failures of duration). These categories of failure can be divided into deficiencies and excesses. The deficiency-failure of attunement is insensitivity—an insensitivity to evidence of benevolence and a failure to perceive that an act of benevolence has occurred. The excess-failure of attunement is oversensitivity—perceiving a certain amount of benevolence where no (or not enough) benevolence has been evidenced. The deficiency-failure of establishment is ingratitude, which can be subdivided into sub-gratitude, non-gratitude, and anti-gratitude. The excess-failure of establishment is overgratitude, which occurs when the magnitude of the cognitive, affective, and behavioral elements of the grateful response are outsized compared to the benevolence to which they are a response, or when such elements arise in response to no benevolence at all. Finally, failures of duration occur when a beneficiary fails to sustain a proper grateful disposition toward a benefactor over time. The deficiency-failure of duration is evanescent gratitude, and it is unclear whether there is an associated excess-failure—that is, whether there is such a thing as overpersistent gratitude. Failures of establishment and failures of duration can be further specified by the particular element(s) of the grateful response in which the failure occurs. When a person finds he fails in any of these ways habitually or regularly as a beneficiary, this habit or regularity amounts to a vice that can be ascribed to that person.[28]

If what I have said is correct, then there is a rich variety of ways in which a person can habitually fail to be grateful, and attending to this variety of gratitude-associated vices is important for several reasons. It may, for instance, be useful in the process of moral education. When we want to help a child develop into a properly grateful person, it helps to know exactly how that particular child tends to stray from the properly grateful disposition. A child who shows insensitivity, for example, is one who needs to be taught to look out for and recognize the evidence that others are being benevolent toward him. A child who shows anti-grateful tendencies, on the other hand, may be keenly sensitive to evidence of the benevolence of others, but he may need to be taught not to envy this benevolence (and should instead, perhaps, be encouraged to match this benevolence with his own). A child who shows good sensitivity and decent affective gratitude but behavioral sub-grateful tendencies needs to be taught that recognition and feelings alone are not enough for gratitude, and he should be approached and coached the same way a goodhearted but lazy child might be. Importantly, moral educators should not assume that just because a child shows no ungrateful tendencies, he needs no moral guidance as far as gratitude goes. Educators should keep an eye out for children who show tendencies toward oversensitivity and overgratitude, making sure such children develop proper levels of self-respect; and educators should avoid urging everyone to instantiate as much gratitude-constitutive behavior and feeling as possible as much of the time as possible.[29]

Recognizing the variety of ways in which a beneficiary can fail to be grateful also helps us make and communicate more fine-grained judgments of those who demonstrate vicious ingratitude. It gives us the language and the concepts, for example, to distinguish between anti-grates and sub-grates. A sub-grate is someone who bears his benefactor goodwill and treats her with beneficence but does not quite demonstrate enough of each to count as fully grateful. An anti-grate, by contrast, is someone who comes to resent his benefactors. Both are rightly called ingrates, but the ramifications of doing favors for one rather than the other are quite different: in particular, doing a favor for an anti-grate may actually endanger the benefactor in a way that doing a favor for a sub-grate would not, since anti-grates respond to benevolence with envy and resentment. Distinguishing these two types of beneficiaries is thus important for us to be able to do when we pass along information to others, and it is something we cannot do effectively if we classify both types of beneficiaries simply as ingrates.

The ability to make these more fine-grained distinctions is helpful not only practically, in our interactions with others, but also theoretically, in the scholarly study of gratitude. It helps us qualify certain widespread generalizations about ingratitude, for example, that are not strictly speaking accurate—or, at least, not as generally apt as they purport to be. Consider, for instance, the claim that ingratitude is among the worst of the moral vices. Hume endorsed this view, writing that "of all crimes that human creatures are capable of committing, the most horrid and unnatural is ingratitude."[30] Kant considered ingratitude (along with envy and malice) "the essence of vileness and wickedness."[31] And Seneca ranked ingrates below thieves and adulterers.[32] These claims do not seem wildly implausible so long as we take anti-gratitude to be representative of ingratitude generally. But they seem far less plausible when said of a mere sub-grate. The moral of the story is that because ingratitude is heterogeneous, philosophers would be wiser to make generalizations about species of ingratitude than about ingratitude *tout court*. My account of the virtue of gratitude and the vices associated with it provides the tools necessary for this.

NOTES

1   For the sake of clarity, throughout this chapter, I will refer to beneficiaries with masculine pronouns and benefactors with feminine pronouns.

2   I make this distinction in Manela (2016a).

3   Those who point this out include Walker (1980–1981) and Manela (2016b).

4   Manela (2015b); Manela (2016a).

5   This goes without saying for those in certain linguistic traditions. For instance, the French word for "grateful," *reconnaissant*, is derived from the verb *reconnaître*, "to recognize." And this insight is not lost on philosophers of gratitude in the Anglophone community. As Fred Berger notes, gratitude "involves at least the recognition of the other's having done something" that qualifies as an act of benevolence (Berger, 1975: 302). See also Walker (1980–1981).

6   There may, of course, be occasions on which a beneficiary sees no direct evidence of a benefactor's motivations. In some such cases, it may be perfectly consistent with proper gratitude to give a benefactor the benefit of the doubt that her motives are benevolent, not selfish. In other contexts, being so generous with the benefit of the doubt may not be warranted—especially when and if there is positive evidence the benefactor was *not* being benevolent.

7   See, for instance, Fitzgerald (1998) and Costello (2009).

8   Positive feelings are not called for, for instance, in cases where the benefactor suffers terribly in benefitting the beneficiary, or in cases where a clumsy would-be benefactor is likely to cause the beneficiary more harm than good, or in cases where a benefactor wants to benefit the beneficiary in a way the beneficiary ashamedly realizes he does not deserve, or in cases where an especially self-abnegating benefactor is willing to accept grossly disproportionate sacrifices on her part for modest gains to

the beneficiary. Some such cases may warrant praise or gratitude to the benefactor, but it seems plausible to say that a beneficiary need not *appreciate* such instances of benevolence, insofar as the beneficiary might prefer a state of affairs in which such benevolence hadn't existed at all. At any rate, it seems true that positive feelings of joy aren't called for in such circumstances.

9   Manela (2015b); Walker (1980–1981).

10 Camenisch (1981).

11 McConnell (1993).

12 Such cases are instances of what Camenisch (1981: 7) calls the "commissive" sense of thanking.

13 Except, perhaps, for the unusual sort of case in which a benefactor has an interest in *not* being thanked or in *not* knowing. In those cases (and perhaps only in those cases), thanking does not seem called for. For an interesting discussion of whether it could be reasonable for a virtuous benefactor to want not to be thanked, see the discussion of John Jarndyce in Robert Roberts' contribution to, this volume.

14 Philosophers who seem to presuppose the incompatibility of a virtue of gratitude and obligations of gratitude include Wellman (1999). Presupposing such an incompatibilism spells trouble for any account of the virtue of gratitude because there are strong arguments for the existence of obligations of gratitude (see Manela, 2015b: §1.). Philosophers can avoid presupposing this incompatibilism as they begin inquiries into gratitude if they are careful to ask what we might call the *of*-question (*whether there are obligations* of *gratitude or a virtue* of *gratitude*) rather than the *is*-question (*whether gratitude* is *a set of obligations or a virtue*), since the second question subtly stacks the deck against the possibility that gratitude could describe *both* a set of obligations *and* a virtue. For other reasons to prefer the *of*-question as a starting point for philosophical inquiry into gratitude, see Manela (2015a: §5).

15 For an extended discussion of a beneficiary's obligation to go out of his way to avoid harming his benefactor, see Manela (2015b: §1).

16 This is one example of the many ways in which the affective and behavioral elements of the grateful response are interconnected.

17 Of course, not every failure to notice evidence of benevolence disqualifies a beneficiary from counting as fully grateful. A blind person who doesn't notice evidence of benevolence because of his blindness doesn't count as ungrateful for that. Still, it seems fair to say that certain kinds of lack of attunement to relevant details are enough to keep a person from counting as fully virtuous. A serial chief executive officer who fails to notice time and again that 90% of the leadership positions in the companies he manages are occupied by men, for instance, seems to fall short of full possession of the virtue of justice, even if he is properly concerned, indignant, and motivated to challenge such gender imbalances whenever they are pointed out to him. By the same token, someone who routinely overlooks clear evidence that people are treating him benevolently falls short of gratitude.

18 Nisters (2012).

19 Ibid.

20 Ungrateful insensitivity is especially likely to lead to this.

21 These distinctions were originally put forward by Thomas Aquinas: II.II.107.

22 Such excesses are especially likely to occur when a beneficiary is oversensitive to evidence of benevolence.

23 This vice, also originally described by Aquinas, has been named *hypergrati- tude* by Nisters (2012). I prefer the term *overgratitude* because that term implies too much gratitude, whereas hypergratitude is a more neutral term, implying only more gratitude than is normal or usual.

24 Ibid.

25 This is one reason it is morally problematic to anthropomorphize and feel grateful toward non-agential natural objects that benefit us. I make this point more fully in Manela, 2018.

26 "Partner" here could be understood as a romantic partner, a friend, a parent, or a mentor.

27 Of course, it seems fair to say that once a beneficiary returns a favor or other- wise performs an act of gratitude for a benefactor, the beneficiary should no longer have the same motivation to benefit his benefactor that he once did. But even after acts of gratitude are carried out, that shouldn't alter the cognitive and affective com- ponents of a grateful response, which should still remain in place in a grateful benefi- ciary. That is, even after acts of gratitude are carried out, we still expect a beneficiary to remember the act of benevolence, and to be disposed to be pleased when he hears things are going well for his beneficiary and upset when he hears things are going poorly. We might even still expect him to have some tendency, albeit one of reduced magnitude, to look for ways to benefit his benefactor beyond what he's already done.

28 It is worth noting here that each of these vices can be more or less localized, more or less context-specific. Just as we can make sense of a person who is grateful to his parents, for instance, we can make sense of someone who is sub-grateful to his parents, overgrateful to strangers, or anti-grateful to siblings as people who show just those failures of gratitude in just those contexts.

29 All this, of course, applies to those interested in self-cultivation as well as moral educators charged with the cultivation of others.

30 Hume (2007: III.I.I).

31 Kant (1979: 218).

32 Seneca (2010: I.10.4).

REFERENCES

Aquinas, Thomas. 2006, *Summa Theologiae: Volume 41, Virtues of Justice in the Human Community: 2a2ae. 101–122*, edited by T. C. O'Brien. New York: Cam- bridge University Press.

Camenisch, Paul F. 1981. "Gift and Gratitude in Ethics." *The Journal of Religious Ethics* 9: 1–34.

Costello, Peter R. 2009. "Towards a Phenomenology of Gratitude—A Response to Jean-Luc Marion." *Balkan Journal of Philosophy* 1: 77–82.

Fitzgerald, Patrick. 1998. "Gratitude and Justice." *Ethics* 109: 119–153.

Hume, David. 2007. *A Treatise of Human Nature*, edited by David Fate Norton. Oxford: Clarendon.

Kant, Immanuel. 1979. *Lectures on Ethics*. Translated by Louis Infield. Cambridge: Hackett.

Manela, Tony. 2015a. "Gratitude." In *Stanford Encyclopedia of Philosophy*, edited by Edward N. Zalta, https://plato.stanford.edu/archives/spr2015/entries/gratitude/.

Manela, Tony. 2015b. "Obligations of Gratitude and Correlative Rights." In Mark Timmons (ed.), *Oxford Studies in Normative Ethics*, pp. 151–170.

Manela, Tony. 2016a. "Gratitude and Appreciation." *American Philosophical Quarterly* 53: 281–294.

Manela, Tony. 2016b. "Negative Feelings of Gratitude." *Journal of Value Inquiry* 50: 129–140.

Manela, Tony. 2018. "Gratitude to Nature." *Environmental Values* 27: 623–644.

McConnell, Terrance. 1993. *Gratitude*. Philadelphia, PA: Temple University Press.

Nisters, Thomas. 2012. "Utrum gratitudo sit virtus moralis vel passio animae or: Gratitude—An Aristotelian Virtue or an Emotion?" In *Politics of Practical Reasoning: Integrating Action, Discourse, and Argument*, edited by Ricca Edmondson and Karlheinz Hülser. New York: Lexington.

Roberts, Robert. 2018. "Gratitude, Friendship, and Mutuality: Reflections on Three Characters in Bleak House." In *The Moral Psychology of Gratitude*, edited by Roberts Robert and Daniel Telech. London: Rowman & Littlefield International, pp. 317–337.

Seneca, Lucius Annaeus. 2010. *On Benefits*. Translated by Miriam Griffin and Brad Inwood. Chicago: University of Chicago Press.

Walker, A. D. M. 1980–1981. "Gratefulness and Gratitude." *Proceedings of the Aristotelian Society* 81: 39–55.

Wellman, Christopher Heath. 1999. "Gratitude as a Virtue." *Pacific Philosophical Quarterly* 80: 284–300.

Chapter 16

Gratitude, Friendship, and Mutuality[1]: Reflections on Three Characters in *Bleak House*

Robert Roberts

INTRODUCTION

Bleak House[2] is a biting critique of the Court of Chancery in Charles Dickens's time; it is a dissertation on documents and their interpretation; it is an exposé of the social evils of the English class system; it is a top-to-bottom panorama of English society—of the vast differences among its parts as well as their intimate interdependence. No doubt it is many other things, as well. But *Bleak House* is also a masterful work of individual and relational moral psychology. It is especially about the complementary virtues of generosity and gratitude, and their vice-counterparts of selfishness, acquisitiveness, and ingratitude. The themes of generosity and gratitude pertain to many members of the novel's large cast, but I will focus on three: John Jarndyce, Esther Summerson, and Harold Skimpole. Jarndyce will be my main specimen, but his relations with the other two are essential to Dickens's exploration of the generosity-gratitude dynamic.

Before I present these characters, let me make some general claims about gratitude and generosity. Here, I'll state these points as theses, without argument. I think *Bleak House* illustrates them, and to that extent provides support for them.

First, gratitude and generosity are complementary virtues[3]: Gratitude is a proper or canonical response to genuine acts and attitudes of generosity; and such generosity is satisfied and completed, so to speak, by expressions of gratitude. We might call this pair the virtues of grace, since both are about gifts—giving and gracious receiving—as contrasted with tit-for-tat transactions characteristic of strict justice. This complementarity does not imply that real generosity never meets with ingratitude, or that virtuous gratitude never errs about the benefactor's generosity. But as a response to real generosity, ingratitude is a failure to appreciate it; and as a response to pseudo-generosity, real gratitude is a distortion, even if a generous one.

Second, in the exchange between generous acts and grateful responses, a mutual attitude arises or is sustained between the parties that is similar to what Aristotle calls *philia*: affection or friendship.[4] I will here call it friendship, though the term is not wholly adequate.

Third, generosity differs from what Aristotle calls liberality (*eleutheria*) and Nietzsche calls *die schenkende Tugend* ("the bestowing virtue").[5] I will call this virtue liberality to distinguish it from generosity.

Fourth, both liberality and generosity have a dominant "expressive" function. They are more than a matter of transferring something good to another person. They express the mind of the giver, and this expressive function makes for the difference between them: generosity and liberality differ in *what* they express. This difference makes for a difference in the canonical response of the beneficiary. To generosity, the canonical response is gratitude; to liberality, servility or resentment.

Fifth, humility is a crucial background virtue for both generosity and gratitude, but not for liberality and its canonical responses. Behind the concern of Aristotle's great-souled man to dominate the beneficiary[6] is the concern for self-importance: the struggle of the liberal person with his beneficiary is a struggle over who is most important. The humility of both the generous and the grateful eliminates the concern for self-importance.[7]

Sixth and last, only in combination with the concept of justice do the notions of generosity and gratitude make sense. A person who is completely without justice will not be able to make personal sense of gratitude and generosity.

ESTHER

Esther Summerson is a model of both generosity and gratitude, but her early life was not auspicious. Unbeknownst to her, she is the illegitimate daughter of beautiful Lady Dedlock, who looks down from one of the highest rungs of English society. The Lady's social position depends on guarding the secret of her shameful past, with which even her husband, Sir Leicester Dedlock, is unacquainted. She thinks her baby died at birth because that is the story told by her dour sister, who reared Esther. Esther's "godmother," as the sister calls herself, tells her nothing about her origins except that she was her mother's disgrace, as her mother was hers. She ensures that Esther's birthdays are days of mourning. On one of those dismal occasions, "I happened to look timidly up from my stitching, across the table, at my godmother, and I saw in her face, looking gloomily at me, 'It would have been far better, little Esther, that you had had no birthday; that you had never been born!'" (64).

But Esther is an affectionate, resolute child, and the early deprivation of love and esteem spurs her to try all the more passionately "to be industrious, contented, and true-hearted, and to do some good to some one, and win some love if I could" (74). Deprivation seems to plant empathy in her nature, and to deepen her appreciation of love when she does receive it. She also has some very good fortune at the secret instigation of John Jarndyce, a wealthy man in late middle age who learns about her situation and pays her way to Greanleaf, a boarding school for girls, where she eventually earns part of her keep by teaching what she has learned to the younger girls. At Greanleaf, she is much loved and valued by faculty, students, and staff alike. After six years at the school, she receives a letter summoning her to take up work as a "companion" to a Jarndyce heiress. Her parting from the school is marked by great demonstrative affection, and she responds by feeling the full magnitude of the undeserved good that she has received from "that Father who had not forgotten me" (74) and from all the people. The new assignment introduces her to Jarndyce and his world, where she again finds much scope for the display of her generous spirit. She becomes the companion of Ada Clare, a cousin of Richard Carstone. Both are current beneficiaries of John Jarndyce's generous concern and support, and heirs of a Jarndyce fortune that is tied up in a complicated Chancery suit over a will.

Esther comes close to being a pervasively grateful person, one who exemplifies the apostle Paul's exhortation to "give thanks in all circumstances" (I Thessalonians 5.18). But not quite. As far as I can see, she never falters by taking the good in her life "for granted"—that is, as hers by default or natural right. She quite consistently thinks of that good as undeserved and as creditable to somebody. But she does sometimes get discouraged by adversity, and at those times she talks to herself, giving herself both internal and external reasons for gratitude,[8] exhorting herself to remember all the good she has received, and to focus on her work and doing her duty. For example, she is secretly in love with a young physician, Allan Woodcourt, and has some hope that he returns her love. But his mother makes it clear to Esther that her son is destined for a woman of better birth, so when she contemplates her prospects, in comparison with the flourishing romance between Ada and Richard, her spirits sink a bit. She responds:

I made up my mind to be so dreadfully industrious that I would leave myself not a moment's leisure to be low-spirited. For I naturally said, "Esther! You to be low-spirited. *You!*" And it really was time to say so, for I—yes, I really did see myself in the glass, almost crying. "As if you had anything to make you unhappy, instead of everything to make you happy, you ungrateful heart!" said I. (288)

Then, while Woodcourt is abroad, she succumbs to smallpox as a result of generously and courageously caring for victims of the disease, which leaves her facial beauty marred and her prospects with Woodcourt further diminished, as she thinks. A kind friend offers his country house for her convalescence:

> Thus, what with being so much in the air, playing with so many children, gossiping with so many people, sitting on invitation in so many cottages . . . and writing long letters to Ada every day, I had scarcely any time to think about that little loss of mine, and was almost always cheerful. If I did think of it at odd moments now and then, I had only to be busy and forget it. I felt it more than I had hoped I should, once, when a child said, "Mother, why is the lady not a pretty lady now, like she used to be?" But when I found the child was not less fond of me, and drew its soft hand over my face with a kind of pitying protection in its touch, that soon set me up again. There were many little occurrences which suggested to me, with great consolation, how natural it is to gentle hearts to be considerate and delicate towards any inferiority. (561–62)

Then she tells the story of a village girl who took unusual care not to humiliate her new husband about his inability to write his name. "Why, what had I to fear, I thought, when there was this nobility in the soul of a labouring man's daughter!" (ibid.). Esther's generous ability to take pleasure in the excellence of others in the midst of her own deprivation lends stability to her virtue of gratitude, a defense against self-pity, by supplying a virtuous external reason for being grateful.

But as far as moral psychology is concerned, I think Esther is less important than the next two characters I will examine. Despite her centrality in the novel, she functions more as a benchmark than as a pungent lesson. Jarndyce is the focal character in this chapter. His generosity has two flaws that interact with the responses of two other characters in the novel with respect to the virtue of gratitude. Esther Summerson and Harold Skimpole are polar opposites with respect to this virtue. In Esther, gratitude is highly developed, in Skimpole, perfectly absent. These three characters taken together yield a number of insights about the virtues of generosity and gratitude.

JARNDYCE

John Jarndyce seems to spend just about full time in philanthropy. Wherever he sees a need, he quietly—often anonymously—does what he can to help, and the help is frequently considerable. Esther's is a case in point. He is genuinely kind hearted, a loving father figure worthy of the affectionate admiration and gratitude that Esther feels toward him. But his generosity has two peculiarities, which we might be inclined to think due to his being *too generous*. His idiosyncratic species of generosity embodies confusions (I will argue) about a pair of symmetrically related emotions: anger (or resentment)[9] and gratitude. He is strongly disinclined to blame others for their faults or even to acknowledge their deficiencies, and he has a decided repugnance to receiving expressions of gratitude for his acts of generosity.

To see how the moral misunderstandings of these two emotions blemish Jarndyce's generosity, let me briefly point out the symmetry in the grammars of anger and gratitude. I express the grammars of the two emotion types in six schematic propositions each, in the first person singular, to show their symmetry.

Gratitude

1 X is a benefit to something I care about.
2 S has acted well in performing or bringing about X.
3 In conferring X, S has acted with good will toward me or something I care about.
4 In conferring X with goodwill, S has put me in a debt of grace to him.
5 S's benevolence and conferral of X show that S is good.
6 I want to express my indebtedness and attachment to S in some token return benefit.

Anger or resentment

1 X is harmful to something I care about.
2 S has acted badly in performing or bringing about X.
3 In doing X, S has acted with ill will or culpable negligence toward me or something I care about.
4 In doing X with ill will, S has come to deserve some corresponding harm.
5 S's disrespect and conferral of X show that S is bad.
6 I want S to get what he deserves in the way of some token return harm.[10]

Anger and gratitude are both "pay back" emotions, good for good, or bad for bad; they both attribute responsibility and hold responsible; both involve an evaluation of the responsible agent.

Anger or resentment. Jarndyce is lavish not only with his time and money but also with the benefit of a doubt. He is so strongly inclined to see the good in people, and to ignore their faults, that he sometimes lends his support to unworthy philanthropic projects. Mrs. Jellyby, for example, exploits one of her children to the permanent detriment of that child's education, and neglects her other children, to spend her time writing letters on behalf of the natives of far-away Borioboola-Gha, in what Dickens calls "telescopic philanthropy"—financed, in part, from Jarndyce's purse. Mrs. Pardiggle, another of Jarndyce's beneficiaries, does not exactly neglect her children (in fact she chides Mrs. Jellyby for this fault) but drags them about with her on her various invasive social work missions, against their will, and trains them in "generosity" by compelling them to give their allowance money to some of her favorite causes.[11]

With Ada and Richard, Esther visits the Jellyby home and sees the filth, disorder, and general family hardship produced by Mrs. Jellyby's "philanthropy." She reports to Jarndyce: "'We thought that, perhaps,' said I, hesitating, 'it is right to begin with the obligations of home, sir; and that, perhaps, while those are overlooked and neglected, no other duties can possibly be substituted for them'" (113). Jarndyce is "floored" at hearing about the Jellyby household, though he admits that he may have sent them on the visit to get such information. He then resorts to a fiction—that the wind, blowing from the east, is causing him some unnamed suffering—a fiction that he employs whenever he is distressed by a situation that involves another person's being blameworthy. The fiction presents his emotion (to himself and to others[12]) as an impersonal discomfort rather than what it really is, namely, something like anger or resentment.

Jarndyce's evasion stems from his generosity, namely the benevolent regard for other people, the well wishing. He wishes not to think ill of people. If one of the things a generous person gives is the benefit of a doubt where badness might be ascribed to the other, still, the clear perception of others' flaws may be necessary to the pursuit of generous activities, because anyone who really wishes others well wants his giving to be efficacious on their behalf. So the generous person chooses really beneficial actions and effective, wise, good-hearted deputies, and discriminates them from less excellent ones. Jarndyce's emotional constitution militates against such discrimination.

One room in his house is the "growlery," where he goes to "growl" when he is feeling out of sorts. Explaining the growlery to Esther, he says, "When I am deceived or disappointed in—the wind . . ." (114). He is about to say "people" but refuses to say it, even in the explanation. The fiction of the east wind allows Jarndyce to avoid feeling anger toward people who exploit philanthropy to satisfy their sense of their own importance. Putting words in his mouth, we might say that for him, these emotions are ungenerous; they seem contrary to wishing people well. Yet he does recognize these people's moral deficiencies.

Jarndyce had fallen into this company, in the tenderness of his heart and his earnest desire to do all the good in his power; but, that he felt it to be too often an unsatisfactory company, where benevolence took spasmodic forms; where charity was assumed, as a regular uniform, by loud professors and speculators in cheap notoriety, vehement in profession, restless and vain in action, servile in the last degree of meanness to the great, adulatory of one another, and intolerable to those who were anxious quietly to help the weak from falling, rather than with a great deal of bluster and self-laudation to raise them up a little way when they were down; he plainly told us. When a testimonial was originated to Mr. Quale by Mr. Gusher (who had already got one, originated by Mr. Quale), and when Mr. Gusher spoke for an hour and a half on the subject to a meeting, including two charity schools of small boys and girls, who were specially reminded of the widow's mite, and requested to come forward with half-pence and be acceptable sacrifices; I think the wind was in the east for three whole weeks. (256–57)

Jarndyce's judgment seems admirably clear when he is thinking of these folks in general, but his policy of veiling the truth from himself in particular cases has the result that his money and time continue flowing down the Jellyby and Pardiggle rat holes—not to speak of the Skimpole rat hole, but more of that later. Emotions lend moral judgment a kind of perceptual immediacy that unemotional moral judgments lack.[13] This immediacy of evaluative perception in the personally harsher emotions is what Jarndyce systematically deprives himself of, in the interest of the spirit of generosity. If he allowed himself to feel occasional episodes of indignation or contempt for Pardiggle's and Jellyby's practices in particular, he would be in a better position epistemically, one that might improve his practice of generosity.

Shall we say that Jarndyce suffers from too much generosity? In Aristotle's doctrine of the mean, he points out that it isn't possible to have too much of a virtue. Whatever someone like Jarndyce has too much of, it isn't a virtue. To say it is too much of a virtue violates the grammar of "virtue." The reckless person doesn't have too much courage, but too much confidence and too little fear, according to Aristotle.[14] If Jarndyce's defect is having too much of something, it would have to be some aspect of generosity like goodwill toward persons. His goodwill is emotionally indiscriminate; it isn't sufficiently nuanced by reflectiveness or wisdom about helping people. He sometimes has goodwill toward the wrong persons, and for wrong reasons, and on wrong occasions. Such nuance, if it is to be emotionally and motivationally embodied, may require the incorporation of complementary uncomplimentary emotions like anger and resentment. And if this is painful, as it will be to a generous heart, it may require some ascetic self-mastery.

Unlike Jarndyce, Esther does allow herself to feel emotions in the neighborhood of anger toward bad parents, of which there are many in *Bleak House*. After a conversation with the oldest Jellyby daughter, the one who has been exploited to the neglect of her education as Mrs. Jellyby's amanuensis, Esther comments, "I must confess that I could not help feeling rather angry with Mrs. Jellyby, myself; seeing and hearing this neglected girl, and knowing how much of bitter satirical truth there was in what she said" (238). Caddy Jellyby's fiancé, the obedient Prince Turveydrop, is about to go off to his evening work in a suburb, which his father might well have shared, had the latter not been busy being the man of "deportment" about town and eating in a French restaurant. Reflecting on an indignant biographical sketch of Mr. Turveydrop by an old lady of his acquaintance, Esther says, "I felt a liking for [Prince Turveydrop], and a compassion for him, as he put his little kit in his pocket—and with it his desire to stay a little while with Caddy—and went away good-humouredly to his cold mutton and his school in Kensington, that made me scarcely less irate with his father than the censorious old lady" (248).

What shall we say about this contrast? Is Esther less generous, or less a grateful person, for her willingness to get angry? Is Jarndyce's unwillingness to perceive people's badness through his emotions really due to an excess of generosity? I have already said that his policy—of giving people the benefit of a doubt regarding their badness—is a legitimate aspect of generosity's benevolence, but I have also said that Jarndyce's generosity would probably be more efficacious if he let himself have this "judgmental" and motivating kind of emotional perception, and that it is a part of generosity to want one's beneficence to be efficacious. Esther mentions compassion in the last quotation, and this emotion is conceptually tied to her anger; the two emotions pick out different aspects of the same situation. In compassion, Esther perceives accurately the suffering of Prince Turveydrop, and in anger, she perceives accurately Mr. Turveydrop's responsibility for that suffering.

Aristotle might say that these two emotions are integrated, in the virtuous personality, by the virtue of practical wisdom. Morally, Esther gets the whole situation right through these two relationally "opposite" emotions (and no doubt others). By contrast, Jarndyce feels the compassion vividly but places the veil of the east wind fiction over the judgmental impression. To this extent, Jarndyce's compassion is morally abstract; it tends toward sentimentality or abstractness, a moral unrealism about suffering. I say this, while affirming that Jarndyce is a very good man. Even his character faults stem from his goodness. But they are faults.

Jarndyce's generosity fits him to survive the Chancery suit with his moral character almost completely intact, in contrast with the majority of the heirs, who are destroyed by it. The main feature of generosity that contributes to this happy prophylaxis is its construal of wealth. The prospect of an inheritance brings out acquisitiveness in most of the heirs. Richard Carstone is the one whose psychological and moral decline we witness most intimately, but others are Tom Jarndyce, Mr. Gridley, and Miss Flite. In the different characters the endless frustrations of the suit occasion a variety of responses: in

Richard, a preoccupying, increasingly unrealistic hope and the foolish investment of his time and his and others' resources; in Tom Jarndyce, despair leading to suicide; in Mr. Gridley, self-destructive rage; in Miss Flite, an apparent loss of touch with reality.

John Jarndyce is protected against the seductions of the lawsuit by the character of his concern about money. He is not unconcerned with it, but he cares about it primarily as a means of helping people. He does not see it as something to be possessed and used by himself in some narrowly private sense. It is possible that some of the destroyed heirs don't conceptualize it in this narrowly private way, either. Richard, for example, is quite prodigal with what money he does have, in view of the fact that he expects to have so much more when the suit is decided. But since these others are less generous than Jarndyce, the suit induces them to abstract from whatever generous considerations they may be attuned to, and to focus concertedly on *getting* the money. Via this acquisitive impulse, the suit becomes preoccupying and dampens whatever generous motives they have. By contrast, Jarndyce's greater steadiness and reliability in seeing wealth as a means of helping prevents an obsessive focus on getting.

The many "philanthropists" in *Bleak House* illustrate the ease with which even doing good can have an "acquisitive," "stingy," selfish character.

> One other singularity was, that nobody with a mission—except Mr. Quale, whose mission, as I think I have formerly said, was to be in ecstasies with everybody's mission—cared at all for anybody's mission. Mrs. Pardiggle being as clear that the only one infallible course was her course of pouncing upon the poor, and applying benevolence to them like a strait-waistcoat; as Miss Wisk was that the only practical thing for the world was the emancipation of Woman from the thralldom of her Tyrant, Man. Mrs. Jellyby, all the while, sat smiling at the limited vision that could see anything but Borrioboola-Gha. (479)

Clearly, the "wealth" involved in this kind of greed is self-importance. The generous person is free not only with his money, time, and the benefit of a doubt but also with crediting others, and with the regard that goes with such crediting. If a philanthropist can credit another philanthropist for genuinely helping people, her attitude toward the other will be gratitude for the work he does. If the credit is *due* the others, then generosity promotes just behavior as well.

None of these uncongenial, self-important "benefactors" is a fit object of gratitude, and the reason is that none of them is generous. Even if, by chance, they should benefit someone, the self their action expresses will, if understood as turned back on its own importance as the last quotation suggests, constitute a forbidding barrier to rational gratitude. Gratitude is an experience of the benefactor's goodwill toward oneself or someone about whom one cares; if that goodwill doesn't come through, the response won't be gratitude; and if by confusion, it gets projected onto an imposter of generosity, it will be misguided and unwise. Mrs. Pardiggle enters the brickmaker's house full of her own importance: "You can't tire me, good people," said Mrs. Pardiggle. . . . "I enjoy hard work, and the harder you make mine, the better I like it." And the object of her laborious charity responds:

> "Then make it easy for her!" [referring to his daughter, who is washing clothes in filthy water] growled the man upon the floor. "I wants it done, and over. I wants a end of these liberties took with my place. I wants an end of being drawed like a badger. Now you're a-going to poll-pry and question according to custom—I know what you're a-going to be up to. Well! You haven't got no occasion to be up to it." (158)

By contrast, Jarndyce's goodwill toward his benefactors, even when misguided, is palpably genuine. And so it elicits gratitude from those with the virtue of gratitude (Esther and Ada, but not Skimpole and Carstone). And probably not Jellyby and Pardiggle, if their self-importance is consistent: gratitude is generous in being directed benevolently toward another and his generous goodwill, rather than turned in on one's own importance. For purposes of gratitude, there is all the difference in the world between a goodwill toward oneself that is misguided and a lack of good will toward oneself.

Let us pull together the points about gratitude that have emerged so far. It is the complement of generosity; in particular, it requires that the beneficiary attribute to the benefactor goodwill toward himself or what he cares about. Consequently, it is incompatible with perceiving the benefactor as motivated overwhelmingly by a concern for self-importance; it thus depends on a degree of humility (unconcern about self-importance) in the benefactor (as perceived by the beneficiary). Gratitude is itself a benevolent attention directed to and appreciative of the benefactor, and so has a generous character.

Thanksgiving. The second peculiarity of Jarndyce's generosity is his animus against receiving expressions of gratitude from his beneficiaries. Just before Esther meets Jarndyce for the first time, she, Ada, and Richard each receive a note from him indirectly warning them against expressing thanks to him when they shall meet him:

> "I look forward, my dear, to our meeting easily, and without constraint on either side. I therefore have to propose that we meet as old friends, and take the past for granted. It will be a relief to you possibly, and to me certainly, and so my love to you."—John Jarndyce. (110–11)

Esther comments that "I had not considered how I could thank him, my gratitude lying too deep in my heart for that; but I now began to consider how I could meet him without thanking him, and felt it would be very difficult indeed" (ibid.). The three discuss this peculiarity of Jarndyce, and Ada dimly remembers a story her mother told when Ada was small, that "he had once done [her mother] an act of uncommon generosity, and that on her going to his house to thank him, he happened to see her through a window coming to the door, and immediately escaped by the back gate, and was not heard of for three months" (ibid.). Often, if a beneficiary seems about to express gratitude for Jarndyce's kindness, he calls in the east wind device. In such cases, the emotion he mistakes for an undifferentiated discomfort seems to be a distressed compassion for the beneficiary.

The first peculiarity of Jarndyce's generosity—that he suppresses angry impressions of others when their faults and shortcomings threaten to elicit such—is not very difficult to explain as originating in generous impulses. Ordinary people's anger and contempt are often ungenerous and always at least a little adversarial, so we can understand how an unusually generous-hearted person, whose moral constitution was a bit one-sided, might exhibit something like Jarndyce's emotional pattern. The second peculiarity is a little harder to understand, and the explanation that I will offer is somewhat speculative with respect to the text of *Bleak House*. Like my explanation of the first peculiarity, it will involve attributing to Jarndyce a misunderstanding that is based in a genuine and generous moral insight. I propose that the second peculiarity stems from his intuitive egalitarianism and a confusion of generosity with liberality.

Here is Aristotle's description of the great-souled man, in the dimension of his generosity (now, rather, liberality) and gratitude:

> And he is the sort of man to confer benefits, but he is ashamed of receiving them; for the one is the mark of a superior, the other of an inferior. And he is apt to confer greater benefits in return [for benefits received]; for thus the original benefactor besides being paid will incur a debt to him, and will be the gainer by the transaction. [The great-souled] seem also to remember any service they have done, but not those they have received (for he who receives a service is inferior to him who has done it, but the great-souled man wishes to be superior), and to hear of the former with pleasure, of the latter with displeasure.[15]

The great-souled man is not an egalitarian, but a highly elitist individual, strongly committed to his own superiority and interested in establishing it by dominating in his relations with others. He conceives the giver of what is not due to be in the dominant position. Perhaps this is because giving what is not due expresses abundance, self-sufficiency, and control, while receiving what is not due (undeserved) indicates want, dependence, and passivity. As a perceptual acknowledgment of having received a good that is not due from someone, gratitude is an emotional admission of defeat in the competition, a feeling of oneself as "bowed down," as Esther says on an occasion when she is feeling especially grateful (75). So the great-souled man wants to be, as much as possible, the giver and not the bowed-down receiver. Inadvertently, Aristotle makes out the great-souled man to be a comical figure, by assuming that the great-souled, like everybody else, have in fact received net undeserved benefits from some others, so that they have to use selective memory to keep up their desired sense of themselves.

The great-souled man's moral orientation with respect to liberality and gratitude says this: (1) Very generally, each person's individual good is to dominate others and (2) a powerful and genteel way of dominating others is to act liberally toward them. This ethical orientation is natural to human beings.[16] Even individuals who have been rather deeply formed in a spiritually egalitarian moral tradition that condemns this elitist view and its emotional manifestations find it cropping up in us. We try humbly to love our neighbor but find that we do enjoy the sense of power over the beneficiary that we get from giving; we take joy not just in giving, but perhaps even more in the social meaning of giving: that it gives us dominance. We want to be generous in the sense of caring more about the beneficiary's well-being than about our own superiority in the situation, but if we are sensitive, we notice that the latter concern ranks disturbingly high. And on the other side of the transaction, we find ourselves uncomfortable when we receive unowed benefits by the grace of an individual giver, because it makes us feel small and weak by comparison. Even if the giver is not enjoying his dominance or successfully covers up this attitude, we feel demeaned and squirm in competition. When we do receive a grace, we express our discomfort by attempting to reciprocate, so as to "even the score"—or better it, as the great-souled man does. Because the debt of gratitude incurred by the generous act can seem humiliating, really generous people often minister to the comfort of their recipients by hiding their role as giver or minimizing the gift. Such kindness has become embedded in our language, which conventionally veils the recipient's debt: "Think nothing of it." "It was nothing." "Don't mention it." "Il n'y a pas de quoi." "De nada." "No hay de qué." Even "you're welcome" may suggest "you come by it well (that is, justly; that is, I have not really be generous with you)."

I am suggesting that Jarndyce's animus against expressions of gratitude stems from a hypersensitivity to the social dynamic exemplified by the great-souled man. Jarndyce's fear or hatred of gratitude is based in one of the concerns basic to a generosity that differs from what I have been calling liberality: a concern for the well-being of the other, conceived in terms of social attitudes: part of the well-being the benefactor wishes for the beneficiary is that she *not* be socially inferior to him. The great-souled man is unconcerned that his giving gifts places the other in the inferior social position—that his winning in the liberality game entails that his "beneficiary" loses out on what *really* matters. He is no more dismayed by this prospect than the championship tennis player feels sorry that his winning the match entails his opponent's losing. But according to the conception of generosity within which Jarndyce's emotions are formed, to wish another well is to wish him not to be inferior in this way.[17] If this reading is right, when someone thanks him for some benefit conferred, the spiritual equality between Jarndyce and his beneficiary seems to him compromised: she is lowered as he is raised, as sure as a teeter-totter. He is put in the dominant position, she in the dominated one. Emotionally Jarndyce cannot tolerate this situation, and so he shuns expressions of thanks. Speaking roughly, we might say that Jarndyce's first peculiarity stems from his concern not to accuse, and his second from his concern not to dominate; both are generous concerns, concerns for the well-being of the other conceived as affected by another's attitude.

But for all its roots in generosity, the second formation is as much a defect as the first, and like the first, it is a defect in generosity. Remember Esther's complaint on receiving Jarndyce's introductory note: "I now began to consider how I could meet him without thanking him, and felt it would be very difficult indeed" (111). Offering a token of gratitude is for the grateful person a need, a satisfaction, a joy, and the benefactor who does not want to accept the expression from his partner needs to have a good reason for refusing her this satisfaction. Reasons can exist, of course. Perhaps the giver is less responsible for the action than the gratitude makes out; perhaps the recipient really *is* in danger of expressing servility rather than gratitude. But if the action was really generous and the gratitude that the beneficiary wants to express matches the action, then to shun expressions of gratitude is ungenerous. In this refusal, Jarndyce seems oddly selective. He takes great joy in others' joys in general, but when it comes to their pleasure of returning gratitude, he regards their desire for pleasure as a threat. Were he fully aware that his discomfort is irrational, then generosity would counsel him to exercise self-denial here, and let the beneficiary thank him even though it distresses him. He might then learn deeper generosity by learning to enjoy properly the other's expressions of gratitude. But if he is genuinely confused about the logic of gratitude and generosity, then his selectivity is not exactly odd and he is not exactly ungenerous. He shuns the expression of thanks out of benevolent concern for the beneficiary; he would not have the fear of gratitude that he has if he were thoroughly "great-souled". His conceptual scheme is an unstable synthesis of two ethical outlooks.

The great-souled man enjoys the gratitude of others because of the impression it gives him of his own superiority. Jarndyce hates the gratitude of others for the same reason. The emotional difference between them is made by the fact that the one wants to be superior to one's neighbors at their expense, and the other wants not to be superior to his neighbors at their expense. What posture would Jarndyce take toward merited gratitude if his ethics were not infected with the great-souled concept of giving? Being the generous person he is, he would rejoice in the other's expression of gratitude for two basic reasons.

First, he wants the gift to be something good and good for the person to whom he gives it; the expression of gratitude is evidence of that goodness, thus making on him an impression that satisfies his benevolence. He might, of course, have such an impression in the absence of any expression of gratitude. Perhaps he simply contemplates the situation, seeing that he has succeeded in doing good to the beneficiary. But joy is an emotion, and emotions are impressions, and signs strengthen impressions; and expressions of gratitude signal the good that has been done, so the expression of gratitude has a special place here in satisfying the impulses of generosity.

Second, and at least equally important, Jarndyce would rejoice in Esther's expression of gratitude as a token of friendship, in mutuality with his act of generosity, which is similarly a token of friendship. In this, contrary to the great-souled philosophy, there is equality between the parties. The fact that the benefactor gives what the beneficiary lacks (money or some other kind of help that requires a special position of power) does not, for the Christian or Stoic or other radical egalitarian, imply that the benefactor is superior to the beneficiary. According to this ethical outlook, the fact of having more or less power in this sense is accidental, having to do with contingent circumstance rather than with any essential identity of the persons involved. Jarndyce is not essentially a rich man, any more than Esther is essentially a quasi-orphan. They are two people, so circumstanced, as it happens, that Jarndyce can help Esther in a certain way. So when she reciprocates, according to her circumstances, with an expression of gratitude, she is no more saying "I admit my inferiority to you" than Jarndyce is saying, by his act of generosity, "I am your superior." On my interpretation of Jarndyce's second peculiarity, he is a very generous man who doesn't understand this point emotionally. And his failure to get it disfigures his generosity. By a deficiency of practical wisdom, he frustrates his beneficiaries and forfeits an aspect of human fellowship.

Jarndyce fails to exemplify what we might call the wise integration of diverse factors in the moral life; or the situational diversity in the single moral life. It is as though one concern—for the freedom of his beneficiary—crowds out an equally important concern—to satisfy the beneficiary's concern to give back in mutuality. Thus, he undermines one of the chief goods of the generosity-gratitude dynamic: its interpersonal bonding. Or the concern to feel benevolently toward the beneficiary crowds out the concern that one's beneficences be genuinely beneficial. Thus, he undermines generosity's commitment to discretion in the choice of beneficiaries and benefits.

Skimpole

The grateful Esther's frustration with Jarndyce is matched by the ungrateful Skimpole's satisfaction with the same. Jarndyce's emotional mismatch with the grateful Esther makes him a perfect match with the ungrateful Skimpole. The interdiction of "judgment" and the horror of thanksgiving in Jarndyce's generosity adapt him for complacency with, and even real enjoyment of, his acquaintance Harold Skimpole. I say "acquaintance," not "friend," because I don't suppose that real friendship with the likes of Skimpole is possible. Friendship has a mutual character of whose emotional dimension Skimpole has constituted himself incapable. The immediate impression he gives has its attractions: he had "a delicate face, and a sweet voice, and there was a perfect charm in him. All he said was so free from effort and spontaneous, and was said with such a captivating gaiety, that it was fascinating to hear him talk" (118). He is not nasty in the overt way the greedy Smallweeds are, but is nevertheless a model of unmutuality and thus of ingratitude and ungenerosity, and one comes to see that, in his genteel and dilettantishly artistic way, he is as nasty as any character in the novel.

Jarndyce has taken him on as another "ward." Skimpole repeatedly makes a point of his unfitness to take the normal adult responsibilities, having no sense, he says, of either time or money. Jarndyce and he share the pleasantly excusing fiction that despite his more than fifty years, he is a mere child in point of responsibility. Jarndyce pays Skimpole's debts, which are many, feeds him, houses him from time to time, provides him company that will appreciate his light self-focused banter, and bails him out of debtor's prison. And to all of these benefits, Skimpole responds without the least degree of gratitude—which suits Jarndyce just fine. Jarndyce had instructed Esther and the others to "take the past for granted," and Skimpole does exactly that to perfection: he seems to lack completely the distinction between what is due one, and what is not.

> He was very fond of reading the papers, very fond of making fancy-sketches with a pencil, very fond of nature, very fond of art. All he asked of society was to let him live. That wasn't much. His wants were few. Give him the papers, conversation, music, mutton, coffee, landscape, fruit in the season, a few sheets of Bristol-board, and a little claret, and he asked no more. He was a mere child in the world, but he didn't cry for the moon. He said to the world, "Go your several ways in peace! Wear red coats, blue coats, lawn-sleeves, put pens behind your ears, wear aprons, go after glory, holiness, commerce, trade, any object you prefer; only—let Harold Skimpole live!" (118–19)

Of course it's the world that supplies this living, in the form of generous people like Jarndyce and some unsuspecting others, and one might suppose that Skimpole thinks the world owes it to him, but I am not sure that he has enough practical concept of debt for this to be true.

I use the word "practical" here as entailing serious inclusion of self. Skimpole does have moral concepts, in the sense that he can speak the language coherently, and he can also use the language to refer to himself. He understands the moral "grammar." But the way he does so makes clear that he himself is not a member of the moral community. A little while before he hits up Esther and Richard to pay a rather large debt to keep him out of prison, he makes the following speech to them:

> "It's only you, the generous creatures, whom I envy," said Mr. Skimpole addressing us, his new friends, in an impersonal manner. "I envy you your power of doing what you do. It is what I should revel in, myself. I don't feel any vulgar gratitude[18] to you. I almost feel as if you ought to be grateful to me, for giving you the opportunity of enjoying the luxury of generosity. I know you like it. For anything I can tell, I may have come into the world expressly for the purpose of increasing your stock of happiness. I may have been born to be a benefactor to you, by sometimes giving you an opportunity of assisting me in my little perplexities. Why should I regret my incapacity for details and worldly affairs, when it leads to such pleasant consequences? I don't regret it therefore."
>
> Of all his playful speeches (playful, yet always fully meaning what they expressed) none seemed to be more to the taste of Mr. Jarndyce than this. (121)

Skimpole understands the moral concepts well, in his way. He knows that gratitude is called for as a response to generous actions. He knows it is a response to things that are perceived as good. He knows that generosity is a virtue, and therefore "enviable."[19] (Though he is disingenuous that *he* envies them their generosity; he in fact wants no part of it.) He knows that the generous person takes pleasure in acting generously. He knows that he too *would* revel in it, were he oriented that way. He knows that the beneficiary is a kind of benefactor of the benefactor. He understands that in the ordinary logic of gratitude and generosity, the beneficiary of generosity owes gratitude to his benefactor.

But he uses this social competence in a completely non-ethical way—to deny that the concept of debt applies to himself—to deny that *he* owes them any gratitude for their kindness. (He delivers this speech to his new "friends" in an "impersonal manner.") In his own case, he conveniently switches from the interpersonal logic of generosity and gratitude to a sort of consequentialism: because of the joy they supposedly take in generously sharing their wherewithal with Skimpole, Skimpole's benefactors already have their reward, so Skimpole owes them nothing. Consequentialist reasoning has its place in ethics, but not here. Gratitude to a benefactor is a matter of personal love; what it gives is essentially expression of self, not payment;

and Skimpole is unwilling to put his heart into the matter in this way. Again, he is disingenuous, sophistical, or ignorant in a deeper way of the beauty of gratitude.

Well, which is it? Is Skimpole disingenuous, or is he ignorant? I think the psychologically plausible answer is—"both." The concept of *understanding* or (which is closely related) *having a concept* is ambiguous, especially in ethics. I have noted two things about Skimpole's grasp of the concepts of gratitude and generosity. One is that he understands them pretty well, and the other is that he uses sophistry to avoid some of their implications, and their application to his own case. If the use of sophistry is intentional, as it seems to be from the playful way Skimpole executes it, this too suggests that in some sense, he does grasp the concepts.[20] One who intentionally uses devices to avoid the implications of a concept must, in some sense, see those implications. He also sees, in some sense, what it would be like to be a grateful person (see above). But clearly, he doesn't *want* to be a grateful person. He doesn't want to feel toward his benefactors what a grateful person feels, to see situations in the interpersonal way a grateful person sees them, or to act expressively as a grateful person acts. This strongly suggests that he doesn't personally (that is, for himself) *see the value* of being a grateful person. He lacks the kind of external reason for gratitude that Esther accesses when, finding little indications of ingratitude in herself, she berates herself and undertakes disciplines to get herself back on track.

If we assume that gratitude is a virtue—a real good for human beings—then we can say that Esther understands something about gratitude that Skimpole misses. Her understanding of the value of gratitude is embodied in her emotions—in the joy she feels when she is able to express gratitude, in the joy and admiration she feels for Jarndyce, in the shame and disappointment she feels when she finds herself being ungrateful. These emotions are perceptions, incipient judgments or bases of judgments about the value of their moral object—in this case, gratitude, her gratitude or lack thereof. Skimpole apparently experiences none of these emotions. Other emotions, like admiration or dismay, might be ways of appreciating someone else's gratitude or ingratitude. Such emotions, based in the concern for, or sense of the importance of, gratitude and generosity, are essential to what we might call the full understanding of the moral concepts. Skimpole understands gratitude and generosity without "fully" understanding them.

Yet even this failure to understand involves moral understanding to the extent that Skimpole feels a kind of pressure to join humanity. His use of sophistry and the fiction that he is but a "child" evince defensiveness. Esther's worldview exerts pressure on him of a kind that witchcraft doesn't typically exert on a scientifically modern western anthropologist. The anthropologist needn't engage in sophistry and fictions to defend herself against the practical implications of magical concepts, though she understands them in much the way that Skimpole understands generosity and gratitude.

Aristotle says that practical wisdom is involved in the structure of each of the moral virtues, and that it is a matter, not just of abstractly intellectual understanding, but of what the subject habitually and in practice aims at. Our comparison of Skimpole and Esther illustrates his points. Despite Skimpole's considerable observer's understanding of the moral concepts, his thoroughgoing ingratitude necessarily impoverishes his practical wisdom.

Skimpole illustrates another point about gratitude: its dependence on the virtue of justice. Generosity and gratitude complement justice in the sense that they turn on the concept of what is not due, and thus depend on a concept of what is due. They introduce a note of grace into a world of tit-for-tat transactions—or they become visible through the introduction of tit-for-tat transactions into a world already characterized by grace. If this is true, and if what I have just argued about moral understanding is right, then you'd need a moral appreciation of what is due to have a proper understanding of gratitude and generosity. Skimpole confirms this connection by lacking justice as abysmally as he lacks the virtues of grace. Consider a sample of Skimpole's musings about a case of flagrant injustice.

> Take the case of the Slaves on American plantations. I dare say they are worked hard, I dare say they don't altogether like it, I dare say theirs is an unpleasant experience on the whole; but, they people the landscape for me, they give it a poetry for me, and perhaps that is one of the pleasanter objects of their existence. I am very sensible of it, if it be, and I shouldn't wonder if it were! (307)

Justice is a matter of people getting what is due them, and the American slaves whose hardships embellish with pleasant "poetry" the landscape of Skimpole's imagination are being deprived of their due as human beings, to put it mildly. The ethical person, upon seriously imagining what the slaves went through (read, for example, Toni Morrison's *Beloved* or Frederick Douglass's *Narrative of the Life of Frederick Douglass*), not only feels the pangs of helpless compassion but also outrage at the injustice of it. Skimpole finds such imagining a nice pastime for a quiet hour "in a shady place."

A person with no sense of justice can have no sense of gratitude. A sensitivity to what is due is a necessary background for appreciating a personal benefit that is not due one—for appreciating the person who gives what he is not under obligation to give as well as the attitude that induces him to give the benefit. Throughout *Bleak House*, Esther's narratives stress her sense of not deserving the various benefits for which she is so thankful. By contrast, Skimpole seems to have no sense of justice at all. He does not even *consider* what is due the American slaves, but also, he does not exactly conceive the things he wants—the music, the claret, the newspapers, a few sheets of Bristol-board—as his *due* in any strict or moral sense; he just calls on the world to give them to him. One of the reasons, therefore, that he has no sense of gratitude, is that he has no sense of justice—even the primitive childish kind of justice that claims it is unfair for him not to have what some peer has.

The person who does have a sense of gratitude may, however, feel gratitude where only justice has been done. That is, out of generosity of attribution, she construes as not due her some benefit that is in fact due her. This spicing of justice-situations with grace is part of civilization, embodied in the polite convention of saying "thank-you" to clerks, nurses, and service people who have done for us only what is required of them. Also, generosity often promotes people's getting justice. Acts of generosity can be acts of justice when they aim at, and bring about, what is due someone. They qualify as acts of generosity because what is due is not due from the one who acts. For example, when Esther undertakes to wash and feed and reads stories to the neglected Jellyby children, she gives them only what is their due as children; yet she acts generously, because these benefits are not due them from her.

CONCLUSION

With the unique power of the novel to depict interacting characters with emotional depth over time, *Bleak House* suggests that gratitude must be understood in its connection with other virtues, especially generosity, but also humility, justice (injustice), friendship, and practical wisdom. Generosity raises the question, so to speak, of the generous attitude toward the beneficiary's grateful impulses. I have proposed that we distinguish generosity from liberality, and that a crucial difference is in the way gratitude in the beneficiary is construed: liberality construes it as servile while generosity construes it generously as a fully respectable and mutual complement; in a word, as an element of friendship. The fundamental equality of benefactor and beneficiary suggests that the difference in roles is "accidental," merely a matter of circumstance and of nothing deeper in the identity of the agents. If this insight is well established in the consciousness of both parties, then both of them exhibit the virtuous humility that generosity and gratitude presuppose, in contrast with the implicit invidiousness of liberality and servility. To be mature in gratitude, the grateful person must also be emotionally alive to justice and injustice, and must therefore be, like Esther Summerson, capable of anger where people are denied what is due them. Without a sense of justice, gratitude will lack the necessary serious contrast between what is owed and what is not owed.

NOTES

1 I am grateful to Baylor University for a sabbatical during which the paper was first drafted, the Self, Motivation, and Virtue Project at the University of Oklahoma and the Templeton Religion Trust for a grant under which this chapter was revised, to Michael Spezio, my co-PI on that grant, for many discussions of issues on which the paper focuses, and to Daniel Telech for very helpful suggestions. The opinions expressed here are the author's and are not necessarily those of the Templeton Religion Trust.

2 *Bleak House*, by Charles Dickens, edited by Norman Page with an introduction by J. Hillis Miller, London: Penguin Books, 1853/1971. Hereafter quotations from this book will be in parentheses in the text.

3 See the paper by Sophie-Grace Chappell in this volume for similar comments.

4 Similar, I say, because Aristotelian elitism, self-sufficiency, and competitiveness taint it, prompting Jean Vanier to say that it lacks "heart" (*Happiness: Aristotle for the New Century*, translated by Kathryn Spink, New York: Arcade Publishing, 184–7). See the chapter by Stephen Darwall in this volume for a similar view.

5 *Thus Spake Zarathustra*, translated by Thomas Common, New York: Random House 1954, Part 1, section 22.

6 See *Nicomachean Ethics*, translated by W. D. Ross and revised and edited by J. L. Ackrill and J. O. Urmson (Oxford: Oxford University Press, 1980), 4.3, especially 1124b10–18. See Chappell, this volume, for a contrasting interpretation of Aristotle.

7 For a discussion of self-importance in its relation to humility and to the genuine importance of a human being, see Robert C. Roberts and Ryan West, "Jesus and the Virtues of Pride" in J. Adam Carter and Emma C. Gordon, editors, *The Moral Psychology of Pride* (Lanham: Rowman & Littlefield, 2017), pp. 99–121.

8 Internal reasons reflect the logic of gratitude, for example, that *I have received a good from a benefactor*, or that *the good I've received isn't owed me*; an external reason is a motive to be grateful that is not internal, for example, that *I need to get on with my work*, and *self-pity is impeding it*; or, *if this laboring man's daughter can be so generous, surely I can stop pitying myself and be grateful.*

9 On the differences and similarities between anger and resentment, see Robert C. Roberts, *Emotions: An Essay in Aid of Moral Psychology* (Cambridge: Cambridge University Press, 2003), 202–204, 214–216.

10 I first discussed this symmetry in "The Blessings of Gratitude" in Robert Emmons and Michael McCullough, editors, *The Psychology of Gratitude* (New York: Oxford University Press, 2004), 58–78.

11 Russell Goldfarb proposes that Jarndyce is not moved by generous motives at all but uses his money to protect his comfortable life against the importunities of people with philanthropic projects—to get people like Jellyby and Pardiggle out of his hair. But this explanation leaves us with an even greater mystery: why Jarndyce involves himself in philanthropic projects in the first place. Why not just retire in comfort to Bleak House and eschew all contact with the world's woes and those annoying do-gooders? Another consideration is that Esther, who is presented as a reliable judge of character, repeatedly extols him for his generosity. Still another

consideration is that Jarndyce, apparently uniquely among the heirs involved in the suit, survives its psychological ravages because he sees money as a means of helping people. See Russell Goldfarb, "John Jarndyce of *Bleak House*" *Studies in the Novel 12* (1980): 144–152.

12 See the discussion of misfelt (affectively erroneous) emotions in Robert C. Roberts, *Emotions: An Essay in Aid of Moral Psychology* (Cambridge University Press, 2003), chapter 4.

13 See Robert C. Roberts, *Emotions in the Moral Life* (Cambridge University Press, 2013), 39–59.

14 *Nicomachean Ethics* 1107a7–8, 1115a6ff.

15 *Nicomachean Ethics* 4.3, 1124b10–15.

16 Chappell (this volume) defends Aristotle against Alasdair MacIntyre's interpretation of Aristotle as endorsing the great-souled man as virtuous. My interpretation of Jarndyce as fearing that gratitude is servile doesn't depend on agreeing with MacIntyre against Chappell. It requires only Jarndyce's awareness of a pathological understanding of human giving and receiving that is starkly represented by Aristotle's description of the great-souled man's interactions with his would-be benefactors and beneficiaries.

17 In Jarndyce's case, this conception is no doubt Christian; Dickens's moral psychology is clearly Christian or Christian-inspired.

18 Might "vulgar" gratitude be obsequious servile "gratitude" as the great-souled man would construe it, such as would correspond to what I have called liberality?

19 See Linda Zagzebski, *Exemplarist Moral Theory* (Oxford: Oxford University Press, 2017), 150–164 on the desirability of the admirable.

20 See the report of Skimpole from inspector Bucket of the detective in chapter 57.

Index

accountability, 9, 139–45, 152, 156
acquisitiveness, 324–25
admiration, 1, 4, 37–38, 72, 83, 110, 147, 202, 320, 333
agency, 78, 79n7, 85, 162, 164, 166–68, 174, 205, 219, 227, 254–55; of children, 164–67; social, 200–201, 206–7
altruism, 164, 208–10, 292
anger, 37, 265, 321–24, 284, 321–23, 335, 336n9
appreciation, 1, 3, 8, 10, 36, 49–50, 74, 76, 78, 84, 86–87, 90–92, 119, 151–52, 154–55, 161, 165, 167, 188, 191n2, 200–201, 223, 238, 269–70, 297–98, 314n8, 319, 326, 333–34
approbation, 147–48, 182–93, 187–88
Aquinas, 123, 139, 263, 284, 314n21, 315n23
Aristotle, 10, 35, 39–40, 45, 48, 123, 230, 255–63, 267n2, 271–72, 274–76, 281, 284, 318, 323–24, 327–28, 334, 336n4, 337n16
Ashton, M. C., 86
Atisa (982–1054 CE), 289
Audi, Robert, 36
authenticity, virtue of, 218; essentialist and existentialist, 10, 217–38

authority, 67–68, 182, 183; second-personal, 156
autonomy, 234, 236, 287

Badhwar, Neera, 44, 49, 52n12, 281
Bartlett, Monica, 282
baseline for determining benefit, 99–101; oughts-based, 100–103, 107, 113n12; pre-interaction, 100–104, 107; rights-based, 100–104, 107, 110; statistical, 100–102, 108
Basu, Rima, 113n10
Bauer, Jack, 10
behavioral outcomes of gratitude, 202–3, 207–8
benefit, 2–3, 8, 19, 23, 28, 30, 35–37, 39, 45–46, 48, 51, 85, 97–99, 101, 118, 120, 125–26, 145, 150, 160–61, 165, 169, 172, 199, 203, 270; morally tainted, 37–38; as a perspectival notion, 101. *See also* baseline for determining benefit
benevolence, 1, 3, 9, 18, 24, 36–37, 52n3, 98, 102, 110, 145–47, 160, 167, 172, 176, 178, 191, 193n11, 280–81, 292, 321; duty of, 63; evidence of, 299, 325

Graver, Margaret, 157n15
great-souled person, 257–58, 327–30
Grotius, Hugo, 63–64, 79n9
growth, 227
guilt, 9–10, 50, 84–85, 139–42, 160,
171, 182, 183, 188, 198, 202–5, 284
Gulliford, Liz, 280–82, 293nn3–4

Harris, Daniel, 73
health benefits of gratitude, 150, 152,
198
Helm, Bennett, 9, 79n3
Herman, Barbara, 60, 62, 79n7
Hieronymi, Pamela, 113n10
Hill, Peter, 282, 286
Hill, Thomas, 43, 46, 48
Hillenbrand, Laura, 105
Hobbes, Thomas, 149, 187
Hohfeld, Wesley Newcomb, 98, 104
holism in the theory of emotions, 180;
methodological, 181, 182, 189
Holland, Rob, 282
Homer, 91–92
honesty, 38, 44, 105, 271–72, 274,
276–78, 286
hope, 80n19, 152, 156, 188, 288
hospitality, 306
Hume, David, 156n7, 157n20, 313
humiliation, 285, 328
humility, 11, 201–3, 280, 282–89, 291,
292n1, 293n7, 318, 326–28, 335,
336n7
Hursthouse, Rosalind, 38, 42
hyper-autonomy, 287, 291

Iacoponi, E., 288
ideology, 255–56, 259
import, 180–81; of norms, 182–84
indebtedness, feeling of, 2, 20, 48, 59,
83, 85–86, 88, 94n4, 199, 201, 203
independence (*autarkeia*), 259, 262–63,
327
indeterminacy of norms, 188–90
indignation, 9, 139, 160, 167, 171–72,
182, 204–5, 284, 323–24

intention to benefit, 2, 29, 166, 176,
180, 188, 254
interdependence, 10, 218, 220, 224,
234–38, 259, 262–63, 287–90
interest satisfaction, 100–102, 104–5,
113n12

Jacobson, Daniel, 107, 114n19
Jecker, Nancy, 123, 125–27
Johnson, B. R., 283
Johnson, S., 284
joy, 1–6, 10, 39, 42, 83, 86, 88,
150–52, 180, 217, 246, 265, 297,
300, 314n8, 328–33
judgment, 247–49
justice, 11, 32n20, 38, 48, 64, 143,
156n7, 171, 174n12, 202, 245, 265,
271, 275–76, 281, 314n17, 317–18,
334–35

Kant, 36, 39, 43, 47–49, 52n5, 62–63,
79, 81n23, 139, 143, 145–46, 149,
276, 313
Karns, Christina, 9, 292
Karremans, Johan, 282
Kass, Amy, 84
kindness, 3–4, 36, 44–46, 49, 51, 69,
98, 106, 115n22, 177, 193, 202, 290,
327–28, 332
Kolodny, Niko, 94n7
Konstan, David, 259–60
Kukla, Rebecca, 146, 156n5

Lance, Mark, 146, 156n5
Language-game, 246–47, 257
Lee, K., 286
Lee, M. T., 283
Levi, Primo, 114n22
liberality, 318
Lincoln, Abraham, 177–79, 190, 192
Loevinger, Jane, 235–36
Løgstrup, Knud Ejler, 153, 155
Lojong, 11, 289–91
love, 6–8, 15, 17, 25–27, 32n18,
41–51, 52n8, 52n14, 52n16, 84, 87,

92–93, 96, 141–42, 145, 152–56,
157n20, 160, 172, 181, 192n9, 222,
229, 245, 257, 268–69, 291, 319,
328, 332; acting from, 41–43, 47–50
Luther, Martin, 284–85
Lyons, Daniel, 96

MacIntyre, Alasdair, 258–63
Macnamara, Colleen, 2, 37, 146–49,
156n2, 174n3, 192n5
Manela, Anthony, 6, 52n7, 71–73, 76,
79n13, 80n20, 119
Martin, Adrienne, 7–8, 80n19, 193n16
Mayr, U., 292
McAleer, Sean, 113n17
McConnell, Terence, 7, 18–20, 62,
97, 105–6, 108, 110, 113nn13–14,
114–15n22, 118–26, 129–31,
133nn1–2, 134n5, 134nn9–11, 177,
192n3
McCullough, Michael, 149, 203
McHugh, Conor, 113n10
McKenna, Michael, 174n3
mentorship, 8, 90–92, 237, 298–99
merit, 36, 40, 49–51, 143–47, 149, 179
Mill, John Stuart, 62–66
money, 6, 72, 92, 122, 200, 207, 262
Moore III, W. E., 292
moral responsibility, 4, 160,
162–63, 165–68, 174n8. *See also*
accountability
moral standouts, 105–6, 108–10,
115n22
moral worth, 39, 43, 48. *See also*
praiseworthiness
Moran, Kate, 79n7
Morgan, Blair, 2
Moss, Matt, 73
motivation, 3–9, 12nn2–3, 15–21,
23–24, 26–27, 30, 31n3, 32n14,
32n19, 36–43, 46–51, 71, 76, 78,
83, 87, 90, 92, 96, 98, 102, 107–10,
112n6, 120–21, 123–24, 133, 161,
163, 166, 169, 172, 183–86, 188–90,
198, 201–3, 205, 207–8, 217–19,

227, 229, 232, 235, 237, 255, 260,
271, 275, 281, 292, 292n2, 298–301,
307, 310, 313n6, 315n27, 323–26,
336n8, 336n11
mutuality, 329–31

Naar, Hichem, 6–7, 32n18
Nam, R. K., 286
narrative, 219, 221–22, 225–31,
233–35; cultural master narratives,
225–26; narrative structure, 229,
231; studies of gratitude, 204–6
Nelkin, Dana, 163–64, 168
norms, communal, 9, 182–84, 186–88,
191; conflict of, 38, 40–41; of
etiquette, 19

obligation, 7–8, 35–36, 41, 48,
139–40, 145, 149, 163, 177, 200,
303–4; filial, 118–20, 123, 127–28;
promissory, 7, 61, 66, 74, 77;
relational structure of, 59–60, 66,
78n2; trustee, 60–62. *See also* duty
ought implies can principle, 131, 163
overgratitude, 308–11
oversensitivity to benevolence, 305–6,
311

Pagano, Maria, 283
parental duty, 118, 125–26, 130, 134n4
Paul, Saint, 293n7
paying a benefit forward, 59, 79n3, 186,
191, 202–3, 207–9, 292–93n2
Pereboom, Derk, 174n8
perspective-taking, 43, 200–201, 204,
206, 232–33
Peterson, Christopher, 149, 288
phronesis. See wisdom, practical
Plato, 276
Portner, Paul, 73
Post, Stephen, 283, 285
Powers, C., 286
praise, 4, 9, 52n4, 110–11, 155, 160,
162–64, 166, 168–69, 171, 174n4,
192n5, 202

About the Contributors

Jack J. Bauer is Professor of Psychology at the University of Dayton. His forthcoming book, *The Transformative Self: Identity, Growth, and a Good Life Story* (Oxford UP), explains how our life stories intersect with cultural ideals of growth to foster specific forms of human flourishing, such as well-being, wisdom, and moral virtue. He is the co-editor of *Transcending Self-Interest: Psychological Explorations of the Quiet Ego* (American Psychological Association Books, 2008).

Agnes Callard is Associate Professor in Philosophy at the University of Chicago. Her primary areas of specialization are Ancient Philosophy and Ethics. Her book *Aspiration*: *The Agency of Becoming* (Oxford UP, 2018) describes the rational process of value-acquisition.

David Carr is Emeritus Professor at the University of Edinburgh, Scotland, UK and currently Professor of Ethics and Education in the Jubilee Centre for Character and Virtues of the University of Birmingham (UK). He has written widely on philosophy and education, especially on the educational implications of virtue ethics and the significance of art and literature for educating moral character.

Sophie Grace Chappell is Professor of Philosophy at the Open University, UK. Her books include *Aristotle and Augustine on Freedom* (Macmillan, 1995), *Understanding Human Goods* (Edinburgh UP, 2003), *The Inescapable Self: An Introduction to Philosophy* (Orion, 2005), *Reading Plato's Theaetetus* (Hackett, 2005), *Ethics and Experience* (Acumen, 2009), and *Knowing What to Do: Imagination, Virtue, and Platonism in Ethics* (Oxford UP, 2014). Her main current research is about epiphanies, immediate and revelatory encounters with value, and their place in our experience and our philosophical ethics.

D. Justin Coates is Associate Professor of Philosophy at the University of Houston. He primarily works on issues related to ethics and the philosophy of action. He is the co-editor of *Blame: Its Nature and Norms* (Oxford UP, 2013) and *Oxford Studies in Agency and Responsibility, Vol 5: Essays on themes from the work of Gary Watson* (Oxford UP, 2019), and his work has appeared in journals such as *Philosophical Studies*, *American Philosophical Quarterly*, and *British Journal for the History of Philosophy*.

Stephen Darwall is that Andrew Downey Orrick Professor of Philosophy at Yale University and John Dewey Distinguished University Professor Emeritus at the University of Michigan. He has written widely on moral philosophy and the history of ethics and is best known for his book, *The Second-Person Standpoint* (Harvard UP, 2006).

Cameron Fenton earned his PhD in Philosophy at Western University in 2018, and works on moral obligations within families. His focus is on the obligations children have to their parents.

Liz Gulliford has a long-standing interest in human strengths and is a Senior Lecturer in Positive Psychology at the University of Northampton, UK. She undertook her doctorate, a critical, interdisciplinary evaluation of positive psychological approaches to strengths and virtues, at Queens' College, University of Cambridge. Liz 's interdisciplinary research has been published in philosophy, psychology and education journals, and in a number of edited volumes.

Bennett W. Helm is the Elijah E. Kresge Professor of Philosophy at Franklin & Marshall College. His work focuses on understanding what it is to be a person and, in particular, the role the emotions and various forms of caring play in our being moral creatures. He is the author of *Emotional Reason: Deliberation, Motivation, and the Nature of Value* (Cambridge UP, 2001), *Love, Friendship, and the Self: Intimacy, Identification, and the Social Nature of Persons* (Oxford UP, 2010), and *Communities of Respect: Grounding Responsibility, Authority, and Dignity* (Oxford UP, 2017).

Christina M. Karns is a neuroscientist at the University of Oregon in the Psychology Department and the Center for Brain Research and Training. Her research utilizes the neuroplasticity of emotions and cognition to support positive and healthy interactions with society and other people. Her work with children, teens, and adults clarifies how attention and self-regulation support healthy neural development and provides an evidence-based foundation for interventions.

Coleen Macnamara is Associate Professor of Philosophy at the University of California, Riverside. Her research lies at the intersection of ethics and moral psychology. Much of her work focuses on the nature and ethics of blame and the reactive attitudes more broadly, but she also has interests in the structure of practical rationality.

Tony Manela is Assistant Professor of Philosophy at Siena College. He has written several articles on the normative ethics and moral psychology of gratitude, and he is the author of the entry "Gratitude" in the *Stanford Encyclopedia of Philosophy*. His scholarly interests include the ethics of giving and receiving, environmental ethics, and biomedical ethics.

Adrienne Martin is the Akshata Murty '02 and Rishi Sunak Associate Professor of Philosophy, Politics, and Economics and George R. Roberts Fellow at Claremont McKenna College. She is the author of *How We Hope: A Moral Psychology* (Princeton UP, 2014).

Terrance McConnell is Professor Emeritus in the Department of Philosophy at University of North Carolina at Greensboro. He is the author of *Gratitude* (Temple UP, 1993), *Moral Issues in Health Care* (Wadsworth, 2nd edition, 1997), and *Inalienable Rights* (Oxford UP, 2000), as well as numerous articles in ethical theory and biomedical ethics.

Hichem Naar is an assistant professor ('Wissenschaftlicher Mitarbeiter') in philosophy at the University of Duisburg-Essen, and a member of the Philosophical Anthropology and Ethics research group in Essen, Germany. His main work is at the intersection of philosophy of mind, action theory, and ethics. In particular, he is interested in the nature of emotions and the role they might play in our practical lives.

Robert Roberts is Distinguished Professor of Ethics Emeritus at Baylor University. His interests include moral psychology, especially of emotions and virtues, and the thought of Søren Kierkegaard. His books include (with Jay Wood) *Intellectual Virtues: An Essay in Regulative Epistemology* (Oxford UP, 2007) and *Emotions in the Moral Life* (Cambridge UP, 2013).

Colin Shanahan received his Masters degree from the University of Dayton studying with Dr. Jack Bauer. He is now studying Existentialist Psychology in a doctoral program at Texas A&M University. His interests in 20th century philosophy and narrative psychology began during his time at Canisius College and form an important framework for his research.

Daniel Telech is a Postdoctoral Fellow at the Polonsky Academy for Advanced Study in the Humanities and Social Sciences, at the Van Leer Jerusalem Institute. He works on issues in ethics, moral psychology, and philosophy of action, particularly on questions about the nature and norms of agent-directed blame and (especially) praise.

Lightning Source UK Ltd.
Milton Keynes UK
UKHW040707081221
395275UK00001B/10

9 781538 158791